The Structure of Modern English

The Structure of Modern English

A linguistic introduction

Laurel J. Brinton
University of British Columbia

John Benjamins Publishing Company
Amsterdam / Philadelphia

The paper used in this publication meets the minimum requirements of American National Standard for Information Sciences – Permanence of Paper for Printed Library Materials, ANSI Z39.48-1984.

Library of Congress Cataloging-in-Publication Data

Brinton, Laurel J.
  The structure of modern English : a linguistic introduction / Laurel J. Brinton.
  p. cm.
Includes bibliographical references and indexes.
  1. English language--Grammar. 2. English language--Phonology. 3. English language--Syntax. I. Title.
PE1106.B75 2000
425--dc21   00-023618
ISBN 90 272 2567 2 (Eur.) / 1 55619 662 8 (US) (Hb; alk. paper)

John Benjamins Publishing Co. · P.O.Box 36224 · 1020 ME Amsterdam · The Netherlands
John Benjamins North America · P.O.Box 27519 · Philadelphia PA 19118-0519 · USA

To Ralph and Monica

Table of Contents

List of Tables xiii

List of Figures xv

Acknowledgments xvii

Foreword xviii

Preface xix
    A note to the student on punctuation xx

UNIT 1
The Study of English

Chapter 1
The Nature of Language and Linguistics

The Nature of Human Language 3
    Fundamental Beliefs about Language 3
    Linguistic Signs 4
    The Rule-Governed Nature of Language 6
    Language Universals, Innateness, and Creativity 6
    Animal Communication Codes 7
The Nature of Grammar 7
    Definition of *Grammar* 8
    Fallacies concerning Grammar 8
Linguistics and the Components of Language 10
Organization of the Book 11

UNIT 2
The Speech Sounds of English

Chapter 2
English Consonants and Vowels

The Spoken versus the Written Form of Language 18
    English Spelling 18
    The Advantages of Speech and Writing 19
The Production of Speech Sounds 20

Consonant Sounds 23
    Classification of Consonants 23
    Consonants of English and their Phonetic Notation 25
Vowel Sounds 34
    Classification of Vowels 34
    Vowels of English and their Phonetic Notation 36
Consonant versus Vowel 42

Chapter 3
English Phonology, Phonotactics, and Suprasegmentals
Phonemes 47
Phonemic Rules 49
Phonological Processes 51
Phonotactics 54
Suprasegmental Features 57
    Stress 57
    Intonation 62
Syllable Structure 65

Unit 3
The Structure and Meaning of English Words

Chapter 4
The Internal Structure of Words and Processes of Word Formation in English
Defining the Word 73
Morphemes 75
    Morpheme versus Morph 75
    Morphemic Analysis versus Morphological Analysis 79
    Allomorphs and Morphemic Rules 82
Processes of Word Formation 85
    Derivation 86
    Reduplication 91
    Conversion or Functional Shift 91
    Compounds 93
    Blends 97
    Back Formations 97
    Shortening 98
    Root Creations 100
Idioms 100

Chapter 5
Grammatical Categories and Word Classes

Grammatical Categories 103
    Number 104
    Gender 105
    Person 106
    Case 107
    Degree 109
    Definiteness 110
    Deixis 111
    Tense 111
    Aspect 113
    Mood 115
    Voice 117
Determining Word Classes 118
    Inflectional and Distributional Tests 119
    Tests Applied to Various Word Classes 120
    Recategorization 124

Chapter 6
Lexical Semantics

Traditional Semantics 129
Basic Semantic Relationships 131
Structural Semantics 134
Semantic Features 138
    Feature Analysis of Nouns 139
    Feature Analysis of Verbal Predicates 143
    Feature Analysis of Modals 147
    Strengths and Weaknesses of Semantic Features 150
Prototypes 151
Semantic Anomaly 153
    Selectional Restrictions 153
    Figurative Language 153

Unit 4
The Structure of English Sentences

Chapter 7
Phrasal Structure and Verb Complementation

Introduction to Phrase Structure Grammar 163
The Form of Phrase Structure Rules 165
Constituents 167

A Phrase Structure Grammar of English 168
    Subject and Predicate 168
    Noun Phrase 169
    Adjective Phrase 172
    Adverb Phrase 175
    Prepositional Phrase 176
    Conjunction 179
    Verb Phrase 181
Review of Phrase Structure Rules 186

Chapter 8
Adverbials, Auxiliaries, and Sentence Types
Adverbials 191
    Adjunct Adverbials 191
    Disjunct Adverbials 193
    Conjunct Adverbials 194
Functions of Postverbal Prepositional Phrases 194
Auxiliary 198
Passive Sentences 201
    Verb Subcategorization and the Passive 202
Yes/No Questions and Negative Sentences 203
    Yes/No Questions 204
    Negative Statements and Questions 205
    Do-Support 205
    Tag Questions 207
Imperatives 208
Review of Phrase Structure Rules 211

Chapter 9
Finite and Nonfinite Clauses
Finite Clauses 215
    That-Clauses 216
    Adverbial Clauses 221
    Wh-Clauses 224
Nonfinite Clauses 238
    Forms of Nonfinite Clauses 239
    Omissions from Nonfinite Clauses 241
    Complementizers in Nonfinite Clauses 241
    Functions of Nonfinite Clauses 244
    Nonfinite Clauses as Complements of V 251
Review of Complex Sentences 256

UNIT 5
The Meaning of English Sentences and their Communicative Functions

Chapter 10
Sentence Semantics
Propositions 264
Thematic Roles 266
    The Expression of Thematic Roles in English 268
    Dual Thematic Roles 271
    Thematic Grids 274
Predications 276
    Descriptive Predicates 276
    Cognitive Predicates 282
    Locative and Possessive Predicates 283

Chapter 11
Information Structuring and Speech Acts
Pragmatics and Syntax 290
    Basic Distinctions 290
    Syntactic Options and Pragmatic Considerations 293
    Information Structuring in a Passage 300
Speech Act Theory 301
    Components of Speech Acts 302
    Taxonomy of Speech Acts 303
    Appropriateness Conditions on Speech Acts 305
    Indirect Speech Acts 307
The Cooperative Principle and Conversational Implicature 312

References 317

Appendices 323

Subject Index 327

List of Tables

Table 2.1:   The Consonants of English   27
Table 2.2:   The Vowels of English   37
Table 2.3:   The Tense and Lax Vowels of English   42
Table 2.4:   Consonant versus Vowel   43
Table 3.1:   Initial Consonant Clusters in English   57
Table 3.2:   Strong and Weak Forms   60
Table 4.1:   The Productive Inflections of Modern English   79
Table 4.2:   Enclitics in English   80
Table 4.3:   Regular Plural Formation in Nouns   83
Table 4.4:   Root Allomorphy   86
Table 4.5:   Semantic Classes of Prefixes in English   87
Table 4.6:   Derivational Suffixes in English   88
Table 4.7:   Syntactic Patterns in English Compounds   95
Table 5.1:   The Nineteen Parts of Speech of English (C. C. Fries 1952)   119
Table 6.1:   Componential Analysis of a Livestock Paradigm   140
Table 6.2:   Componential Analysis of (a) Types of Garments and (b) Bodies of Water   141
Table 6.3:   Feature Analyses of Sample Nouns   142
Table 6.4:   Typology of Situation Types   144
Table 6.5:   Epistemic and Deontic Meanings of the Modal Auxiliaries   149
Table 6.6:   Core and Peripheral Members of the Category "Vehicle"   152
Table 6.7:   Examples of Selectional Restrictions   154
Table 7.1:   Expansions of NP   170
Table 7.2:   Expansions of AP   172
Table 7.3:   Expansion of (a) AdvP and (b) PP   176
Table 7.4:   Conjunction   180
Table 7.5:   Expansions of VP   186
Table 8.1:   Specifiers of the Verb (Active)   199
Table 8.2:   Specifiers of the Verb (Passive)   201
Table 9.1:   *That*-Clauses   216
Table 9.2:   Adjunct Adverbial Clauses   222
Table 9.3:   Forms of the Interrogative *Wh*-Complementizer   226
Table 9.4:   Relative Clauses   230
Table 9.5:   Indirect Questions   236

Table 9.6:   Controlled and Indefinite PRO in Nonfinite Clauses   242
Table 9.7:   *Persuade-*, *expect-*, and *want*-type Verbs in English   255
Table 10.1: Ø-, 1-, 2-, 3-, and 4-Place Predicates   265
Table 10.2: The Syntactic Expression of Thematic Roles in English   269
Table 10.3: Thematic Grids for English Verbs   275
Table 10.4: Stative, Inchoative, and Causative/Agentive Forms   281
Table 11.1: Focusing Operations in English   299
Table 11.2: Types of Speech Acts and their Appropriateness Conditions   308
Table 11.3: Sentences Conventionally Used in the Performance of Indirect Directives   311

List of Figures

Figure 1.1: Organization of the Text   12
Figure 2.1: The Vocal Tract with (a) Velum Raised and (b) Velum Lowered   21
Figure 2.2: Configurations of the Larynx: (a) Voiceless (Exhalation), (b) Voiced, and
               (c) Whispered   22
Figure 2.3: Some Places of Articulation   25
Figure 2.4: The Diphthongs of English (Approximate Starting and Ending Points)   40
Figure 4.1: Types of Morphemes   76
Figure 4.2: Types of Morphs   77
Figure 6.1: A Hierarchy of Fish Hyponyms   135

Acknowledgments

I would like to acknowledge Distance Education and Technology of the University of British Columbia for permission to use materials which I originally prepared for a distance education course as the basis of this text and accompanying workbook.

I am grateful to my colleagues, Lilita Rodman and Leslie Arnovick of the University of British Columbia, and to Barbara Dancygier and Lynne McGivern, who tested parts of the text and workbook in their classrooms, to my research assistant, Patte Rockett, who assisted me at various stages in the production of the manuscript, and to my students, who offered critiques and corrections of the material.

Alan Doree of the University of British Columbia did the painstaking work of preparing the numerous tree diagrams; I am appreciative of the diligence and care he took with them. I am also very grateful to my husband, Ralph Brands, who produced some of the figures in the text and whose computer expertise saved me hours of frustration.

Finally, I would like to thank Kees Vaes of John Benjamins, who was the type of editor that every author hopes to have.

Foreword

Although this is not a Revised Version of my textbook, a third print run has provided me with the opportunity to correct a number of misprints in the text itself and in the CD-ROM exercises. A list of these corrections can be found on the publisher's web site: www.benjamins.com/JPB/ or my web site: http://www.english.ubc.ca/~lbrinton/

Laurel Brinton
Vancouver, July 2003

Preface

The following text gives a full introduction to English sounds, grammar, and vocabulary. It begins with a study of the distinctive sounds of English (*phonology*). It turns next to an analysis of the structure of English words and their classification (*morphology*) as well as the classification of English words and their grammatical modification. This is followed by an exploration of the meaning of English words (*lexical semantics*). The next section is taken up with a detailed analysis of English sentence structure (*syntax*) from a generative perspective. The text then looks at the interaction of syntax and semantics (*sentence semantics*) and considers the functions and contexts of language use (*pragmatics*). A chapter outlining the importance of a knowledge of the structure of English for teaching and learning (*pedagogy*) is also included on the accompanying CD-ROM.

This textbook is addressed to advanced undergraduate (and graduate) students interested in contemporary English, including those whose primary area of interest is English as a second language, primary or secondary-school English education, English literature, theoretical and applied linguistics, or speech pathology. For this reason, this textbook, unlike many other introductory linguistics textbooks, emphasizes the empirical facts of English rather than any particular theory of linguistics. Furthermore, the text does not assume any background in language or linguistics. Students are required to learn the International Phonetic Alphabet as well as the technical vocabulary of grammar and linguistics, but all necessary terms and concepts are presented in the text.

Upon completion of this textbook and accompanying workbook, students will have acquired the following:

1. a knowledge of the sound system of contemporary English;
2. an understanding of the formation of English words and of their grammatical modification;
3. a comprehension of the structure of both simple and complex sentences in English;
4. a recognition of complexities in the expression of meaning, on both the word and sentence level; and
5. an understanding of the effects of context and function of use upon the structure of the language.

The textbook is divided into eleven chapters. Chapter 1 briefly examines the discipline of linguistics and the nature of human language and grammar. After a consideration of the means of production of human speech sounds, Chapter 2 studies the consonant and vowel sounds of English and methods of their phonetic transcription. Chapter 3 continues discussion of the English sound system, considering sound combinations, stress, intonation, and syllable structure; it also examines phonological rules in English and the concept of the *phoneme* (distinctive sound of a language). Chapter 4 explores the internal structure of words, the concept of the *morpheme* (meaningful unit of a language), and the varied processes of word formation in English. Chapter 5 begins by defining the grammatical categories and looking at the grammatical modification of English words and ends with a study of the means of word classification in the language. Chapter 6 surveys a number of traditional and structural approaches to word meaning and includes a discussion of figurative language. Chapter 7 treats the syntax of the simple sentence, looking at the internal structure of the noun, adjective, adverb, and prepositional phrase, complement structures in the verb phrase, verb types, and grammatical functions. Chapter 8 continues to treat the syntax of the simple sentence, including adverbial modifiers and verb premodifiers, and then examines the structure of passive, interrogative, negative, and imperative sentences. The syntax of the complex sentence is dealt with in Chapter 9, including *that*-clauses, *wh*-clauses (*wh*-questions, relative clauses, and indirect clauses), and nonfinite clauses (infinitival and participial clauses). Chapter 10 turns to the question of sentence meaning, understood in terms of thematic roles and predication analysis. Chapter 11 looks at two quite different approaches to the question of the function of language in context: information structuring and speech act theory.

A CD-ROM accompanies this textbook. It includes:

1. a complete workbook with self-testing exercises; and
2. a chapter on pedagogical applications of the material presented in the textbook.

Answers for all of the self-testing exercises are provided. At relevant points in each chapter in the text, students are directed to complete specific exercises and are advised to do so before continuing with the chapter. The exercises should provide a check on students' understanding and progress. The additional chapter discusses the changing role of linguistics in the teaching of English, reviewing arguments both in favor and opposed to explicit grammatical instruction for native and nonnative speakers and considering the importance of grammatical knowledge for both the teacher and the learner.

At the end of each chapter, students are also directed to readings that provide more detailed or enriched content on certain topics or supplemental help in understanding the content of the chapter.

A note to the student on punctuation

Various punctuation conventions are used in this textbook with which you may not be familiar.

It is the practice to distinguish between words (or parts of words) which are "mentioned" rather than used. Using words is what we do whenever we speak, but mentioning words is what we do when we refer to words as words or to the forms of words, rather than evoking their meanings. For example, try reading the following sentences:

> The word paper has five letters. Court has several different meanings. The feminine suffix -rix is almost obsolete. The clause whatever you do is an indefinite relative clause.

You may have had some difficulty reading these sentences. The reason for your difficulties is that these sentences contain word forms which are mentioned rather than used. The convention in printed texts is to italicize these mentioned forms, as follows:

> The word *paper* has five letters. *Court* has several different meanings. The feminine suffix *-rix* is almost obsolete. The clause *whatever you do* is an indefinite relative clause.

Note the this convention makes these sentences much easier to read. (In handwriting, mentioned forms are underlined.) This use of italics differs from the use of quotation marks to repeat the exact words of a spoken or written text, e.g., "convention" occurs two times in the previous paragraph.

Italics denote all linguistic forms which are used as examples within a sentence. However, it is not the practice to italicize examples which are set off from the sentence, as in the following:

> Below are two structurally ambiguous sentences:
>> Visiting relatives can be tiresome.
>> Flying planes can be dangerous.

When the actual sound of the word is being referred to, the International Phonetic Alphabet is used. To distinguish such representations from regular writing, they are enclosed in square brackets (or slashes), e.g.:

> The word *read* is pronounced [rɛd] or [rid].

Single quotation marks are used to give the meaning or gloss for a word; e.g., the word *garrulous* means 'tiresomely talkative'.

Another convention in linguistic works is the use of capitals to denote all the forms of a single word, thus WORK stands for *works, work, working, worked*. Capitals are also used for phonological and semantic features. These usages will be explained in more detail within the text.

Unit 1

The Study of English

CHAPTER 1

The Nature of Language and Linguistics

■ Chapter Preview

The chapter begins by looking at the nature of human language, starting from certain fundamental beliefs we share concerning the naturalness, power, and function of language and
moving towards a more scientific analysis of human language as a system of arbitrary vocal
signs, having the qualities of universality, innateness, and creativity. Particular attention is
given to the rule-governed nature of language. Language is also seen as uniquely human. The
ambiguous term *grammar* is then defined and a number of fallacies concerning grammar are
disputed, for example, that one type of grammar is simpler than another, or that changes in
grammar involve deterioration in a language. Finally, the discipline of linguistics is examined,
with its division in five components, corresponding to the levels of language: phonology,
morphology, syntax, semantics, and pragmatics.

■ Commentary

The Nature of Human Language

Linguists understand language as a system of arbitrary vocal signs. Language is rule-governed,
creative, universal, innate, and learned, all at the same time. It is also distinctly human. We
will look at what is meant by each of these terms in some detail, but before doing so, let's
briefly examine some preconceptions about language that a lay person might bring to the
study of language.

Fundamental Beliefs about Language

As speakers of language, we all have certain deep-seated notions concerning the nature of
language. Like all such fundamental beliefs, these are often wrong, though they contain a
germ of truth. For example, as literate beings, we tend to equate language with writing. But
there are significant differences, not only between oral sounds and written symbols, but also
between spoken and written syntax or vocabulary. More importantly, we assume that there is
some necessary, inevitable, or motivated connection between a word and the thing it names.
This assumption lies behind the belief that names tell us something about the bearer of that
name (for example, when one utters a statement such as "She doesn't look like a Penelope!")

or that a change in status must entail a change in name (for example, the custom — now changing, of course — for a woman to adopt her husband's surname upon marriage). It also lies behind the thought, which we may all probably be guilty of having at times, that a foreign language is somehow perverse and idiotic, while our own language is natural and sensible.

Because we believe that there is an inevitable connection between a word and the thing it represents, the word is very powerful: names are extremely important (as we see in the Old Testament Genesis) and the possession of language can be very dangerous (as we see in the Old Testament story of the Tower of Babel). We avoid naming certain taboo objects explicitly because doing so might invoke the object named; in addition, we may avoid directly naming things which we fear or stand in awe of, such as God, our parents, or dangerous animals, and things which are unpleasant or unclean, such as birth, death, bodily parts and functions, or disease. Instead, we substitute euphemisms. Even if we recognize that names do not, in fact, invoke the objects they name, there is a sense in which language has the effect of action. That is, by means of language alone we can perform an action, as for example when you say, "I nominate Alex". We will examine this phenomenon in Chapter 11.

Finally, we generally think of language as functioning to give expression to our thoughts ("language as a vehicle for thought"), to transmit information (the "communicative function"), or perhaps to provide the raw material for works of literature (the "narrative function"). But language has many more functions, for example, to get others to do things, to express emotions or feelings, to maintain social intercourse (as in greetings or talk about the weather — the "phatic" function), to make promises, to ask questions, to bring about states of affairs, to talk to oneself, and even to talk about language itself, what is known as metalanguage 'language turned back on itself', which is common in everyday life, not just among linguists. The idea that language simply expresses thought is a result of the philosophical and logical tradition, which treats language as a collection of propositions consisting of referent(s) and a predication which have truth-value (are true or false). However, in normal language use, speakers are not always committing themselves to the truth of a proposition; in fact, they do so only in the case of assertions or statements. Likewise, the idea that language has a communicative function, that it conveys new information, derives from its use in fairly restricted contexts, such as in the classroom or the newspaper, or when gossiping. In fact, the most important and frequent function of language is probably its phatic function.

Linguistic Signs

In the view of linguists, human language consists of **signs**, which are defined as things that stand for or represent something else. Linguistic signs involve sequences of sounds which represent concrete objects and events as well as abstractions. Signs may be related to the things they represent in a number of ways. The philosopher C. S. Peirce recognized three types of signs:

a. **iconic**, which resemble the things they represent (as do, for example, photographs, diagrams, star charts, or chemical models);
b. **indexical**, which point to or have a necessary connection with the things they represent (as do, for example, smoke to fire, a weathercock to the direction of the wind, a symptom to an illness, a smile to happiness, or a frown to anger); and

c. **symbolic**, which are only conventionally related to the thing they represent (as do, for example, a flag to a nation, a rose to love, a wedding ring to marriage).

It turns out that there is very little in language which is iconic. Onomatopoeic words, which resemble the natural sounds they represent, are a likely candidate. However, while "bow-wow" might represent the sound of a dog in English, for example, other languages represent the sound quite differently (for example, "guau" in Spanish or "amh-amh" in Irish). So even such words seems to be highly conventionalized. Certain aspects of word order are indeed iconic. In the following sentences, we would normally assume that the words, phrases, or clauses represents the temporal and causal order in which the events took place:

> Susie went to New York, Montreal, and Toronto.
> Sybil became ill and left the party.
> She ate dinner, read the newspaper, and watched TV.

For example, in the second sentence, we assume that Sybil became ill before she left the party and/or she left the party because she became ill. Note the very different interpretation we give to *Sybil left the party and became ill*. Or in the sentence *If you do well on this exam, you will get a good grade in the course*, we know that the condition precedes the consequence, both in the sentence and in real life. Iteration can also sometimes be iconic, as in *The car repairs became more and more expensive*, where the repetition of *more* has an intensifying effect.

A few aspects of language are indexical, such as the demonstrative pronouns *this* or *that*, which point to the things they represent as close to or far away from the speaker, or adverbs such as *now* and *then*, which denotes the moment of speaking or after (or before) the moment of speaking, respectively.

Most language, however, is symbolic. Ferdinand de Saussure — a Swiss scholar whose work is often said to have been the beginning of modern linguistics — stated that the relation between the linguistic sign and what it signifies is conventional or **arbitrary**. By an arbitrary connection, he meant that the sequence of sounds constituting a word bears no natural, necessary, logical, or inevitable connection to the thing in the real world which it names. Speakers must agree that it names that thing. Since there is no motivation for the connection, speakers must simply learn it. Speakers of English, for example, have entered into a social agreement that the word *apple* stands for a particular fruit; there is no resemblance between the sound of the word and the appearance or taste of the fruit. However, like all social agreements, such as those concerning dress or manners, linguistic agreements can be changed: English speakers could, for example, agree to call an apple a *pall*. In recent years, English speakers have agreed to replace quite a number of words which were felt to have acquired derogatory or negative connotations, such as the replacement of *crippled* by *handicapped* or *disabled*, or the replacement of *manic-depressive* by *bipolar disorder*.

■ *Self-Testing Exercise: Do Exercise 1.1.*

The Rule-Governed Nature of Language

Language consists of signs occurring not in a random collection, but in a system. A system consists of smaller units which stand in relation to each other and perform particular functions. These smaller units are organized on certain principles, or rules. For this reason, language is said to be rule-governed. The rules of a language, or its underlying system, are inferable from the observable patterns of the language. This underlying system constitutes what is called grammatical **competence**, which is part of native speakers' implicit knowledge, their "internalized grammar"; while grammatical competence is complete and perfect, it should be remembered that speakers' actual use of language, what is called **performance**, may be quite incomplete and imperfect.[1] A helpful analogy that might be made is to the score of a symphony — which, like competence is perfect and unchanging — and to the orchestra's playing of the symphony — which, like linguistic performance, may be inexact or may contain errors and which changes on each occasion of playing.

The rules of language act as a kind of constraint on what is possible in a language. For example, in the area of syntax, the rules of English permit *I like soap operas* or *Soap operas I like*, but not **Like soap operas I* (* means ungrammatical, not permitted by the rules of the language). In respect to word formation, *overnight* is a possible verb expressing a length of time (as in *The climbers overnighted on a rock ledge*), but *midnight*, since it expresses a point in time, is not a possible verb (as in **The revelers midnighted in the streets*). The phonological rules of English would permit the word *prace* (though it does not exist), but would not generate the word **psabr*. Furthermore, we know by the morphological rules of the language that if *prace* were a verb, the past tense would be *praced*, pronounced with a final "t" sound (not the "d" or "ed" sound that is found in other past tense forms), and if *prace* were a noun, the plural would be *praces*, pronounced with a final "ez" sound (not the "s" or "z" sound that is found in other plural forms).

Language Universals, Innateness, and Creativity

A more general set of constraints on language is known as language **universals**. These are features of language which are not language-specific; that is, they would be found in all languages of the world. Because of the surface diversity of languages, however, the search for language universals has proceeded slowly. We do know, for example, that, if one considers the order of the three main sentence elements, the subject (Su), the verb (V), and the object (O), there are only three basic word orders that occur with any frequency among world languages, namely, SuVO, SuOV, and VSuO, even though logically three other orders would be possible (VOSu, OVSu, OSuV). It may turn out to be the case that certain grammatical categories (such as number), functions (such as subject), and processes (such as passive) are universal. One consequence of the notion of universals is that language appears to be more motivated (that is, iconic) than previously assumed.

Inherent in the notion of universals is the belief that human language is **innate**, that we are born with an inborn capacity for language acquisition and are genetically equipped to learn a language (not a specific language, but human language in general). This "genetic predisposition" to learn a language is thought to account for the speed and ease with which children learn their first language during a crucial period of language acquisition (birth to age four), despite the fact that the linguistic data that they hear is incomplete, that they receive no negative evidence, and that they are seldom explicitly "taught" or corrected. Of course, children must be exposed to a language in order to acquire it, so language is in part learned as well as innate. Universals are clearly a consequence of the genetic endowment of human beings for language. A current scholarly debate is whether this innate capacity for language is part of more general cognitive strategies, such as spatial perception, or is contained in a separate language faculty, or "module"; the answer is not yet in. (On the usefulness of speakers' innate knowledge in the teaching of English, see the chapter on pedagogy on the CD-ROM.)

Despite the general and language-specific constraints on the form of language, we also consider language to be **creative**, or infinite. The first aspect of creativity is that human beings can produce and understand novel sentences and sometimes even new words. In fact, it is likely that no sentence that you have read so far in this text is one that you have encountered before. The second aspect of creativity is that we can create sentences of (theoretically) infinite length (as in the nursery rhyme *This is the dog that worried the cat that killed the rat that ate the malt that lay in the house that Jack built*), although there are obviously practical limits on length.

Animal Communication Codes

Finally, human language is uniquely human. Language is what distinguishes human beings from other animals. While many animals have codes of communication, these differ in important ways from human language. Most animal language is indexical and "stimulus-bound", depending on the necessary presence of concrete stimuli. The topic of conversation must be present in the immediate environment; it cannot be displaced in time or space. Animal communication codes may also be iconic and natural, but they are not symbolic. Furthermore, although the codes may be structurally quite complex, they are finite, not infinite or creative; there is a closed repertory of utterances. (Although some chimpanzees have been observed to use American Sign Language creatively, this may have been merely accidental.) The codes are acquired exclusively through genetic transmission, not learned, whereas, as we have seen, human language is both innate and learned. Animals always give primary responses, while human beings often give secondary responses, reacting to how something is said rather that what is said. Human beings may also use language to refer to abstractions or nonexistent entities; they can use language to lie, exaggerate, or mislead; and they can use it metalinguistically. None of these is possible within an animal communication code.

The Nature of Grammar

As well as having a number of misconceptions about the nature of language, lay people often have a different definition of the term *grammar* than linguists do.

Definition of Grammar

It is important at the outset to be clear about the meaning of the ambiguous term *grammar*. In linguistics, the term is used to refer to the rules or principles by which a language works, its system or structure. Speakers of a language all have an internalized grammar (their competence), whether they can articulate the rules of the language or not. And unless they have studied their language in a formal context, they probably can't. Throughout the ages, grammarians and linguists have been attempting to formulate the speakers' grammar in a set of rules, though it is probably fair to say that they have not yet been able to do so completely for any language. This sense of grammar is known as **descriptive grammar**. You have probably been exposed to a different sense of grammar known as **prescriptive grammar**, which involves attempts to establish and maintain a standard of correctness in the language, to "prescribe" (dictate) and "proscribe" (forbid) certain ways of speaking; but this has little to do with the actual working of the language. It is only in a prescriptive sense that we can talk about "good" grammar or "bad" grammar; prescriptive grammar involves value judgments based on factors external to language — such as, social class or level of education (a topic discussed in more detail in the chapter on pedagogy on the CD-ROM).

The difference between descriptive grammar and prescriptive grammar is comparable to the difference between **constitutive rules**, which determine how something works (such as the rules for the game of chess), and **regulatory rules**, which control behavior (such as the rules of etiquette). If the former are violated, the thing cannot work, but if the latter are violated, the thing works, but crudely, awkwardly, or rudely. That is, if you move the pawn three spaces in a single move, you cannot be said to be playing chess, but if you eat off your knife, you can eat adequately, but you are being rude or vulgar. Analogously, if you say *Cat the the dog chased* you are not speaking English; the sentence is ungrammatical. Hearers might well have trouble understanding you (Is the dog chasing the cat or the cat chasing the dog?). However, if you say *He did good on the exam*, your sentence is grammatical and would be understood by all, but many people would find your sentence unacceptable; they would consider it "bad", "nonstandard", or "incorrect" English.

On the role of prescriptivism in language teaching, see the chapter on pedagogy on the CD-ROM.

Fallacies concerning Grammar

There are some fallacies concerning the nature of grammar which are widely believed. One fallacy is that there are languages that have "no" grammar or "little" grammar. If grammar is defined as the principles by which a language operates, it must be recognized that every language has a grammar and that each language's grammar is completely adequate. It is certainly true that there are different types of grammars — such as the widely divergent grammars of Chinese, German, Turkish, or Cree — but these are all equally operative.

A related fallacy is that certain types of grammars are simpler and hence more "primitive" than others, while other grammars (particularly grammars which make use of inflections, or word endings, to express distinctions) are more complex and hence more advanced. This view was widely held in the eighteenth and nineteenth centuries, but was dispelled by the discovery that supposedly primitive languages (for example the American Indian languages) had extremely complex grammars and that the earliest form of the Indo-European languages, which has been reconstructed, probably had a more elaborate inflectional system than classical languages such as Greek, Latin, and Sanskrit. In fact, it is unclear how a concept such as grammatical "simplicity" would be defined: is it, for example, simpler to add an inflection to a word or to express the same concept with a separate word, as English often does? That is, is *the dog's tail* or *the tail of the dog* simpler? It also seems to be the case that if one area of the grammar of a language is "simple", other areas are usually more "complex" in compensation. The number of variant forms of the English verb, for instance, is quite small, usually only four (e.g., *work, works, worked, working*). Compared even with another so-called analytic language (one which has few inflections) such as French, then, the English verb is inflectionally very simple. But the auxiliary phrase in English balances matters out by being very complex: there may be as many as four auxiliaries preceding the main verb, and these must occur in a certain order and form (e.g., English can produce phrases as complex as *might have been being worked*). Moreover, if one language makes a grammatical distinction that another language appears not to, further examination of the second language often reveals that it makes the same distinction, but in a different way.

Another fallacy about the form of grammars, which was also current in the eighteenth and nineteenth centuries, was that grammars should be logical and analogical (that is, regular). So strong was this belief that there were a number of attempts to eliminate supposedly illogical features of English grammar, such as the use of two or more negatives for emphasis, which was common prior to the eighteenth century, but was then judged by principles of logic to make a positive. While some of this "language engineering" was successful, grammars do not naturally follow logical principles. There is some drive towards regularity in language, as when children make "analogical mistakes", producing a regular form such as *take/taked* for the irregular *take/took*; the same process operates over time in languages, as when *bōc/bēc* in Old English (similar to *goose/geese*) is replaced by *book/books* in Modern English. However, there are opposing forces — often changes in pronunciation — which serve to make language irregular, so no perfectly regular language exists.

A fallacy about changes in grammar is that they result in deterioration, or, alternatively, evolution. Again, it would be difficult to define what is meant by grammatical "evolution" or "deterioration". There is no doubt that languages change over time, sometimes in quite radical ways, but the changes do not seem to entail an advancement or a loss of any kind; the status quo is maintained. Furthermore, changes in language are not entirely random, but often proceed in certain predictable ways (known as *drift*) and by a number of quite well-understood mechanisms.

It is often believed that people are taught the grammar of their native language, but in fact little conscious teaching of grammar occurs in the critical period of language learning, apart from rather sporadic corrections of wrong forms (as in, "it's not *tooken* but *taken*"). Children learn the language by hearing instances of it, and, it is now believed, constructing their own "internalized" grammar.

Three further fallacies concerning grammar which have already been touched on are that there are completely random differences among the languages of the world (the notion of language universals calls this view into question), that the sentences a person produces directly reflect his or her grammatical knowledge (the distinction between competence and performance underlines the incorrectness of this view), and that there is only one sense of the term *grammar* (we saw above that we need to recognize both prescriptive and descriptive grammars as well as the linguist's as opposed to the speaker's grammar).

■   *Self-Testing Exercise: Do Exercise 1.2.*

Linguistics and the Components of Language

Linguistics is defined as the study of language systems. For the purposes of study, language is divided into levels, or **components**. These components are conventional and, to some extent, arbitrary divisions of linguistic investigation, and although they are interrelated in complex ways in the system of language, we treat them more or less separately. They constitute the framework which organizes this textbook.

The first component is **phonology** (from the Greek word *phōnē* meaning 'sound, voice'), the study of the speech sounds of a particular language. A subdivision of phonology is **phonetics**, the study of the speech sounds of human language in general, either from the perspective of their production (*articulatory phonetics*), their perception (*auditory phonetics*), or their physical properties (*acoustic phonetics*). Although speech is a continuum of sound, it is possible to break it into different types of sounds, known as consonants, vowels, and semivowels; we will study how these different sounds are articulated, as well as how other features of sound, including stress and pitch, are superimposed over these sounds. Since the repertory of human speech sounds is quite large (but not unlimited — there are physical constraints on the sounds human beings are capable of producing), no language makes use of all possible speech sounds, but instead selects a limited set. Furthermore, within this limited set of sounds, certain sounds will be distinctive, that is, make a difference in meaning (such as the "t" sound and "k" sounds in *tap* and *cap*), while others will be nondistinctive and predictable variants (such as the slightly different "t" sounds in *stop* and *top*). Phonetics and phonology are perhaps the most exact areas of linguistic study.

Since the writing system of English does not provide us with a one-to-one correspondence between oral sound and written symbol, we need a tool for representing human sounds in an regular way when studying phonology; the International Phonetic Alphabet (the IPA) has been invented for this purpose. In it, each written symbol represents one, and only one, speech sound, while each speech sound is represented by one, and only one, written symbol. We will begin by learning this special alphabet.

The second component of language is **morphology** (from the Greek word *morphē* 'form'). Morphology is the study of the structure or form of words in a particular language, and of their classification. While the concept of a word is intuitively clear, it is not easy to define it objectively (is *ice cream* one word or two?), and morphology must begin by trying to formulate such a definition. Morphology then considers principles of word formation in a language: how sounds combine into meaningful units such as prefixes, suffixes, and roots, which of these units are distinctive and which are predictable variants (such as *a* and *an*), and what processes of word formation a language characteristically uses, such as compounding (as in *roadway*) or suffixing (as in *pavement*). Morphology then treats how words can be grouped into classes, what are traditionally called *parts of speech*, again seeking some objective criteria — either of form or of meaning — for sorting the words of a language into categories. We will study all of these questions in respect to the form of words in English.

The third component of language is **syntax** (from Greek *suntassein* 'to put in order'). Syntax is the study of the order and arrangement of words into larger units, as well as the relationships holding between elements in these hierarchical units. It studies the structure and types of sentences (such as questions or commands), of clauses (such as relative or adverbial clauses), and of phrases (such as prepositional or verbal phrases). Syntax is an extensive and complex area of language, and nearly one-third of the textbook is devoted to the study of English syntax. The two components of morphology and syntax are sometimes classified together as *grammar*.

The fourth component of language is **semantics** (from Greek *sēmainein* 'to signify, show, signal'). Semantics is the study of how meaning is conveyed, focusing either on meanings related to the outside world (*lexical meaning*) or meanings related to the grammar of the sentence (*grammatical meaning*). It is perhaps the least clear-cut area of linguistic study. In studying meaning, we consider both the meaning of individual words (*lexical semantics*) and the meaning which results from the interaction of elements in a sentence (*sentence semantics*). The latter involves the relationship between syntax and semantics. A further area of study, which is also treated here, is the meaning relationships holding among parts in an extended discourse (*discourse semantics*).

A fifth component of language, not part of the traditional subdivision but added in recent years, is **pragmatics** (from Greek *pragma* 'deed, affair', from *prassein* 'to do'). Pragmatics is the study of the functions of language and its use in context. As was pointed out above, language, in addition to serving to communicate information, actually has a variety of functions, including the expression of emotion, the maintenance of social ties, and even the performance of action (a statement such as *I declare you guilty* uttered by a judge). Furthermore, in any context, a variety of factors, such as the age, sex, and social class of the interlocutors and their relationships of intimacy and power, influence the form of language used. We will consider this fairly wide-open field from two different perspectives.

Organization of the Book

This book examines the structure of Modern English starting with the smallest units and working toward larger units. Thus, we begin with the phonological level (individual sounds), move to the morphological level (sounds combined into words and meaningful parts of words), and then to the syntactic level (words combined into phrases, clauses, and sentences). The relation of sentences within the larger discourse is the subject matter of pragmatics. Since meaning derives from aspects of phonological structure, from words and clauses, and from larger textual structures, we consider aspects of the semantic component as it relates to all of the levels. However, since meaning is most strongly associated with lexical items and syntactic structures, a section on word semantics follows the morphological section, and a section on sentence semantics follows the syntax section. This approach may be schematized as in Figure 1.1.

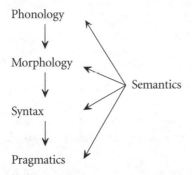

Figure 1.1. Organization of the Text

There are many different ways to study language, or different approaches, which can be termed schools of linguistics. Each has certain characteristics and certain strengths. In studying the different linguistic components, we use methods of analysis formulated within different schools of linguistics. Such an eclectic approach seems desirable because some theories are better suited to deal with certain areas than others. Traditional grammar (an approach to the study of language dating from Greek times) underlies much of our treatment, but our approach to both phonology and morphology will be primarily structuralist (an approach to the study of language dating from the 1930s to the 1950s), and our approach to syntax will be overtly generative (an approach to the study of language dating from the late 1950s to the present).

■ Chapter Summary

Now that you have completed this chapter, you should be able to:

1. describe the characteristics of human language;
2. differentiate between iconic, indexical, and symbolic signs;
3. distinguish between different senses of the word *grammar*;
4. describe common fallacies about language and grammar; and
5. define the study of linguistics and its subparts.

■ Recommended Additional Reading

The topics discussed in this chapter are generally addressed in introductory linguistics textbooks, such as Fromkin and Rodman (1993, Chapter 1), Finegan (1999, Chapter 1),

Akmajian et al. (1995, Chapter 1), O'Grady and Dobrovolsky (1996, Chapter 1) or in treatments of English linguistics, such as Klammer and Schulz (1995, Chapter 1), Delahunty and Garvey (1994, Chapter 1) and Kaplan (1995, Chapter 1). On the definition of language, see Crystal (1997).

You may find a dictionary of linguistics, such as Crystal (1996) or Trask (1993), a very useful reference while reading this textbook. Hurford (1994) is a dictionary/grammar, with extensive examples from English as well as exercises and answers.

The best modern traditional grammar of English is Quirk et al. (1985), which also exists in a shorter students' form (Greenbaum and Quirk 1990). Older traditional grammars of English based on historical principles are those by Curme (1931, 1935; and a shorter form 1947), Jespersen (1909–49; and a shorter form 1933), and Poutsma (1904–26) — German, Danish, and Dutch speakers, respectively! Very useful grammars of English that are primarily traditional in orientation are those intended primarily for teachers of English as a second language, such as Celce-Murcia and Larson-Freeman (1999) or Larson-Freeman (1997).

A prescriptive (but very intelligent) approach to English usage can be found in Fowler (1983). For a humorous take-off on Fowler, see Thurber (1931).

Structural accounts of English include Francis (1958), Fries (1952), and Strang (1968). Bloomfield (1933) and Sapir (1921) are classic — and very readable — structural accounts of language in general. More contemporary 'structural' accounts are Huddleston (1984; 1988). References to generative accounts of English may be found in later chapters on phonology and syntax.

If you would like to read the writings of Ferdinand de Saussure, they can be found in a modern translation (Saussure 1988). A very readable discussion of the human language capacity is Pinker (1994).

■ Notes

1. The distinction between competence and performance corresponds roughly to what Saussure called *langue* and *parole*.

Unit 2

The Speech Sounds of English

CHAPTER 2

English Consonants and Vowels

■ Chapter Preview

This chapter begins with a discussion of some of the differences between writing and speech, what each medium can and cannot express. It then examines the production of human speech sounds, with a detailed look at the egressive pulmonic system. The criteria for analyzing consonant sounds are explained. An inventory of the consonant sounds in English and explication of the method of their phonetic transcription follows. Vowels sounds are next classified, with a description of what vowel sounds English has and how they are transcribed. The chapter ends with discussion of the difficulty of distinguishing vowels and consonants by either formal or functional means.

■ Commentary

As defined in Chapter 1, phonetics is the study of speech sounds in general. It has three subdivisions:

– the study of how sounds are made or the mechanics of their production by human beings (articulatory phonetics);
– the study of how sounds are heard or the mechanics of their perception (auditory phonetics); and
– the study of the physical properties of the speech waves which constitute speech sound (acoustic phonetics).

In this chapter, after briefly examining how speech sounds are made, we will turn to **phonology**, the study of the speech sounds in a particular language, in our case, the inventory of sounds constituting the sound system of English, including consonants, vowels, and glides. Our study of English phonology will continue in the next chapter with a consideration of the distinctive and nondistinctive sounds in English as well as of sound combinations and syllable structure in the language.

The Spoken versus the Written Form of Language

The initial step in the study of the sound system of a language is to distinguish between speech and writing. This is often a difficult distinction for literate people to make since we are tempted to consider the written form as equivalent to language. But speech and writing are, in fact, two quite distinct media of language. Speech is temporally prior, both in the history of humankind and in the history of the individual. Languages existed for millennia before writing systems were invented. We learn to speak effortlessly, but must struggle to learn to write; many, in fact, do not learn to write yet are fluent speakers of the language. It is salutary to remember that even in Shakespeare's day the majority of English speakers were illiterate, yet verbally proficient enough to understand Shakespeare's word plays. Some languages have no written form, but all languages have spoken forms. Moreover, a variety of writing systems are used to record the languages of the world, some languages have more than one writing system, and even very closely-related languages may use very different writing systems.

English Spelling

That writing is often an imperfect means of representing speech is perhaps most obvious in the well-known inadequacies of English spelling. If we compare the actual sounds of English with the **orthography**, the graphic symbols or letters used in writing, we find the following discrepancies:

- one sound can be represented by a variety of letters, as with the vowel sound in *meat*, *meet*, *city*, *key*, *ceiling*, *people*, *niece*, *evil*, and *quay*;
- one letter can represent a variety of sounds, as with *d* in *damage*, *educate*, *picked*;
- a letter or letters may represent no sound at all, as in *knee*, *gnat*, *lamb*, *receipt*, *right*, *honor*, *rhyme*, *psalm*, and *salmon*;
- two or more letters may represent a single sound, as in *throne*, *chain*, *edge*, *shore*, *nation*, *itch*, *inn*, *school*, *eat*, *friend*, *too*, *leopard*, *cause*, *blood*, or *lieutenant*;
- a letter may simply indicate the quality of a neighboring sound, as in *dinner* vs. *diner* (where a double or single *n* indicates the quality of the preceding vowel) or *dine* vs. *din* (where the presence or absence of final *e* indicates the quality of the preceding vowel);
- a single letter may represent two or more sounds, as in *box* (x=ks); and
- some sounds have no graphic representation, as with the initial sounds in *universe* and *one*.

■ *Self-Testing Exercise* 2.1: Examining the reasons for the marked incongruity between sound and spelling in English makes for a fascinating historical study. Read the brief discussion and do the self-testing exercise on the CD-ROM.

For the study of speech sounds, therefore, orthographic systems are clearly inadequate. We need a system of recording sounds in which a single written symbol represents one and only one speech sound and in which a single sound is represented by one and only one written symbol. For this reason, the **International Phonetic Alphabet (IPA)** was invented in 1888 (and revised in 1989). It is based on the Roman alphabet primarily, with some symbols from other writing systems, as well as some invented symbols and diacritics (marks added to symbols). The recording of the sounds of a language in the IPA is called **transcription**. Much of this chapter will be concerned with the transcription of English using the IPA.

The Advantages of Speech and Writing

It is important to keep in mind, however, that each medium of language — speech and writing — fulfills different functions and has certain advantages. On one hand, the oral medium expresses certain meaning features that cannot always be recorded in the written medium:

1. emphasis: indicated by syllable stress in speech and very inexactly by underlining in writing, as in *I want thát one, not this one.*
2. sentence type: indicated by intonation (pitch) in speech and very crudely by end punctuation in writing, as in the difference between *He said he would help.* and *He said he would help?* (though often different word orders distinguish different sentence types such as questions or commands);
3. homographs: words that are spelled the same but pronounced differently, for example, *sewer* 'one who sews'/'a conduit for sewage' or *hót dòg* 'a sausage'/*hót dóg* 'an overheated canine';
4. paralanguage: tones of voice and vocal qualifiers: indicated by shouting, growling, whispering, drawling, and so on;
5. variations in pronunciation resulting from dialect or idiolect (an individual's unique dialect);
6. kinesics: indicated by body movement, facial expressions, and gestures;
7. performance errors, slips, or hesitations;
8. features of the speech situation, such as the relation of the speaker and the hearer; and
9. intimacy and personal contact.

In reading over the above list, you might have thought of dialogue in novels or plays as an exception. However, dialogue is always very stylized and conventionalized. For example, tones of voice, kinesics, contextual features, and many performance errors must be explicitly described. If dialogue were faithfully to represent the performance errors of real conversation, it would be nearly incomprehensible; the transcribed conversation would be quite incoherent. Features of regional or social dialect are also imperfectly represented (as in *Ah'm tahrd* for a Southern American pronunciation of *I'm tired*), frequently by the use of eye dialect, or the use of unconventional spelling to suggest a nonstandard dialect but actually approximating actual pronunciation, such as *bekuz, nite, wuz, sez.*

On the other hand, there are aspects of language which writing expresses but speech cannot:

1. historical changes: older pronunciations preserved in the spelling, such as *comb, gnat,* or *taught*;
2. words: indicated by spaces, sometimes disambiguating ambiguous phonological sequences such as *nitrate/night rate, syntax/sin tax,* or *homemade/home aid*;
3. homophones: words which are pronounced the same but spelled differently, such as *bear/bare, meat/meet,* or *maid/made*;

4. related words or affixes which sound different, such as *photograph, photography, photo-graphic* or the past tense affix *-ed* in *rated, walked, robbed*;
5. a greater range of vocabulary, more complex syntax, and greater refinement of style, resulting in part from the planning permitted by the situation of writing;
6. language free of performance errors (which, in fact, we often are not consciously aware of in the spoken form);
7. a standard language without dialectal differences, allowing easier communication among diverse groups;
8. permanency: permitting the keeping of historical annals, the recording of laws, and the writing of other permanent records.

Incidentally, it is because of points (1) and (7) above that the many attempts at spelling reform in the history of the English language have been unsuccessful. For example, we will see below that certain modern dialects of English do not pronounce the "r" in words such as *part* or *par*, while others do, although historically all dialects pronounced the "r". If spelling were to represent pronunciation more closely, then which dialect's pronunciation should become fixed in the orthography?

The Production of Speech Sounds

Keeping in mind the primacy of speech, we will now consider how we make speech sounds. Speech sounds are produced using, but modifying, the respiratory system. When speaking, the number of breaths per minute increases, with a shorter inspiration and longer expiration period. A greater amount of air is expelled, with a gradual decrease in the volume of air and fairly constant pressure. Importantly for the production of sound, the air is often impeded at some point or points on its way out.

English and most languages of the world use the **egressive pulmonic system**, but other air stream mechanisms are possible. *Egressive*, as opposed to *ingressive*, refers to the fact that sound is produced when air is exiting, not entering, the lungs. *Pulmonic* refers to the use of the lungs as the power source. In speaking, air is expelled from the lungs by a downward movement of the ribs and upward movement of the diaphragm using the intercostal muscles. The air travels up the bronchial tubes to the trachea, or "wind pipe", and through the larynx, or "Adam's Apple". The larynx contains a valve which functions in conjunction with the epiglottis to close off the trachea while you are eating. This valve has been adapted for the purposes of speech; it is known as the **vocal cords**. The vocal cords are two muscles stretching horizontally across the larynx, attached to cartilage at either end that controls their movement. The vocal cords are relatively open during normal breathing, but closed during eating. The space between the cords when they are open is known as the **glottis**. The vocal cords of men and of women are of different lengths: 1.7 cm for women, 2.3 for men. This, as we will see later, accounts in part for the different vocal qualities of men and women. Air continues past the larynx into the pharynx, whose only real function is as a connector and resonator.

The air then moves into the vocal tract (see Figure 2.1), consisting of the **oral** and **nasal cavities**. The oral cavity, that is, the mouth, is a resonator and a generator of speech sounds via the articulators, which may be active (moving) or passive (stationary). The **active articulators** include the following:

- the tongue, divided into the tip (or apex), and moving backwards, the blade (or lamina), the front, the back or dorsum, and the root: the tongue modifies the shape of the cavity, acts as a valve by touching parts of the mouth to stop the flow of air, and is shaped in various ways to direct the flow of air.
- the lower lip (the combining term is *labio-*, as in *labiodental*): the lip may be placed against the upper teeth, or, together with the upper lip may be closed or opened, rounded or spread.

The **passive articulators** include the following:

- the teeth (*-dental*): both upper and lower.
- the roof of the mouth, which is divided into the alveolar ridge (*alveolo-*), which is 1 cm behind the upper teeth, the hard palate (*-palatal*, as in *alveolopalatal*), which is the domed, bony plate, the soft palate, or velum (*-velar*), which is the muscular flap at the rear, and the uvula (*-uvular*), which is the tip of the velum.
- the pharynx, or back of the throat, which is used by some languages (but not English) in producing speech sounds.

If you run your tongue back along the top of your mouth from your teeth, you should be able to feel your alveolar ridge and to distinguish your palate from your velum.

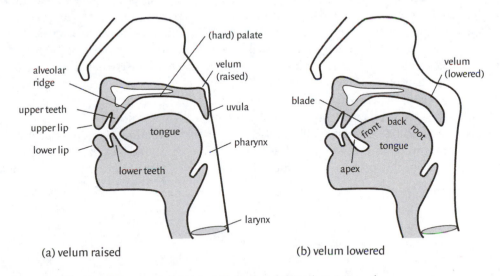

(a) velum raised   (b) velum lowered

Figure 2.1. The Vocal Tract with (a) Velum Raised and (b) Velum Lowered

A useful feature of the velum is that it is movable. If it is raised against the back of the pharynx (called *velic closure*), then air passes out only through the oral cavity (see Figure 2.1a). This is known as an **oral sound**. If it is lowered (called *velic opening*), then air can pass out through the other cavity, the nasal cavity, that is the nose (see Figure 2.1b). If air passes out of the nose exclusively, a **nasal sound** is produced, but if air passes out of both the nose and the mouth, a **nasalized sound** is produced. People who have a "nasal quality" to their voice probably have incomplete closure of the velum at all times, so that a little air is always able to escape through the nose. Also, when you have a cold and your velum is swollen, you will have imperfect velic closure and hence a nasal voice, but you will also not be able to produce exclusively nasal sounds since your nose is blocked and will substitute oral sounds (e.g., "b" for "m").

Let us return, for a few minutes, to the larynx and the vocal cords to see how they function in producing sounds. When the cords are widely separated and fairly taut, no noise is produced. This is known as an *open glottis* and produces a **voiceless sound** (see Figure 2.2a). However, the vocal cords may also be set in vibration ("phonation"), and this produces a **voiced sound** (see Figure 2.2b). They vibrate open and shut as air passes through. Vibration is begun by initially closing the vocal cords completely, but with the cords fairly relaxed. Air pressure builds up below the cords and blows then apart. Then the pressure decreases and the cords close again; these events occur in rapid succession. Women's vocal cords, being smaller, vibrate more rapidly, normally 190–250 Hz (times/second), while men's larger vocal cords vibrate 100–150 Hz. When the vocal cords are vibrating, you can feel a vibration and hear a buzzing. To do so, place your fingers on your larynx or cup your hands over your ears and say *sa-za-sa-za*. You should sense the vibration of the cords with the *z* but not the *s*. A *closed glottis* occurs when the vocal cords are brought completely together once and the air stream is interrupted. This produces a speech sound we will consider later called a *glottal stop*.[1]

Whispering involves bringing the vocal cords close together, keeping them fairly taut but not vibrating them. Air is restricted through a small triangular passage between the arytenoid cartilages, and this produces a hissing sound (see Figure 2.2c). To produce a breathy voice, the vocal cords never close completely but are in vibration; hence, there is a murmuring sound. A creaky voice results from voicing with slow, regular vibration, whereas a harsh voice results from excessive tension in the vocal cords and irregular vibration. A hoarse voice usually results from swelling of the vocal cords producing irregular vibration and incomplete closure; the larger size of the vocal cords may also result in a lower pitched voice.

Two other features of sound are **loudness** and **pitch** (or **intonation**). Loudness is related to the pressure and volume of air expelled; as these increase, the sound becomes louder. Pitch is a matter of the quality of the sound, which is a consequence of the frequency of the sound

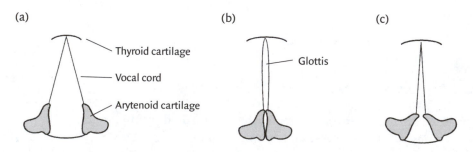

(a)   (b)   (c)

Thyroid cartilage

Vocal cord

Arytenoid cartilage

Glottis

Figure 2.2. Configurations of the Larynx: (a) Voiceless (Exhalation), (b) Voiced, and (c) Whispered.

wave emitted. Every person has a natural frequency and range. Men's voices tend to have a lower pitch than women's due to the larger size of their vocal cords, which vibrate more slowly. Pitch can be modulated by altering the tension on the vocal cords and changing their length. Pitch decreases when the vocal cords are elongated and tensed and increases when they are relaxed, hence shorter. Most human voices have a range of about two octaves.

Consonant Sounds

Speech is a phonetic continuum, a continuous, smoothly flowing set of movements, not a set of discrete and isolated movements. It is convenient, however, to segment the speech chain in syllables, and to divide these in turn into consonants and vowels. A syllable consists necessarily of a vowel; optionally, it may begin and/or end with a consonant. A vowel is the nucleus or acoustic high point of a syllable; it is articulated for a longer time than surrounding consonants. While vowels tend to continue the airstream, consonants tend to break it. We begin our study of speech sounds with consonants, since they are somewhat easier to describe. We will look first — in abstract — at how consonants are articulated before examining in detail the specific consonants of English.

Classification of Consonants

A **consonant** is defined as a speech sound which is articulated with some kind of stricture, or closure, of the air stream.

Consonants are classified according to four features:

1.   the state of the glottis: in vibration (voiced) or open (voiceless);
2.   the state of the velum: lowered (nasal) or raised (oral);
3.   the place of articulation: where the stricture occurs (place of maximum interference) and what articulators are involved; and
4.   the manner of articulation: the amount of stricture, whether it is complete, partial (called close approximation), or relatively open (open approximation).

The term *approximation* refers to the two articulators approaching, or "approximating", one another.

In describing the **place of articulation** for consonants, it is traditional to list the active and then the passive articulator. Consonants involve a rather large number of discrete places of articulation (see Figure 2.3):

1.   **bilabial:** the lips are brought together (the lower lip is active); the tongue is not involved but remains in the "rest position" (its position when you say *ah* for the doctor) — e.g., the sound of *b* in English;
2.   **labiodental:** the lower lip is brought up against the upper front teeth; again the tongue is in rest position — e.g., the sound of *f* in English;
3.   **interdental:** the tip of the tongue (or apex) protrudes between the teeth or touches the back of the upper teeth — e.g., the sound of *th* in English;
4.   **dental:** the tip of the tongue touches the back of the upper teeth;

5. **alveolar:** the tip of the tongue makes contact with the alveolar ridge — e.g., the sound of *d* in English;
6. **alveolopalatal:** the front, or blade, of the tongue is raised to an area between the alveolar ridge and the palate — e.g., the sound of *sh* in English;
7. **palatal:** the front of the tongue is brought up against the palate — e.g., the sound of *y* in English;
8. **velar:** the back, or dorsum, of the tongue is brought into contact with the velum — e.g., the sound of *g* in English;
9. **uvular:** the back of the tongue touches the uvula;
10. **pharyngeal:** the root of the tongue (specifically, the epiglottis) is moved backwards against the wall of the pharynx; and
11. **glottal:** the vocal cords, functioning as articulators, make a brief closure.

While the dental, uvular, and pharyngeal places are not used for the articulation of English consonants, they are used in other languages: e.g., the dental place of articulation is used for Spanish "t", the uvular for German "r" and a French fricative, and the pharyngeal for a fricative in Arabic.

Two places of articulation may also be used at the same time — what is called coarticulation — as in the case of **labiovelars**, which involve the lips, on one hand, and the tongue and velum, on the other.

Each of the various places of articulation just examined may combine with a number of different **manners of articulation** to produce consonant sounds:

1. **stop:** (oral stop) involving complete closure of two articulators with the velum raised (velic closure) — e.g., the sound of *p* in English;
2. **nasal:** (nasal stop) involving complete closure of two articulators with the velum lowered (velic opening) — e.g., the sound of *n* in English; for every stop position in English, there is a nasal articulated in the same position (homorganic);
3. **fricative:** (or *spirant*) involving close approximation of two articulators; the air stream is partially obstructed so that a turbulent airflow is produced, resulting in a hissing or rubbing sound — e.g., the sound of *s* in English;
4. **affricate:** consisting of a stop released slowly into a homorganic fricative — e.g., the sound of *ch* in English; this sound is analyzed either as a complex or a simple sound;
5. **trill:** (or *roll*) involving complete closure alternating intermittently with open approximation, that is, a rapid vibration of the active articulator against the passive articulator (this sound in not common in English except for the Scottish "r" made with an apical trill);
6. **flap:** (or *tap*) involving momentary complete closure in which the active articulator strikes the passive articulator only once; it is one strike of a trill and similar to a stop except that the tongue is more tense and controlled than in a stop; and
7. **approximant:** one articulator approaches another but generally not to the extent that a turbulent air stream is produced; there is usually open approximation in the three different types of approximants:

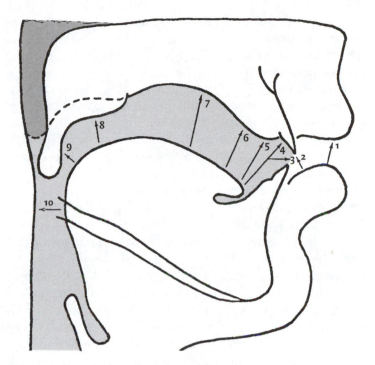

1. bilabial
2. labiodental
3. interdental
4. dental
5. alveolar
6. alveolopalatal
7. palatal
8. velar
9. uvular
10. pharyngeal

Figure 2.3. Some Places of Articulation

a.   **lateral**: involving complete closure of the central portion of the vocal tract, with the lateral passage of air; the air may pass around the sides with no stricture (open approximation) — e.g., the sound of *l* in English — or, in languages other than English, with some stricture (close approximation)

b.   **retroflex**: involving the underside of the tongue curling back behind the alveolar ridge towards the palate — e.g., the sound of *r* in English; laterals and retroflexes are called *liquids*;

c.   **glide** (or **semivowel**): involving a glide to or from a vowel; this sound is articulated like a vowel (with no stricture) but functions as a consonant to begin or end syllables — e.g., the sound of *w* in English.

Consonants of English and their Phonetic Notation

We will now consider what combinations of voicing, place of articulation, and manner of articulation are utilized in the articulation of consonants in English. Remember that not all possible combinations are used in all languages, though certain combinations (such as interdental stop, perhaps, or a velar trill) might be physiologically impossible.

As you read the following section, you should consult the consonant chart in Table 2.1. On the consonant chart, following common practice, the places of articulation are listed across the horizontal axis (roughly corresponding to a cross-section of the mouth viewed from the left, with the front of the mouth on the left and the back of the mouth on the right);

the manners of articulation are listed along the vertical axis, moving in a rough way from greatest stricture at the top to lesser amounts of stricture as one moves down. Voiceless consonant are listed above voiced ones, where applicable. It is not necessary to specify the state of the velum since all consonants are oral except the nasals. Note that in giving a technical description of a consonant sound, it is traditional to list voicing, then place, then manner; get into the habit of describing the consonants in this order from the very beginning.

CAUTION: In learning the sounds of English and, especially, in transcribing English words, you must not allow yourself to be influenced by the written form. Because of the imperfect correspondence between sound and spelling in English mentioned above, the spelling will often lead you astray or confuse you. You must try to function entirely in an oral context. You must also try to say words with a natural and relaxed pronunciation. There is a strong tendency when reading words or saying them in isolation to give them an overly formal and even distorted pronunciation. Try to speak as you do naturally in casual conversation. Do not whisper the words, either, as you cannot distinguish between voiced and voiceless sounds when whispering.

This section, in addition to surveying the consonant inventory of English, will teach you the phonetic alphabet symbol used to transcribe each of the consonants. We will use the modified version of the IPA used in North America. For the most part, you will be asked to give what is called **broad transcription** rather than **narrow transcription**. As the names imply, broad transcription merely records the grosser features of sound, whereas narrow transcription records all the nuances and finer aspects of sound, though not performance factors such as drunken slurs, loudness, and so on. Although it is common to enclose broad transcription between slashes, such as /kæt/ for *cat*, and to use square brackets for narrow transcription, such as [kʰætʼ], we will generally use the square brackets exclusively.

In the **stop series** of English, there are paired voiced and voiceless stops produced in three locations:

1. the voiced bilabial stop [b] (as in *band*, *ember*, *mob*) and the voiceless bilabial stop [p] (as in *pound*, *open*, *coop*);
2. the voiced alveolar stop [d] (as in *danger*, *eddy*, *loud*) and the voiceless alveolar stop [t] (as in *tangle*, *otter*, *moat*); and
3. the voiced velar stop [g] (as in *grass*, *rugged*, *rug*) and the voiceless velar stop [k] (as in *carrot*, *election*, *luck*).

As you can see, all of these stop sounds are represented in the IPA with Roman alphabet symbols. The bilabial stop is made by bringing the lips together, the alveolar by bringing the tip of the tongue up against the alveolar ridge, and the velar by bringing the back of the tongue up against the soft palate. Because the air stream is completely blocked, you cannot actually hear stops until you open your mouth to release them into a vowel. Released stops are called *plosives*. Furthermore, the articulation of stops cannot be maintained; their articulation is instantaneous. Practice saying all of these sounds.

The stops share certain features. First, the voiced stops are articulated for a shorter period than the corresponding voiceless stops. Compare the final stops in the left-hand column with those in the right-hand column:

Table 2.1. The Consonants of English

Manner of Articulation		Bilabial	Labiodental	Interdental	Alveolar	Alveolo-palatal	Palatal	Velar	Glottal
						Place of Articulation			
Stop	voiceless	p			t			k	?
	voiced	b			d			g	
Nasal		m			n			ŋ	
Flap					ɾ				
Fricative	voiceless		f	θ	s	š (= ʃ)			h
	voiced		v	ð	z	ž (= ʒ)			
Affricate	voiceless					č (= tʃ)			
	voiced					ǰ (= dʒ)			
Approximant	lateral				l				
	retroflex				r (= ɹ)				
	glide or semivowel	w					y (= j)	w	h

The symbols in parentheses represent the IPA symbols in cases where they differ from the symbols used in this book.

ca<u>b</u> [b]	ca<u>p</u> [p]
ca<u>d</u> [d]	ca<u>t</u> [t]
ra<u>g</u> [g]	ra<u>ck</u> [k]

You should find that the final consonants on the left take less time to pronounce than those of the right. Second, the three voiceless stops have two variants each. Note the following underlined sounds:

s<u>p</u>ot	<u>p</u>ot
<u>s</u>team	<u>t</u>eam
<u>s</u>cud	<u>c</u>ud

In the right-hand column are **aspirated** versions of the stops given in the left-hand column; aspiration means that you release a small puff of air after articulating these sounds. If you hold your fingers or a small piece of paper in front of your mouth, you should be able to feel, or see, the puff of air. As we will see in the next chapter, the occurrence of aspiration is entirely predictable, with the aspirated versions occurring word or syllable initial before a stressed vowel.[2] In narrow transcription, aspiration is indicated with a diacritic or mark added to the letter, in this a case a superscript "h", hence [p^h, t^h, k^h]. Third, voiced stops may be partially devoiced at the end of words; anticipating the following silence, we stop voicing part way through the sound. Devoicing is indicated with a diacritic called an "under-ring" [̥]; thus the "b" in *rub* could be represented [b̥]. Or we may simply not release the stop at the end of a word, though we can still somehow distinguish the different stops even when they are unreleased. Try saying *rap, rat,* and *rack* without releasing the stops; the words should still be distinctive even though the initial consonant and vowel are the same. Unreleased stops in narrow transcription are indicated with a superscript "corner" [̚]. Stops are also unreleased frequently before other stops, as in *apt, captain, rubbed, rubdown, necktie, act,* and, *mugged.* Note that you don't actually release the [p̚, b̚, k̚, g̚] here but move directly to the next stop.

The alveolar stops also behave in several distinctive ways. First, when [t] occurs between two vowels (in the intervocalic position), as in *pity, Betty, little, latter, better, writer, city* or *pretty*, it is normally voiced in both American and Canadian English, though not in British English. Say the following words and note whether they are homophones for you:

bitter — bidder	atom — Adam
latter — ladder	shutter — shudder
metal — medal	petal — pedal/peddle
litre — leader	coated — coded
wetting — wedding	conceited — conceded

If you have the same sound in both, you likely have either a [d] sound or a sound called an alveolar flap. This is represented by a "fish hook r" [ɾ]. It is voiced and sounds very much like a [d], but is more rapid and has more force since the tongue is tapped against the alveolar ridge once rapidly and forcefully. As we shall see below, flapping does not occur when the [t] or [d] precedes *-en* and perhaps not before *-el/-le.*

Second, when [d] precedes the "th" sound, it is often made as a dental stop (with the tongue against the back of the teeth) rather than as an alveolar sound (with the tongue against the alveolar ridge). We do so because we are anticipating the following interdental sound (discussed below). Note the different position of your tongue when you say the "d's" in the following words:

wide [d]	width [d̪]
bread [d]	breadth [d̪]

The sounds in *width* and *breadth* are much like the dental sounds of Spanish or French. They are represented in narrow transcription with a subscript under the phonetic symbol which looks very much like a tooth, called a subscript "bridge" [d̪].

The velar place of articulation for [k] and [g] in fact ranges over quite a large area of the mouth. We anticipate the vowel that follows and articulate the velar stop either further forward towards the palatal region (as in the first two columns below) or further back in the velar region (as in the second two columns):

gill	kill	cool	goof
game	came	cull	good
gad	cat	coat	goat

A final stop, which is unpaired, is the glottal stop. It is a stop produced by bringing the vocal cords together and blocking the air stream at this point. A glottal stop is by definition voiceless and is represented by [ʔ]. You will articulate two glottal stops when you say *uh-uh* meaning 'no', transcribed [ʌʔʌʔ], but none when the word means 'yes', transcribed [əhʌ]. A glottal stop quite often precedes a final voiceless stop, so that *trip* would be pronounced [trɪʔp]. Some speakers of North American English and British English produce [ʔt] or [ʔ] instead of [t] before *-en* or *-el/le* in words such as *beaten, fatten, battle,* or *bottle.* Cockney speakers produce [ʔ] alone in final position instead of an unreleased stop after a vowel in words such as *rap, rat,* or *rack* and intervocalically where others have a flap in words such as *city* or *pretty.*

The **nasal series** consists of three nasal consonants articulated in the same positions as the three sets of oral stops. In fact, the only difference between stops and nasals is that in producing the nasals, the velum is lowered so that air is released through the nose. The nasals in English are all voiced, though other languages have voiceless nasals:

1. the bilabial nasal [m] as in *mad, omen, room*;
2. the alveolar nasal [n] as in *nose, onerous, loan*; and
3. the velar nasal [ŋ] as in *singer, ring* (or the Chinese surname *Ng*).

To produce the bilabial nasal, your lips are brought together, as for [b], but air is allowed to escape through the nose. Note that with the nasals you can maintain their articulation (as long as you have air). The alveolar nasal [n] is articulated with the tongue in the same position as for [d]. The velar nasal is a bit more difficult to produce in isolation since in English it never begins a word. Put your tongue in position to articulate [g], but then release air through your nose. In the case of the velar nasal, we encounter our first phonetic symbol not borrowed from the Roman alphabet; it is represented by an "n" with a tail called an "eng" [ŋ]. Another thing to note about the velar nasal is that it is always found before an orthographic *k* or *g*, though the *g* may not be pronounced in final position (e.g., *anger, sinking, sink, sing*).

As with the alveolar stop, the alveolar nasal may have a dental variant when it occurs before the interdental sound th. Contrast the "n" sounds below:

ten [n]   tenth [n̪]
moon [n]   month [n̪]

The first is articulated with the tongue against the alveolar ridge, the second with the tongue against the back of the upper teeth.

Another feature of the alveolar nasals is called nasal release. This occurs when the nasal follows a homorganic stop (a stop produced in the same place of articulation), hence the sequences [tn] and [dn]. In nasal release the stop is released directly into the nasal; that is the tongue is kept against the alveolar ridge and the velum is lowered. There is no separate release of the stop. Say the following words and note how you move from the stop to the nasal: *fitness, Whitney, kidney, goodnight*. In narrow transcription, nasal release is represented with a superscript "n": $[t^n]$ and $[d^n]$.

The next set of sounds is the **fricative series**. English is unusual among the languages of the world in having a very large and diverse class of fricatives. There are voiced and voiceless fricatives produced in four positions:

1. the voiced labiodental fricative [v] (as in *virtue, oven, love*) and the voiceless labiodental fricative [f] (as in *fool, offer, rough*).
2. the voiced interdental fricative [ð] (as in *then, lather, lathe*) and the voiceless interdental fricative [θ] (as in *thigh, author, froth*). The voiced version is represented with an Irish symbol (adopted by the Anglo-Saxons) called an "eth" or barred "d" and the voiceless version is represented with the Greek letter theta.
3. the voiced alveolar fricative [z] (as in *zero, ozone, ooze*) and the voiceless alveolar fricative [s] (as in *sorry, passive, rice*).
4. the voiced alveolopalatal fricative [ž] (as in *equation, rouge*) and the voiceless alveolo-palatal fricative [š] (as in *shirt, marshal, rush*). These sounds are represented by the Roman alphabet symbols with a diacritic called a "hachek", a Czech word meaning 'little hook'; the symbol for the voiceless sound an "s-wedge" and for the voiced sound is called a "z-wedge". Note that these are not the IPA symbols (which are [ʃ] "esh" = 'long s' for the voiceless fricative and [ʒ] "yogh" for the voiced), but [š] and [ž] are more commonly used in North America.

The labiodental fricatives [v] and [f] are made by bringing the lower lip up against the upper teeth, the interdental fricatives [ð] and [θ] by protruding the tip of the tongue out between the upper and lower teeth. Interdental fricatives are quite uncommon among the European languages and often cause difficulty for nonnative speakers. Even for native speakers, it may be difficult to distinguish between the voiced and voiceless variants. Listen carefully to the contrast in the following words:

bathe [ð] ~ bath [θ]
either [ð] ~ ether [θ]
then [ð] ~ thin [θ]

One rule of English which may help you to some extent in distinguishing these sounds is that the voiced interdental fricative is found at the beginnings (word initial) of only certain types of words, namely articles, demonstratives, pronouns, adverbs, and conjunctions, such as *the*, *that*, *they*, *there*, *though*, but never nouns, adjectives, or verbs. The sound is found in the middle and at the end (word medial and word final) of all words. There are no restrictions on the occurrence of the voiceless interdental fricative.

The alveolar fricatives [z] and [s] are made by bringing the tip of the tongue up towards the alveolar ridge, as with [t, d, n], but not closing off the flow of air entirely. The alveolo-palatal fricatives [ž] and [š] are made by bringing the tongue up towards the region between the alveolar ridge and palate. To feel the difference in tongue position between the alveolar and the alveolopalatal fricatives, say [s]–[š] and [z]–[ž] in sequence. You should feel your tongue moving back slightly; it is also flattening out a bit. But you should also note a further difference: the alveolopalatal sounds involve quite marked rounding of the lips, called *labialization*. While [s], [š], and [z] are found in all positions in words, [ž] is restricted in its occurrence: it is never found in initial position in English words, only in French words used in English such as *genre*.

As with alveolar [t] and [n], the alveolar fricatives may be dentalized before an interdental. Note the position of your tongue when you say *esthetic* or *is this*; you are likely articulating [s̪] or [z̪].

While English has quite an elaborate set of fricatives, there are some possible fricatives that it does not make use of, such as the bilabial fricatives [ɸ] or [β] (you can make these by putting your mouth in position to say [p] or [b] but allowing some air to escape — you will feel a slight tingling in your lips) and the velar fricatives. The voiceless velar fricative [x] is found in some dialects of English, for example, in the Scottish pronunciation of *loch*, also in the proper pronunciation of German *Bach*. English speakers usually substitute their closest sound, [k], for the latter. The voiced velar fricative [ɣ] is also found in German.

Fricatives can be divided into two subclasses based on the amount of acoustic energy released in articulating them. One subclass, the **sibilants**, is produced by constricting the air and then directing it over a sharp edge, namely the teeth. This yields a sound with more acoustic energy, hence louder and higher in pitch than other fricatives; sibilants are perceived as loud hissing sounds. Sibilants include [s, z, š, ž] as well as the affricates (see below). The nonsibilants involve constriction of the air but no sharp edge; they are consequently much quieter with less hissing. They include [f, v, θ, ð]. Say these different sounds and note the acoustic difference. Sibilants are also differentiated articulatorily from nonsibilants in that they are made with a grove or slight trough along the center line of the tongue.

The **affricate series** consists of only two sounds in English:

1. the voiced alveolopalatal affricate [ǰ] (as in *jury*, *lodger*, *barge*); and
2. the voiceless alveolopalatal affricate [č] (as in *chin*, *pitcher*, *itch*).

Note that these are represented by Roman alphabet symbols with hachek diacritics called a "c-wedge" and "j-wedge". As defined earlier, affricates are produced by articulating a stop and then releasing it into a fricative: you can produce the English affricates by saying the alveolar stops and releasing them immediately into the corresponding alveolopalatal fricative — [t] then [š], [d] then [ž]. For this reason, these sounds are sometimes represented [tš] and [dž] (or [tʃ] and [dʒ] in the IPA), suggesting they are complex sounds. We are interpreting them as single sounds, not clusters, however.[3]

Affricates, fricatives, and stops all belong to a larger class of sounds called *obstruents*. They are grouped together because they behave similarly. For example, as mentioned in the case of stops, voiced obstruents are articulated for a shorter time than voiceless obstruents, and voiced obstruents at the end of words are partially devoiced.

The **approximant series** in English includes three sets of quite different sounds all articulated with open approximation (no real restriction on the airflow). English approximants are generally voiced, so it is not necessary to specify this feature in their description. The alveolar lateral, the sound in *lick*, *alloy*, *mall*, is represented by [l]. To feel what the tongue is doing when you articulate this sound, say [d] and then [l]; you should feel the sides of your tongue drop, allowing air to pass around the sides. There is actually quite a lot of variability in the place of articulation of [l], that is, in the place in the central portion of the mouth where the air is blocked, ranging from the alveolar to the palatal region. Note the position of your tongue when you pronounce the "l's" in the following columns of words:

leaf   loom
late   loan
lack   lawn

The laterals in the first column are produced further forward in the mouth than the laterals in the second column because you are adjusting to the vowel which follows: the first are "front" vowels and the second "back" vowels (see the next section). The lateral is produced even further back in the mouth, in the velar region, when it follows rather than precedes a vowel; listen to the lateral in the following words: *kiln*, *cool*, *feel*, *bell*. These words contain what is called a dark l, or velarized l, represented with a "superimposed tilde" [ɫ] (in contrast to the clear l in the words given before). Another feature of "l" is lateral release, which like nasal release (see above), occurs when the lateral follows a homorganic stop, namely [d] or [t]. The stop is released directly into the lateral, as in *sadly*, *fiddler*, *butler*, *cutlass*, *atlas*; this phenomenon is represented in narrow transcription with a superscript l, [dˡ] and [tˡ].

The second type of approximant is the glide, or semivowel. There are two glides in English; they occur only at the beginning of syllables. The palatal glide is the sound in *yes*, *canyon*. We will represent this sound as [y], though the IPA uses [j]. It is produced by raising the tongue in the palatal region. The velar glide is the sound in *will*, *aware*; it is represented [w]. Note that when you say this sound, your tongue is raised in the velar region, but you also have strong labialization, or lip-rounding. For this reason, it would be more accurate to describe it as labiovelar, and for that reason, the symbol is included on the consonant chart (Table 2.1) in both the velar and (bi)labial places of articulation. Now say the following sets of words:

which	witch
where	wear
whale	wail

Do you have different sounds at the beginning of the words in the two columns? If not, you are using the sound [w] in both. But if you do, you are using the sound [w] for the second column but the sound [ʍ] (or "inverted w"), a voiceless labiovelar fricative, for the first column. That is, your mouth is in roughly the same configuration as for [w] but with no voicing or with the air slightly constricted at the glottis. In Old English this sound was written *hw* rather than *wh*; the Old English spelling fairly closely approximates what you are doing in articulation.

The third kind of approximant is the retroflex. The description of the English retroflex is rather difficult, and there is no completely satisfactory treatment. It is probably best to call it an alveolar retroflex: the tongue curls back somewhat, and there is also some amount of labialization. It is the sound in *river, area, measure*. We will represent it [r], though the IPA symbol for this sound is a "turned r" [ɹ].[4] A number of dialects of English are what are called nonrhotic, or r-less, dialects (including standard British English and the dialects of American English spoken in New York, the South, and parts of New England). In these dialects, [r] is omitted preconsonantally and word finally, as in *part* or *far*. Such dialects often have a linking r, [r] inserted before a vowel in the next or the same word, as in *the idea(r) is*. They may also have an intrusive r, [r] inserted preconsonantally after a vowel, as in *wa(r)sh*. Most dialects of American and Canadian English, however, consistently retain [r]; they are rhotic dialects.

The last consonant sound is the *h* sound found in *hard, ahead*. It also poses some difficulty for description. It is often described as a voiceless glottal fricative, since the air is partially obstructed by bringing the vocal cords together producing a kind of rough breathing; this is the analysis of the IPA, and hence [h] is included on your consonant chart in the appropriate box. It is the only voiceless fricative without a voiced counterpart. Another way to understand the sound is as a kind of voiceless vowel, which is homorganic with the following vowel (in fact, [h] occurs only syllable initial before a vowel in English). That is, you put your mouth in position to say the following vowel; then you constrict the air momentarily before setting the vocal cords in motion to produce the voiced vowel. Note the position of your tongue and lips when you say [h] in each of the following words, each with a different vowel:

heed		hoop
hid		hood
hate	hut	home
head		horse
hat		hot

For this reason, [h] can also be considered a voiceless glottal approximant (it would be the only voiceless approximant), and could be written with the appropriate vowel symbol with a devoicing diacritic [̥].

This completes the inventory of consonants in English. In our discussion, we have also mentioned various phonological processes which alter the basic sound of consonants; diacritics are used in addition to the consonant symbols to denote these processes:

[̥]	devoicing
[ʰ]	aspiration
[~]	velarization
[̪]	dentalization
[̚]	unreleased

In the following chapter, we will discuss in more detail when and why these phonological changes occur.

■ Self-Testing Exercise: Do Exercise 2.2.

Vowel Sounds

Turning now to vowels, we will again consider the articulation of vowels in abstract before examining the specific vowels found in English. In articulatory terms, vowels are sounds articulated with no obstruction of the air stream, that is, with open articulation. There is lack of central closure of the air stream, though the tongue may come into contact with the teeth on the sides. In acoustic terms, vowels are sounds that vary in pitch, which is determined by the quality of the sound wave. Pitch is modified by changing the shape of the resonating chamber (the oral and, sometimes, the nasal tracts) by changing the position and shape of tongue and lips and by lowering or raising the velum. In functional terms, vowels constitute the nucleus, or necessary, part of the syllable.

Classification of Vowels

Although there are fewer vowels than consonants, their classification is more difficult for several reasons. First, vowels are articulated not by putting the articulators into discrete configurations, but by shaping the tongue in the mouth. Hence, there is theoretically an infinity of different vowel sounds, forming a continuum with no distinct boundaries. Second, there is significant regional and individual variation in the inventory of vowel sounds; in fact, phonologically, different dialects of English are distinguished primarily by their inventory of vowels, while the inventory of consonants is quite consistent across dialects.[5] Third, authorities differ in their analyses of vowel sounds and in their methods of transcribing vowels; several (not entirely compatible) systems of vowel transcription are currently in use. Fourth, we can produce acceptable vowel sounds without the full complement of articulatory gestures, for example, with our teeth clenched or without the required lip rounding. Fifth, differences in length combine with differences in quality in distinguishing vowels, but it is not always easy to separate these differences. Sixth, it is quite difficult to tell where the tongue is when a vowel is produced; in fact, phonologists do not find an exact correlation between position of tongue postulated by the classificatory system for vowels and measured auditory qualities, especially for the central and back vowels.

In some respects, however, vowels are easier to classify than consonants. For consonants, we must consider four criteria: voicing, orality/nasality, place, and manner of articulation. For vowels, we need to consider only one criterion. Vowels are always voiced (except h, when it is analyzed as a voiceless vowel, or vowels in the environment of voiceless stops, which may be partially devoiced). Vowels are also oral; English does not regularly use nasalized vowels (though in the presence of nasal consonants, vowels may be nasalized). In manner of articulation, vowels are all produced with open approximation. Therefore, we need only consider place of articulation, here understood rather differently than it is for consonants: not what articulators are used and where stricture occurs, but where the tongue is. In articulating vowels, the tongue is primary, though other articulators may change the size and shape of the resonating chamber: the larynx can move up and down slightly, the velum can be raised or lowered (giving one or two resonating chambers), the lower jaw is also raised or lowered in conjunction with the tongue position (moving through the close, half-close, half-open, and open positions as the tongue is lowered), and the lips can be open and closed, also in conjunction with the tongue position, as well as **rounded** (pursed) or **unrounded** (spread). The rounding of the lips has the double effect of changing the shape of the opening and lengthening the resonating chamber.

In classifying vowels, however, it is generally sufficient to talk about the position of tongue, or, specifically, about the position of the highest point of the tongue. The tongue is convex, with the front and back humped and the tip hanging down. The high point is measured on two axes: a horizontal, or front-back axis, and a vertical, or high-low axis. The vowel chart in Table 2.2 below, which is a schematic representation of a side-view of the mouth (viewed from the left), shows these two axes. The front-back axis is divided into three positions, **front, central,** and **back,** which ranges from the center of the palate to the back of velum. The high-low axis is divided into from four to six positions, either the four positions of the jaw noted above or two positions in each of three sections, **high, mid,** and **low**. We will use the latter classification. There are thus 36 possible vowel positions, including the choice between rounded and unrounded vowels in each position.

There are also two kinds of vowels. A **monophthong** is a single or simple vowel sound constituting the nucleus of a syllable. The position of the tongue is more or less static, and there is a relatively constant acoustic property, or pitch, to the sound. A **diphthong** consists of the tongue gliding from one vowel position to another within a single syllable; it is produced as one continuous sound, not as a succession of sounds. By definition, a diphthong involves a change in the position of the tongue, and it may involve a change in the shape of the lips as well. In articulating diphthongs, we may make use of vowel positions not used in articulating monophthongs. There is quite a large range of beginning and ending points for diphthongs. Because of the movement of the tongue, the articulation of a diphthong, unlike that of a monophthong, cannot be maintained; a diphthong is not necessarily longer (does not take more time to articulate) than a monophthong, though diphthongs are frequently, and erroneously, called "long vowels" in school. Diphthongs always make use of one of the two semivowels, [y] and [w], hence their name of "glide"; we will, however, transcribe the semivowels in diphthongs using the symbols for their vowel equivalents [ɪ] and [ʊ]. The glide component of a diphthong is considered nonsyllabic since it is shorter and less sonorous; the vowel component is considered syllabic since it is the nucleus or high point of the sound. There are two types of diphthongs. A falling diphthong consists of a syllabic portion followed by a nonsyllabic portion, or a vowel followed by a glide. Because the glide is acoustically less prominent than the vowel, the diphthong is considered to be "falling"; the term has nothing to do with tongue position, which in fact usually rises. A rising diphthong consists of a nonsyllabic portion followed by a syllabic portion, or a glide followed by a vowel.

Vowels of English and their Phonetic Notation

We will now consider which of the possible vowel positions are used in English by surveying the vowel inventory of English and learning the phonetic alphabet symbol used to transcribe each vowel. Combined with your consonant transcription skills acquired in the previous section, you will by the end of this section be able to transcribe entire words and sentences as well as read broad phonetic transcriptions.

As you read the following section, you should consult the vowel chart in Table 2.2. For ease in learning the sound represented by each symbol, a sample word containing that sound is given on the chart. You might find it useful to memorize these words, so that when faced with an unknown vowel sound you can check whether it rhymes with your sample word. If no word appears next to a symbol in the chart, this means that the sound does not generally occur as a monophthong in English, but only as the nucleus in diphthongs, which are listed below the vowel chart. In giving a technical description of English vowels, it is traditional to begin with the high-low position, then give the front-back position, and finally list features of tenseness and rounding.

CAUTION: Be sure to pronounce all of the sample words carefully. Because of the dialectal and individual diversity noted above for vowel sounds, you might find you do not pronounce all of the words the same way as indicated. Strike out any examples which are not appropriate for you. The vowels given are essentially "General American".

We will begin with the monophthongs, moving from front to back. The **front vowels** are produced with the high point of the tongue in the palatal region. The front vowels of Modern English are all unrounded. In the high front area, there are two vowels:

1.   the high front tense vowel represented with a Roman alphabet lower case *i* [i]; this is the "long e" sound of words such as *heed, he, bead, heat, keyed*. This sound is sometimes analyzed as a diphthong [iy], but we will consider it a monophthong.
2.   the high front lax vowel represented with a Roman alphabet small capital I [ɪ]; this is the vowel in words such as *hid, bid, hit, kid*.

Try saying the two sounds in succession and note the position of your tongue. In the mid front area, there are two possible vowels, only one of which is found as a monophthong in English:

1.   the upper-mid front vowel represented with a Roman alphabet lower case *e* [e] is the sound in German *leben* 'to live', French *été* 'summer', or Spanish *leche* 'milk'. If we compare the French and Spanish words with English *ate* or *lay*, we find that the English sound is really a diphthong; the tongue is not in a constant position, but moves to a glide at the end of the sound. Most dialects of English have no "pure e".
2.   the lower-mid front vowel represented with Greek epsilon [ɛ] is the sound in *head, bed, neck, bet, hair, care*. It is a very common vowel in English.

Table 2.2. The Vowels of English

Monophthongs

[handwritten left margin: where tongue tip touches roof of mouth]
[handwritten right margin: → ranges from centre of palate to back of velum]

	Front	Central	Back
High (close)			
tense	i seat	ɨ just (adv)	u pool
lax	ɪ sit		ʊ put
Mid			
upper	e *[handwritten: été / not present]*	ə but, tuba	o
lower	ɛ set	ʌ putt	ɔ port
Low (open)			
	æ sat	a	ɒ pot ɑ father

Diphthongs

eɪ late	aɪ file	oʊ loan
ɪu cute	aʊ fowl	ɔɪ foil

*[handwritten: * if there's no associated sample word, then the vowel sound exists as part of a diphthong]*

In the low front area, there is one vowel in English: the low front vowel represented by the Old English symbol called "æsc" or "ash" [æ]; it is the sound in words such as *lamb*, *hat*, *rap*, *fast*, *tram*. Ash is a ligature, that is, a single letter formed by linking two letters, in this case *a* and *e*; you should practice making ash with a single stroke starting in the upper left-hand corner. This sound is very susceptible to regional variation, especially between British and North American English.

The vowels are fairly evenly spaced in front. Say each of the front vowels in succession from the top. As you do so, notice that your lower jaw drops as your tongue is lowered, so that by the time you reach [æ], your mouth is open quite wide. You may also notice your tongue moving back a little, as the lower front vowels are articulated slightly back of the upper ones.

The tongue is in the palatal-velar region when articulating the **central vowels**, all of which are unrounded. In the mid central area, there are two sounds. Both of these are "ah" sounds, but they occur in different contexts:

1. the upper-mid central vowel represented by the Hebrew letter "schwa" [ə]. This sound is found in unstressed syllables and before [r], as in *sofa*, *tuba*, *roses*, *but*, *herd*, *her*, *bird*, *hurt*, *pert*. This vowel is often a **reduced vowel**; that is, another vowel sound will be centralized to schwa when it loses stress, as in the case of the sound underlined in the following words (stress is indicated by the acute accent mark ´):

catástrophe [æ]	catastróphic [ə]
depréciate [i]	déprecate [ə]
locátion [eɪ]	lócative [ə]
propóse [oʊ]	próposition [ə]
oblíge [aɪ]	óbligation [ə]
allége [ɛ]	allegátion [ə]
absólve [a]	absolútion [ə]

In unstressed syllables, there is a strong tendency for [ɪ] to be reduced to schwa except before velars and [l], as in *college, comic, spinach*. But you will find great variation between [ɪ] and [ə], and even [ɛ], in unstressed syllables. A variant of schwa is the high central vowel represented by "barred i" [ɨ]. This is the reduced vowel found in very casual speech, as when you say the adverb *just* as opposed to the adjective *just*: compare *He just arrived* and *He is a just person*. You should note that the vowel in the adverb is somewhat higher. You might also have [ɨ] in the second syllable in the following words: *chicken, women, roses, college*.

2. the lower-mid central vowel represented by a "inverted v" [ʌ]. This sound occurs only in stressed syllables, as in *cut, bud, hut, putt, mud*. This sound is lower and somewhat further back than schwa; in fact, it is sometimes analyzed as a lower-mid back vowel.

In the low central area, there is one sound, represented with a Roman alphabet lower case *a* [a], but it does not generally occur as a monophthong in American English; it is used as a starting point for diphthongs, as we will see later.[6] It is the sound you might find in German *machen*. Because it is somewhat further forward than the mid central vowels, it is sometimes analyzed as a front vowel in other systems of transcription.

The **back vowels** are all articulated with the back of the tongue in the velar region. In English, the back vowels are all rounded, except one. These are two high back vowels:

1. the high back tense vowel represented by a Roman alphabet lower case u [u]. It is the vowel sound in words such as *who, booed, boot, hoot, cooed, do*. Note the strong rounding of your lips when you pronounce this vowel. In some systems of transcription this vowel is analyzed as a diphthong with a following glide [uw], but we will consider it a monophthong.
2. the high back lax vowel represented by Greek upsilon [ʊ], the sound in *hood, put, good, look, could*. If you say the high back tense vowel [u] and then the high back lax vowel [ʊ], then you should notice both that your tongue is lower and that your lips are somewhat less rounded. Historically, [ʊ] has become [ʌ] in many words, so that words which appear from the spelling to contain short u do not, such as *fun, run, luck, spun, gun, cuff, gull, dull*; exceptions are *u*'s between labials and [l], [š] or [č], which remain [ʊ], such as *full, pull, mull, wool, bull, push, bush*, or *butcher*.

When we reach the mid and lower back areas, the vowel situation becomes considerably more murky: there is great dialectal differences as to which vowels are found as well as differences of opinion concerning their transcription. In the mid back area, there are two possible vowels:

1. The upper-mid back vowel is represented by a Roman alphabet lower case [o]; it is the sound in German *Boot* 'boat' or French *eau* 'water', *chaud* 'hot'. But it does not exist as a monophthong in most dialects of English, only as the beginning point of a diphthong, the sound found in, for example, *boat*. As you say that vowel, you should notice that your tongue is not in a constant position, but rises at the close; your lips will also round more at the end.
2. The lower-mid back vowel is represented by a backwards c, called an "open o", [ɔ]. While this vowel is common in many dialects of English, in some dialects, it occurs only

before [r], as in *Morse* (cf. *moss* with [a]), *port* (cf. *pot*), *gorse* (cf. *gosling*). (In some systems, [ɔ] is considered a low back vowel.)

In the low back area, there are again two possible vowels:

1. the low back unrounded vowel represented by a lower case script *a* [a]. This is the vowel found in *father* and, for many speakers, also in *hot, cod, body, bomb, hard, bard, heart, card*. Note that this is the only back vowel which is not rounded.
2. the low back rounded vowel represented by an upside down script *a* [ɒ]. Speakers of British and Canadian English may have this sound in the words given immediately above, except *father*. Say these words and try to determine whether your vowel is the rounded version [ɒ] or the unrounded version [a].[7]

British English and some dialects of American English distinguish the vowels in the following sets of words, using [ɔ] in the first column and [a] or [ɒ] in the second:

cawed	cod
caught	cot
auto	Otto
awed	odd
taught	tot
naught	not

However, Canadian English and some dialects of American English do not distinguish the vowels. Say these words and determine whether they are homophones for you. Now try to say the back vowels in order from the top — [u–ʊ–o–ɔ–a] — noticing how your tongue drops, your jaw lowers, and your lips gradually unround.

This completes the inventory of monophthongs of English. We turn now to the diphthongs. English has six diphthongs, five of which are falling diphthongs, and one of which is a rising diphthong. As you read the following explanations, look at Figure 2.4, which shows the beginning and ending points of the various diphthongs.

1. The low central to high front (lax) diphthong [aɪ] is the sound found in *hide, high, bide, height, eye, sigh, tired, hire*. This sound was probably called "long i" in school, but it is really a falling diphthong ending with the [y] glide.
2. The low central to high back (lax) diphthong [aʊ] is the sound in *how, bowed, cowed, out, down*. Note that your lips round at the end on the [w] glide.

There is a phenomenon affecting these two diphthongs which characterizes Canadian English; for this reason, it is often called *Canadian raising*, though it is also found in American dialects, such as those of tidewater Virginia and Cape Cod. In Canadian raising, the beginning point of these two diphthongs is somewhat higher, closer to the mid central region, so that the resulting diphthongs are [ʌʊ] and [ʌɪ], as in the typical Canadian pronunciations of the following:

[aʊ] > [ʌʊ]	*out, south, mouse, couch*
[aɪ] > [ʌɪ]	*rice, type, tight, wife*

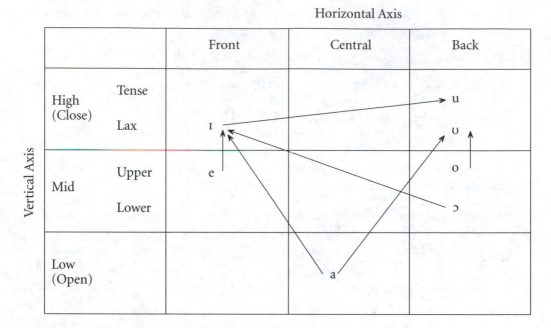

Figure 2.4. The Diphthongs of English (Approximate Starting and Ending Points)

However, this raising occurs only before voiceless consonants, so that speakers have a contrast between a raised diphthong for the words in the first columns below and an unraised diphthong for the words in the second columns where the consonant following is voiced:

[ʌʊ]	~	[aʊ]		[ʌɪ]	~	[aɪ]
house		houses, (to) house		knife		knives
mouth		mouths, (to) mouth		advice		(to) advise
spouse		(to) espouse		tripe		tribe
lout		loud		ice		eyes
bout		bowed		write		ride

3. The (upper-)mid front to high front (lax) diphthong [eɪ] is the sound in *hay, hate, bayed, mate, gate, late*. This sound has traditionally been called "long a", but it is, in fact, a falling diphthong. It substitutes for a "pure e" sound.

4. The (upper-)mid back to high back (lax) diphthong [oʊ] is the sound in *bode, hoe, boat, coat, no*. Known traditionally as "long o", it is a falling diphthong ending in a [w] glide; note that your lips round with the glide.

5. The (lower-)mid back to high front (lax) diphthong [ɔɪ] is the sound in *ahoy, Boyd, boy, ploy*. It too is a falling diphthong.

6. The high front (lax) to high back (tense) diphthong [ɪu] is the sound in *hued, cute, cued, few, pure, fury*. It is the only rising diphthong of English: it begins with a [y] glide and concludes with a [u] vowel.

Quite a common phenomenon for many speakers is the loss of the [y] glide (or "yod-dropping"), that is, a shift from [ɪu] to [u], what can be called **monophthongization**, after alveolar consonants, as in *Sue*, *suit*, *new*, *stew*. Note that if monophthongization occurs, the following words are homophones:

Tue(sday)	two, to
due, dew	dew, do
lieu	loo

In other environments, the diphthong is maintained, as in the words below, where [ɪu] in the first column contrasts with [u] in the second:

pew	poo
cute	coot
view	voo(doo)
beaut(y)	boot
few	phoo(ey)
music	mood
cute	coot

■ *Self-Testing Exercises:* Do Exercises 2.3, 2.4, and 2.5.

Two additional features of vowels still need to be discussed. The first is the feature of vowel **tenseness**. Tenseness is a rather controversial concept, but it is generally thought to refer to the degree of tension in the muscles of tongue, which affects the total volume of tongue, and is responsible for small variations in vowel quality. Tense vowels are longer, higher, and more marginal, while lax vowels are shorter, lower, and slightly more centralized. More important-ly, tense and lax vowels can be distinguished by their occurrence in certain types of syllable. An open syllable is one which does <u>not</u> end in a consonant, though it may optionally begin with one or more consonants. A closed syllable is one which ends in one or more consonants; again it may or may not begin with consonants. While both tense and lax vowels can occur in unstressed syllables of any kind and in stressed closed syllables, only tense vowels can occur in stressed open syllables; lax vowels cannot occur in stressed open syllables. Thus, we can classify the vowels of English into the following two categories (see Table 2.3; note that the asterisk marks an impossible sequence, here a lax vowel in an stressed open syllable).

Again, the back vowels are a bit confusing: for speakers who have [ɔ] only before [r], then it will be lax, and for those who distinguish between [a] and [ɔ], [a] may also be lax.

The second feature is that of vowel **length**, the time spent in articulating a vowel. Unlike many languages, English does not distinguish between long and short vowel pairs. While there is some difference in length, this is always predictable. It has been found that syllables in English are always the same lengths; they always take the same amount of time to articulate. But we have already seen above that voiced and voiceless obstruents at the ends of words are different length, voiceless being longer than voiced. In such words, then, in order to compensate for the length of the consonants, the vowel length differs, keeping the length of the syllable constant:

Table 2.3. The Tense and Lax Vowels of English

Tense	Lax	Open Syllable	Closed Syllable
i	ɪ	ki, *kɪ	kin, kɪt
eɪ	ɛ	keɪ, *kɛ	keɪk, kɛč
	æ	*kæ	kæt
	ə, ʌ	*kə, *kʌ	kərt, kʌt
u	ʊ	ku, *kʊ	kut, kʊk
oʊ		moʊ	koʊt
ɔ, a		sɔ, ma/paʊ	kɔt, ka/kʊt
aɪ		laɪ	kaɪt
aʊ		kaʊ	kraʊd
ɔɪ		kɔɪ	kɔɪl
ɪu		kɪu	kɪut

Vo C$_{vl}$ vowel shorter — obstruent longer   seat   safe   lace
Vo C$_{vd}$ vowel longer — obstruent shorter   seed   save   laze

(C = consonant, Vo = vowel, vd = voiced, vl = voiceless.) Final sequences of consonants also take longer to articulate than single consonants, as you would expect (initial consonants seem to have no effect). Moreover, vowels in open syllables will be longer than those in closed syllables. These facts combined give us the following, entirely predictable, sequence of vowel length:

long	half-long	short	
CVo	> CVoC$_{vd}$ >	CVoC$_{vl}$ >	CVoCC
see	seed	seat	ceased
lay	laid	late	laced
mow	mowed	moat	most

Vowel length may be indicated by diacritics: [ː] for long, [ˈ] for half-long, and nothing or [˘] for short. Alternatively, a macron [̄] may indicate a long vowel.

Consonant versus Vowel

The speech sounds can be viewed in two ways, either in respect to function or in respect to form. Vowels always have a function that can be described as "syllabic": they constitute the obligatory nucleus of a syllable. They are louder, longer, more sonorous, and acoustically more prominent than consonants, which initiate or arrest (release or end) syllables. Consonants, which are optional, are shorter and acoustically less prominent. They generally have a "nonsyllabic" function. In respect to form, vowels are articulated with no restriction of the air stream, or with open approximation. Most consonants are articulated with some restriction of the air stream.

However, we have already seen that the distinction between consonant and vowel is not entirely distinct: glides are articulated as vowels but function as consonants. Further difficulty results from the fact that certain consonants have a syllabic function; that is, they are like a vowel in being able to stand alone in a syllable (without any other vowel). These consonants include the liquids and the nasals. They are commonly syllabic following a consonant at the end of a polysyllabic word. We indicate syllabic function by a subscript bar [ˌ]. Read the following words; you should notice that the second syllable may contain a [ə] vowel or no vowel at all. In the second instance, the consonant serves the function of a vowel:

[l̩]   fizzle, muddle, muscle, kettle
[n̩]   reason, beaten, sudden, and (said rapidly)
[ŋ̍]   Jack and Kate (said rapidly), lookin' good
[ɾ̩]   ladder, butter, runner
[m̩]   solemn, rhythm, prism, film (for some speakers)

Note that nasal release and lateral release may yield syllabic consonants. Syllabic [l̩] and [n̩] occur following alveolars, but generally not following labials and velars. Syllabic [ŋ̍] and [m̩] are rare in this function.

Table 2.4. Consonant versus Vowel → *don't bother w/ chart*

Traditional Classification

Consonants	Vowels		
p t k ʔ	i	u	aʊ eɪ
b d g	ɪ ə ʊ		aɪ oʊ
m n ŋ	ɛ ʌ ɔ		ɔɪ ɪu
f θ s š č h	æ a ɒ		
v ð z ž ǰ			
w r l y			

Classification by Function

Always nonsyllabic	Syllabic or nonsyllabic	Always syllabic
p t k ʔ	m n (ŋ)	i u
b d g	r l	ɪ ʊ
f θ s š č h		e ə o
v ð z ž ǰ		ɛ ʌ ɔ
w* y*		æ a a ɒ

Classification by Form

Close approximation	Open approximation		
p t k ʔ	w y	i u	aʊ eɪ
b d g	r l	ɪ ə ʊ	aɪ oʊ
m n ŋ	h	ɛ ʌ ɔ	ɔɪ ɪu
f θ s š č	æ a ɒ		
v ð z ž ǰ			

* When syllabic [w] = [ʊ] and [y] = [ɪ].

Therefore, consonants and vowels do not seem to be distinguished clearly by function:[8] some consonants may function as vowels, as the nucleus of a syllable, in certain situations. Consonants and vowels are also not distinguished by form, that is by manner of articulation: some consonants, namely approximants, are articulated as vowels with open approximation. Table 2.4 gives the traditional classification followed by classifications based on function (syllable/nonsyllabic) and on form (articulated with closure in the vocal tract).

■ *Self-Testing Exercise:* Do Exercise 2.6. For more advanced work in phonological analysis, read the discussion of "distinctive features" on the CD-ROM and do the problems in Exercise 2.7.

■ Chapter Summary

Now that you have completed this chapter, you should be able to:

1. list the differences between the written and oral media of communication;
2. describe the human speech apparatus and production of speech sounds;
3. give a technical description of English consonants and vowels and provide the phonetic symbol for each;
4. discuss the classification of consonants and vowels using both formal and functional criteria; and
5. transcribe English words in broad transcription.

■ Recommended Additional Reading

A very clear discussion of articulatory phonetics and English consonants and vowels may be found in MacKay (1991). A more detailed discussion of English phonetics, including a treatment of different dialects, is Giegerich (1992, Chapters 1, 2, 3, 4, and 5).

Textbooks which you might like to consult include Kreidler (1989, Chapters 2, 3, and 4), Ladefoged (1993, Chapters 1, 2, 3, and 4, pp. 75–88), and O'Grady and Dobrovolsky (1996, Chapter 2, pp. 15–37, and Chapter 3, pp. 82–89). Murray (1995, Chapter 1) includes exercises with answers. Delahunty and Garvey (1994, Chapter 12) discusses the differences between spoken and written language.

For definitions of any of the terms used in this chapter, see Crystal (1996) or Trask (1995) and for a clear and concise explanation of any of the phonetic symbols used here, see Pullum and Ladusaw (1996).

On the difference between speech and writing, see Biber (1988), especially Chapters 2 and 3.

■ Notes

1. Two other air stream mechanisms may be used in producing certain sounds in other languages, the "glottalic" system and the "velaric" system. In the latter, for example, the tongue is raised against the velum and at the same time at a point further forward in the mouth, trapping air. Moving the tongue downward rarefies the air, and when the tongue is released, air rushes in to produce an ingressive sound. There are at three types of such sounds, called *clicks*, in languages of southern Africa (Bantu, Xhosa, Zulu, and Bush-Hottentot). These include the bilabial click (the "kissing" sound), the alveolar click (the "tut-tut" or "tsk-tsk" sound of disapproval), and the lateral click (the sound made to spur a horse on). Although we use these sounds, of course, they are not regular speech sounds.

2. Another place in which aspiration may occur is in final position following [s] or [f], as in *soft, clasp, risk*. We will not be concerned with this environment for aspiration.

3. The affricates are treated as single sounds rather than as consonant clusters because they are the only sequences that can occur both word initially and word finally, and they are the only sequence of stop + fricative that can occur word initially (see the next chapter on "Phonotactics").

4. In the IPA, the symbol [r] represents the alveolar trilled *r* one finds in many languages.

5. This book does not include any detailed description of the dialects of English. Two recent publications on this topic are Wells (1982) and Cheshire (1991). For a discussion of issues of "dialect", "idiolect", "standard/nonstandard" and the teaching of English, see the chapter on pedagogy on the CD-ROM.

6. The sound [a] does occur as a monophthong in the dialect of older New England speakers, replacing [æ] before fricatives or nasal plus fricative combinations, as in *half, last, laugh, bath*, or *dance*, and as a lengthened vowel in Southern American dialects, replacing the diphthong [aɪ], as in *fine* [faːn] or *right* [raːt].

7. If you have [ɒ], then it is likely that [a] is restricted to the position before [r], as in *part*.

8. Because the traditional classification of sounds rests on both formal and functional criteria, it has proved useful in phonological work to break sounds down into smaller components. These are known as *phonological*, or *distinctive*, *features*. This alternative way of describing sounds originated in the "Prague School" of structural linguistics which flourished between the wars. It was promoted in America by a linguist named Roman Jakobson and later incorporated into the approach know as "generative phonology" by Noam Chomsky and Morris Halle in their influential book, *The Sound Pattern of English* (1968). While this approach is considered somewhat too advanced for this text, you may find out more about it in Exercise 2.7 on the CD-ROM and in the sources listed in the "Recommended Additional Reading" section.

CHAPTER 3

English Phonology, Phonotactics, and Suprasegmentals

■ Chapter Preview

This chapter begins with a discussion of the notions of the phoneme (distinctive sound) and allophone (predictable variant). A number of phonemic rules for specific English phonemes and their allophones are stated. The chapter then treats the topic of phonological rules, which account generally for allophonic variation in English. This is followed by a description of the constraints on possible positions for sounds and possible sound combinations in English. It then treats the features of stress and intonation in English, features which extend over more than one sound. The characteristics of stress are defined, the rules of stress placement in English are explained briefly, and the functions of stress in different domains — morphology, syntax, and discourse — are described. The pitch patterns of different sentence types are exemplified, and intonation is related to the presentation of information in an English sentence. The chapter ends with a discussion of English syllable structure — a level of structure intermediate between the sound and the word.

■ Commentary

Phonemes

You will recall that we defined phonology as the study of the distinctive sounds in a language, and although we have mentioned in passing the difference between certain distinctive and nondistinctive variants (for example, between [tʰ] and [t]), we have not discussed this subject in any detail. The concept of distinctiveness is captured by the notion of a **phoneme**. A phoneme is a distinctive or contrastive sound in a language. What "distinctive" means in this context is that the sound makes a difference in meaning and has communicative value. Different phonemes make contrasts in words. For example, [n], [l] and [t] are all phonemes because they serve to make contrasts in words, as in *nab, lab, tab*. Here we see how the phonemes of a language are determined, by means of what are called *minimal pairs*. A minimal pair is a set of different words consisting of all the same sounds except for one. The one sound which contrasts is then determined to be a phoneme since it makes a difference in **meaning** (it differentiates one word from another). For example, we could set up what is called a *phonetic environment*, a sequence of sounds such as [æt]. If we then establish a blank slot word initially, [_æt], and substitute different consonants in this slot, we can see if we get different words. If we do, then each of these consonants is a phoneme. Examine the following:

[_æt] *pat, bat, sat, mat, gnat, fat, that, vat, cat* ...

We can conclude that [p], [b], [s], [m], [n], [f], [ð], [v], and [k] are all phonemes. And *bat* and *cat*, for example, are a minimal pair. The same can be done for vowels with a phonetic environment such as [p_t]:

[p_t] *pit, peat, pate, pot, pout, put, putt, pat, pet* ...

We can conclude that [ɪ], [i], [eɪ], [a], [aʊ], [ʊ], [ʌ], [æ], and [ɛ] are all distinct phonemes.

Phonemes are said to be unpredictable, since their occurrence depends on what word you want to say rather than by any phonological rule. That is, whether [b] or [k] occurs in the environment [_æt] depends on whether you wish to refer to the nocturnal flying mammal or to the family feline, not on whether the sound occurs in the context of [æ] or word initially or any other factor which is solely phonetically determined. Phonemes are also said to be in **parallel distribution** since they occur in the same (or "parallel") phonetic environments. Note that an ideal writing system would be phonemic, where each alphabetic symbol stands for one and only one phoneme.

There is some debate about the nature of the phoneme. One view is that it has some psychological validity; it is a concept in the mind. Another view is that it is an abstraction, or an ideal sound. A third view is that it refers to a class of sounds which are phonetically similar (but not identical) and have the same phonological function. The last two views are probably the easiest to comprehend, and they have the further advantage of incorporating the notion of the allophone. An **allophone** (from *allos* 'other' *phōnē* 'sound') is a predictable variant of a phoneme. Allophones are the individual members of a class of sounds (a phoneme), or the pronounceable or concrete realizations of an abstraction (a phoneme). We speak of the phonetically similar variants of a sound as the "allophones of a (a particular) phoneme". To take a real example from English, consider the aspirated [tʰ] and the nonaspirated [t] discussed in the previous chapter. They are phonetically very similar, but not identical. Allophones are nondistinctive (noncontrastive) variants of a phoneme, since substituting one allophone for another allophone of the same phoneme will not lead to a different word. Replacing [tʰ] with [t] in *top*, or [t] with [tʰ] in *stop*, will not lead to different words, just a slightly odd-sounding one. (Of course, substituting one allophone for another allophone of a different phoneme would result in a different word; replacing [tʰ] with [kʰ] in *top* would give *cop*.)

Allophones of a phoneme are predictable: they are conditioned by the phonetic environment, which determines the appearance of one or another allophone. Thus, we can say that the aspirated version of [t] is predicted by its position word (or syllable) initially before a stressed vowel; the nonaspirated version is predicted by all other phonetic environments. We can say that allophones are positional variants, which are in **complementary distribution**, meaning that where one occurs the other does not. They never occur in the same environment, always in different environments. They never overlap in distribution;

rather, their distributions "complement" (or 'complete') one another. Our examples [tʰ] and [t] never occur in the same position: [tʰ] occurs syllable initial, and [t] occurs in all other environments. Thus, we can conclude that [tʰ] and [t] are allophones of the phoneme /t/. We enclose the phoneme in slashes to indicate that it represents a class of sounds, or an abstraction, and thus cannot be pronounced; in fact, for this reason, we should really use another symbol such as /T/ between the slashes since the phonetic alphabet symbol represents a pronounceable sound and the phoneme is not that. However, it is usual to use the phonetic alphabet symbol.

Note that *environment* in the context of phonemes and allophones is limited strictly to **phonetic** features, though it can refer to a number of such features; for example, it can refer to the position of the sound in the word or syllable (e.g., syllable initial or word final), the nature of the surrounding sounds (e.g., between vowels, following a voiceless stop, before an approximant), or even the placement of stress.

In contrast to the rule that allophones never occur in the same environment, they my sometimes be in "free variation". For example, stops may or may not be released word finally. A speaker will release or not release them arbitrarily, and whether or not they are released makes no difference in meaning.

Phonemes and allophones are always language- (or dialect-)specific. For example, in Greek [ɪ] and [i] are allophones of the same phoneme, while in English they are distinct phonemes. In Japanese [l] and [r] are allophones of the same phoneme, hence the difficulty many native Japanese speakers have with these two distinct sounds in English. In some dialects of English, specifically those which do not distinguish *pin* and *pen*, [ɪ] and [ɛ] are allophones of the same phoneme.

Finally, while the phonemes of a language constitute its inventory of distinctive sounds, languages might also have a few marginal phonemes. These are sounds which occur in only a limited number of words. For example, one might consider the voiceless velar fricative [x] occurring in words such as *Bach* as a marginal phoneme for some speakers of English.

Phonemic Rules

The predictability of the allophones of a phoneme can be stated in terms of a rule, called a **phonemic rule**. The rule stipulates the different environments in which each allophone is found. It can be formalized as follows:

$$/x/ \rightarrow [y]/$$
$$[z]/ \text{ elsewhere}$$

The symbol between slashes /x/ represents the phoneme, and the symbols in square brackets represent the allophones [y] and [z]. The arrow → means 'is realized as' or 'has the allophones'. Thus, this rule reads "the phoneme x has the allophones y and z". Furthermore, the slash / means 'in the environment'. Following the slash, the phonetic environment in which the allophone is found is stated. Such environments are quite varied, and they are generally abbreviated in some way, e.g.:

# —	(= word initial)
— #	(= word final)
Vo—Vo	(= between vowels)
C—	(= following a consonant)

(# = word or syllable boundary.) The dash here stands for the position of the allophone. The environment of the last allophone is always stated as "elsewhere", or all other environments. The "elsewhere allophone" is the one with the widest distribution, the one found in the greatest variety of environments. Note that "elsewhere" includes all environments **excluding** the environments already listed above in the rule; you always read the rule from top to bottom.

Let's look at some actual examples of phonemic rules in English, reviewing details that were presented in the previous chapter:

1. Since /h/ may be analyzed as a voiceless vowel homorganic with the following vowel, we could write a rule for the predictable variants of this phoneme as follows:

/h/ →	[i̥]/—i	heed
	[ɪ̥]/—ɪ	hid
	[æ̥]/—æ	hat
	[u̥]/—u	who
	[ʊ̥]/—ʊ	hood
	etc.	

Remember that the diacritic [̥] indicates devoicing.

2. The voiceless stop /p/ has a number of variants:

/p/ →	[pʰ]/ #—Vó	port, party, computer, apart
	[p̚]/ —{C$_{stop}$, #}	cap, rope, capped, opt, scepter
	[p]/ elsewhere	sport, spring, apron, proclaim, tipsy

(Vó = stressed vowel.) Remember that the diacritic for aspiration is [ʰ] and that for unreleased it is [̚]. This rule says that the phoneme /p/ is realized as aspirated [pʰ] syllable initially before a stressed vowel; it is unreleased [p̚] before another stop consonant or word finally, and it is [p] in all other environments.

3. The voiceless stop [t] has more variants than /p/:

/t/ →	[tʰ]/ #—Vó	tongue, return, attend
	[tⁿ]/ —[n, n̩]	fitness, mitten
	[tˡ]/—[l]	atlas, butler
	[ɾ]/ Vó—{Vo, [ɹ], [l̩]}	city, matter, bottle
	[t̪]/ —[ð, θ]	at that, eighth
	[t̚]/ —{C$_{stop}$, #}	footprint, hatpin, rat, root
	[t]/ elsewhere	stop, try, twin, attract, matron

Remember that the diacritic for dentalization is [̪] and that for syllabic function is [̩]. This rule reads that the phoneme /t/ has as its allophone an aspirated [tʰ] syllable initially before a stressed vowel, a nasal-released [tⁿ] before [n] or syllabic [ṇ], a lateral-released [tˡ] before [l] (and for some speakers before [ḷ]), a flap between a stressed vowel and a vowel or syllabic liquid, a dentalized [t̪] before interdental consonants, an unreleased [t̚] word finally, and [t] in all other contexts.[1]

Note that a stressed vowel must precede a flap, so that in the following sets of words, there is flapping in the first but not in the second column, where the stressed vowel follows rather than precedes t:

[ɾ]	[t]
phótograph	photógrapher
fráternize	fratérnal
átom	atómic

In casual speech a flap may also occur between two unstressed vowels as in *cávity*, *chárity*, *próperty*, *vísiting* (cf. visitátion).

4.   The phoneme /n/ also has a number of predictable variants:

/n/ →	[ɱ]/—C_labiodental	infamous, information, confirm
	[n̪]/—C_interdental	month, ninth, in the
	[ŋ]/—C_velar	incongruous, increase, income
	[ṇ]/ C_obstruent—#	leaden, madden, kitten, listen
	[n]/ elsewhere	noise, pound, tons, funny, pin

The symbol [ɱ] represents a labiodental nasal — try articulating one! Also try to write this rule out in prose.

5.   The rule for vowel length, which is predictable and hence phonemic, can be stated as follows:

/Vo/ →	[Voː]/ —#	fey	grow	eh
	[Voˑ]/ —C_vd	fade	brogue	Abe
	[Vo]/ elsewhere	face, faced	broke, broast	ape, aced

Recall that the diacritics for length are [ː] for "long" and [ˑ] for "half-long". Elsewhere could also be stated in terms of the two environments where short vowels occurs: —C_vl and —CC(C)(C).

Phonological Processes

There are often more general processes of phonological change involved in allophonic variation. These may apply to classes of sounds which share one or more features and may be stated in terms of **phonological rules** similar in formalism to phonemic rules. The motivation behind many, though not all, phonological rules is ease of articulation, in which the speaker wishes to minimize his or her articulatory effort. This results in **assimilation**, where two neighboring (usually adjacent) sounds become more like one another in respect to one or more phonetic feature. Below are some examples of phonological rules, stated first in prose, then in abbreviated form using the formalism of rules. (It is also possible to state these rules in terms of the distinctive features; see Exercise 3.2. Often the use of distinctive features makes clear how assimilation is working.)

1.   All consonants are <u>labialized</u> before rounded vowels:

$/C/ \rightarrow [C^w]/ \text{—} V_{rounded}$

[^{w}] is the diacritic for labialization. C includes stops (*pool, boot, tool, dote, coke, good*), fricatives (*thorough, food, voice, sew, zoo, shone*), affricates (*chose, jury*), nasals (*note, moan*), and liquids (*lute, rude*) ([r] is by nature labialized). $V_{rounded}$ includes [u, ʊ, oʊ, ɔ, ɔɪ, ʋ].

2.   Liquids and nasals have a <u>syllabic</u> function following a consonant word finally:

$/l, r, m, n/ \rightarrow [ḷ, ṛ, m̩, ṇ]/ C_{obstruent}\text{—}\#, C_{nasal}\text{—}\#$

We saw this rule operating above in the case of the allophones of /n/. Examples of this rule are [m̩] in *chasm*, [ṇ] in *button, omen*, [ḷ] in *paddle, camel, tunnel* and [ṛ] in *latter, hammer, runner*. We must specify obstruents and nasals in the phonetic environment of the rule above rather than consonants in general in order not to generate syllabic forms following liquids, as in *curl, turn, kiln, firm*, and *film* (though some speakers have [fɪlm̩]).

3.   Alveolar sounds are <u>dentalized</u> before an interdental:

$/s, t, d, n, l/ \rightarrow [s̪, t̪, d̪, n̪, l̪]/\text{—}\{ð, θ\}$

Examples of this rule are [s̪] in *sixth*, [t̪] in *eighth*, [n̪] in *tenth*, [l̪] in *wealth*, and [d̪] in *width*.

4.   Approximants and nasals are <u>devoiced</u> following a voiceless consonant:

$/y, w, r, l, m, n/ \rightarrow [y̥, w̥, r̥, l̥, m̥, n̥]/ C_{vl}\text{—}$

Note that the natural class of sonorants identifies the group of sounds which all undergo devoicing in this context. Examples of this rule are [w̥] in *twin, twelve*, [y̥] in *few, cute*, [l̥] in *play, claim*, [r̥] in *try, pry*, [n̥] in *snore*, and [m̥] in *smart*.

5.   Velars are <u>fronted</u> (to the palatal region) in the environment of a front vowel:

$/k, g, ŋ/ \rightarrow [k̟, g̟, ŋ̟]/ \text{—} V_{front}, V_{front}\text{—}$

[̟] is the diacritic for fronting. Examples of this rule are [k̟] in *key, kit, kept, cape, cat, pick, peek*, [g̟] in *geese, give, get, gate, gad, fig, rag*, and [ŋ̟] in *ring, rang*.

6.   Vowels are <u>nasalized</u> before a nasal:

$Vo \rightarrow Ṽo/ \text{—}[n, m, ŋ]$

The diacritic for nasalization is [˜].[2] Examples of this rule are [ʌ̃] in *sun*, [ĩ] in *sin*, [æ̃] in *Sam*, and [ũ] in *soon*.

7. [l] is velarized (becomes the "dark l") after a vowel or other approximant:

    /l/ → [ɫ]/ V—, [r]—

8. Front vowels are retracted (articulated further back) before [ɫ]:

    Vo → Vo̠/ —[ɫ]

The diacritic for retracting is [̠]. Examples of this rule are [i̠] in *seal*, [ɪ̠] in *sill*, [e̠ɪ] in *sail*, [ɛ̠] in *sell*, and [æ̠] in *Sally* (compare *seat, sit, same, set, Sam* where the same vowels are not retracted).

9. Voiceless stops are aspirated word or syllable initially before a stressed vowel:

    /p, t, k/ → [pʰ, tʰ, kʰ]/#—Vó

10. Alveolar obstruents become alveolopalatal obstruents before [y] in the following syllable:

    /t, d, s, z/ → [č, ǰ, š, ž]/—#[y]

Palatalization is extremely common word internally:

[t] > [č]	posture, digestion, Christian
[d] > [ǰ]	individual, residual, educate, soldier
[s] > [š]	passion, tissue, anxious, mission
[z] > [ž]	occasion, leisure, vision, fusion

Palatalization may also occur between words in rapid speech: [č] *don't you*, [ǰ] *would you, do you*, [š] *miss you, bless you*, [ž] *as yet, as usual*. Sometimes it occurs even when there is no syllable break, as in the pronunciation of *tune* as [čun]. Palatalization must include the rule of "yod-dropping" which deletes the [y] of the following syllable; we have already encountered this rule in the monophthongization of [ɪu] to [u].

11. Lax vowels [ɪ, ɛ, æ, ə, ʌ, ʊ] when unstressed are reduced to [ə]:

    V_lax → [ə]/ when unstressed

Examples of vowel reduction can be seen in the underlined vowels in the following pairs of related words:

átom/atómic	mélody/melódic/melódius	
[æ ə]/[ə a]	[ɛ ə/[ə a]/[ə oʊ]	
Cánada/Canádian	órigin/oríginal	cómedy/comédian
[æ ə]/[ə eɪ]	[ɔ ə]/[ə ɪ]	[a ə/[ə i]

(Contrast the examples above with the unstressed vowels in the following words. Since they are tense, they are not reduced: *geography, psychology, calico, vacation*.)

12. [ə] may be deleted when followed by a liquid or nasal beginning the next syllable:

    [ə] → Ø/ —#[l, r, n, m]

Examples of this rule are the underlined vowels in *police*, *parade*, *suppose*, *gorilla*, *every*, *evening*, *generally*, *botany*, and *family*. The syllable following the deleted vowel generally carries some degree of stress. Unlike the preceding rules, which are obligatory, this rule is optional.

If we consider the rules above, we see that there is assimilation in voicing, as in rule (4) above, assimilation in place of articulation, as in rules (3, 5, 7, 8, and 10), and assimilation in manner of articulation, as in rule (1 and 6). The deletion of a segment (12) or reduction of vowels (11) is probably also motivated by ease of articulation. Not all rules are clear cases of assimilation, however, as in rule (9), in which a segment (aspiration) is added, or rule (2).

■   *Self-Testing Exercises: Do Exercises 3.1 and 3.2.*

Below is a summary of the diacritics introduced in this chapter:

devoicing [̥]   labialization [ʷ]
aspiration [ʰ]   fronting [̟]
unreleased [̚]   nasalization [̃]
dentalization [̪]   retracting [̠]
syllabic [̩]   velarization [~]
length [ː] [ˑ]

Phonotactics

Phonotactics are the constraints on positions and sequences of sounds in a language. Phonotactics are always language-specific; that is, combinations of certain sounds may be permitted in another language which are not permitted in English, such as [pn] beginning a word.

When discussing the possible positions of sounds in a language, we need to refer to word initial, medial, and final positions, as well as other positions, such as syllable initial, or other factors, such as the occurrence of a sound in monosyllabic or polysyllabic words. In the previous chapter, we considered in passing some of the constraints on the positions of sounds in English. Let's review those constraints:

1. [ŋ] is never word initial; originally, [ŋ] was an allophone of [n] occurring before [k] and [g], a cluster which could not occur word initially. Additionally, [ŋ] is word medial only after a stressed vowel;
2. [ž] is never word initial (except in French words such as *gendarme*). It is common word medially, and fairly rare word finally. Note that [š] (a native sound in English) is common word initially, as in *sure*, *sugar*, *shirt*;
3. [h], [y], and [w] are always syllable initial before a stressed vowel. They occur syllable finally only as part of a diphthong;
4. [ð] is word initial only in certain pronouns, adverbs, prepositions, demonstratives, and the definite article, never in nouns, verbs, and adjectives. Otherwise, it occurs freely word medially and word finally;
5. syllabic nasals and liquids [m̩, n̩, l̩, r̩] are never word initial; and
6. unreleased stops occur only word finally or before another stop.

This is not an exhaustive list of the restrictions, but it covers the most important ones.

When discussing the possible sequences or combinations of sounds in a language, we are primarily concerned with the combinations of consonants, called *consonant clusters*, which may begin or end a syllable. In English we find that initial consonant clusters are much more restricted than final consonant clusters. In initial position, the phonotactics of English do not allow the following sequences:

- stop + stop, such as [pt],
- stop + nasal, such as [pn],
- nasal + stop, such as [np],
- stop + fricative, such as [ts],
- fricative + stop, such as [ft], except where the fricative is [s] (or in obviously "foreign" words such as *shtick*).

The only permitted sequences are the following:

- voiced or voiceless stop + approximant,
- voiceless fricative + approximant,
- [s] + voiceless stop, but no other voiceless fricative,[3] and no voiced stops,
- [s] + nasal.

There is only one possible combination of three consonants:

- [s] + voiceless stop + approximant.

The results of these restrictions are recorded in Table 3.1. Some of the combinations occur quite infrequently, such as [skl]. The gaps in the table represent either systematic gaps or accidental gaps. Systematic gaps can be explained by a general rule, such as the restriction against two labials occurring together — which rules out [*pw], [*bw], and [*spw] (note that [w] is treated as a labial) — and the restriction against two alveolars/dentals occurring together — which rules out *[tl], *[dl], *[θl], and *[stl] (note that [θ] is treated as a dental, but [r] is not). Accidental gaps include those sequences which do not violate any general principle but which simply do not occur in English, such as [stw], [hl], or [hr]. Interestingly, the latter two sequences did occur in an earlier period of English, as in Old English *hlūd* 'loud' and *hnutu* 'nut', but were subsequently lost. Speakers of some dialects — those who do not distinguish between *whale* and *wail* — have also simplified [hw] > [w]. The [s] + approximant and [š] + approximant series may be explained by a general restriction against [š] + approximant, with [šr] representing the labialization of [s] > [š] before [r]. Note that [šl] occurs in a nonnative word such as *schlepp, schlemiel*, [šm] in *schmooze, schmuck*, [šn] in *schnapps, schnauzer*, [šw] in *schwa*, and [sr] in *Sri Lanka*. Finally, can you explain why [sŋ] does not occur? Is it a systematic or an accidental gap?

You might have noticed that the approximant [y] has been omitted from the discussion. The reason for this is that it occurs following a consonant only in combination with the vowel [u]. In fact, it may occur following a wide variety of consonants, voiced or voiceless. Therefore, [y] is not considered to participate in consonant clusters:

py *pew*		ty *tune*	ky *cute*
by *beauty*		dy *duty*	gy *gules*
my *music*		ny *news*	* ŋy
fy *few*	θy *thew*	sy *sue*	* šy
vy *view*	* ðy	* zy	* žy

(Note that in some dialects [y] is lost following alveolars. Also, only certain dialects have [y] following [č] and [ǰ].) [θy] and [gy] are rare and almost obsolete. By the way, do you know the meaning of *gules* or *thew*?

Final consonant clusters are freer and more complex than initial clusters, containing up to four consonants. Space does not permit an exhaustive listing, but some possible combinations of two consonants are the following:

– liquid + consonant, as in *harp, harm, horse, hurl, help, helm, else* ([lr] does not occur since [r] must precede [l]);
– nasal + obstruent, as in *bend, bent, pins, tenth, lamp, rink*;
– obstruent + obstruent, including fricative + stop (as in *lift*), stop + fricative (as in *lapse*), fricative + fricative (as in *leaves*), and stop + stop (as in *apt*).

Not all possible combinations of these sounds occur, however; e.g., [m] precedes [p, f] only and [ŋ] precedes [k, g] only, while in all other instances the nasal preceding the obstruent is [n]. Certain of these clusters are indicative of a particular grammatical context; thus, the cluster of fricative + fricative or voiced consonant + [z] always indicates a noun plural or possessive or third person singular of the verb and voiced consonant + [d] always indicates the past tense or past participle of a verb.

Sequences of three consonants include:

– three obstruents (stop + fricative + stop), as in [dst] in *midst*;
– nasal + two obstruents, including nasal + fricative + stop, as in [nst] in *rinsed*, nasal + stop + fricative, as in [mps] in *glimpse*, and nasal + stop + stop, as in [mpt] in *prompt*;
– liquid + two obstruents, including liquid + stop + fricative, as in [rps] in *corpse*, liquid + stop + stop, as in [lpt] in *helped*, liquid + fricative + fricative, as in [lvz] in *shelves*, and liquid + fricative + stop, as in [rst] in *first*.

Sequences of four consonants occur, though they tend to be simplified by speakers, e.g.:

[mpst] glimpsed	[ndθs] thousandths
[ksθs] sixths	[ksts] texts

As you can see, in these cases, the fourth consonant is always an inflectional ending added to a word ending in three consonants. Words ending in four consonants without an inflectional ending are rare, if not impossible.

Native speakers of a language intuitively know the permissible and nonpermissible sequences (it is part of their linguistic competence); newly-created words will always follow the phonotactic principles of the language: thus, while *pnark* could never be created in

Table 3.1. Initial Consonant Clusters in English

pl	please	bl	black	*tl		*dl		kl	class	gl	glue
pr	prank	br	brown	tr	trace	dr	dry	kr	crew	gr	grow
*pw		*bw		tw	twin	dw	dwell	kw	queen	gw	Gwyn
sp	spy			st	stove			sk	sky		
spl	splat			*stl				skl	sclerosis		
spr	spring			str	string			skr	scream		
*spw				*stw				skw	square		
sm	smart			sn	snore			*sŋ			
fl	flow	*θl		sl	slow	*šl		*hl			
fr	free	θr	throw	*sr		šr	shrimp	*hr			
*fw		θw	thwart	sw	swear	*šw		hw	where		

English, *plark* could be. Borrowed words which have not been fully assimilated into English may have nonEnglish sequences, such as [kn] in *Knorr*. It is usual, however, to make the borrowed word conform to the phonotactics of English by eliminating nonEnglish clusters, such as [ps] in *psychology*, which becomes [s], and [ts] in *Zeppelin*, which becomes [z]. Remember also that while certain sequences of sounds are not possible in English, they are humanly possible and may be found in other languages, for example, initial [ts], [kn], [gn], [bd], [ps], [pf], [pn] in German.

Suprasegmental Features

Suprasegmental features are those articulatory features which are superimposed over more than one segment (i.e., vowel or consonant); they include stress and intonation.

Stress

Every word spoken in isolation has at least one stressed syllable. In articulatory terms, **stress** involves a rise in air pressure; an increase in the activity of the respiratory muscles forces more air out of the lungs during the articulation of a particular syllable. There may also be an increase in the activity of the larynx, resulting in higher pitch. In acoustic terms, the stressed syllable is perceived as longer, louder, and of higher pitch. The term *stress* is sometimes used interchangeably with *accent*, but *accent* should not be confused here with the other use of the term to refer to dialect features (as in "a British accent").

Certain languages in the world have an accentual system based on pitch difference, not stress differences. That is, syllables carry varying levels of pitch, and pitch differences alone can distinguish words. These *tonal* languages include Chinese, Thai, West African languages, and Amerindian languages. But English has stress accent.

To find the stressed syllable in English, say a polysyllabic word and tap your finger at the same time. You will naturally tap on the stressed syllable. The reason for this is that it is easier to produce one increase in muscular activity in conjunction with another, so you use your respiratory muscles and your hand muscles simultaneously. If you try to tap on an unstressed syllable, you will get a distortion in the pronunciation of the word. Try saying the following word while tapping your finger (the stressed syllable is marked):

  abóminable   pátriarchy   exécutive   confidéntial   interpretátion

The rule for stress in Germanic words is very simple: words are always stressed on the first syllable (as in *ápple, fáther, húnger*), except prefixed verbs, which are stressed on the root syllable (as in *forgét, belíeve, withdráw*). However, English has borrowed many words from the Romance languages, which have a different stress principle: stress falls on the penultimate syllable, as in *admónish*, unless there are two consonants or a tense vowel at the end, as in *adápt, exíst*. The result is that the stress system of Modern English is now very complex, and accent is not entirely predictable.

Traditionally, different degrees, or levels, of stress are differentiated:

  primary (level 1)   marked by an acute accent (´)
  secondary (level 2)   marked by a grave accent (`)
  unstressed (level 3)   unmarked or marked by a breve (˘)

For example, if you say *computation* in isolation or at the end of a sentence, the *ta* syllable will carry the strong stress, but the *com* syllable will also carry a seemingly weaker stress. What is actually happening here is superimposition of an intonational pattern (discussed in the next section) called a *tonic accent* onto the last stressed syllable. So we say that *ta* carries **primary stress** and *com* carries **secondary stress**, thus *còmputátion*. Secondary stress is sometimes difficult to hear, but generally it will be separated by at least one syllable — either before or after — from the syllable carrying primary stress, as follows:

  intérrogàte   àccidéntal   ínventòry
  còncentrátion   épilèpsy   hallùcinátion

That is, secondary stress will occur in words where the stressed syllable is followed by two or more syllables or where the stressed syllable is preceded by two or more syllables.

In transcription, the IPA system of marking stress is the use of a superscript tick **before** the primary stressed syllable and a subscript tick before the secondary stressed syllable, e.g., *eligibility* [ˌɛlɪjəˈbɪləti], or only primary stress is indicated. Unstressed syllables are not marked.

Stress is a meaningful feature of speech in respect to both words and word groups in English. It has functions in the province of morphology, syntax, and discourse:

1.   Stress distinguishes different parts of speech, as in the corresponding nouns (with initial stress) and verbs (with final stress) below:

noun	verb
próduce	prodúce
áddress	addréss
ímport	impórt
ínsult	insúlt
súrvey	survéy

íncline   inclíne
éxport   expórt

There are also derivationally-related pairs that show the same stress pattern: *concéive* (V) and *cóncept* (N), *procéed* (V) and *prócess* (N), or *preténd* (V) and *prétense* (N). But note that there are many exceptions: *respéct* and *rewárd* are both a noun and a verb; *cómment* is both a noun and a verb; and *díffer* and *defér* are different verbs; compare also *belíeve* (V) and *belíef* (N).

2. Stress distinguishes a word from a phrase (idiom), as in the corresponding sets below:

WORD	PHRASE
N (conversion)	V + Particle
wálkout	to wálk óut
púshover	to púsh óver
rípoff	to ríp óff
cáve-in	to cáve ín
N (compound)	A + N
hótdòg	hót dóg
bláckbòard	bláck bóard
híghcháir	hígh cháir
V (conversion)	A + N
to stónewall	stóne wáll
to bláckball	bláck báll
to máinstream	máin stréam

A word, as we shall see in the next chapter, has only one primary stress, while a phrase has more than one.

3. Stress patterns in derivationally related words distinguish parts of speech:

N (concrete)	N (abstract)	A
díplomat	diplómacy	diplomátic
phótograph	photógraphy	photográphic
mónotone	monótony	monotónic
télegraph	telégraphy	telegráphic
N	A	
pícture	picturésque	
jóurnal	journalése	

That is, the affix affects the placement of stress.

4. Stress is not unrelated to full vowels; unstressed vowels may or may not be reduced to [ə], while stressed vowels are generally full (see above):

expláin [eɪ]   explanátion [ə]
emphátic [æ]   émphasis [ə]

Table 3.2. Strong and Weak Forms

word	strong	weak	example of weak form
and	[ænd]	[ənd, ən, n̩]	I've got to make dinner and clean up.
too, to	[tu]	[tə]	She went to her office.
can	[kæn]	[kən]	I can help you.
at	[æt]	[ət]	Betsy's staying at home today.
as	[æz]	[əz]	He's as happy as possible.
could	[kʊd]	[kəd]	I could be there in ten minutes.
than	[ðæn]	[ən]	She is richer than I am.
you	[yu]	[yə]	Would you give me a hand?
had	[hæd]	[(h)əd]	I had better leave now.
would	[wʊd]	[(w)əd]	Jack would know the answer.
are	[ar]	[ər, ɾ]	We are going to Florida next week.
them	[ðɛm]	[(ð)əm]	Tell them to stop making so much noise.

Sometimes we have full and reduced versions (**strong** and **weak forms**) of the same words (see Table 3.2). The weak forms occur when the word is unstressed. As function words, the words given in Table 3.2 are generally unstressed in a sentence unless they are contrastive.

There are also strong and weak forms of sequences:

I am > I'm   [aɪæm > aɪəm > aɪm]
you are > you're [yuar > yuwər > yɾ]
she is > she's   [šiɪz > šiɪz > šiz]
it is > it's   [ɪtɪz > ɪɾɪz > ɪts]

Note the voicing assimilation in the last case.

The vowel in the second half of a compound noun is reduced:

[mæn] > [-mən]   foreman, policeman, draftsman
[lænd] > [-lənd] Finland, England, highland
[fʊl] > [-fəl]   helpful, thoughtful, rightful
[badi] > [-bədi] somebody, anybody, nobody

However, conscious factors, such as the newness of a word, may prevent an expected reduction, as in *superman* or *madman* and *Disneyland* or *Newfoundland*, which usually contain full vowels, though *madman* is variable and Canadians invariably pronounce *Newfoundland* with a full vowel. Reductions of other forms may likewise be predictable, as in the cases of *a*, *the*, *to*, which are reduced when they occur before a word beginning with a consonant:

a   [ə] a cup   vs.   [æn] an apple
the [ðə] the man vs.   [ði] the apple
to   [tə] to jail vs.   [tu] to university

Remember that the reduction of vowel sounds is not due to "sloppiness" or "laziness", but is completely natural. You may have observed that when nonnative speakers do not reduce vowels as we would expect, their speech indeed sounds "foreign" and nonEnglish.

5.   Stress is used for contrastive emphasis, often indicated in writing by italics or underlining:

I want the r<u>é</u>d one, not the blue one.
He c<u>á</u>n, but he won't finish his work.

The second example shows that we usually don't stress verbs but must stress an accompanying auxiliary verb.

6.   Stress may be used in a discourse to signal new as opposed to old (given) information. For example, in a discussion of what food is wanted by the addressee for dinner, the speaker might use any of the questions below:

Do yóu want pizza for dinner?
Do you want pízza for dinner?
Do you want pizza for dínner?

If the old information — the topic — concerns having pizza for dinner, then the first sentence might be used to question specifically whether the addressee wants it ("you" as opposed to "your brother"). If the topic concerns the addressee's wants for dinner, then the second sentence might be used to question what food he or she wants ("pizza" as opposed to "spaghetti"). If the topic concerns having pizza for some meal, then the third sentence might be used to question which meal pizza should be served at ("dinner" rather than "lunch"). The third sentence — in which the last noun in the clause receives the greatest prominence — is also the most neutral version of this question, where no particular item is being unduly stressed (as we shall see in the next section). (We will consider this aspect of stress in more detail in Chapter 11.)

There is some amount of dialectical variation in the placement of stress. For example, the following words receive different stress placement in British and North American English. Decide which syllable is stressed for you: *ánchóvy, prépáratory, gáráge, lámentable, ápplicable, mústáche, mágazíne, advértisement, córóllary* [ˈkɔrələri] or [kəˈrʊləri]. There is a fairly general rule in British English that secondary stress is omitted on *-ory/-ary* and, as a consequence, the penultimate syllable is lost in words ending in [-(ə)ri], as in *secretary, laboratory, obligatory, military,* and *dictionary.*

■ Self-Testing Exercise: Do Exercise 3.3.

When we speak entire sentences, we do not, in fact, stress every word. Try doing so and see how unnatural it sounds. Instead, we stress only certain words, and unstress others. Generally, we place stress on the major parts of speech, or content words (the nouns, verbs, adjectives, and adverbs), and remove stress from the minor parts of speech, or function words (the prepositions, conjunctions, pronouns, articles, and so on). Consider the following sentence:

In autumn, the dry, yellow leaves fall from the trees.

We would expect *autumn, dry, yellow, leaves, fall,* and *trees* to carry stress, and *in, the,* and *from* not to. Moreover, in English these stresses fall as much as possible at regular intervals, making English a "stress-timed" language. The amount of time necessary for an utterance depends upon the number of stressed syllables, with unstressed syllables occupying much less time than stressed ones. Say the following sentences and note where the stresses fall. Observe that certain content words which one might expect to carry stress do not do so:

> A fúnny thing háppened on the wáy to the fórum.
> Fíve pretty gírls kissed fífteen handsome bóys.
> Thís is the hóuse that Jáck búilt.

Variations in the placement of stress within an individual polysyllabic word may also result from the position of the word in a sentence. Note the difference in stress for the following adjectives if they occur before the noun (in attributive position) or if they occur following the verb (in a predicative position), in the slot indicated:

> *Alex is an* _____ *person*   *Alex is very* _____
>   ártificial   artifícial
>   ábsent-mínded   absent-mínded
>   arístocratic   aristocrátic

Because the placement of stress in a sentence is a matter of spacing out the stresses as evenly as possible and because it is usual to place stress near to the end of the sentence in English, on the last major of speech, *pérson* carries stress; as a consequence, stress on the preceding adjective is placed as far from it as possible, on the first or second syllable. In contrast, since *véry* carries emphatic stress, the stress on the following adjective is placed as late as possible, on the penultimate syllable.

Intonation

Like stress, intonation is a meaningful suprasegmental feature of speech. **Intonation** refers to patterns of pitch variation in a sentence. It does not refer to the discrete pitches of different vowels, to pitch accent, nor to physiologically determined variations in pitch due to the size and shape of a person's vocal apparatus (e.g., the difference in pitch between men's and women's voices). The pitch patterns of intonation are similar to tunes distributed over sentences in an organized and systematic way. They affect the meaning of the sentence as a whole by indicating different sentence types, such as statements or questions. Intonation is represented in a gross fashion in writing by punctuation marks: ?, . ! ; —. Intonation patterns may also indicate the attitude or relation of the speaker to the hearer as well as various contextual features. Therefore, though intonation is a phonological feature, its meaning lies within the province of syntax and pragmatics. Intonation patterns differ quite substantially among different dialects of English, for example between British and American or American and Canadian English. Note that you cannot usually determine the national dialect of a singer because the tunes of the music supercede the distinctive intonational patterns of English sentences.

    In studying intonation, it has been the practice to recognize either different levels of pitch (generally four levels) or different intonational contours, described as **falling** or **rising**.

Using the latter approach, we identify a number of different pitch patterns, which convey different meanings:

– long falling: expresses finality, conclusion, affirmation, agreement;
– short falling: expresses an attenuated or qualified conclusion;
– long rising: expresses questioning and a lack of finality;
– short rising: expresses some degree of reservation or functions as a signal of attentiveness (continuation marker);
– rising-falling: expresses finality with added emotion (e.g., emphasis. enthusiasm, certainty, annoyance); and
– falling-rising: expresses querulousness, skepticism, reservation.

We can see the meaning of these pitch patterns even in a one-word sentence:

long falling: Yes. "The answer is 'yes'".
short falling: Yes. "The answer is 'yes', but I am impatient with your question or find it unimportant".
long rising: Yes. "Did you say 'yes'"?
short rising: Yes. "Perhaps". Or "Please go on — I'm listening".
rising-falling: Yes. "I'm certain".
falling-rising: Yes. "I'm doubtful".

Of course, we normally speak in sequences longer than an individual word. In analyzing intonation patterns, we need to divide longer sequences of discourse into **tone groups**. Tone groups are not necessarily syntactic, but correspond to units of information. A single tone pattern continues over a particular tone group. There may be more than one tone group per sentence. The number of tone groups may vary depending on style: in more formal, deliberate, or pompous style, there are a greater number of tone groups than in more colloquial styles. Consider the following sentence:

She sat by the window in the late afternoon,// reading a letter.

Here there are two tone groups, corresponding to syntactic units, both with falling intonation. A more formal style might consist of three tone groups:

She sat by the window// in the late afternoon,// reading a letter.

Each tone group contains a **tonic syllable**, which carries the major shift in intonation. Usually, the tonic syllable is the last stressed syllable in the tone group. It expresses the information which the speaker considers new (unknown) and most important, as in the following sentences where the tonic syllable is underlined:

Did you get the job? vs. Did you lose your job?
I visited my mother. vs. I visited your mother.

Let's now examine pitch patterns in different sentence types. In each example the tonic syllable is underlined.

1.   A statement has a long falling intonation pattern.
     a.   A whale is a <u>mam</u>mal. (Here the topic of the conversation is whales. What the speaker is adding to the conversation is that these animals are mammals — as opposed to fish — so "mammal" is new information.)
     b.   A <u>whale</u> is a mammal. (Here "mammal" is the topic, and "whale" is new information.)
     A command also has falling intonation when compliance is expected:
     a.   Close the <u>win</u>dow!
     b.   Take your <u>seats</u>!

2.   A *yes/no* question has a long rising intonation pattern, since it expects an answer.
     a.   Do you want some <u>cof</u>fee?
     b.   Do you want <u>cream</u> in your coffee?
     c.   Do you want <u>cof</u>fee or tea?
     d.   Do you want <u>cof</u>fee,// or <u>tea</u>? (This actually represents two *yes/no* questions, the second being a kind of afterthought to the first.)
     e.   You are giving up <u>cof</u>fee? (Note that this is not syntactically a question, but the intonation shows that it is functioning as one.)
     f.   You bought a new <u>car</u>,// <u>eh</u>? (The particle *eh* and the rising intonation turns this statement into a question.)
     An echo question, which asks for the repetition of what has been said before, also has long rising or falling-rising intonation.
     a.   He said <u>what</u>?
     b.   You did <u>what</u>?

3.   A *wh*-question has a long falling intonation pattern (like a statement) since this type of sentence does not ask for but rather presupposes an answer.
     a.   Where did you put the <u>paper</u>? (This is the neutral emphasis.)
     b.   Where did <u>you</u> put the paper? (This focuses on "you" as new information.)

4.   A tag question has two tone groups; the first half is syntactically a statement, while the second half is syntactically a question (we will look at the construction of these questions in Chapter 8).
     a.   You will <u>help</u>,// <u>won't</u> you? (This follows the expected pattern where the first tone unit has (short) falling intonation because it is a statement and the second tone unit has (short) rising intonation because it is a *yes/no* question.)
     b.   He bought a <u>paper</u>,// <u>didn't</u> he? (This is not a real question, but merely asks for confirmation, so unlike (a), the second tone unit has long falling intonation.)

5.   An alternative question consists of two tone groups as well, the first having question intonation and the second statement intonation:
     a.   Did you buy a <u>paper</u>,// or <u>not</u>? (The first pattern is long rising, and the second long falling. The second tone unit acts as a statement added as a kind of afterthought.)
     b.   Do you want a <u>dough</u>nut,// or a <u>muf</u>fin?

6. A list has a number of tone groups with short rising intonation pattern indicating that the discourse continues:
   a. I bought some apples,// oranges,// and peaches. (The last tone group is falling because this is a statement. Long falling intonation on the first two tone groups yields a very slow, deliberate, solemn style, while long rising intonation of these tone units yields a highly dramatized style, often used when addressing children.)
   b. Do you want an apple, an orange, or a peach? (The last tone group is rising because this is a *yes/no* question.)

   Complex sentences have a similar pattern — short rising followed by the appropriate end intonation — whether the subordinate clause precedes or follows the main clause:
   a. When she arrived home// she opened the mail.
   b. She turned off the radio// when he called.

7. A question expressing great doubt or surprise has a falling-rising intonation pattern.
   a. Are you sure? (The vowel of the tonic syllable may be elongated.)
   b. It's raining?

8. A statement expressing great certainty has a rising-falling intonation pattern.
   a. (I've told you several times) I don't know.
   b. (You have to wear your jacket) It's raining.

9. When a vocative (a term of address) or a parenthetical is added to a tone unit, the preceding intonation pattern generally continues over it.
   a. Did you catch what she said, Jerry?
   b. We're in for some hard times, I think. (In this case, there may also be short rising intonation on the parenthetical to lighten up the utterance.)

■ *Self-Testing Exercise: Do Exercise 3.4.*

Syllable Structure

We will end this chapter by examining the unit intermediate between sounds (meaningless segments) and affixes/words (meaningful segments), namely the **syllable**. The syllable represents a level of structure intuitively recognized by speakers of the language; it figures importantly in the rhythm and prosody of the language. As noted earlier, a syllable consists obligatorily of a vowel (or syllabic consonant); this is the acoustic peak, or **nucleus**, of the syllable and potentially carries stress. As discussed above, a syllable may optionally begin with one to three consonants — the **onset** of the syllable — and may close with one to four consonants — the **coda** of the syllable:

(C) (C) (C) Vo (C) (C) (C) (C)

The nucleus and coda together form the rhyme. Syllable structure can be represented in the form of trees, as in the diagrams below for *spring* and *quartz* (Sy = syllable, On = onset, Rh = rhyme, Nu = nucleus, Co = coda):

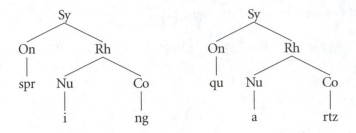

With polysyllabic words, the question of syllable division arises. If there is no medial consonant, the syllable division falls between the vowels, as in *po.et* or *gi.ant*:

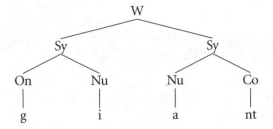

(W = word. For simplicity, we will ignore the intermediate level of the rhyme.)[4] If there is one medial consonant, and stress follows the consonant, the medial consonant forms the onset of the second syllable, as in *ba.ton* or *a.bout*:

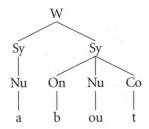

However, if stress falls on the initial syllable, speakers syllabify sometimes with the consonant as coda of the first syllable, sometimes as onset of the second, as in *read.y/rea.dy* or *rig.id* or *ri.gid*. The consonant is said to be **ambisyllabic** (*ambi-* Greek for 'both'), belonging to both syllables:

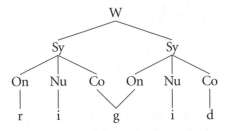

Ambisyllabicity may occur as well when the syllable preceding and following the consonant are both unstressed, as in *man.i.fest/man.if.est* or *or.i.gin/or.ig.in*. Of course, the first consonant is also ambisyllabic:

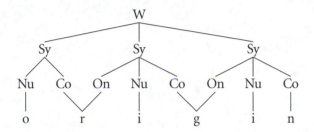

When a consonant cluster occurs word medially and stress falls on the vowel following, the consonants form the onset of the second syllable (compare *about* above), as in *su.blime* or *re.strain* (not *rest.rain, res.train* or *sub.lime;*[5] * *subl.ime* would not be possible since * *bl* is not a possible final cluster):

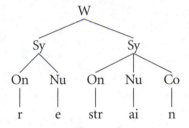

When stress falls on the vowel preceding the consonant cluster, the cluster forms the onset of the second syllable with the initial consonant being ambisyllabic (compare *rigid* above), as in *mi.stress/mis.tress* or *na.sty/nas.ty* (but not *nast.y* or *mist.ress*):

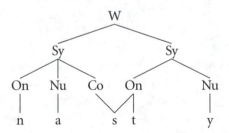

However, if the consonant cluster is not a possible initial cluster in English, the consonants are split between the two syllables, as in *at.las* (not * *a.tlas*), with the longest possible sequence (according to phonotactic constraints) forming the onset of the second syllable, as in *em.blem* (not *emb.lem* or * *e.mblem*).

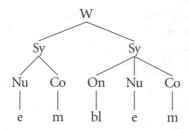

■   *Self-Testing Exercise:* Do Exercise 3.5.

A phenomenon similar to ambisyllabicity arises not at syllable boundaries, but at word boundaries, in cases of apparent ambiguity, as in these well-known examples:

my train/might rain	this kid/the skid
mice fear/my sphere	syntax/sin tax
that scum/that's come	not at all man/not a tall man
night rate/nitrate	an aim/a name
Grade A/gray day	we dressed/we'd rest
lighthouse keeper/light housekeeper	that's tough/that stuff

For example, the sequence of sounds [aɪskrim] could be divided as follows:

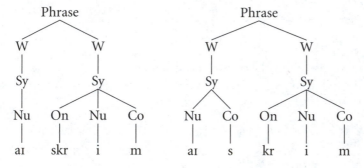

That is, [s] could form the coda of the first word or the onset of the second word, just as in ambisyllabicity, a consonant can form the coda of the first syllable or the onset of the second. Nonetheless, various phonetic features seem to permit disambiguation of these sequences.[6] For example, the [k] in *ice cream* would be aspirated, whereas that in *I scream* would not be. Vowel length would distinguish *my train* (with [aɪ:]) from *might rain* (with [aɪ]); nasalization and vowel quality would distinguish *an aim* (with [æn]) from *a name* (with [ə]), and stress would distinguish *líghthòuse kéeper* from *líght hóusekèeper*.

■ Chapter Summary

Now that you have completed this chapter, you should be able to:

1. write rules for phonemes of English, given appropriate data;
2. identify a number of phonological processes at work in English;
3. state the restrictions on positions of sounds and combinations of sounds in English;
4. determine the placement of primary and secondary stress in English words;
5. describe the different functions of stress in English;
6. identify the tonic syllable and pitch pattern within a tone group; and
7. determine the syllable structure of English words.

■ Recommended Additional Reading

Useful discussions of English phonology can be found in Ladefoged (1993, Chapter 4, pp. 88–96, and Chapter 5), MacKay (1991, Chapters 7 and 8), Kreidler (1989, Chapters 5–7, 9–10, 13–14), Giegerich (1992, Chapters 6–10), and O'Grady and Dobrovolsky (1996, Chapter 2, pp. 37–43, and Chapter 3, pp. 59–82, 90–94). Murray (1995, Chapter 2) is an elementary discussion, complete with exercises and answers. A generative approach to English phonology is Carr (1999). General linguistics treatments of phonology include Hawkins (1984), Lass (1984), and Katamba (1989). For a more detailed discussion of English intonation, see Crystal (1969), Couper-Kuhlen (1986), and, for a more individualistic account, Bolinger (1986).

■ Notes

1. We are ignoring certain variants of /t/ such as the preglotalized version, which might replace the unreleased stop, and the glottal stop, which might replace the nasal- or lateral-released stop.
2. Note that both nasalization and velarization are indicated with a "tilde" diacritic, except that in the first case, the tilde is placed above the phonetic letter and in the second case it is superimposed over the letter.
3. The sequence [sf], always spelled *sph*, occurs in a few words of Greek origin, such as *sphere* and *sphinx*.
4. While is it conventional to use the symbol σ for "syllable" and Σ for "word", for the purposes of this introductory text, I am using the more intuitively more obvious "Sy" and "W".
5. Syllabification practices used in dictionaries are conventional and not entirely phonologically based. Often, morphological boundaries are also used in establishing syllables. This would be the case for *sublime*, where the prefix *sub-* would be recognized for the purposes of syllabification.
6. Such phenomena used to be explained by postulating a suprasegmental feature called "juncture", a kind of pause which demarcated the boundary between words and which differed from the pauses between sounds within words ("open" versus "close" juncture).

The Structure and Meaning of English Words

CHAPTER 4

The Internal Structure of Words and Processes of Word Formation in English

■ Chapter Preview

This chapter first introduces the criteria used for distinguishing a word from a phrase. It then considers the internal structure of words, making use of the abstract notion of a morpheme (meaningful unit) and the concrete notion of a morph. The different types of morphemes and morphs are described. It is shown that there is not always a correspondence between the morphemes and morphs of a word and that morphemes may be realized in different ways as morphs. The chapter then introduces allomorphs (predictable variants) of morphemes, and the writing of morphemic rules is explained. Both stem and root allomorphy is treated. The next section of the chapter explores the different processes of word formation in English, focusing on the complexities of derivation and compounding; minor processes of word formation — reduplication, conversion, blending, shortening, and root creations — are treated in less detail. The chapter ends with a brief discussion of idioms.

■ Commentary

Defining the Word

We move now from an examination of the smallest segments of language (sounds) to the larger units (words, which Leonard Bloomfield defined as "minimal free forms"). However, since speech is a phonetic continuum, without pauses between words (we generally pause between larger syntactic units such as phrases or clauses), we need some means of determining the boundaries of words. We all have an intuitive feel for the words of the language and we think immediately of the written word, but even nonliterate speakers can divide the speech chain into words. Thus, there must be some formal criteria for wordhood which all speakers use. These might be of various kinds:

1. Orthographic: a word is what occurs between spaces in writing.
2. Semantic: a word has semantic coherence; it expresses a unified semantic concept.

3. Phonological:
    a.   potential pause: a word occurs between potential pauses in speaking. Though in normal speech, we generally do not pause, we may potentially pause between words, but not in the middle of words.
    b.   stress: a word spoken in isolation has one and only one primary stress.
4. Morphological: a word has an internal cohesion and is indivisible by other units; a word may be modified only externally by the addition of suffixes and prefixes.
5. Grammatical: words fall into particular classes.
6. Syntactic: a word has external distribution or mobility; it is moved as a unit, not in parts.

We can see the usefulness of these criteria if we look at some problematical examples of word delimitation:

grapefruit	son-in-law
travel agency	money-hungry
good-for-nothing	look over

By the criterion of orthography, *grapefruit* would be considered a single word, as would hyphenated forms such as *good-for-nothing* or *money-hungry*, while phrases such as *travel agency* or *look over* must be considered as multiple words, or phrases. Yet by the second criterion, semantic unity, the words and the phrases all appear to be equally unified conceptually. The discrepancy is especially apparent if you compare *grapefruit* with related concepts such as *passion fruit* or *bread fruit*. In fact, the conventions of spacing between words, as well as hyphenation practices, are often quite arbitrary in English. As well as being hyphenated, *good-for-nothing* and *son-in-law* meet the syntactic criterion of wordhood: they are moved as a single unit. However, they differ in respect to the morphological criterion; while *good-for-nothing* always behaves as a single word, with external modification (*two good-for-nothings*, *good-for-nothing's*), *son-in-law* is inconsistent, behaving as a single word when made possessive (*son-in-law's*), but as a phrase, that is, with internal modification, when pluralized (*sons-in-law*). The third criterion, a single primary stress, would seem to be the most reliable, but even here compound adjectives such as *money-hungry* pose a problem: they have two primary stresses and are phonologically phrases but are treated orthographically, morphologically, and syntactically as single words. "Phrasal verbs" such as *look over* also present an interesting case. Though having many of the qualities of a phrase — internal modification occurs (*looked over*), material may intercede between the parts (*look over the information*, but also *look the information over*), and both *look* and *over* receive primary stress — phrasal verbs seem to express a unified semantic notion, the same as expressed in this case by the single word *examine*. As this chapter progresses, we examine these problems in more detail.

Another difficulty when treating words is the term *word* itself, which may be used in a number of different ways:

1. It may refer to the word form, the physical unit or concrete realization, either the orthographical word (which is underlined or italicized in writing when it is mentioned rather than used) and the phonological word (which may be uttered or transcribed).

2.   It may refer to the **lexeme**, which is rather like a dictionary entry. A lexeme includes all inflected forms of a word. It is thus a kind of abstraction or class of forms and is indicated by small capitals, as in the following examples:

> WALK — *walk, walks, walked, walking*
> RUN — *run, runs, ran, running*
> SING — *sing, sings, sang, sung, singing*

Note that since the lexeme is an abstraction, it is conventional to choose one of the inflected forms to represent it, such as the infinitive of the verbs given above or the singular of nouns.[1]

The same word form may in fact represent different lexemes. A homonym is a single orthographic and phonological word standing for two lexemes, as *bear* is either the verb or the noun. A homograph is a single orthographic word (but separate phonological words) standing for two lexemes, as *lead* is either the noun [lɛd] or the verb [lid]. A homophone is a single phonological word (but separate orthographical words) standing for a single lexeme, as [bɛr] is either the noun *bear* or the adjective *bare*.

The same lexeme might also have quite distinct word forms, as in the case of the definite article THE, represented by [ði] or [ðə], or the indefinite article A/AN, represented by [eɪ], [ə], [ən], or [æn].

3.   Finally, *word* may also refer to a morphosyntactic word (or grammatical word). A morphosyntactic word consists of a lexeme and associated grammatical meaning. For example, *put* is three morphosyntactic words:

> I put the garbage out every week. (PUT + present)
> I put the garbage out yesterday. (PUT + past)
> I have put the garbage out already. (PUT + past participle)

Note that it is more general for the different grammatical meanings to be represented by different word forms: e.g., *sing* (SING + present), *sang* (SING + past), and *sung* (SING + past participle).

By the criteria discussed in this section, would you analyze *passer-by* as a word or not?

Morphemes

We begin the study of morphology by taking words as given and examining their internal structure.

Morpheme versus Morph

We must start by identifying the **morpheme**, the smallest meaningful unit in a language; the morpheme is not necessarily equivalent to a word, but may be a smaller unit. Like the phoneme, the morpheme refers to either a class of forms or an abstraction from the concrete forms of language. A morpheme is internally indivisible; it cannot be further subdivided or analyzed into smaller meaningful units. It has internal stability since nothing can be interposed in a morpheme. It is also externally transportable; it has positional mobility or free distribution, occurring in various contexts. Morphemes are represented within curly braces { } using capital letters for lexemes or descriptive designations for other types of morphemes.

There are a number of types of morphemes, as shown in Figure 4.1.

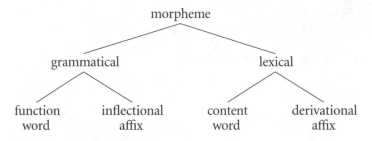

Figure 4.1. Types of Morphemes

This classification is based primarily on meaning. **Lexical morphemes** express lexical, or dictionary, meaning. They can be categorized into the major lexical categories, or word classes: noun, verb, adjective, or adverb. They constitute open categories, to which new members can be added. Lexical morphemes are generally independent words (free roots) or parts of words (derivational affixes and bound roots). **Grammatical morphemes** express a limited number of very common meanings or express relations within the sentence. They do not constitute open categories; they can be exhaustively listed. Their occurrence is (entirely) predictable by the grammar of the sentence because certain grammatical meanings are associated with certain lexical categories, for example, tense and voice with the verb, and number and gender with the noun. Grammatical morphemes may be parts of words (inflectional affixes) or small but independent "function words" belonging to the minor word classes: preposition, article, demonstrative, conjunction, auxiliary, and so on, e.g., *of*, *the, that, and, may.*

In the case of the morpheme — which is an abstraction — we must also recognize the level of the **morph**, the concrete realization of a morpheme, or the actual segment of a word. We must do so because sometimes a morpheme has no concrete realization, although we know that it exists. In such cases, we speak of a **zero morph**, one which has no phonetic or overt realization. There is no equivalent on the level of the phoneme. For example, the past tense *let* consists of the morpheme {LET} plus the morpheme {past}, although the past tense morpheme has no concrete expression in this case. Or plural *fish* consists of the morphemes {FISH} + {pl}, although the plural morpheme has no concrete realization. Note that morphs are represented by word forms or phonetic forms. We say that a morpheme is "realized" as a morph.

Just as there are different types of morphemes, there are different types of morphs (see Figure 4.2).

This classification is based primarily on form. A **free morph** may stand alone as a word, while a **bound morph** may not; it must always be attached to another morph. A free morph is always a **root.** That is, it carries the principal lexical or grammatical meaning. It occupies the position where there is greatest potential for substitution; it may attach to other free or bound morphemes. Examples of roots are underlined in the following words:

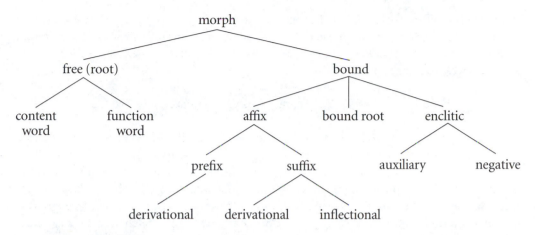

Figure 4.2. Types of Morphs

> unavoidably
> overgrown
> disheartened
> reclassify

Roots are also occasionally bound morphs. These are called **bound roots**. Bound roots are often foreign borrowings that were free in the source language, but not free in English. For example, in the following sets of words, we would all intuitively identify the root *-vert*, *-mit*, or *-ceive* (in part because it occurs in a number of words, as do the prefixes):

> -vert: con<u>vert</u>, re<u>vert</u>, sub<u>vert</u>, intro<u>vert</u>, per<u>vert</u>
> -mit: trans<u>mit</u>, com<u>mit</u>, re<u>mit</u>, ad<u>mit</u>, o<u>mit</u>, sub<u>mit</u>
> -ceive: con<u>ceive</u>, per<u>ceive</u>, re<u>ceive</u>, de<u>ceive</u>

However *-vert*, *-mit*, and *-ceive* cannot stand alone as independent words, and we would also find it very difficult to state the meaning of any of these roots, unless we know Latin, from which these words derive: *-vert* is from Latin *vertere* meaning 'to turn', *-mit* is from Latin *mittere* meaning 'to send', while *-ceive* is from Latin *capere* meaning 'to seize'. Bound roots may also be native English, as with *-kempt* (< *unkempt*) and *-couth* (< *uncouth*), where the positive form no longer exists. The term *etymene* has been coined because bound roots can be said to have meaning only if you know their history, or etymology.

Unlike a root, an **affix** does not carry the core meaning. It is always bound to a root. It occupies a position where there is limited potential for substitution; that is, a particular affix will attach to only certain roots. English has two kinds of affixes, **prefixes**, which attach to the beginnings of roots, and **suffixes**, which attach to the end of roots. Some languages regularly use "infixes", which are inserted in the middle of words. In Modern English, infixes are used only for humorous purposes, as in *im-bloody-possible* or *abso-blooming-lutely*. Historically, the *-n-* in *stand* is a "nasal infix" indicating present tense; note that it does not occur in the past tense *stood*. While it might initially be tempting to analyze the vowel alternation indicating plural (as in *man, men*) or past tense (as in *sing, sang*) in Modern English as a kind of infix, note that the vowels actually replace the existing vowels; hence, this exemplifies the morphological process of replacement.[2]

■ *Self-Testing Exercise:* To practice identifying roots, prefixes, and suffixes, do Exercise 4.1.

Affixes may be of two types, derivational or inflectional, which have very different characteristics. A **derivational affix** in English is either a prefix or a suffix. There may be more than one derivational affix per word. A particular derivational affix may attach to only a limited number of roots; which roots it attaches to is not predictable by rule, but highly idiosyncratic and must be learned. A derivational affix has one of two functions: to convert one part of speech to another (in which case, it is called **class changing**) and/or to change the meaning of the root (in which case, it is called **class maintaining**). Such affixes function, then, in word formation and are important in the creation of new lexemes in the language. They always precede an inflectional affix. An **inflectional affix** in English is always a suffix. A particular inflectional affix attaches to all (or most) members of a certain word class. The function of inflectional affixes is to indicate grammatical meaning, such as tense or number. Because grammatical meaning is relevant outside the word, to the grammar of the entire sentence, inflectional affixes always occur last, following the root and any derivational affixes, which are central to the meaning or class of the root. A distinction can be made between productive inflections, which would attach to any new word entering the language to express a particular grammatical category, and nonproductive, or remnant, inflections, which are found on select members of a class, but would never be added to a new word. As shown in Table 4.1, the productive inflections of Modern English are very limited.

Some examples of nonproductive inflections are the plural vowel alternation *tooth–teeth*; the *-most* superlative of *foremost*; the *-en* past participle of *write-written*; or the past tense-vowel alternation of *ring-rang*.

■ *Self-Testing Exercises:* To learn to identify inflectional suffixes, do Exercise 4.2. Then to better understand the difference between inflection and derivation, do Exercise 4.3.

An **enclitic** is a kind of contraction, a bound form which derives from an independent word and must be attached to the preceding word. In English, we have two kinds of enclitics: auxiliaries, which are attached to the preceding subject, and the negative *-n't*, which is attached to the preceding auxiliary. These are exemplified in Table 4.2.

Some languages have "proclitics", originally free words which must be attached to the word which follows; the articles in French are proclitics, e.g., *la auto* > *l'auto*. Also, the archaic forms in English *'twas* (< *it was*) or *'tis* (< *it is*) contain proclitics.

Finally, a root must be distinguished both from a **base**, which is a root plus associated derivational affixes, to which derivational affixes are added, and from a stem, a root plus associated derivational affixes, to which inflectional affixes are added.

Table 4.1. The Productive Inflections of Modern English

plural number	*-s*	} Noun
possessive case	*-s*	
present (nonpast) tense, 3rd p sg	*-s*	} Verb
past tense	*-ed*	
past participle	*-ed*	
present participle	*-ing*	
comparative degree	*-er*	} Adjective
superlative degree	*-est*	

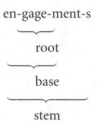

Words are analyzed morphologically with the same terminology used to describe different sentence types:

- a simple word has one free root, e.g., *hand*;
- a complex word has a free root and one or more bound morphs, or two or more bound morphs, e.g., *unhand, handy, handful*;
- a compound word has two free roots, e.g., *handbook, handrail, handgun*; and
- a compound-complex word has two free roots and associated bound morphs, e.g., *handwriting, handicraft.*

Morphemic Analysis versus Morphological Analysis

The importance of the distinction between morph and morpheme is that there is not always a one-to-one correspondence between morph and morpheme, and morphemes can combine or be realized in a number of different ways. We can thus analyze words in two different ways: in **morphological analysis**, words are analyzed into morphs following formal divisions, while in **morphemic analysis**, words are analyzed into morphemes, recognizing the abstract units of meaning present.

If we start first with nouns, we would arrive at the two analyses of each of the following words:

	Morphological Analysis	Morphemic Analysis
writers	3 morphs *writ/er/s*	3 morphemes {WRITE} + {-ER} + {pl}
authors	2 morph *author/s*	2 morphemes {AUTHOR} + {pl}
mice	1 morph *mice*	2 morphemes {MOUSE} + {pl}

Table 4.2. Enclitics in English

auxiliaries

> will, shall > 'll
> would, had > 'd
> is, has > 's
> are > 're
> have > 've
> am > 'm
> was > *'s

negative -*n't*

won't	wouldn't	
?shalln't	shouldn't	
can't	couldn't	
?mayn't	?mightn't	
mustn't		
hasn't	haven't	hadn't
isn't	aren't	*am't (ain't)
wasn't	weren't	
?oughtn't		
*usedn't		
needn't		
?daren't		

fish	1 morph *fish*	2 morphemes {FISH} + {pl}
children	2 morphs *child/ren*	2 morphemes {CHILD} + {pl}
teeth	1 morph *teeth*	2 morphemes {TOOTH} + {pl}
man's	2 morphs *man/s*	2 morphemes {MAN} + {poss}
men's	2 morphs *men/s*	3 morphemes {MAN} + {pl} + {poss}

You should note that the morphemes, since they are abstractions, can be represented any way one wants, but it is customary to use lexemes for roots and descriptive designations for inflectional morphemes, such as {pl} rather than {-S} for the plural marker and {poss} rather than {-S} for the possessive marker, since these can often be realized by a number of different forms. The descriptive designations that we will use should be self-evident in the following discussion (also see the list of abbreviations in Appendix I).

A noun such as *sheep* raises a difficulty for morphemic analysis, since it is either singular or plural. Should we postulate two morphemic analyses?

> {SHEEP} + {pl}
> {SHEEP} + {sg}

This seems a good idea. If we postulate a morpheme for singular, even though it is never realized, we can account for number systematically. Thus, we will analyze all singular nouns as containing an abstract {sg} morpheme, so that *man's* above would have the analysis {MAN} + {sg} + {poss}, *writer* the analysis {WRITE} + {-ER} + {sg}, and *author* the analysis {AUTHOR} + {sg}.

Let us look at how morphological and morphemic analysis work in adjectives:

	Morphological Analysis	Morphemic Analysis
smaller	2 morphs *small/er*	2 morphemes {SMALL} + {compr}
smallest	2 morphs *small/est*	2 morphemes {SMALL} + {supl}
better	1 morph *better*	2 morphemes {GOOD} + {compr}
best	1 morph *best*	2 morphemes {GOOD} + {supl}

(Here, compr = comparative degree and supl = superlative degree, as will be discussed in the next chapter.) Again, we need to postulate a morpheme positive degree {pos}, even though it is never realized, to account systematically for the inflected forms of adjectives:

good	1 morph *good*	2 morphemes {GOOD} + {pos}

For verbs, the two analyses work as follows:

	Morphological Analysis	Morphemic Analysis
worked	2 morphs *work/ed*	2 morphemes {WORK} + {past}
		2 morphemes {WORK} + {pstprt}
wrote	1 morph *wrote*	2 morphemes {WRITE} + {past}
written	1 morph *written*	2 morphemes {WRITE} + {pstprt}
working	2 morphs *work/ing*	2 morphemes {WORK} + {prsprt}
		3 morphemes {WORK} + {gerund}+ {sg}
put	1 morph *put*	2 morphemes {PUT} + {past}
		2 morphemes {PUT} + {prsprt}

(Here, pstprt = past participle, prsprt = present participle; see further Chapter 9.) Note that we have to analyze *-ing* verbal forms not only as present participles, but also as "gerunds", or verbal nouns, as in *Swimming is good exercise.* Since gerunds are functioning as nouns, they may sometimes be pluralized, e.g.:

sittings	3 morphs *sitt/ing/s*	3 morphemes {SIT} + {gerund} + {pl}

(Gerunds will be discussed in more detail in Chapter 9.) We need to postulate a morpheme {pres}, which is never realized, to account coherently for the distinction past versus present:[3]

work	1 morph *work*	2 morphemes {WORK} + {pres}
write	1 morph *write*	2 morphemes {WRITE} + {pres}

The morphemic analysis of pronouns is somewhat more complicated:

	Morphological Analysis	Morphemic Analysis
we	1 morph *we*	3 morphemes {1st p} + {pl} + {nomn}
him	1 morph *him*	4 morphemes {3rd p} + {sg} + {m} + {obj}
its	2 morphs *it/s*	4 morphemes {3rd p} + {sg} + {n} + {poss}

(Here, nomn = nominative case and obj = objective case; see the following chapter.)

Morphemes combine and are realized by one of four **morphological realization rules**:

1.   agglutinative rule — two morphemes are realized by morphs which remain distinct and are simply "glued" together, e.g., {WRITER} + {pl} > *writers*
2.   fusional rule — two morphemes are realized by morphs which do not remain distinct but are fused together, e.g., {TOOTH} + {pl} > *teeth*
3.   null realization rule — a morpheme is never realized as a morph in any word of the relevant class, e.g., {sg} on nouns, which never has concrete realization in English.
4.   zero rule — a morpheme is realized as a zero morph in particular members of a word class, e.g., {SHEEP} + {pl} > *sheep*. Note that in most other members of the class noun, {pl} has concrete realization as -*s*.

Examples from above of the four different morphological realization rules are the following:

   agglutinative: {WORK} + {past} > *worked*
   fusional: {WRITE} + {past} > *wrote*
   null: {WORK} + {pres} > *work*
   zero: {PUT} + {past} > *put*, {PUT} + {pstprt} > *put*

More than one rule may operate in a single word, as {MAN} + {pl} + {poss} > *men's* is created by both a fusional and an agglutinative rule.[4]

■   *Self-Testing Exercise:* Do Exercise 4.4.

Allomorphs and Morphemic Rules

Let us turn now to a further aspect of morphemes. Just as phonemes have predictable variants, called allophones, morphemes have predictable variants called **allomorphs**. Allomorphs are the members of the class, morpheme, or the phonetic realizations of the abstraction, morpheme. Allomorphs are semantically similar and in **complementary distribution**. They needn't be phonologically similar, however. Allomorphs are predicted, or "conditioned", in one of three ways:

–   **phonologically conditioned**: the appearance of a particular allomorph is predictable from the phonetic environment;
–   **grammatically conditioned**: the appearance is unpredictable phonologically but is determined by the grammar of the language; or
–   in **free variation**: allomophs may be used interchangeably in a particular environment, (or otherwise known as "contextually conditioned").

Let's consider the following example involving regular plural formation in nouns in English, as shown in Table 4.3.

Although the orthographic form of the plural is -*s* or -*es* in all cases, you will notice that the phonological form of the plural morpheme in column A is [əz], in column B [s], and in column C [z]. Thus, there are three allomorphs of the plural morpheme. These allomorphs

Table 4.3. Regular Plural Formation in Nouns

A	B	C	
bushes [š]	maps [p]	knobs [b]	rays [eɪ]
buses [s]	cats [t]	rods [d]	sofas [ə]
mazes [z]	racks [k]	logs [g]	toys [ɔɪ]
judges [ǰ]	ropes [p]	seals [l]	keys [i]
matches [č]	laughs [f]	mirrors [r]	news [ɪu]
boxes [s]	paths [θ]	pans [n]	lathes [ð]
garages [ž]		tombs [m]	coves [v]
rouges [ž]		rings [ŋ]	

are phonetically similar, as well as semantically similar, all expressing the concept 'more than one'. It is also necessary to determine how these allomorphs are conditioned. If they are phonologically conditioned, there must be something about the phonetic environment of the noun which determines the choice of allomorph. In fact, it is the final sound of the root of the noun which is the determining factor. Note that in column A, all of the nouns end with a fricative or an affricate, in column B, with a voiceless consonant, and in column C, with a voiced consonant or vowel. We can refine this information and state it in terms of a **morphemic rule** similar in form to a phonemic rule (as in Chapter 3). This rule will also account for the allomorphs of the possessive morpheme (as well as of the 3rd p sg pres morpheme on verbs and contractions of 3rd p sg pres of *have* and *be*):

{pl} → [əz]/ sibilants —
      [s]/ voiceless consonants —
      [z]/ elsewhere

Note that it is inaccurate to say that [əz] occurs after fricatives, since certain fricatives such as [f] take the [s] allomorph while others such as [v] take the [z] allomorph. But the sounds found in column A [s, z, š, ž, č, ǰ] constitute a natural class called "sibilants". And remember that the rule is read downward, so that "voiceless consonants" in the second line would exclude any voiceless consonants already included in the first line among sibilants. As with phonemic rules, we specify one allomorph as "elsewhere". This is the form with widest distribution or the one found in the most diverse phonetic environments, in this case, after voiced consonants and vowels. It should also be the form from which the other forms can be derived with the simplest set of phonological rules. For example, if we take [z] as the underlying form,[5] then we need the following rules to derive the other forms:

1. a declustering rule which inserts schwa between two sibilants (giving the [əz] allomorph); and
2. a devoicing rule which devoices [z] when it immediately follows a voiceless consonant (giving the [s] allomorph).

Note that the rules must be applied in this order. If we take [s] as the underlying form, we need a voicing rule (if the ending follows a voiced sound) and then a declustering rule. If we take [əz] as the underlying form, we need a schwa deletion rule (if the ending does not follow a sibilant) and a devoicing rule. These latter rules are less natural than the declustering and devoicing rules initially suggested.

Certain noun plurals are grammatically conditioned:

Ø	fish, sheep, deer
vowel alternation	mice, lice, geese
-en	children, brethren, oxen
foreign plurals	
-a	phenomena, data, criteria
-i	stimuli, alumni
-ae	alumnae, formulae
-ices	indices, appendices
-es	bases, axes
-im	kibbutzim, cherubim

These endings are not productive, but are linguistic fossils, or remnant forms. Note that if a noun such as *mouse* took a productive ending, it would be the [əz] allomorph, *child* would take [z], and *tooth* would take [s].

A problem for the morphemic rule of plural allomorphs in English is provided by the following sets of words, all ending in [f] in the singular:

wolf — wolves	leaf — leaves
knife — knives	loaf — loaves
sheaf — sheaves	wife — wives
elf — elves	life — lives
shelf — shelves	calf — calves
thief — thieves	self — selves

We would expect the plural allomorph to be [s] in all cases, given the final voiceless consonant of the root, as in the following words:

belief — beliefs	chief — chiefs
proof — proofs	safe — safes

What we find instead is the plural allomorph [z], with a concomitant voicing of the final root consonant. In some cases, we find variation between the phonologically expected and unexpected forms:

wharf — wharfs/wharves	dwarf — dwarfs/dwarves
hoof — hoofs/hooves	scarf — scarfs/scarves

A similar irregularity appears in the following words, where the expected [əz] allomorph is found, but there is voicing of the final root [s]:

house — houses	blouse — blouses

It is interesting to note that in these cases, the possessive morpheme -s is altogether regular: *wolf's, knife's, life's, thief's, elf's,* and so on.

How do we account for these irregularities in the plural forms? We could have a morphological realization rule which changes final voiceless fricatives to voiced fricatives when {pl} is added. However, such a rule would have to apply generally to all roots ending in voiceless fricatives, and it does not. Instead, we say that there are two predictable variants of the root, what is called **root allomorphy**. The two allomorphs of the root are grammatically conditioned, by the presence of either a following {sg} and {pl} morpheme

    {lif} → [liv]/ —{pl}
       [lif]/ elsewhere

Note that "elsewhere" would include the environment before both {sg} and {poss}. Hence, this form has the widest distribution. Actually, the —{pl} environment is too restricted since we also have voicing when a verb is formed from the noun (for example, *to shelve, to calve, to halve*); this even occurs in some cases where there is no voicing in the noun plural (as in *to believe, to prove, to grieve*).

A similar kind of root allomorphy can be seen in cases of shifts from noun to verb where (a) the nominal forms have [s] and the verbal forms have [z], or (b) the nominal forms have [θ] while the verbal forms have [ð] (see Table 4.4). Assuming that the voiceless form is the base form, morphemic rules for these forms would be as follows:

    {haʊs} → [haʊz]/ [ᵥ]—   {bæθ} → [bæð]/ [ᵥ]—
       [haʊs]/ elsewhere   [bæθ]/ elsewhere

Finally, it is interesting to note that bound roots may show root allomorphy; for example, -*cept* is a predictable variant of -*ceive* before -*ion*, as in *conception, perception, reception,* and *deception.*

Generally, English is not rich in allomorphy, though we have inherited quite a lot of it with the Latinate vocabulary that we borrowed, as you shall see in Exercise 4.5. However, two other examples of native allomorphy are the [ðə]/[ði] variants of the definite article {THE} — can you determine how these are conditioned? A further example of root allomorphy is *staves/staffs* (< *staff*), where the root-allomorphic plural and the regular plural have become semantically distinguished, the former being restricted to music.

■ Self-Testing Exercise: To practice writing morphemic rules, do Exercise 4.5.

Processes of Word Formation

English has a number of means by which morphs combine or are altered to form new words. However, only two of these processes of word creation, derivation and compounding, are responsible for significant numbers of new words.

Table 4.4. Root Allomorphy

(a)	N:		V:		(b)	N:		V:	
	N:	house	V:	to house		N:	bath	V:	to bathe
		blouse		to blouse			cloth		to clothe
		use		to use			breath		to breathe
		excuse		to excuse			mouth		to mouthe
		advice		to advise			teeth		to teethe
		abuse		to abuse			wreath		to wreathe

Derivation

The addition of a word-forming affix (a prefix, a suffix, and, in some languages, an infix) is called **derivation**. We have already looked at the features of derivational affixes (in contrast to inflectional suffixes). The addition of a derivational affix to a root produces a new word with one or more of the following changes:

–   a phonological change (including stress change): *reduce > reduction, clear > clarity, fuse > fusion, photograph > photography, drama > dramatize, relate > relation, permit > permissive, impress > impression, electric > electricity, include > inclusive*;
–   an orthographic change to the root: *pity > pitiful, deny > denial, happy > happiness*;
–   a semantic change, which may be fairly complex: *husband > husbandry, event > eventual, post > postage, recite > recital*; and/or
–   a change in word class.

In English, derivational affixes are either prefixes or suffixes. They may be native (deriving from Old English) or foreign (borrowed along with a word from a foreign language, especially French). Their productivity may range from very limited to quite extensive, depending upon whether they are found preserved in just a few words and no longer used to create new words or whether they are found in many words and still used to create new words. An example of an unproductive suffix is the -*th* in *warmth, width, depth*, or *wealth*, whereas an example of a productive suffix is the -*able* in *available, unthinkable, admirable*, or *honorable*. But which affix attaches to which root is always quite arbitrary and unpredictable; it is not a matter of rule but must be stated separately for each root (as, for example, in a dictionary). That is, derivation is part of the lexicon, not part of the grammar of a language.

Only three prefixes, which are no longer productive in English, systematically change the part of speech of the root:

a-	N/V > A	*ablaze, asleep, astir*
be-	N > V	*betoken, befriend, bedeck*
en-	A/N > V	*enlarge, ensure, encircle, encase, entrap*

Other prefixes change only the meaning of the root, not its class. Prefixes fall into a number of semantic classes in English, depending upon the meaning that they contribute to the root, as shown in Table 4.5. Note the difference between privation and negation: a privative prefix expresses the reverse of an action (as in *undo*) or the absence of a quality (as in *amoral*

Table 4.5. Semantic Classes of Prefixes in English

(a)	Time	
	pre-	prearrange, presuppose, preheat
	after-	aftershock, afterthought, afterglow
(b)	Number	
	tri-	tricycle, triannual, triconsonantal
	multi-	multinational, multilingual, multimillionaire
(c)	Place	
	in-	infield, in-patient, ingrown
	inter-	interconnect, interbreed, interlace
(d)	Degree	
	super-	supersensitive, supersaturated, superheat
	over-	overanxious, overconfident, overdue
(e)	Privation	
	a-	amoral, apolitical, asymmetric
	un-	unlock, untie, unfold
(f)	Negation	
	un-	unafraid, unsafe, unwise
	anti-	antisocial, antitrust, antiwar
(g)	Size	
	micro-	microcosm, microchip, microfilm
	mini-	miniskirt, minivan, minimall

'without morals'), whereas the negative prefix expresses 'not' (as in *immoral* 'not moral'). The list given in Table 4.5 is not an exhaustive one; other semantic categories would be needed to classify all the prefixes of English, such as "completeness" (e.g., *fulfill*), "reversal" (e.g., *counterattack*), or subordination (e.g., *vicechair*). Furthermore, some prefixes may fit into more than one category; e.g., *under-*, expresses both degree (in *underpayment*) and place (in *underwater*). Prefixes may often attach to more than one part of speech, e.g., *mislead* (V) and *misfortune* (N).

Of the prefixes given in Table 4.5, *after-*, *in-*, *over-*, and *un-* are native English, while *pre-*, *inter-*, *super-*, and *mini-* are Latin and *tri-*, *a-*, *micro-*, and *anti-* are Greek.

Suffixes have two functions: to change the meaning of the root and to change the part of speech of the root. Those changing meaning alone include the diminutive suffixes *-ling*, *-let*, *-y* (in *princeling, piglet, daddy*), the feminine suffixes *-ess, -ette, -rix, -ine* (in *actress, usherette, aviatrix, heroine*) — which, for social and cultural reasons, are now falling out of use — and the abstract suffixes, making an abstract noun out of a concrete noun, *-ship, -hood, -ism* (in *friendship, manhood, hoodlumism*), as shown in Table 4.6a. More often, however, suffixes change the word class of the root. As shown in Table 4.6b and c, the suffix may produce a noun from a verb or an adjective; such a suffix is called a **nominalizer**. This constitutes the largest set of class-changing suffixes. A highly productive nominalizer is the agentive suffix -*er*, which may be added to many verbs to produce agent nouns. A suffix which produces a verb from a noun or an adjective is called a **verbalizer**, as exemplified in Table 4.6d, while one which produces an adjective from a noun, a verb, or another adjective is called an **adjectivalizer** and is exemplified in Table 4.6e, f, and g. The smallest set of class-changing prefixes is the **adverbializer**. In addition to those shown in Table 4.6h, another adverbializer in English is the old inflectional possessive ending -*s* in *nowadays, nights, once,* and *thereabouts.*

The formation of complex words is not always entirely predictable or regular. For example, -*ist* is typically added to common nouns (e.g., *cyclist*) and occasionally to proper nouns (e.g., *Platonist*). The addition of -*ist* results in a phonetic change [-ɪst] and a semantic

Table 4.6. Derivational Suffixes in English

(a)	N > N	
	-hood	neighborhood, brotherhood, girlhood
	-ship	championship, membership, kinship
	-ism	idealism, patriotism, fanaticism
(b)	V > N	
	-ment	arrangement, judgment, advancement
	-er	worker, helper, leader
	-(c)ation	legalization, simplification, taxation
(c)	A > N	
	-dom	freedom, officialdom, Christendom
	-ness	happiness, cleverness, bitterness
	-ity	legality, purity, equality
(d)	A/N > V	
	-ify	pacify, simplify, purify
	-ize	prioritize, publicize, centralize
(e)	N > A	
	-y	flowery, thirsty, bloody
	-ous	poisonous, famous, glamorous
	-ful	delightful, sinful, pitiful
(f)	V > A	
	-ive	supportive, generative, assertive
	-able	acceptable, livable, changeable
	-ful	hopeful, thankful, useful
(g)	A > A	
	-ish	greenish, fortyish, coldish
	-ly	goodly, sickly, lonely
(h)	A/N > Adv	
	-ward	homeward, eastward, downward
	-ly	quickly, terribly, gradually
	-way(s)	sideway(s), anyway(s), someway

change 'one connected with X'. However, some words have an additional phonetic change, as in *Platonist* above or in *publicist, historicist* (< *public, historic*), where the final [k] consonant changes to [s]. The semantics of -*ist* words is also more complex than first suggested since such words may denote persons adhering to a theory (e.g., *anarchist, realist, hedonist*), persons exercising a scientific profession (e.g., *linguist, dentist, psychiatrist, botanist*), or persons addicted to an ideology (e.g., *perfectionist, extremist, nationalist, fascist*). In the last category would fall *racist, sexist, lookist,* or *ageist*, which denote not just people addicted to race, sex, looks, or age, but those who make discriminations or hold prejudices based on these qualities. Note too that many such words have acquired negative connotations (as has, in fact, the notion of 'addiction'). The morphology of -*ist* words is also not entirely regular; some -*ist* words are related to abstract nouns ending in -*y* (e.g., *botany, psychiatry*) and some to ones in -*ism* (e.g., *realism, fascism*), while some -*ist* words take an -*ic* adjectivalizer and others do not (e.g., *hedonistic,* *dentistic). And the combination of -*ist* with a particular root is not predictable: while *balloonist* and *cyclist* are possible, for example, *boatist and* *skatist* are not. The suffix -*ist* is often in competition with either *(i)an* (e.g., *pedestrian, grammarian, barbarian*) and -*ite* (e.g., *suburbanite, socialite, Troskyite*). In the case of a follower of Darwin, all three forms — *Darwinian, Darvinist,* and *Darvinite* — exist.

Finally, the false morphological division of words may result in more or less productive suffixes, which one scholar calls "splinters", as in the following:

ham/<u>burger</u> > cheeseburger, fishburger, mushroomburger
alc/<u>oholic</u> > workaholic, chocaholic
mar/<u>athon</u> > workathon, telathon, swimathon, walkathon
pano/<u>rama</u> > autorama, motorama
caval/<u>cade</u> > aquacade, motorcade
<u>heli</u>/copter > heliport, helidrome, helistop

(These might also be analyzed as blends; see below.)

Derivation can be stated in terms of lexical rules:

mis- + align (V) + -ment > misalignment (N)
image (N) + -ine + -ary > imaginary (A)
false (A) + -ify > falsify (V)

Or they can be expressed by tree diagrams, which have the advantage that they indicate the hierarchical arrangement and order of derivation of complex words.[6] Possible representations of the derived form *nonsmoker* are the following:

nonsmoker

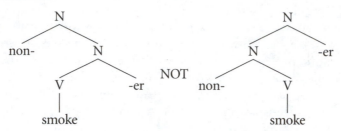

The reason that the second derivation is impossible is that one must be able to stop at any point in the derivation and still have a word of English. The second derivation produces the nonword *nonsmoke*. The form *unimpressionable* has two possible derivations:

unimpressionable

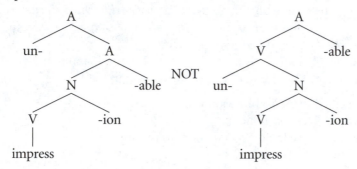

(Here we are not analyzing *impress* into its bound root -*press* and prefix *im-*.) Again, the second derivation produces the nonword *unimpression*. Look at the two possible trees for *informality*:

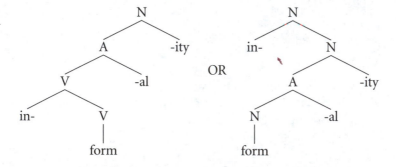

While neither derivation produces a nonword, the reason for preferring the second derivation in this case is semantic. *Informality* means not having the quality of form and is related to the noun *form*. The prefix is negative. It is not related to the verb *inform*, which does not contain a negative prefix. Compare the following derivations of *information*:

information

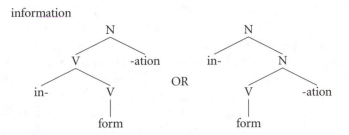

OR

Again, there are semantic reasons for preferring the first derivation here, since *information* is related to the action of informing, not to a formation.

■ *Self-Testing Exercises:* Do Exercises 4.6 and 4.7 on derivation.

Reduplication

Reduplication is a process similar to derivation, in which the initial syllable or the entire word is doubled, exactly or with a slight phonological change. While reduplication is not a regular process of word formation in English, it is in other languages, such as the perfect *tetegi* formed from the present *tango* in Latin or the past *haíhald* formed from the present *haldan* in Gothic. In English, reduplication is often used in children's language (e.g., *boo-boo, putt-putt, choo-choo*) or for humorous or ironic effect (e.g., *goody-goody, rah-rah, pooh-pooh*). Three different kinds of reduplication can be identified:

1. exact reduplication: *papa, mama, goody-goody, so-so, hush-hush, never-never*;
2. ablaut reduplication in which the vowel alternates while the consonants are identical: *criss-cross, zig-zag, ping-pong, tick-tock, flip-flop, mish-mash, wishy-washy, clip-clop, riff-raff*; and
3. rhyme reduplication in which the consonants change while the vowel remains the same: *helter-skelter, hodge-podge, fuddy-duddy, razzle-dazzle, boogie-woogie, nitty-gritty, roly-poly.*

Recent reduplications have been formed with two meaningful parts, for example, *flower-power, brain drain, culture vulture,* or *heart smart.*

Conversion or Functional Shift

A **functional shift** is the **conversion** of one part of speech to another without the addition of a suffix. It is sometimes said that a zero (∅) derivational suffix is added (since it is usual for derivational suffixes to change the part of speech, as discussed above). The only concrete change that may occur in a functional shift is a change in stress.

The following kinds of functional shifts can be found in English:

V > N	(a) run, drive, walk, bruise, cut, break, look, call, dump, spy, bite, sneeze
N > V	(to) man, head, shoulder, telephone, lust, contact, ship, sign, skin, mail
A > V	(to) weary, better, empty, idle, dirty, bare, quiet, tame, lower
N > A	blue-collar (worker), plant (supervisor), paper (shredder), head (bookkeeper)
A > N	(the) poor, rich, (a) daily, double, given, private
Prt > V	(to) down, up, off, thwart

("Prt" denotes "particle", a super-class of words including prepositions, adverbs, and some conjunctions, as will be discussed in Chapter 5.) Less common kinds of conversions are a preposition to a noun (*ins and outs*), an adverb to a noun (*whys and wherefores, the hereafter*), or even a prefix to a noun (*pros and cons*). Once a word has been converted, it can normally take the inflections of the new class, for example, *two runs, telephoned/telephoning, dirtied*.

What happens semantically when a word is converted may be quite varied. For example, in the V > N shift, an action is treated as an object or thing, though the emphasis may be on the action (e.g., *an attack, a fight, a kiss, a kick, a groan*), the result of the action (e.g., *an award, a find, a break, a bruise, a crease*), the person performing the action (e.g., *a spy*), the time of the action (e.g., *the spring, the fall*), the place of the action (e.g., *a sink, a drain, a speak-easy*), or the range of the action (e.g., *an overlap*). Note that with such shifts, actions become easily countable (e.g., *two kisses, several fights*). With the N > V shift, the new verb may denote the thing which is moved to a location (e.g., *to paint, to water*) or from a location (e.g., *to milk, to skin*), or the location to which the thing is moved (e.g., *to bottle, to box*) or from which it is moved (e.g., *to mine*); it may also refer to the instrument of the action (e.g., *to lock, to mail, to whistle, to rattle*). A > V gives the inchoative ('to become X') or the causative ('to cause to become X') meaning (see Chapter 10). The shift N > A expresses the quality associated with some entity, while A > N treats a quality as an entity (and hence quantifiable).

It is often difficult to know in conversions which is the original (or basic) form and which the converted form. Sometimes semantics or morphological modification will offer a clue. When the noun is primary, the verb necessarily includes the meaning of the noun. Thus, *to butter toast with margarine* sounds odd because the converted verb *butter* includes the meaning of the noun. Similarly, *to garage the car in the shed* is not entirely natural. However, *to anchor the ship with a rock* or *to comb one's hair with one's fingers* is acceptable because the verb is original and the noun derived by conversion. What do you think in the case of *to hammer the stake with a rock*? Is the noun or the verb original? Another distinguishing feature is the regularity of inflection. Converted forms will always take the regular, productive inflection, never a remnant or irregular inflection. For example, *grandstand, highlight*, or *highstick* may be either nouns or verbs. Since the past tense forms are *grandstanded, highlighted*, and *highsticked*, we conclude that the verb must be derived from the noun; otherwise, the past tense would be *grandstood, highlit*, or *highstuck*. In contrast, the past tense of *deepfreeze* is *deepfroze*, not **deepfreezed*, and thus the noun must derive from the verb.

Stress changes accompany the conversion of phrasal verbs to nouns and adjectives:

V + Prt > N   comeback, runoff, takeover, make up, rundown, standby, showoff, runaway
V + Prt > A   throw-away, tow-away, see-through, run-down, built-in, run-on

The primary stress on the particle is lost in each case. Another set of converted forms shows a difference in stress, with stress on the first syllable (prefix) of the noun and the second syllable (root) of the verb:

Verb	Noun
condúct	cónduct
rebél	rébel
permít	pérmit
recórd	récord
objéct	óbject

Note that unstressing of the syllable may also lead to reduction of the vowel.

A special kind of functional shift is what we may call **commonization** (the technical name is "antonomasia"), in which a proper noun is converted into a common word. A proper noun, naming a real or fictional person or place, tribe, or group, may undergo commonization to a noun, verb, or adjective, often with no phonological change:

> N: cashmere, china, sandwich, odyssey, valentine, bourbon
> V: lynch, pander, canter, welsh
> A: maudlin, zany, frank

In other cases, however, a derivational suffix is added to convert the noun into the appropriate part of speech:

> N: sad*ism*, chauvin*ism*, marion*ette*
> V: tanta*lize*, pasteur*ize*
> A: quix*otic*, platon*ic*, spart*an*, machiavell*ian*

Compounds

A **compound** is the combination of two or more free roots (plus associated affixes). Both **phrases** (such as *kick the bucket, hit the road, sit tight, run the gamut, under the weather*) and compounds consist of more than one free root and may be semantically opaque. However, unlike a phrase, where the free roots are joined in a single syntactic unit but remain distinct words, a compound is considered a single word. Our usual means of distinguishing a compound word from a phrase are not always reliable. English orthography is indeterminate because compounds can be written as a single word or as two words, hyphenated of not, e.g., *icecream, ice cream, ice-cream*. Moreover, the semantics of compounds are not very helpful; we expect compounds, since they are single words, to have a semantic unity, but phrases may have equally cohesive semantics. Compare *shipyard* and *automobile assembly plant*; the compound and the phrase might be considered equally unified notions. It is sometimes pointed out that the order of elements in a compound tends to be nonliteral, while in a phrase it is literal, as in the difference between *forthcoming* and *come forth*, or *offputting* and *put off*, but this rule cannot be extended very far. A better means of differentiation is internal coherence, since compounds are externally modified (at the single word boundary), whereas phrases may be internally modified (at any of the word boundaries). For example, the plural of the compound *manhole* is *manholes* not **menhole*, with the plural marker at the end, whereas the plural of the phrase *man-of-war* is *men-of-war* not **man-of-wars*, with the plural marker internal to the phrase. Another good means of distinguishing compounds is their external mobility; that is, they move in a sentence as a whole, not in parts. For example, the compound *cross-examination* moves as a unit (*The lawyer conducted the cross-examination, The cross-examination was conducted by the lawyer*), while part of the phrase *check out* may be moved (*He checked out the witness, He checked the witness out*). However, stress seems to offer the most reliable means of distinguishing a compound from a phrase. As a single word, a compound will carry only one primary stress, whereas a phrase, as a group of words, will carry more than one primary stress. The second half of the compound carries secondary stress and the vowel may be reduced (see Chapter 3). Compare the stress patterns in the following sets:

Compound	Phrase
stónewàll	stóne wáll
sáfeguàrd	sáfe guárd
bréakdòwn	bréak dówn

This principle holds for compound nouns and some compound verbs. Compound adjectives, however, may carry more than one primary stress, as *duty-free* or *child-proof*.

Both the semantics and the syntax of compound are complex. Often the semantics of compounds are not simply a sum of the meaning of the parts; that is, if we know the meaning of the two roots, we cannot necessarily predict the meaning of the compound, as in *firearm*, *highball*, *makeup*, or *handout*. Note the various ways in which the meanings of the roots of these compounds interact with *home*:

homeland — land which is one's home
homemade — something which is made at home
homebody — someone who stays at home
homestead — a place which is a home
homework — work which is done at home
homerun — a run to home
homemaker — a person who makes (cares for) the home

The syntax of compounds is even more complex. Any combination of parts of speech seems possible, with almost any part of speech resulting. One principle which holds is that the word class of the compound is determined by the **head of the compound**, or its rightmost member, whereas the leftmost member carries the primary stress. The only exception to this rule is a converted compound. Look at the syntactic patterns of compounding shown in Table 4.7.

Other rarer patterns include V + V > A (*make-believe*) and V + V > V (*freeze-dry*). Note that in addition to combining two roots, compounds may contain derivational or inflectional affixes; when the present or past participle inflectional suffix (represented by -*ing* and -*en* in Table 4.7) is added to a verb, the resulting unit functions as an adjective. Compounds may also involve conversions and back formations (discussed later in this chapter).

■ *Self-Testing Exercise:* Do Exercise 4.8 on compounding.

A problem for the differentiation of compounds and phrases is the **phrasal verb**. Older English preferred prefixed verbs, such as *forget, understand, withdraw, befriend, overrun,*

Table 4.7. Syntactic Patterns in English Compounds

Compound Nouns

N + N > N	airplane, lipstick, deathblow, figurehead, peppercorn
V + N > N	cut-throat, spoil-sport, leapfrog, drawbridge, crybaby
A + N > N	madman, fast-food, software, hotbed, mainland, busybody
Prt + N > N	background, in-crowd, off-Broadway, afternoon
Prt + V > N	outcast, downpour, outbreak, offspring (converted prefixed or compound V)
V + Prt > N	put-down, drop-out, lockout, sit-in, fallout, runaway (converted phrasal V)
N + -'s + N > N	bachelor's degree, bull's eye, housemaid's knee
V + -ing + N > N	spending money, closing time, freezing point
N + V + -ing > N	handwriting, housekeeping, foxhunting (gerund)
N + V > N	bloodshed, bus-stand, sunrise, handshake, nosebleed (converted V)
N + V + -er > N	hairdresser, nutcracker, landowner, peacemaker

Compound Verbs

N + V > V	babysit, carbon-date, head-hunt, skydive, housekeep (backformations)
A + V > V	free-associate, double-book, fine-tune, whitewash (backformations)
Prt + V > V	outdo, overcook, underrate, overeducate
A + N > V	strong-arm, blacklist, brownbag, mainstream (converted N)

Compound Adjectives

N + A > A	headstrong, childproof, duty-free, lifelong, carsick
A + A > A	bittersweet, icy-cold, red-hot, social-economic
N + N > A	seaside, coffee-table, back-street (converted N)
A + N > A	redneck, blue-collar, solid-state (converted N)
V + Prt > A	tow-away, see-through, wrap-around (converted phrasal V)
N + V + -ing > A	man-eating, seed-bearing, heart-breaking, life-giving
A + V + -ing > A	easygoing, hard-hitting, good-looking, quick-cooking
N + V + -en > A	manmade, hand-woven, housebroken, crest-fallen
A + V + -en > A	high-born, widespread, far-fetched, new-found
A + N + -ed > A	cold-blooded, thick-skinned, double-barreled

outdo, offset, and *uproot* (note the position of stress on the root morpheme rather than on the prefix), but prefixing of verbs is not productive in Modern English, except for those with *out-* and *over-*. Modern English favors verbs followed by postverbal particles, such as *run over, lead on, use up, stretch out,* and *put down.* Like compounds, phrasal verbs have semantic coherence, evidenced by the fact that they are sometimes replaceable by single Latinate verbs, as in the following:

break out — erupt, escape	think up — imagine
count out — exclude	put off — delay
take off — depart, remove	egg on — incite
work out — solve	put out — extinguish

Furthermore, the meaning of the combination of verb and particle in the phrasal verb may be opaque, that is, not predictable from the meaning of the parts. Often, the difference in meaning between the simple and the phrasal verb is 'completive'; the phrasal verb expresses termination or completion of the action:

burn vs. burn down, up, on, out	work vs. work out, up
eat vs. eat up, through	wash vs. wash up, down, out
pay vs. pay up, off	read vs. read through

Unlike compounds, however, phrasal verbs exhibit internal modification (*burn down/burned down*, *burning down*), carry two primary stresses (*wórk óut*), and behave syntactically like phrases since the particle may move after the object, or an adverb may intercede between the verb and the particle:

He burned down the house.
He burned the house down.
He burned the house right down.
cf. *He burned right down the house. *He burned right the house down.

For these reasons, we must conclude that phrasal verbs are phrases, not compounds.

A further problem in the analysis of compounds is **phrase compounds**, such as *lady-in-waiting, dog-in-the-manger, forget-me-not, has-been, whiskey-and-soda, bubble-and-squeak,* or *son-in-law*, which are generally written as compounds and have semantic unity. But they are usually internally modified like a phrase, as in the *ladies-in-waiting*. When they are inflected for the possessive, however, they seem to show external modification like a compound, as in *son-in-law's (new car)*. Historically, this has not always been so: prior to the sixteenth century, such phrases had internal modification in the possessive, as in *kings crown of England* (= 'king of England's crown'), which has the possessive ending *-s* on *king*. Then it became possible to add the possessive ending to an entire phrase, a construction called the "group genitive". What precedes the possessive ending need not be a single-word compound but can be a phrase, as in *my neighbor next door's dog*, or even a clause, as in *a woman I know's niece*. By no criteria would *my neighbor next door* be considered a compound. Thus, phrase compounds seem to be phrasal in nature.

Another problem of historical interest is **amalgamated compounds**. These are words which in origin are compounds, but which in the course of time have become fused and no longer separable into two distinct parts. Some examples are the following:

barn < bere 'barley' + ærn 'place'
halibut < hālig 'holy' + butte 'flatfish'
garlic < gar 'spear'+ lēac 'leek'
orchard < ort (Lt. hortus) 'garden' + geard 'yard'
cobweb < coppe 'kind of spider' + web
midrif < mid + hrif 'belly'
midwife < mid 'with' + wīf 'wife'
mildew < mele 'honey' + dew

In the last four examples only half of the compound is opaque; the other half is identifiable. Nonetheless, since they are no longer recognizable as compounds, all are considered single, unanalyzable morphemes.

The distinction between compounding and derivation can also be problematical from a historical perspective, since many suffixes and prefixes derive from originally free roots. For example, -*hood* comes from Old English word *hād* meaning 'condition'. But since it no longer exists as an independent word, we can safely consider -*hood* a suffix. More troublesome are prefixes such as *over-*, *under-*, *out-*, or *in-* (in *over-skilled, underpayment, outcast, infield*), which also exist as independent prepositions and adverbs in current English. It is best, I think, to consider them prefixes in the cases just given.

Blends

A **blend** involves two processes of word formation, compounding and clipping. Two free words are combined and blended, usually by clipping off the end of the first word and the beginning of the second word, although sometimes one or the other morpheme is left intact. Blends are sometimes called "portmanteau" words. Examples of blends are the following:

sm(oke) + (f)og	>	smog
mo(tor) + (ho)tel	>	motel
spr(ay) + (tw)ig	>	sprig
tw(ist) + (wh)irl	>	twirl
trans(fer) + (re)sistor	>	transistor
sky + (hi)jacker	>	skyjacker
motor + (caval)cade	>	motorcade
perma(nent) + frost	>	permafrost
docu(mentary) + drama	>	docudrama
para(chutist) + trooper	>	paratrooper
film + (bi)ography	>	filmography

In the last six examples, where one half remains intact, it might also be possible to analyze -*jacker*, -*cade*, *perma-*, *docu-*, and -*para*, and -*ography* as new (and perhaps productive) derivational affixes attached to free roots.

Back Formations

In **back formation**, speakers derive a morphologically simple word from a form which they analyze, on the basis of derivational and inflectional patterns existing in English, as a morphologically complex word. For example, by analogy with the very common derivational pattern in English in which the agentive suffix -*er* is added to a verb to produce a noun (*sing* + -*er* > *singer, work* + -*er* > *worker, buy* + -*er* > *buyer*), verbs have been formed from the following nouns by the removal of an agentive suffix, as in *sightseer* − -*er* > *sightsee, babysitter* − -*er* > *baby-sit*, or *typewriter* − -*er* > *typewrite*. Since the nouns predate the verbs in these cases, we say that the verbs are "back-formed". Back formation is thus the opposite of derivation: C−B>A as opposed to A+B>C. Without a knowledge of the history of an individual word, it is usually impossible to know whether related forms result from derivation or back formation. In many cases of back formation a presumed affix is removed which is in fact not truly an affix, as in the following words where the *-or, -ar,* and *-er* are not the agentive suffix, but part of the root: *orator − -er > orate, lecher + -er > lech, peddler + -er > peddle, escalator + -er > escalate, editor + -er > edit, swindler + -er > swindle, sculptor + -er > sculpt, hawker + -er > hawk.* These mistakes are also called back formations. Note that some of them are colloquial or marginal, while others are fully accepted.

Other examples of back formations are the following, where presumed derivational suffixes such as *-ion, -al, -ive, -ance/ence,* and *-asm* have been removed:

self-destruction > self-destruct	vivisection > vivisect
resurrection > resurrect	connotation > connote
emotion > emote	intuition > intuit
transcription > transcript	paramedical > paramedic
sedative > sedate	enthusiasm > enthuse
surveillance > surveille	reminiscence > reminisce

In the case of *joyride < joyriding* or *henpeck < henpecked,* inflectional affixes (*-ing* and *-ed*) have been removed.

Shortening

The three types of shortening — acronyms, initialisms, and clipped forms — have in common the deletion of sound segments without respect to morphological boundaries. That is, parts of words, but not usually entire morphemes, are deleted.

Clipping. A **clipping** is the result of deliberately dropping part of a word, usually either the end or the beginning, or less often both, while retaining the same meaning and same word class, as in the following examples:

end

mimeo < mimeograph	hack < hackney
deli < delicatessen	porn < pornography
mike < microphone	whiskey < whiskeybae
gin < jenever ('juniper')	condo < condominium
rehab < rehabilitation	fax < facsimile
fan < fanatic	mitt < mitten

beginning

burger < hamburger	venture < adventure
spite < despite	gin (cotton gin) < engine
cello < violoncello	Viet Cong > Cong

beginning and end

fridge < refrigerator
flu < influenza
shrink < head-shrinker

The word *taxicab* has provided two clipped forms, *taxi* and *cab*, depending on whether the beginning or the end was clipped. Sometimes a word or part of a word in a phrase is clipped:

women's lib < women's liberation   paper boy < newspaper boy
high tech < high technology   movie < moving picture
narc < narcotics agent   chauvinist < male chauvinist

A diminutive affix may be attached to the clipped form, as in *movie, jammies, hankie,* and *nightie.* A clipping may leave behind a prefix or suffix rather than (part of) the root:

ex < ex-husband
bi < bi-sexual
bus < omnibus

In the last example, *bus* is actually part of the dative plural inflectional ending *-ibus* of the Latin word *omnis,* meaning 'all'.

Clipping is generally not sensitive to morphological boundaries, though it does usually reflect phonological processes, selecting the longest possible syllable, what is called a maximal syllable, such as *narc* rather than *nar.*

Clippings often begin life as colloquial forms, such as the clipped forms *prof* (< *professor*), *gym* (< *gymnasium*), *chem* (< *chemistry*), *psych* (< *psychology*), or *lab* (< *laboratory*) one hears on campus, but many have become fully accepted in the standard language and are no longer recognized as clipped forms.

Acronyms and initialisms. An extreme form of clipping results in acronyms and initialisms. In an **acronym**, the initial letters of words in a phrase are pronounced as a word, as in the following examples:

WASP < W(hite) A(nglo)-S(axon) P(rotestant)
SALT < S(trategic) A(rms) L(imitation) T(alks)
NATO < N(orth) A(tlantic) T(reaty) O(rganization)
AIDS < a(cquired) i(mmune) d(eficiency) s(yndrome)
radar < ra(dio) d(etecting) a(nd) r(anging)
laser < l(ight) a(mplification) (by) s(timulated) e(mission) (of) r(adiation)
sonar < so(und) na(vigation) r(anging)

Note that acronyms are not formed in an entirely systematic way; a word or words may be skipped, or the first two letters of a word may be chosen, always in order to produce a word which conforms to English phonotactics. Acronyms are written with capital letters when formed from a proper noun. In an **initialism**, the initial letters of words in a phrase are pronounced as letters, as in *r.s.v.p., a.m., p.m., B.C., A.D., v.d., b.m.* (What are the sources of these initialisms? Check a dictionary if you are uncertain.) Sometimes an initialism may involve only a single word, as in *i.d.* or *t.v.* Proper nouns are indicated with capitals. Initialisms are almost always written with periods between the letters, except in a few cases such as *okay* or *o.k.* and *emcee* or *m.c.*, in which the form is treated variously as an acronym or an initialism.

Root Creations

The rarest form of word formation is **root creation**, the invention of an entirely new root morpheme. Brand names are the most likely examples of root creations, but when examined closely, they often prove to be based on existing words or names or to follow patterns of word formation such as shortening. A few recent root creations are *granola*, *quark*, and *googol*. Onomatopoeic words, which in their pronunciation are imitative of animal sounds (e.g., *bow-wow*, *baa*, *cuckoo*, *moo*, *meow*) or other natural sounds (e.g., *twitter*, *gulp*, *hiss*, *sizzle*, *squeak*, *boom*, *blab*), can presumably be created at will as the need arises, though they are highly conventionalized and language-specific. Some new words are considered **literary coinages**, such as Shakespeare's *multitudinous* or *dwindle*, Milton's *sensuous* or *oblivious*, and Spenser's *blatant* or *askance*. However, it is often difficult to know whether an author actually invented the word or whether he or she was simply the first to record it in writing.

■ Self-Testing Exercise: Using a dictionary, when necessary, identify the processes of word formation in Exercise 4.9.

Idioms

A final consideration in regard to words is the existence of special kinds of phrases called idioms. An **idiom** is a sequence of words which functions as a single unit; it is syntactically fixed and semantically conventionalized. Examples include the following:

spill the beans	saw logs	shoot the breeze
keep tabs on	add fuel to the fire	lose one's cool
steal the show	bite the dust	rock the boat
take stock of	flog a dead horse	hold your horses
sit tight	find fault with	take heart
take fright	hit the road	run the gamut
be under the weather	let the cat out of the bag	be dead to the world

Idioms are frequently quite informal. No, or little, variation is allowed in the words that constitute the phrase, so that you can't say, for example, *hold your stallions, *bite the dirt, *shoot the wind, or *spill the rice. The semantics of the idiom are usually not predictable from the meaning of the individual words; this is what linguists call "noncompositionality". For example, you can't calculate the meaning of 'being sick' or 'feeling ill' from the meanings of *under* and *weather*. The meaning of idioms is often thought to be metaphorical or proverbial; they are emotionally-charged rather than neutral in meaning. (Note that when the wording of an idiom is changed, as in *spill the rice* above, the phrase can be interpreted only literally.)

Since idioms are not like free syntactic phrases — which can be accounted for the syntactic and semantic rules of the grammar — but are rather more like single words, the question arises as to whether they should be treated in the morphological component of the grammar, that is, whether they should be treated as unanalyzable wholes. The difficulty with doing so is that there appear to be degrees of idiomaticity, with some idioms permitting syntactic changes and some being more literal in meaning than others. *Pull some strings*, for example, seems to be much less idiomatic than *shoot the breeze* in respect to its flexibility:

> internal modification:
>> She pulled some important strings for him.
>> ?They shot a little breeze today.
> fronting on object:
>> Those strings, he won't pull for you.
>> *The breeze, we shot yesterday
> passive:
>> Some strings were pulled for him.
>> *The breeze was shot yesterday by us.

I don't intend to propose an answer to the question of the analysis of idioms here, but to leave it for you to ponder. Some scholars distinguish between "collocations", fixed groups of words, and true idioms. How do you think we should account for them in our grammar?

■ Chapter Summary

Now that you have completed this chapter, you should be able to:

1. give the criteria used to distinguish a word from a phrase;
2. define the different types of morphemes and morphs;
3. analyze a word into its constituent morphs and morphemes and specify how the morphemes are concretely realized as morphs;
4. differentiate a morpheme from an allomorph;
5. write a morphemic rule for the allomorphs of a morpheme in English;
6. explain and identify the most common processes of word formation in English; and
7. analyze derived and compound words into their constituent morphs.

■ Recommended Additional Reading

Still the most complete treatment of English morphology is Marchand (1969). More readable and more contemporary treatments are Adams (1973) and Bauer (1983, see especially Chapter 7). A classic discussion of morphology in the structuralist tradition may be found in Bloomfield (1933, Chapters 13 and 14) with many interesting examples. General linguistic accounts of morphology are Matthews (1991) and Bauer (1988), and advanced treatments of morphology in a generative framework are Jensen (1990) and Spencer (1991).

Textbooks which you might want to consult for a somewhat different perspective are Brown and Miller (1991, Chapter 15), Klammer and Schulz (1995, Chapter 3), Finegan (1999, Chapter 2, pp. 41–53), Kaplan (1995, Chapter 3), and O'Grady and Dobrovolsky (1996, Chapter 4, pp. 111–39).

■ Notes

1. In Latin dictionaries, on the other hand, verbs are listed in their 1st p sg pres tense forms; thus, the verb 'to love' is listed as *amo* 'I love' not as *amare* 'to love'.

2. Historically, these vowel alternations result from phonological processes called "umlaut" and "ablaut", respectively.

3. The 3rd person singular form *works* or *writes* causes some difficulty for our analysis. Would we need to propose the following analysis for *works*: {WORK} + {pres} + {sg}? If we do this, we would also have to postulate a {pl} morpheme, which is never realized. However, we won't do this, but will assume that -*s* is added by a rule of grammar, that of concord, which copies the feature of number from the noun subject to the verb.

4. There are often historical explanations for the fusional and zero rules; for example, the plural of *goose* was originally the result of an agglutinative rule in *gōs + -*iz* > *gōsiz (the asterisk here indicates a reconstructed form), but the form has undergone sound change and loss, so that the modern speaker now perceives it as fusional, {GOOSE} + {pl} > GEESE.

5. Remember that the underlying form need not correspond to the actual historical form.

6. In writing or reading these tree diagrams, you should work from the bottom up; that is, you should begin with the root and then add the prefixes and/or suffixes.

CHAPTER 5

Grammatical Categories and Word Classes

■ Chapter Preview

The first half of the chapter defines the grammatical categories (number, person, gender, case, degree, definiteness, deixis, tense, aspect, mood, and voice) and the distinctions within each category, explaining how each of these categories is expressed in the different parts of speech in English. The second half of the chapter considers the classification of words using formal (inflectional and distributional) tests. Tests for the categories of noun, adjective, verb, auxiliary, and particle are examined.

■ Commentary

Grammatical Categories

In the previous chapter, we introduced the distinction between lexical and grammatical morphemes, but apart from listing the inflectional affixes of English, we were — in our discussion of the processes of word formation — primarily concerned with lexical morphemes. We return now to grammatical morphemes, focusing on the diversity of their meanings and forms in English. You will recall that grammatical morphemes may be either free roots (function words) or bound affixes (inflectional suffixes). Semantically, grammatical morphemes express grammatical notions such as number or tense, what are called the **grammatical categories**. In this section, we will look in more detail at the different grammatical categories, the terms of each category (the distinctions made within each category), and the means by which they are expressed in English. In synthetic languages, such as Classical Latin or Greek, the grammatical categories are expressed almost exclusively by inflectional endings, whereas in analytic languages, such as Modern English or Modern French, the grammatical categories are expressed primarily by word order (the position of a word in a sentence) and by function words, as well as by a few inflections.[1] A phrase containing a function word which is functionally equivalent to an inflection is called a **periphrasis**, or **periphrastic form**. For example, in English, we can express the possessive either by an inflection -'s (as in *Alicia's cat*) or by a periphrasis with *of* (as in *the leg of the table*)

Let us look first at the concept of a grammatical category, which is rather difficult to define. It is important to keep in mind that a grammatical category is a linguistic, not a real-world category, and that there is not always a one-to-one correspondence between the two, though they are usually closely related. For example "tense" is a linguistic category, while "time" is a category of the world. While past tense usually expresses past time (as in *I saw a movie last night*), the past-tense auxiliary in the following expresses future time: *I wish you would go*. And the present-tense verb of *I leave tomorrow* expresses future time. Furthermore, grammatical categories can be either formal or notional categories. In the first case, they are identified by the formal distinctions made in a language solely by means of inflection. By these criteria, English, for example, would be said to have only two tense distinctions, past and present (as in *work/worked*). In the second case, however, there is assumed to be a universal set of grammatical categories and terms, which may or may not be expressed in a language by different means. For example, the universal tense distinctions might be considered to be past, present, and future. These are expressed in English by means of inflection and, in the case of the future, by periphrasis (as in *will work*). It is assumed that languages will express different sets of grammatical distinctions and will do so in different ways. Furthermore, we can differentiate between overt and covert categories. Overt categories have explicit or formal realization on the relevant part of speech, such as past tense in English verbs (the *-ed* inflection), while covert categories are expressed only implicitly by the cooccurrence of particular function words, such as future tense in English verbs (the *will* auxiliary occurring with the verb). Finally, we must decide whether a distinction is expressed systematically and regularly in a language, by a regular grammatical marker, or whether it is expressed idiosyncratically and lexically, by the meaning of content words. The distinction "dual" (the concept of 'two'), which is expressed grammatically separately from plural in many languages, can be expressed in Modern English only with the lexical items *both* or *two*, not by an inflection or function word. However, in Old English, dual was expressed grammatically by special forms of the personal pronouns, that is, by *wit* 'we two' and *git* 'you two'.

The following inventory of grammatical categories proceeds through the nominal categories (number, gender, person, case, degree, definiteness) and then the verbal categories (tense, aspect, mood, and voice).

Number

The first category, number, is relatively simple. There are two terms of this category in English: **singular** (the concept of 'one') and **plural** (the concept of 'more than one'). Number is expressed by inflection, generally by *-s*:

– in count nouns (*dog/dogs*)
– in demonstratives (*this/these, that/those*)
– in the 1st and 3rd p of personal pronouns (*I/we*), possessive determiners (*my/our*), possessive pronouns (*mine/ours*), and reflexive pronouns (*myself/ourselves*), but not in the 2nd p.

Note that for historical reasons the idiosyncratic forms of the personal pronouns are considered "inflected forms", though they do not always contain separable inflectional endings. Number is also expressed by distinct forms of certain pronouns and adjectives:

–   singular: *every, each, someone, anybody, a/an*
–   plural: *all, many, few, several, most*

Number is also expressed in a limited way in verbs, by the singular *-s* of the 3rd p which occurs in the present but not in the past tense (*he writes* versus *they write, he wrote*). Number is expressed more fully in the inflected forms of the verb 'to be' (singular *am, is, was*, plural *are, were*), which because of its high frequency, tends to preserve inflections more fully than do other verbs. (Note: the history of the English language has involved a gradual loss of inflections in all parts of speech.)

The concept of **generic number**, which incorporates both singular and plural and is used when one doesn't want to specify number, is expressed in English in three ways:

a.   the definite article + singular noun (*The tiger may be dangerous*),
b.   the indefinite article + singular noun (*A tiger may be dangerous*), and
c.   Ø article + plural of count nouns or singular of mass nouns (*Tigers may be dangerous* or *Gold is valuable*).

Finally, an "odd" use of number is use of the plural when singular is denoted, in the so-called "royal *we*" or "editorial *we*".

Gender

English has a rather straightforward system of gender called **natural gender**, as opposed to the seemingly less motivated system called **grammatical gender**. Grammatical gender, the system found in German, French, or Italian, for example, as well as in an earlier stage of English, appears to be arbitrary; here, gender is not related to the sex of the object denoted but is really just a means of subclassifying nouns as masculine/feminine or masculine/feminine/ neuter, as in German *das Mädchen* (n) 'the girl' or French *le jour* (m) 'the day' or Italian *la vita* (f) 'the life'.[2] In contrast, natural gender depends on the sex of the object in the real world. In this system, we distinguish **masculine, feminine, common** or dual (m or f), and **neuter** (sexless) genders.

In English, gender is expressed by inflection only in personal pronouns, and only in the 3rd person, singular *he, she, it*; the 1st and 2nd person forms *I, we*, and *you* are common gender, while the 3rd person plural form *they* is either common gender or neuter (*the people … they, the boats … they*). Relative and interrogative pronouns and some other pronouns inflectionally express a related category of animacy (animate/inanimate): *who, whom* vs. *what, which, somebody/one* vs. *something, anybody/one* vs. *anything*. Distinctions of animacy are variable, but commonly speakers distinguish between human beings and higher animals (*the {woman, dog} who …*) and lower animals and inanimate things (*the {ant, stone} which …*).

In nouns, gender is generally a covert category shown by the cooccurrence of relevant pronouns: *the boy … he, the girl … she*. Note that there is nothing about the morphological form of the nouns *boy* and *girl* which would indicate that they are masculine or feminine gender. (This is generally the case in languages with grammatical gender as well; it is the accompanying article, not the shape of the noun, which reveals its gender.) However, gender may also be expressed overtly on the English noun in a number of limited ways:

1. by derivational suffixes, such as the feminine suffixes -*ine* (*hero/heroine*), -*ess* (*god/goddess*), -*rix* (*aviator/aviatrix*), and -*ette* (*suffragist/suffragette*) or the common gender suffixes -*er* (*baker*), -*ist* (*artist*), -*ian* (*librarian*), -*ster* (*prankster*), and -*ard* (*drunkard*);
2. by compounds, such as *lady-, woman-, girl-, female-, -woman* or *boy-, male-, gentleman-, -man*;
3. by separate forms for masculine, feminine, and common genders, such as *boy/girl/child* or *rooster/hen/chicken*; and
4. by separate forms for masculine and feminine genders, such as *uncle/aunt, horse/mare, bachelor/spinster* and proper names such as *Joseph/Josephine, Henry/Henrietta*.

You can see that none of these means is systematic. It is significant that the feminine is always derived from the masculine, except in the case of *widow/widower*, presumably because women outlive men. In the case of *ballerina*, there is no simple masculine form. Also, it is typical for the masculine form to double as the common gender form, as with *horse*, though in the case of *goose/gander* or *drake/duck*, the feminine form is the common gender form, presumably because the female is more important in the barnyard economy.

The marked use of the feminine gender with ships, cars, countries, fortune, art, music, and nature in Modern English is sometimes considered a remnant of grammatical gender. But it is better seen either as a kind of personification or what George Curme calls "gender of animation", by which the object is animated and an emotional attachment is expressed. The use of neuter gender with babies (*What a cute baby. What's its name?*) or callers (*A person is calling for you. Who is it?*) is an expediency used when the gender is unknown.

The lack of a common gender for the 3rd person singular, especially for use following a singular indefinite pronoun such as *each* or *every*, has long been a source of difficulty in English. Traditionally, the masculine form has been used for the generic (e.g., *Every child should put on his coat*), but this expediency is now out-of-favor. In fact, the use of the plural *their*, which is gender-neutral but which violates number agreement (e.g., *Every child should put on their coat*), is found very early, while forms such as *his or her* or *his/her* (e.g., *Every child should put on his or her coat*) are newer attempts to correct this deficiency.[3]

Person

The category of person is quite simple. Three terms are recognized:

1st person: the speaker, person speaking;
2nd person: the addressee/hearer, person spoken to; and
3rd person: the person or thing spoken about.

Person distinctions are expressed by the inflected forms of the pronouns, for example:

– personal pronouns:	*I*	*you*	*he, they*
– personal possessive determiners:	*my*	*your*	*his, their*
– personal possessive pronouns:	*mine*	*yours*	*his, theirs*
– personal reflexive pronouns	*myself*	*yourself*	*himself, themselves*

Person is also expressed inflectionally in the singular, present tense, indicative of verbs by the -*s* inflection on the 3rd person: *I write* vs. *she writes*. It is also expressed more fully in the verb 'to be': *I am/was, we are/were* (1st person), *you are/were* (2nd person), *he/she/it is/was, they are/were* (3rd person). Nouns are all 3rd person, but this is shown only covertly by the cooccurrence of pronouns: *the house … it (*I, *you), the houses … they (*we, *you)*.

The form *one* expresses **generic person** (all persons) in English, but since it is often considered rather formal, we can also use the 1st p pl, 2nd p, or 3rd p pl forms in a generic sense:

one: *One doesn't do that.*
we: *We always hear too late.*
you: *You never can tell.*
they: *They'll find a cure for cancer soon.*

The generic *you* is the most common in informal usage. Finally, a few apparently deviant uses of person are the following:

3rd p for 2nd p: *your excellency, your honor*
3rd p for 1st p: *present company, the writer, your teacher, Caesar* (spoken by Caesar himself)
1st p for 2nd p: *we won't do that anymore, will we* (spoken by a parent to a child)

Case

Case is one of the more difficult categories. It may be defined rather simply as an indication of the function of a noun phrase, or the relationship of a noun phrase to a verb or to other noun phrases in the sentence. Case is most fully expressed in the personal and interrogative/relative pronouns, which distinguish **nominative case** (the function of subject), **genitive case** (the function of possessor), and **objective case** (the function of object) by different inflected forms:

-   nominative: *I, we, you, he, she, it, they, who*;
-   genitive: *my/mine, our/ours, his, her/hers, its, their/theirs, whose*; and
-   objective: *me, us, you, him, her, it, them, whom*.

There is no distinction between the nominative and objective form of *it*, nor of *you* (though historically the nominative form was *ye*, as in the archaic expression *Hear ye, hear ye*). The genitive includes forms which function as determiners, such as *my* and *our*, as well as forms which function as pronouns, such as *mine* or *ours*.

Nouns differentiate inflectionally between the nongenitive, or **common, case** and the genitive:

cat, cats   cat's, cats'
man, men   man's, men's

While orthographically there appear to be four distinct forms of nouns when singular and plural, common and genitive case are considered, you should keep in mind that the apostrophe is merely orthographic so that the forms *cats, cat's,* and *cats'* are phonologically indistinguishable. Only irregular plurals such as the noun *man* actually distinguish four forms.

Beyond this, nouns can be said to distinguish nominative and objective case only by word order, by placing the noun before or after the verb, respectively, in the usual positions for subject and object in an Subject–Verb–Object language such as English. Hence, in the sentence *The ship struck the dock*, "the ship" could be called nominative case and "the dock" objective case, though morphologically both are common case. This ordering principle is so strong that it may even override grammatical principles. The sentence *Who did you see?* is more natural than the grammatically correct *Whom did you see?* because in this structure the object (*who*) precedes rather than follows the verb, so the nominative form *who* is preferred. Another case distinction which can be made is **dative case** (the function of indirect object); this is really a subcategory of the objective case. It is shown by periphrasis with *to* or *for* or by word order (V iO dO): *He gave the book to Jane, He gave Jane the book*.

What I have just presented is a simplified picture of case usage. There are other traditional cases, such as the "instrumental" or "ablative", which I have not mentioned because they are expressed only periphrastically in Modern English, for example, with the prepositions *with* or *from*. There are also many conventional uses of cases, such as use of the nominative case after the verb 'to be' (e.g., *It is I*). In addition, the case functions are semantically complex: the same function can be expressed by different cases, as in instances where the concept of possession is expressed by either the genitive or dative case (e.g., *The book is mine, The book belongs to me*), or one case can express several different functions or meanings.

The genitive case is an excellent example of this latter situation. It does not simply express the notion of possessor, but it indicates a variety of other notions. The following types of genitives have been identified, based on the meaning relationship holding between the noun in the genitive and the head noun:

possessive genitive: *Felix's car*
subjective genitive: *the Queen's arrival*
objective genitive: *the city's destruction*
genitive of origin: *Shakespeare's plays*
descriptive genitive: *person of integrity*
genitive of measure: *an hour's time, a stone's throw*
partitive genitive: *a member of the crowd*
appositive genitive: *the city of Vancouver*

Only the first, the possessive genitive, expresses the prototypical meaning of the genitive: *Felix owns his car*. In contrast, the "subjective genitive" expresses the same relation as a subject does to a verb (*the Queen arrives*), while the "objective genitive" expresses the same relation as a direct object does to a verb (*X destroys the city*); it is certainly not the case that the Queen owns her arrival or that the city owns its destruction. The phrase *the shooting of the hunters* is ambiguous between subjective and objective genitive readings because it can mean either 'the hunters shoot X' or 'X shoots the hunters'. *The child's picture* is likewise ambiguous — has the child drawn the picture or has someone taken the picture of the child? The "genitive of origin" expresses the source, person, or place from which something originates. An expression such as *the woman's book* could be ambiguous between the possessive genitive and the genitive of origin — does the woman own the book or has she written the book? The "descriptive genitive" is usually expressed periphrastically; the genitive noun is often equivalent to a descriptive adjective, as in *man of wisdom*='wise man'. The "genitive of measure" expresses an extent of time or space, the "partitive genitive" the whole in relation to a part. Finally, the genitive noun of the "appositive genitive" renames the head noun.

Although the genitive can be expressed inflectionally with *'s* or periphrastically with *of* NP, it is not always possible to substitute one means of expression for the other. For example, while *the Queen's arrival* = *the arrival of the Queen*, *a person of integrity* ≠ **an integrity's person* or *a stone's throw* ≠ *a throw of a stone*. Certain types of genitives, such as the partitive, descriptive, or appositive, are typically expressed only periphrastically. Another complex aspect of the genitive is the **double genitive**, in which periphrastic and inflectional forms cooccur: *a friend of Rosa's, no fault of his*. The double genitive is necessarily indefinite (**the friend of Rosa's*) and a human inflected genitive (**a leg of the table's*). It normally has a partitive sense (='one friend among all of Rosa's friends), though it is also possible to use it when Rosa has only one friend. Contrast *a portrait of the king's* (='one among all the portraits (of others) that the king owns') and *a portrait of the king* (='a portrait which depicts the king').

Degree

Degree, unlike the nominal categories that we have been discussing, is a category that relates to adjectives and adverbs. It has three terms, **positive, comparative**, and **superlative**. While positive degree expresses a quality, comparative degree expresses greater degree or intensity of the quality in one of two items, and superlative degree expresses greatest degree or intensity of the quality in one of three or more items. The positive degree is expressed by the root of the adjective (e.g., *big, beautiful*) or adverb (e.g., *fast, quickly*) — that is, it is null-realized — while the comparative and superlative degrees are expressed either by inflection or by periphrasis (using *more, most*):

positive	Ø	big	fast	beautiful	quickly
comparative	-er, more	bigger	faster	more beautiful	more quickly
superlative	-est, most	biggest	fastest	most beautiful	most quickly

Whether the inflection or the periphrasis is used depends upon the phonological shape of the root: monosyllabic forms are inflected as are disyllabic forms ending in -*y* (e.g., *holier*), -*er* (e.g., *bitterer*), -*le* (e.g., *littler*), -*ow* (e.g., *narrower*), and -*some* (e.g., *handsomer*); all other forms occur in the periphrasis, including adverbs ending in -*ly* (e.g., **quicklier*). Lesser degree can be expressed periphrastically with *less* and *least*, as in *less big, least beautiful*. Sometimes, the three degrees of a particular word are expressed by different roots, as in *bad/worse/worst* or *good/better/best*. This is called **suppletion**. The paradigm of the adjective *old* (*older/elder, oldest/eldest*) shows irregularities but is not suppletive; the irregular forms *elder/eldest* are specialized semantically to refer to familial relations, while the regular forms *older/oldest* are used in all other functions. An interesting set of inflected forms is *nigh, near, next*; the positive form has been lost, the old comparative has become the positive, new comparative and superlative have developed (*near/nearer/nearest*), and the superlative form no longer exhibits degree.

For semantic reasons, not all adjectives can be inflected for degree, such as *perfect, unique, round, full, empty, married,* and *dead.* These adjectives are incomparable because they express absolute qualities. Something is either 'dead' or not; it cannot be more or less dead. Superlatives such as *most unique* are thus logically impossible, though one frequently hears such forms, where either *most* can only be understood as an emphatic or *unique* can be understood as meaning 'unusual'. Likewise, a form such as *best time, rudest remark,* or *closest of friends* often expresses a high degree rather than a true comparison, with the superlative equivalent to 'very'. Finally, it is also common to hear the superlative used in the comparison of two items, as in *put your best foot forward.*

Definiteness

The concepts of definiteness and indefiniteness are intuitively quite simple: definite denotes a referent (a thing in the real world denoted by a noun) which is known, familiar, or identified to the speaker and hearer, while indefinite denotes a referent which is novel, unfamiliar, or not known. If we consider nouns on their own, definiteness is a covert category, obvious only in the cooccurrence of an article with a noun, either the **definite article** *the* or the **indefinite article** *a/an,* though all proper nouns and most pronouns are intrinsically definite. In actual practice, definiteness can be quite confusing. First, it intersects with the category of specificity, specific denoting a particular entity in the world and nonspecific denoting no particular entity. Frequently, specificity coincides with definiteness (*the car* = 'a particular car known to the hearer') and nonspecific coincides with indefiniteness (*a car* = 'no particular car, not known to the hearer'), though other combinations are possible.[4] Second, article usage in English is complex and in many instances arbitrary. There are several different uses for each article, articles are often omitted, and there are dialectal differences in the use of articles. Thus, article usage can be an area of grammar which is very difficult for non-native speakers to master.

In broad outline, the major uses of *the* are the following:

1. for something previously mentioned: *yesterday I read a book … the book was about space travel;*
2. for a unique or fixed referent: *the Prime Minister, the Lord, the Times, the Suez Canal;*
3. for a generic referent: *(I love) the piano, (We are concerned about) the unemployed;*
4. for something which is part of the immediate socio-physical context or generally known: *the doorbell, the kettle, the sun, the weather;*
5. for something identified by a modifying expression either preceding or following the noun: *the gray horse, the house at the end of the block;* and
6. for converting a proper noun to a common noun: *the England he knew, the Shakespeare of our times, the Hell I suffered.*

The first use listed above is known as the **anaphoric**, or 'pointing back', use of the definite article. Many times, however, the definite article is omitted, for example, with institutions (e.g., *at school*), with means of transportation (e.g., *by car*), with times of day (e.g., *at noon*), with meals (e.g., *at breakfast*), and with illnesses (e.g., *have malaria*), and it is not always possible to predict when such omissions will occur.

The major uses of *a/an* are the following:

1. for something mentioned for the first time (see above);
2. for something which cannot or need not be identified: *(I want) a friend*;
3. for a generic referent: *(He is) a teacher*;
4. equivalent to 'any': *a (any) good book*;
5. equivalent to 'one': *a week or two*; and
6. for converting a proper noun to a common noun: *a virtual Mozart, another China.*

Deixis

Though not traditionally recognized as a grammatical category, deixis might be added to the list. From the Greek word meaning 'to point', deixis denotes the marking of objects and events with respect to a certain reference point, which is usually the time and place of speaking (the speaker's here and now). There are four different types of deixis: personal, spatial, temporal, and textual. **Personal deixis** is expressed in the personal pronouns: *I* vs. *you* vs. *he*. As *I* denotes the person speaking, the referent of *I* changes depending on who is speaking; the referent of *I* is always related to the specific speech situation. (This deictic use of personal pronouns contrasts with their anaphoric use in texts, as in *the boy … he*.) An interesting modification of personal deixis is for social purposes, to mark a person who is socially close to or remote from the speaker, such as the use of *tu/vous* in French or *du/Sie* in German. *You* may also be nondeictic in its generic use (see above). **Spatial deixis** is expressed in certain verb pairs, such as *come/go* or *bring/take*, denoting direction towards or away from the speaker, or in adverbs and demonstratives, such *here/there/(yon)* or *this/that*, denoting position near to or far from the speaker. **Temporal deixis** is expressed by various adverbs relating to the time of speaking: *now, then, yesterday, today, tomorrow, this morning*. It is also expressed by tense, as we shall see below. The final type of deixis, **textual deixis**, is expressed by the articles or demonstratives, as in the following: *I rode the roller coaster. {This, the ride} was very exciting*. Here *this* or *the ride* refers back in the text to the sentence preceding it.

■ Self-Testing Exercise: Do Exercise 5.1 on nominal categories.

Tense

We turn now to categories that relate strictly to the verb. The first such category is **tense**, which, in simple terms, is the linguistic indication of the time of an action. In fact, tense establishes a relation: it indicates the time of an event **in respect to** the moment of speaking (or some other reference point). If we consider the time line below, for example, we see that a past-time statement, such as *It rained*, or a future-time statement, such as *It will rain*, denotes a situation that did hold before the present moment or will hold after the present moment, respectively:

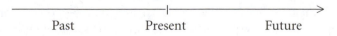

| Past | Present | Future |

This relational aspect of tense makes it a deictic category, since whether a situation is past, present, or future depends upon the moment of speaking and changes as that moment changes.

Before looking at tense more closely, we should remember that tense is not the only means of expressing time in language; adverbs are commonly used for this purpose. These temporal adverbs may be either deictic, expressing time in relation to the speaker and moment of speaking, such as *yesterday/today/tomorrow* (i.e., past, present, future), or nondeictic, expressing absolute time, either calendric, such as *Tuesday*, or clock, such as *at 4:00*. Tense, on the other hand, is always deictic.

The only tense distinction expressed inflectionally in English is that between present and past, as in *walk/walked* or *sing/sung*, even though it is conventional to talk about a three-way distinction between past, present, and future tense. However, the future is expressed periphrastically and thus is not formally parallel to the past and present.

Beginning with an examination of the uses of the **present** tense form in English, we find that it is not, in fact, used to denote actions which are actually going on at the present time. For this, the present progressive is used, as in *I am reading at this moment*, not **I read at this moment*. Instead, the present is used for the expression of a number of other types of temporal as well as nontemporal situations; for this reason, the term **nonpast** is preferred to *present*:

1. habits: *I walk to work everyday. She smokes. We eat dinner at 6:00.*
2. states: *She lives at home. I like chocolate. I believe you. I have lots of work to do. The dog sees well. I feel sick.*
3. generic statements: *Beavers build dams. Tigers are ferocious.*
4. timeless statements: *The sun sets in the west. Summer begins on June 21st. Two plus two is four.*
5. gnomic (proverbial) statements: *A stitch in time saves nine. Haste makes waste.*
6. future statements: *We leave tomorrow. I see the doctor this afternoon.*
7. instantaneous commentary: *He shoots; he scores. Now I beat in two eggs. He pulls a rabbit out of the hat.*
8. plot summary: *Hamlet dies at the end of the play. Emma marries Mr. Knightley.*
9. narration in the present (the "historical present"): *Then he says …*
10. information present: *I hear/see that Manfred has been promoted.*

A habit indicates a series of events that are characteristic of a period. These events constitute a whole. For habits to exist, the event (of walking to work, smoking, etc.) need not actually be going on at the present moment. States include nondynamic situations such as emotional states (*love*), cognitive states (*understand*), perceptual states (*feel*), bodily sensations (*ache*), and expressions of having and being (*own, resemble*). A generic statement predicates something of a numerically generic subject. Note that the difference between a state such as *I am happy* and a generic statement such as *Tigers are ferocious*, in addition to the nongeneric/generic subject, is that the state refers to a specific situation and can occur with adverbs such as *still, already, not yet*. Timeless statements express eternal truths and laws of nature. Gnomic statements express proverbs, which though similar to eternal truths, aren't necessarily timeless. Futures expressed with the simple present generally refer to situations that are predetermined and fixed. Instantaneous commentary occurs in sports reporting, cooking demonstrations, and magic shows, though the progressive is also possible in these contexts. This is the only use of the nonpast form for actions actually going on at the current moment. The present is used in summarizing works of literature and in talking about artists as artistic figures, though not as actual persons (*Shakespeare is the greatest writer in English* vs. *Shakespeare was born in Stratford on Avon*). The historical present is the use of present tense for narrating informal stories and jokes, though it is being used increasingly frequently in serious literature. Finally, the information present is the use of present tense with verbs of hearing or seeing where one might expect the past tense.

The uses of the **past** are much more unified. Generally, it denotes an event or a state in past time, as in *Haydn composed the symphony in 1758* or *Handel lived in England for a number of years*; note that this past time is divorced from, or distinct from, the present moment. The past tense is also the usual tense of narration (even for narratives set in the future!). The past tense may denote a past habit (when an appropriate time adverbial is used), though there is also a special past habitual form, *used to*, as in *I drove to work last year, I used to drive to work*. But the past tense may also be used nontemporally for politeness to denote the present or the future (e.g., I *was hoping you would help*) and in hypothetical statements to denote the future or the unreal (e.g., *If you studied more, you would do better*). These are "modal" uses of the past, as we will discuss more fully below.

As noted above, the **future** tense is expressed noninflectionally by a variety of periphrases:

1. *will/shall* + infinitive: *I will help you tomorrow.*
2. the simple present: *The party begins at 4:00.*
3. the present progressive: *We're having guests for dinner.*
4. *be going to, be about to* + infinitive: *The child is going to be sick. The boat is about to leave.*
5. *shall/will* + the progressive: *I will be moving next week.*

All of the forms of the future carry subtle differences in meaning. For example, *It's going to rain today* or *It's about to rain* might be uttered while looking up at a threatening rain cloud, while *It will rain today* could only be the prediction of the meteorologist or a report of this person's prediction, but **It rains today* is distinctly odd because it denotes the future as fact, or predetermined, and as punctual, and the progressive *It's raining today* could not function as a future in this instance either. *It will be raining today (when you want to mow the lawn)* is possible if it denotes a situation surrounding another event. Note that commands (e.g., *Wash the dishes!*) always carry a future meaning as well since you cannot command someone to do something in the past nor to be doing something at the present moment. Despite the designation of future as a tense, however, it bears a closer relation to modality than to tense since it expresses what is not (yet) fact (see below).

Aspect

The category of aspect is one more often applied to languages such as Russian or Hopi, but it is, in fact, equally applicable to English since the so-called "compound tenses", the perfect and the progressive, are better treated as expressions of the aspect. Aspect (which translates the Russian term for 'view') can be defined as the view taken of an event, or the "aspect" under which it is considered, basically whether it is seen as complete and whole (**perfective aspect**) or as incomplete and ongoing (**imperfective aspect**). The simple past tense in English is perfective in aspect since it views events as complete and whole, e.g., *Yesterday, I drove to town, ran some errands, and visited with my friends.* The **progressive** periphrasis, consisting of *be* + the present participle, presents actions as in progress, ongoing, and incomplete (not yet ended). It thus expresses imperfective aspect. It is the usual way to express a situation happening at the very moment of speaking, which by definition is incomplete. However, depending upon the temporal nature of the situation expressed by the verb (a topic to be treated in more detail in the next chapter) — in essence, whether it is punctual or durative — the progressive may denote somewhat different situations:

1. a continuous activity: *She is swimming. They were cleaning the house when I called.*
2. a repeated activity (iterative aspect): *He is bouncing the ball. The light was flashing when I entered the house. He is breaking dishes (*a dish). People (*a person) will be leaving early.*
3. a process leading up to an endpoint: *The child is finishing the puzzle. She was solving the problem when she was interrupted.*

Note that in all cases, the activity in question is ongoing and hence not complete, either at the present moment or in reference to some time in the past (expressed in the *when*-clause). The progressive is generally incompatible with static situations since they are nondynamic and hence cannot been seen as ongoing or in progress, e.g., **I am liking chocolate, *I am having lots of work to do.*[5]

Both the meaning and categorization of the other periphrasis in English, the **perfect**, consisting of *have* + the past participle, pose difficulties for scholars. However, it is widely agreed that the perfect is an aspect category (rather than a tense category) and that it presents the "current relevance" of a past event. The past event is relevant either by its continuation into the present (and beyond) or by its results in the present. Whether it is one or the other depends again on the inherent temporal nature of the situation expressed by the verb's lexical meaning:

continuative: I have lived here since childhood. (state)
    She has sung in the choir for ten years. (habit)
    The preacher has talked for the last hour. (continuous activity)
    The child has coughed all night. (iterated activity)

resultative: She has recovered from the flu. (activity with a necessary endpoint)
    I have lost my keys. (punctual event)
    I have read the novel. (activity with a neccessary endpoint)
    Our dog has just been run over. (cf. Our dog was just run over.)(punctual event)

In the case of the continuative perfect, the state or event has duration; it continues from the past into the present and possibly beyond. In the case of the resultative perfect, the event is completed, but has some significance to the present. Thus, while *I have eaten breakfast (today/ *yesterday)* would imply that one is still full (and could be said only in the morning), *I ate breakfast (today/yesterday)* would have no such implication (and could be said at any time of the day or subsequent days). Similarly, *I have lost my keys* could not be uttered if one had subsequently found one's keys, though *I lost my keys* could be. Expressions such as *I have read that novel* belong to the subcategory of "perfect of experience", in which the event took place at least once in the past and has some results — though perhaps not tangible results but merely results in the memory of the subject — in the present. The last example of the resultative perfect given above (*Our dog …*) belongs to the subcategory of the perfect which one linguist calls "hot news perfect"; here, the simple past would be equally possible (and would be more common in North America).

The aspectual periphrases combine with tense forms — tense is expressed on the auxiliary verb — to give the following forms:

- present progressive: *she is singing* (action ongoing at the present moment);
- past progressive: *she was singing* (action ongoing at some moment in the past);
- future progressive: *she will be singing* (action to be ongoing at some moment in the future);
- present perfect: *she has sung* (past action with results in the present);
- past perfect: *she had sung* (past action with results at some past moment or completed prior to some past moment "past-in-the-past"); and
- future perfect: *she will have sung* (future action with results at some future moment or completed prior to some future moment "past-in-the-future").

The two aspectual periphrases may also combine in the order perfect + progressive, as in *I have been reading the novel for the last hour*, to express an action which has been ongoing from some moment in the past to the present (and possibly beyond). What would the past + perfect + progressive (e.g., *I had been reading the novel for the last hour*) and future + perfect + progressive (e.g., *I will have been reading the novel for the last hour*) mean?

A number of other aspectual periphrases in English distinguish the beginning of situations (*ingressive aspect*), the continuation of situations (*continuative aspect*), and the end or termination of situations (*egressive aspect*), e.g., *It started/continued/stopped raining* (these aspects will be treated further in Chapter 10). In contrast to the perfect aspect, we can recognize a *prospective aspect* consisting of *be* + infinitive, e.g., *she is to see her doctor tomorrow*. The *habitual aspect*, which views a situation as repeated on different occasions, has been treated in the discussion of the nonpast and past tenses above.

Mood

Mood is rather difficult to define, but it can said simply to be an indication of the speaker's attitude towards what he or she is talking about, whether the event is considered fact (*indicative*) or nonfact (*subjunctive, imperative*). Nonfact encompasses a number of different degrees of reality, including wishes, desires, requests, warnings, prohibitions, commands, predictions, possibilities, and contrary-to-fact occurrences.

The **indicative** is expressed by the simple form of the verb. In earlier stages of English, the **subjunctive** was expressed by special inflected forms of the verb, but in Modern English, only remnant forms of the subjunctive remain: these are identifiable by the lack of -*s* in the 3rd p sg pres (since historically the ending was an -*e* which was gradually lost) and by use of *be* for all persons and numbers of the present tense and of *were* for the past tense. Examples of remnant inflected subjunctives in main clauses tend to be highly formulaic, such as *God save the Queen, Have mercy on us, Suffice it to say,* or *Far be it from me.* While a form such as *God save the Queen* might resemble a command to God to save the Queen, it differs from a command in having an explicit 3rd p subject; furthermore, it would be quite presumptuous to command God to do anything. Remnant subjunctives in dependent clauses tend to be restricted to a few contexts:

– *that*-clauses following verbs such as *insist, suggest, recommend, move, beg, ask, be required* (*I recommend that he leave*); adjectives such as *advisable, imperative, desirable* (*It is advisable that he leave*); and nouns such as *decision, requirement, resolution* (*It is a requirement that that he leave*).
(Note that the indicative would be *I recommend that he leaves*; it is only in the 3rd p sing that the difference between indicative and subjunctive is obvious since the other persons and numbers have no *-s* ending on the verb. The subjunctive following verbs such as *suggest* and *recommend* seems to be the only fully productive usage in Modern English, though not in British English.)
– *if*-clauses: *If she had the time …, If we were rich …, … as if he liked it, if only he were smarter …*
– clauses following verbs of wishing: *I wish I were rich.*

The latter two cases are past subjunctives expressing a hypothetical or unreal condition. Because the verb is always past tense, these uses resemble the "polite" use of the past tense discussed above (the use of the past tense without past time reference, e.g., *I was wondering whether you would write me a letter of recommendation*). In many subordinate clauses, the indicative is gradually replacing the subjunctive, as in *If I was rich* rather than *If I were rich.* Subjunctives in *whether-, though-,* or *lest*-clauses are now obsolete (e.g., *I wonder whether that be true or not*). Another means of expressing the subjunctive is by means of inversion: *Had I the time …*

In Modern English, the subjunctive has been replaced by other modal forms containing modal auxiliaries or their phrasal equivalents, as in *He may leave, You shouldn't wait, Would you pass the salt?, It might rain, You ought to try harder.* Modal adverbs such as *maybe, possibly,* or *perhaps* are also used, as are modal adjectives such as *possible, probable,* or *necessary.* A more colloquial, but very common, means of expressing the subjunctive is by the use of first-person parentheticals, or what have been called comment clauses: *He would be happy to help, I think* or *You're right, I guess.*

The **imperative** is a subclass of the subjunctive which expresses direct commands. In English the imperative has a special syntactic form: it is a subjectless sentence containing a bare form of the verb, as in *Go!, Be quiet!, Don't disturb me!* The imperative is addressed to a second person *you.* There are also an imperative with *let's* addressed to the 1st person plural, to oneself and to others present, as a kind of suggestion (e.g., *Let's see a movie tonight*) and an imperative with *let* addressed to the 3rd person (e.g., *Let him see to that*). The 1st person with *let's* must be distinguished from a true 2nd p command *Let us see a movie tonight,* spoken, for example, by children to their parents.

Voice

The category of voice, though usually considered a category of the verb, is actually relevant to the entire sentence. Voice is an indication of whether the subject is performing action of the verb or being something (**active voice**) or whether the subject is being affected by the action or being acted upon (**passive voice**). While the active is expressed by the simple forms of the verb, the passive is expressed periphrastically:

– by *be* + the past participle, as in *The report was written (by the committee)*; or
– by *get* + the past participle, as in *The criminal got caught (by the police)*.

The difference between the *be*-passive and the *get*-passive is that the former focuses on the resultant state ('the report is in a written state') while the latter focuses on the action bringing about the state. In the passive, the logical subject — the agent — moves out of the position of grammatical subject and is relegated to a *by*-phrase. However, it is common to delete the *by*-phrase in the passive, to omit mention altogether of the agent who performed the action. This is a manifestation of one of the rhetorical functions of the passive (see Chapter 11).

Another distinction of voice is the middle voice, in which the action of the verb reflects back upon the subject; in English, the middle is generally expressed with a reflexive pronoun (a form in *-self*), which indicates the sameness of the subject and the object, as in *Henry shaved (himself)*, *Terry bathed (herself)*, *Felicia cut herself*. A form which is sometimes called a "middle" is what Otto Jespersen calls a **notional passive**; this is a sentence which is active in form but passive in meaning: for example, *The shirt washes easily* (='the shirt is easily washed'), *these oranges peel easily* (='these oranges are easily peeled'), *the cake should cook slowly* (='the cake should be slowly cooked'). Note that nearly all notional passives contain a manner adverb. They differ from regular passives in that, not only do they occur without explicit agents, there is never even an implicit agent (**these oranges peel easily by you*). Another place where forms may be active in form but passive in meaning are some infinitives, such as *these apples are ready to eat* (='these apples are ready to be eaten') or *there are the dishes to do* (='there are the dishes to be done'). A construction such as *that movie is filming in Vancouver*, which is also active in form but passive in meaning (='that movie is being filmed in Vancouver') is a remnant or an earlier period when there was no progressive passive construction (as in *the customers are being served*) but instead a simple progressive was used (as in *the customers are serving well*).

In conclusion, we can approach the categories from a different perspective by noting which different parts of speech each of the grammatical categories is relevant to:

– nouns: number, gender, case, (person), and definiteness;
– pronouns: number, gender, case, and person;
– adjectives and some adverbs: degree; and
– verbs: number, person, tense, aspect, mood, and voice.

No grammatical categories are relevant to prepositions and conjunctions, which are invariable.

■ Self-Testing Exercises: Do Exercise 5.2 on verbal categories and Exercise 5.3 as a review.

Determining Word Classes

We have completed our examination of the internal structure of words, but there remains one aspect of morphology that we have yet to examine: the classification of words into what are known variously as word classes, lexical categories, or parts of speech. Traditionally, eight parts of speech are recognized: noun, verb, adjective, adverb, pronoun, preposition, conjunction, and interjection (or article). The reason for eight parts of speech is that the first Greek grammarian recognized that number of parts of speech in Classical Greek. Changes in the inventory of parts of speech have subsequently been required to account for other languages, but the number eight has remained constant. The traditional parts of speech are identified by a mixed combination of criteria, both notional (according to the meaning of words) and formal (according to the form, function, or distribution of words). The notional criteria are particularly problematical. For example, nouns are traditionally said to name people, places, and things, but they also denote abstractions (e.g., *truth, existence*), nonentities (e.g., *void, vacuum*), and events (e.g., *picnic, race, thunderstorm*). In fact, parts of speech are purely a matter of language, not of the external world; they do not correspond in a one-to-one way with things in the real world. We tend to equate nouns with things and verbs with events, but there are other languages which make different correspondences, for example, between nouns and long duration — e.g., *house* (N), *live* (V)— and verbs and short duration — e.g., *kick* (V), *fist* (N). Furthermore, the inventory of parts of speech does not appear to be universal, but differs from language to language (Vietnamese has 12, Nootka has 2 parts of speech). The student of language should not bring preconceptions about parts of speech to bear on a particular language. Approaching English as if it were an unknown language, the linguist C. C. Fries determined that there were 19 parts of speech in English (see Table 5.1). He did so using the formal tests that we will examine below (I have supplied the names for the categories).

Finally, the traditional analysis of parts of speech seems to suggest that all parts of speech are of the same semantic and functional importance. However, as we saw when we examined morphemes, words fall into one of two quite different categories: **content (lexical) words** or **function (grammatical) words**. To repeat the characteristics of these two classes, content words carry the primary communicative force of an utterance, are open or productive classes, and are variable in form (inflected); their distribution is not definable by the grammar. Content words fall into the major parts of speech, including nouns, verbs, adjectives, adverbs, and some pronouns. Function words carry less of the communicative force of an utterance. They express grammatical meaning (by relating sentence parts); they express the terms of grammatical categories (the meanings often expressed by inflections), and their distribution is definable by the grammar. They are closed or unproductive classes and are generally invariable in form (except demonstratives, modals, and some pronouns). Function words fall into the minor parts of speech, including prepositions, conjunctions, interjections, particles, auxiliaries, articles, demonstratives, and some adverbs and pronouns.

Table 5.1. The Nineteen Parts of Speech of English (C. C. Fries 1952)

Class 1: (noun)
Class 2: (verb)
Class 3: (adjective)
Class 4: (adverb)
Class A: *the, this, a/an, both our, every, two, each,* etc. (determiners)
Class B: *may, might, can, will,* etc. (modals)
Class C: *not*
Class D: *very, rather, pretty, quite,* etc. (degree adverbs)
Class E: *and, or, but, rather,* etc. (coordinating conjunctions)
Class F: *at, by, for, from,* etc. (prepositions)
Class G: *do*
Class H: *there* (existential *there*)
Class I: *when, why, where,* etc. (*wh*-words)
Class J: *after, when, although,* etc. (subordinating conjunctions)
Class K: *oh, well, now, why* (discourse markers)
Class L: *yes, no*
Class M: *look, say, listen*
Class N: *please*
Class O: *let's*

Inflectional and Distributional Tests

Because of the problems associated with notional definitions of the parts of speech, we need some formal means for determining the word classes of a language. Two types of tests have been developed in structural linguistics as an objective (formal), not subjective (notional), means of determining the parts of speech.

In a **distributional test**, words that fill the same syntactic slot, that is, fit into the same syntactic position and function, are considered to belong to the same class of words. In such a test, semantics is ignored as much as possible. For example, the words *large, green, exciting,* and *damaged* belong to the same class because they all fill the following test frame, while the other words do not:

The _____ book is on the shelf.

large	*read	*man
green	*while	*up
exciting	*very	*oh
damaged	*that	*him

Note that this test is very similar to the test frame used to identify phonemes that we discussed in Chapter 3.

In an **inflectional test**, all words that take a particular inflectional suffix are considered to belong to the same class of words. This test depends, of course, on the prior identification of the inflectional suffixes of a language. Thus, for example, *big* takes the inflection *-er*, but *hand, arrive, and,* and *him* do not:

The _____ {-er, -est} book

bigger	*hander	*ander
bigger	*hander	*ander
biggest	*arrivest	*himest

Derivational morphology is generally not very helpful in such a test because it is highly idiosyncratic and individual in its combinatory possibilities, though extremely productive derivational affixes such as the agentive -*er* on V's and the adverbial -*ly* on A's are of some use. Moreover, inflectional tests have fairly limited applicability in a language such as English, which has very few inflections. They are also suitable only for the major parts of speech since the minor parts of speech are invariable.

Distributional and inflectional tests must be used in combination, because words belonging to the same class may not meet all of the tests. When words meet *most* tests for a particular class, but fail to meet some, then we have evidence for the **subcategorization**, or subclassification, of a particular word class.

Tests Applied to Various Word Classes

Noun. Inflectional tests for the category **noun** (N) include the plural -*s* inflection and the genitive -'*s* inflection. The plural inflection attaches to certain types of nouns, but not to others:

count noun: *pencils, dogs, hats*
proper noun: **Susans, *Jims, *Seattles*
mass (noncount) noun: **honeys, *rices, *golds*
abstract noun: **existences, *friendships, *musics*
collective noun: *committees, herds, *furnitures*

Proper nouns are distinguished from common nouns in that they denote a unique referent; they cannot, therefore, be pluralized. Count nouns denote items that are individuated and can be pluralized and counted, while mass (noncount) nouns denote substances that exist in bulk or unspecified quantities. While they may be divided into portions (*a spoon of honey, a cup of rice, an ounce of gold*), in their bulk form, they cannot be counted. Note that some mass nouns name continuous substances (e.g., *honey, gold*), whereas other names substances whose parts are generally too small or insignificant to be counted (e.g., *rice, sand*). Abstract nouns are distinguished from concrete nouns in that they denote things which are not tangible and cannot be known through the senses; they are often mass as well. Collective nouns name groups of individuals which together form a unit. Collectives are generally countable, though some are not. Thus, we see that the plural inflectional test serves as an important means of subcategorizing nouns.[6] The genitive inflection can be added to all kinds of nouns, though it is sometimes a bit odd with inanimates (e.g., ?*the cupboard's back* vs. *the back of the cupboard*).

We can consider three distributional tests for the category noun:

1.   Det _____

That is, nouns can follow a subclass of words called **determiners** (Det), which include articles (such as *a, the*), demonstratives (such as *this, that*), possessives (such as *my, her*), and quantifiers (such as *many, several*). The occurrence of nouns with determiners depends on their subclass and number:

– proper nouns never follow a determiner (*the Seattle)
– single count nouns always follow a determiner (*the dog*, *dog)
– plural count nouns may or may not follow a determiner (*dogs*, *the dogs*)
– mass nouns may or may not follow a determiner (*the honey, honey*), though they never follow the indefinite article (*a honey)
– collectives behave either like count nouns (*herd, herds, the herd, the herds*) or like mass nouns (*furniture, the furniture*, *a furniture*)

Quantifiers are rather complex since some are restricted to mass nouns (e.g., *{much, a little, a large amount of, less} gold/*dogs*), while others are restricted to count nouns (e.g., *{many, a few, several, a large number of, fewer} dogs/*gold*) and others may occur with both (e.g., *{more, most, a lot of} dogs/gold*).[7]

2.   A _____

Plural count nouns and mass nouns may follow an adjective (*fierce dogs, sticky honey*), but single count nouns and proper nouns cannot (*big dog*, *beautiful Seattle*).

3.   Det A _____

All nouns except proper nouns can follow the sequence of determiner and adjective (*the big dog, two fierce dogs, the sticky honey*, *the beautiful Seattle*). There are a number of other elements which can occur in the noun phrase (NP), but these three distributional tests are sufficient for our purposes here. (We will consider the structure of the NP in Chapter 7.)

Adjective. Inflectional tests for the category **adjective** (**A**) include the comparative -*er* and the superlative -*est* degree endings, as in *larger/largest* or *prettier/prettiest*. As discussed earlier in the chapter, some adjectives cannot take these inflections for phonological reasons, while other are excluded for semantic reasons. Another difficulty with this inflectional test is that it admits certain adverbs, such as *late/latest, sooner/soonest*, though not others *quicklier/quickliest*. As we discussed in the previous chapter, -*ly*, though a common derivational suffix added to adjectives, does not function as an inflectional test.

Distributional tests for the category of adjective include the following:

1.   Det _____ N

This is called the attributive position of adjectives, the position preceding the noun (as in *the fierce dog*). A few adjectives, such as *afraid, asleep*, or *afire*, cannot appear in this position. Another position in which adjectives are found is the following:

2.   V$_{cop}$ _____

This is called the predicative position of adjectives, following a copula verb (see below) in the predicate of a sentence (as in *the dog is fierce*). A few adjectives cannot appear in this position, such as *principal, utter, mere, outright, entire*, or *same*. Also note that certain adjectives have quite different meanings in attributive and predicative positions, e.g., *That poor heiress has no friends* vs. *That girl is very poor*. Adjectives may also follow a subclass of words called **degree words (Deg)**, or intensifiers:

3.   Deg _____

Degree adverbs include *so, too, very, somewhat, rather, quite, slightly, highly, moderately, completely, awfully, incredibly,* or *unbelievably* (as in *very fierce dog*). Also included among the degree adverbs are the periphrastic forms for degree, *more* and *most*. The degree word and the adjective together form the adjective phrase (AP). A problem with this test is that it will also include most adverbs, as in *very quickly, quite soon,* or *most helpfully*.

Verb. The category of **verb (V)** has the greatest number of inflectional tests of all the word classes:

1.   the present participle *-ing*, which attaches to all verbs;
2.   the 3rd p sg pres *-s*, which also attaches to all verbs;
3.   the past tense *-ed*, which attaches to "weak" verbs, but not to "strong" verbs (which form their past tense by vowel alternation) or to other irregular verbs; and
4.   the past participle *-ed*, which likewise attaches to weak, but not to strong verbs (which may take the nonproductive ending *-en* or some other ending).

The agentive suffix *-er*, though a common ending to verbs, is not inflectional; in fact, there are many members of the class which cannot take it, e.g., **knower, *hurter, *realizer,* or **beer* (< *be* + *-er*).

There are several distributional tests for the category verb; these serve to subclassify verbs. Certain verbs, known as transitive verbs, such as *buy, break, learn, give,* or *hit*, may precede noun phrases:

1.   _____ NP

Other verbs, known as intransitive verbs, such as *appear, run, rise, arrive,* or *fall*, cannot precede noun phrases:

2.   _____ #

(The pound sign # indicates a clause boundary; in other words, no word needs to follow an intransitive verb, though an adverb often does.) A third subclass of verbs, known as copula verbs (or "linking verbs"), such as *seem, feel, become, appear,* or *happen*, precede adjective phrases. The copula *be* may also precede a noun phrase.

3.   _____ AP/NP

A final distributional test applies to all verbs. They may follow the periphrastic marker of the infinitive *to* (which replaces the infinitival inflectional ending *-an* in older English):

4.   to _____

(We have treated the different types of verbs cursorily, since they will be treated in some detail in Chapter 7.)

■ *Self-Testing Exercise:* In order to explore the tests for verbs more fully, do Exercise 5.4.

Adverb. The category of **adverb (Adv)** is rather difficult to differentiate. A small number of what are traditionally recognized as adverbs take the comparative inflectional endings -*er* and -*est*, but most are uninflected. In respect to distribution, adverbs are very free:

> Maria worked quickly.
> Maria completed the work quickly.
> Maria quickly completed the work.
> Quickly Maria completed the work.

It is traditional to say that an adverb modifies verbs, adjectives, and other adverbs. However, the possible distributional tests for adverb as modifier are inadequate: _____ A would include adjectives as well (as in *large, fierce dog*); _____ Adv would isolate the subclass of degree words only; and _____V would draw in nouns, auxiliary verbs and *not*. Adverbs also "modify" entire sentences, such sentence adverbs may occur in initial and final position in the sentence (hence _____S or S_____) as well as medially at major breaks:

> Surprisingly, Maria (surprisingly) completed the work (surprisingly).

In fact, there is considerable overlap in word forms among adverbs and other parts of speech. For example, *since* and *before* may have the following functions:

> adverb: He hasn't been here since. I've never seen it before
> preposition: I haven't seen him since lunch. I saw him before his exam.
> conjunction: He's been asleep since I arrived. I spoke to her before she left.

Because of this overlap and because of the difficulty of isolating adverbs from other parts of speech, some scholars have proposed a larger category of **particle (Prt)**, or adposition, which would include **prepositions (P)**, some adverbs, some conjunctions, and the particles of phrasal verbs. There would be no inflectional tests for this category, because these words are generally invariable, but there are several distributional tests:

1.   right _____
     look it right up (particle of phrasal verb)
     go right home (adverb)
     land right on top (preposition)
     he left right after the music started (conjunction)
2.   measure phrases _____
     three feet behind me (preposition)
     twice before (adverb)
     he was here two hours before I was (conjunction)

3. _____ NP
    <u>in</u> the garden (preposition)
    <u>after</u> the man leaves (conjunction)
    blow <u>out</u> the candle (particle of phrasal verb)
    (Note that this test does not distinguish particle from verb.)
4. _____ P
    out of   up from
    away with   up from under

The last test works for prepositions, but not for the other members of the category of particle.

■ *Self-Testing Exercise:* **Do Exercise 5.5.**

Recategorization

A major difficulty for word classification is that the same word can often belong to different parts of speech. The word *round*, for example, can function as a noun, an adjective, a verb, a preposition, and perhaps even an adverb:

N	a <u>round</u> of parties
A	a <u>round</u> table
V	<u>round</u> off the figures
Prep	come <u>round</u> the corner
Adv	come <u>round</u> with some fresh air

We can account for some of these forms by functional shift, or conversion, but we might also have to say that there are a number of homophones here.

A related problem is how to deal with an expression such as *the good, the bad, and the ugly*. The forms *good*, *bad*, and *ugly* seem to be functioning as nouns because they follow a determiner, but they are unlike nouns in the following respects:

– they do not pluralize (*the bads)
– the possessive is odd (ˀ*the bad's horse*)
– they do not follow an adjective (**the remarkable good*)[8]

In some respects, they behave like adjectives in that they can follow a degree adverb (*the remarkably/truly good*) and perhaps be inflected for degree (ˀ*the best, the worst, the ugliest*). There would appear to be four possible ways to analyze these forms:

1. There are two distinct lexemes in each case, a noun and an adjective, which are homophones.
2. The forms are adjectives with an understood, or elliptical, noun such as *ones*.
3. The adjectives have been recategorized as nouns.
4. The forms belong to the class of adjective, but syntactically function as nouns.

While the first analysis works, it is a cumbersome solution and it does not serve to show how the adjective and the noun forms might be related (which intuitively we feel they are). The second analysis looks appealing, but it has problems since sometimes you would have to understand a singular noun *one* rather than *ones* (e.g., *the {deceased, Almighty, accused, departed} one*), while at other times, the adjective refers to an abstraction and hence *one* seems inappropriate (*the known *one*). Between the third and fourth analyses, the fourth seems preferable; if recategorization had occurred, one would expect the recategorized word to have all of the behavioral characteristics of its new class, including its inflectional forms. Since it doesn't, it seems that these forms are still lexical adjectives, but are functioning as nouns in this instance.

Recategorization can occur both within a class (from one subcategory to another) or between classes. For example, the subcategory of a noun can be shifted in the following ways:

–   from abstract to concrete: *a beauty* (= 'a horse'), *a youth* (= 'a boy'), *a personality* (= 'a well-known person')
–   from mass to count: *wines, milks, difficulties, hairs*
–   from proper to common: *the Susans I know* (= 'the women named Susan whom I know'), *an Einstein* (= 'a genius'), *a Benedict Arnold* (= 'a traitor')

Again, to account for the shift from mass to count noun, there are four possibilities:

1.   A word such as *difficulty* would be entered in the dictionary as two separate lexemes, one mass and one count.
2.   The count noun is understood as having an elliptical quantifying expression, e.g., *(pieces of) cake* = *cakes*.
3.   The mass noun has been recategorized as count.
4.   The mass noun is functioning syntactically as a count noun.

The first analysis has the inelegance noted for the first analysis above. The second analysis runs into difficulties because it would be necessary to postulate a different quantifying expression for each shifted noun, as in <u>bottles</u> *of wine*, <u>glasses</u> *of milk*, or <u>strands</u> *of hair*, while in some cases, there does not appear to be any quantifying expression, as with *difficulties*. Furthermore, the plural forms occasionally refer to types not quantities, as in *the wines of France* or *the teas of China*. One would also have to shift the plural inflection from the elided quantifier to the noun by some yet unknown syntactic process. However, in contrast to the case of *the good*, it seems plausible to explain the shift in this case as a true instance of recategorization since the words behave both inflectionally and distributionally like count nouns.

■   *Self-Testing Exercise:* Do Exercise 5.6 on recategorization.

In conclusion, there appear to be a number of general problems with the inflectional and distributional tests that we have been discussing. First, there is an inherent circularity to the tests: the first test frame usually contains some word class, such as "determiner" in the test for noun; we are then assuming what we are trying to prove. Or the first test frame contains some lexical item; in this case, meaning (which we were trying to exclude) necessarily enters in. We must also ignore certain violations (which subcategorize words) and take certain tests as the basic one for a category. But there are no reasons, on inflectional and distributional grounds, why one test should be more important than any other. Finally, it is not clear how far subcategorization should be taken: we could conceivably continue until each word is a separate subclass, though doing so would not be very useful. Despite these difficulties, the inflectional and distributional tests discussed here represent a more precise means of categorization than does the traditional approach.

■ Chapter Summary

Now that you have completed this chapter, you should be able to:

1. define the grammatical categories and their terms;
2. say how the terms of each grammatical category are expressed in English (by means of inflection, periphrasis, word order, and so on) and in which parts of speech; and
3. apply the inflectional and distributional tests for the categories noun, adjective, verb, auxiliary, and adverb in English.

■ Recommended Additional Reading

Both of the topics treated in this chapter are generally covered in traditional grammars of English (see the references in Chapter 1). A very clear account of tense, aspect, and modality in English is Leech (1987), while Hirtle (1982) provides an interesting account of number in English. The classic structuralist treatment of parts of speech is Fries (1952, pp. 65–141). Introductory textbooks which include good discussions on both grammatical categories and word classes are Kaplan (1995, Chapters 4 and 5), Brown and Miller (1995, Chapter 16), Delahunty and Garvey (1999, Chapter 5 and 6), Klammer and Schulz (1995, Chapters 4 and 5), and Finegan (1999, Chapter 2, pp. 35–41, 56–60, and Chapter 6, pp. 202–209). Lyons (1968, Chapter 7) includes a thorough discussion of grammatical categories in general, while Hurford (1994) defines the grammatical categories in English.

■ Notes

1. Languages are situated on a cline between these language types. A language such as Modern German, for example, is more synthetic than Modern English but more analytical than classical Latin. Modern French is probably somewhat more synthetic than Modern English.
2. Historically, there is probably motivation for grammatical gender since it serves as a means of subcategorizing nouns. However, for the contemporary speaker, the motivation is generally not obvious.
3. Given the frequency of the use of *they/their* as a common gender singular form in contemporary English, it might even be possible to argue that it has developed a singular sense in addition to its

plural sense, similar to the development of *you*. If so, it is like *you*, which grammatically continues to take plural concord.

4. This topic is taken up in more detail in Chapter 11.

5. There are a number of "marked" uses of the progressive with state verbs, such as to change a state verb into a dynamic one (e.g., *Fred is being very silly* = 'behaving in a silly way'), to indicate a temporary state (e.g., *She is living with her parents this summer*), to denote a waxing or waning state (e.g., *Gasoline is costing a lot these days, I'm understanding economics better now*), or for purposes of politeness (e.g., *I'm not recalling your name*).

6. Apart from problems of recategorization, which are discussed below, the mass/count distinction involves quite a number of complexities of number, which cannot be treated in detail here (but see any standard reference grammar of English). For example, some mass nouns are plural in form and take a plural verb (e.g., *brains, savings, wages, ashes*), some singular nouns end in *-s* and take a singular verb (e.g., *news, politics, mumps, dominoes*), nouns denoting singular bipartite items end in *-s* and take a plural verb (e.g., *scissors, binoculars, pajamas, pants*), and some singular nouns may follow plural numerals (e.g., *five staff, six offspring, two bear*). Collective nouns may be count (e.g., *family, team*), mass and singular in form (e.g., *shrubbery, gentry*), or mass and plural in form (e.g., *groceries, leftovers*); moreover, collective nouns take a singular verb or a plural verb depending on whether the collective is seen as a unit or an abstraction (e.g., *The family is a dying institution*) or whether the individual members of the collectives are emphasized (e.g., *The family are all coming home for Christmas*), though there are some dialectal differences here as well.

7. It is amusing to observe that the usage of all supermarkets — in their signs for express lanes which declare "nine items or less" — ignores the distinction between mass and count. These signs should, of course, read "nine items or fewer". Rather than seeing this usage as an "error", we should probably consider it a "change in progress".

8. A possible counterexample is *the working poor*, with a present participle functioning as an adjective.

CHAPTER 6

Lexical Semantics

■ Chapter Preview

This chapter first considers some common assumptions about word meaning. The technical terms that linguists use in naming various relationships holding between words and sentences are introduced. The chapter then examines one way of approaching the problem of lexical meaning called *structural semantics*. The inherent meaning of nouns, verbs, and modal auxiliaries is next analyzed, breaking down their meaning using a given set of lexical features. Weaknesses with the notion of lexical features are briefly considered, as well as an alternative approach based on prototypes. Semantic restrictions on the combinations of words and the concept of semantic anomaly are then discussed. The chapter ends with an enumeration of the different types of figurative language, focusing on how metaphors are recognized and interpreted.

■ Commentary

Semantics is the study of linguistic meaning. We can study meaning on a number of different levels: **lexical semantics** is the study of the meaning of individual words (lexical items) in isolation; **sentence semantics** is the study of the meaning of a sentence, of the semantic relationships holding among the parts of sentence; and **text (discourse) semantics** is the study of the meaning of extended discourse (spoken or written), of the semantic relationship holding among utterances. In this chapter, we will be concerned with the semantics of words, focusing on lexical rather than grammatical meaning (the latter was treated in the previous chapter). However, we can only sample a number of different approaches towards lexical semantics, such as structural semantics, semantic features or components, and prototypes since a coherent and complete theory of semantics has yet to be formulated. Once we have treated the syntax of the sentence, we will consider sentence semantics (Chapter 10), and after that, we will turn to some aspects of discourse semantics (Chapter 11).

Traditional Semantics

We begin by looking at some of our preconceptions about meaning. This approach to meaning, which can be termed **traditional semantics**, like traditional grammar, tends to be prescriptive and is embodied in our attitudes towards dictionaries.

The first preconception of traditional semantics is that the meaning of an utterance consists of a sum of the meaning of its parts; therefore, if we don't know what an utterance means, we assume that we simply have to look the words up in a dictionary. In popular thinking about language, there is one correct and accepted meaning for each word in the language; people generally rely upon dictionaries to provide this "correct" meaning and to act as arbiters of meaning. However, such a view is probably mistaken in its assumption that there is one "true" meaning for a word. Even if such unequivocal meanings existed, dictionary makers would have no direct access to them; they can only consult usage (often aided now by the use of computerized collections of the language) to see what meanings words are being used with. Word meanings are a matter of both social agreement (see Chapter 1) and use, and are thus imprecise and fluid. Native speakers do not always agree on the meanings of words, even common words, and dictionaries cannot be expected to record individual variation in word meanings; for example, for different speakers, *brother-in-law* may refer to one's sister's husband, husband's brother, and/or wife's brother, or any combination of these meanings. Meanings may change more rapidly than can be recorded in dictionaries, despite the best efforts of lexicographers; for example, if asked the meaning of the word *desultory*, most people would respond with the meaning 'aimless, slow, casual', as in *He walked along in a desultory manner*; yet many dictionaries, including the *Oxford English Dictionary*, list its meaning as 'skipping about, jumping, flitting'. While this is its original meaning and its meaning at an earlier period of the language, it is not, at least judging from contemporary quotations, its current sense.[1] Finally, the traditional view of semantics also ignores many aspects of meaning apart from the meanings of words, such as the function of meaningful phonological features (i.e., stress and intonation), the meaning of the grammatical structure of the utterance, and the significance of the communicative context (pragmatics).

A second assumption of traditional semantics is that the correspondence between a word and a thing is simple and direct. In fact, the relation between a word and the world may be quite complex. For example, *disappointment* names an emotional state, but to understand the word we must know that this is the state which results from one's hopes or expectations of something pleasant not being satisfied. The word *widow* denotes a type of woman, but again we must know something about the history of that woman, that she was married and that her husband has died. To understand meanings of the word *stingy* or *lazy*, as well as their negative associations, we must know something about the cultural values of the English-speaking linguistic community. Even the meaning of the expression *apple core* depends upon our knowledge of the way in which apples are typically eaten in our society!

A third assumption of traditional semantics — and perhaps the most problematical one— is that words name things or objects in the real world, that meaning is always in reference to phenomena outside language. In fact, many words do not name things at all, such as words denoting abstractions or nonentities, or function words. Linguists believe that a clear distinction must be made between the **extension** of a word, the set of entities that a word denotes in the world (its referents) — if it denotes any entity at all — and the **intension** of a word, the set of properties shared by all the referents of a word, their defining characteristics. This distinction is important because the extension may be the same while the intension differs: e.g., the same man may be denoted by *Mr. Jones, my neighbor, that man mowing the* *lawn*, or *an accountant*. In contrast, the intension may be the same while the extension differs: e.g., *I* always names the property of being the speaker, but the extension differs as the speaker shifts or *the Prime Minister of England* always name the same position within the government of England, but over time, the extension differs.

A final assumption of traditional semantics is that it is possible to treat the meanings of individual words separately. However, words refer to things in the real world not directly, but by means of concepts existing in the mind, or meanings internal to language (linguistic meaning) — what is known as the **sense** of a word — and words enter into various sense relationships with other words in the language. For example, words expressing movement towards and away from the speaker form a network based on directionality and transitivity:

	towards speaker	away from speaker
intransitive	come	go
transitive	bring	take
	?	send

Likewise, words expressing vision form a network based on the distinction between chance happening and willful act as well as duration:

	happening	act
longer duration	see	look (stare, gawk)
shorter duration	glimpse	glance

In these networks, the meanings of the words are interdependent; it is impossible to know the meaning of *look*, for example, without also knowing the meaning of the word *see*.

■ Self-Testing Exercise: Do Exercise 6.1.

Basic Semantic Relationships

As speakers of the language, we all have an implicit understanding of a number of semantic relationships that hold between either words or sentences in the language. Let's examine briefly the technical terms that linguists use to describe the different types of relationships.

1. **Paraphrase**: one statement is a paraphrase of another when it has the same meaning as another, as *Philip purchased an automobile* is a paraphrase of *Philip bought a car* (we will look at synonymy — sameness of meaning between words — below).

2. **Entailment**, or implication: one statement entails another when the second is a logically necessary consequence of the first, as *Alan lives in Toronto* entails *Alan lives in Canada*. Note that the relationship of entailment, unlike that of paraphrase, is one-way: it is not the case that *Alan lives in Canada* entails *Alan lives in Toronto*.

3. **Inclusion**: one statement includes another, as *I like fruit* includes *I like apples*. Again, this relationship is unidirectional: *I like apples* does not include *I like (all) fruit*.

4.   **Contradiction**: a statement or sequence of statements is logically contradictory; that is, if one is true, the other must be false, as *He is an orphan* contradicts *My parents are living* or *I spit out the beer I swallowed* is internally contradictory.

5.   **Anomaly**: a sentence has no meaning in the everyday world; it violates semantic rules, for example, *He swallowed a dream* or *The rock giggled*. (We will examine anomaly below, as some apparent anomaly is actually figurative language.)

6.   **Lexical ambiguity**: a word allows more than one meaning in context, as in *an old friend*, which may denote a friend who is aged or a friend who one has known for a long time (two different meanings of *old*), or *a large bill*, which may denote a large beak of a bird or a large check at a restaurant (two different words *bill*), or *he lost his head*, which may mean that he became discomposed (a metaphorical interpretation) or that he was decapitated (the literal interpretation).[2]

7.   **Denotation/connotation**: words have literal or referential meanings (denotation) but also evoke feelings, attitudes, or opinions (connotations). The following words, whose denotations are similar if not identical, carry differing connotations, either good or bad:

soldier — warrior	relax — loaf
insect — bug	hound — dog
illness — disease — ailment — condition	generous — extravagant
fat — obese — plump — portly — stout — substantial	

For example, some air blowing through a window is called a *draft* when it is cold and undesired, but a *breeze* when it is cool and desired; a *plan* points to careful foresight, while a *scheme* suggests deviousness or manipulation. Sometimes the connotations of words are associated with their language of origin, as in the sets below, deriving from English, French, and Latin, respectively:

fire — flame — conflagration
fear — terror — trepidation
rise — mount — ascend
ask — question — interrogate

In any but the most mundane uses of language, connotations are an important aspect of meaning. Words may also carry social meaning, indicators of the identity of the speaker (age, sex, social class, race) or the formality of the context. These are also significant to the meaning of a discourse.

8.   **Polysemy**: a word has more than one meaning out of context; the meanings are related to one another, e.g.:

court: 'enclosed area', 'retinue of a sovereign', 'judicial tribunal';
mouth: 'opening through which an animate being takes food', 'the part of a river which empties into a lake or sea';
bug: 'insect', 'enthusiast', 'electronic device for eavesdropping', 'design defect in a computer';
fire: 'to burn or ignite', 'to shoot a gun', 'to discharge from one's employment'.

9.   **Homonymy**: two words sound and are written the same but are different in meaning, e.g.:

bark₁ 'outer covering of wood'   bark₂ 'harsh sound, uttered by a dog'
sound₁ 'noise'   sound₂ 'body of water'   sound₃ 'free from defect'
band₁ 'thin strip for encircling an object'   band₂ 'group of people'
swallow₁ 'to ingest'   swallow₂ 'a type of bird'

Homonyms represent different entries in a dictionary, while the different meanings of a polysemous word are listed under a single entry. However, without consulting a dictionary, it is often difficult to distinguish between polysemy and homonymy, that is, when one is dealing with two meanings for a single word or two different words. If the two forms belong to different parts of speech, one can usually conclude that they are homonyms. In the case of polysemy, the meanings are related (either literally or figuratively), though the connection between different meanings may sometimes be difficult to perceive (as in the meanings 'a series of connected mountains' or 'a unit for cooking' for *range*). In some cases, the meanings may have become so far apart from one another over time that an originally single word is divided into two dictionary entries (as in *pupil* 'a student' and *pupil* 'the opening in the center of the iris of the eye').

10.   **Part-whole**: a word denotes part of a whole, as *fender* is to *car*, *week* is to *month*, *head* is to *body*, *branch* is to *tree*, *binding* is to *book*. This has been termed "meronymy" (Cruse 1986).

11.   **Presupposition**: what is assumed beforehand by an utterance, or what is taken for granted, is said to be presupposed. The test for presupposition is that when an utterance is negated, what is presupposed remains true; what is presupposed "holds up under negation". Minimally, the existence of the thing or person talked about (the topic) is presupposed, as in *My teacher gave a boring lecture*, where the existence of teacher is presupposed; when negated — *My teacher didn't give a boring lecture* — the teacher is still assumed to exist, though a lecture may or may not have been given (she may have given an exciting lecture or she may have led a discussion). Individual words may carry presuppositions:

Have <u>another</u> cup of coffee (presupposes that addressee has already had a cup of coffee).
You should hit him <u>back</u> (presupposes the he has hit the addressee).
I <u>responded</u> to him (presupposes that he has asked the speaker something).
I read the article <u>again</u> (presupposes that the speaker has already read the article at least once).
I {<u>continued, stopped, finished</u>} drawing (presupposes that the speaker was drawing in the time immediately preceding the moment of speaking).
I <u>resumed</u> drawing {presupposes that the speaker was drawing in some time not immediately preceding the moment of speaking).
I {<u>began, started</u>} drawing (presupposes that the speaker was not drawing in the time immediately preceding the moment of speaking).
They have a bigger house <u>than</u> we do (presupposes the existence of both their house and our house).

If what is presupposed does not hold, then presupposition failure occurs, and the communication is pragmatically odd. In a *wh*-question, everything is presupposed except the information requested:

> Where did you put the paper? (presupposes that the addressee put the newspaper somewhere).

Indirect questions have the same presupposition: *I asked where she put the paper.* Compare a *yes/no* question such as *Is Karen attending the conference?*, where only the existence of Karen is presupposed.

Entire propositions may also be presupposed when they are expressed in the complement clauses of what have been termed **factive** expressions:

> It is {tragic, exciting, amusing, terrible, odd, significant, relevant, a bother} that it is raining.
> I {regret, am happy, remember, concede, understand, hear, learn, notice, resent, accept, appreciate, deplore, tolerate} that it is raining.

Notice that it is impossible to add **but it isn't raining* to the above statements since they presuppose that it is raining. An entire proposition may also be presupposed if it is nominalized (*His refusal to help annoyed me, What annoyed me was his refusal to help*). If the proposition of the complement clause is not presupposed, the expression is **nonfactive**:

> I {believe, guess, think, agree, doubt, fear, imagine, assert, am dreaming} that it is raining.
> It {appears, seems, chances, is likely, is possible, is certain, it true/false, probable} that it is raining.

Both factive and nonfactive contrast with counterfactive, which denotes an event that has not occurred and probably will not occur, as in *She pretended to be listening, He wishes that he were rich.*

It is important to distinguish presupposition from entailment. The clearest distinguishing test is that entailment does not hold up under negation. Thus, *Alan does not live in Toronto* does not entail that *Alan lives in Canada* (in fact, he may live anywhere).

■ *Self-Testing Exercise:* Do Exercise 6.2.

Structural Semantics

One description of the meaning relationships of words in a language is that of the British linguist John Lyons and is called *structural semantics*. Lyons recognizes three major types of relationship: synonymy, hyponymy, and oppositeness.

The concept of **synonymy** is, of course, well-known and intuitively obvious; it denotes sameness in meaning, or sense, as with the words:

unhappy/sad	huge/enormous
correct/right	casual/informal
prisoner/convict	present/gift
flourish/thrive	donate/contribute

Synonymy is context-dependent: *pedigree* refers only to animals, while *ancestry, genealogy,* and *lineage* refer only to human beings, and *descent* may refer to either; *carcass* refers only to animals, *corpse* only to human beings. Two words may have the same meaning in a particular context, but not necessarily in all contexts; for example, *pale/light* and *peel/skin* are synonymous in *The shirt is {pale/light} in color* or *the {peel, skin} of the orange is thick* but not in *The book is {light, *pale} in weight* or *the girl's {skin, *peel} is sunburned.* Synonymy ignores the connotations of words and recognizes only their denotations. In fact, many synonyms differ only in respect to their connotations, as in *horse/steed/nag.* Synonyms may also differ in degree or intensity, as in *rain/showers/sprinkles/downpour.* Synonmy also ignores stylistic aspects — the colloquial, familiar, or formal register of the word — or its social or geographic dialect distribution. Consider the following sets of synonyms and note the differences in formality among the terms as well as their distribution in Canadian, American, or British English:

> sofa, couch, chesterfield, davenport
> privy, loo, w.c., bath/rest/washroom, toilet
> dear, expensive, costly

Hyponymy is a relation of inclusion or entailment. A **superordinate term** (or "hypernym") includes a set of **cohyponyms** (the prefix *hypo-* is Greek for 'below', the prefix *hyper-* is Greek for 'above', though to avoid confusion Lyons uses the corresponding Latin prefix *super-*). For example, the referents of the superordinate term *red* include the referents of the cohyponyms *scarlet, crimson, vermilion, pink, maroon,* and so on. In contrast, a hyponym entails the superordinate term, but not vice versa: *vermilion* entails *red,* though *red* does not entail *vermilion.* If *roses* is a hyponym of the superordinate term *flowers,* then *I bought some roses* entails *I bought some flowers,* but *I bought some flowers* does not entail *I bought some roses.* The meaning of the hyponym includes the meaning of the superordinate term. Another way to understand the concept of a superordinate term is as the name of a class of entities, as *musical instrument* is a class term including *piano, violin, flute, guitar, drum, cello, marimbas, accordion,* and so on. There may be different levels of hyponyms, a hierarchy, as shown in Figure 6.1. The lower one moves in this hierarchy, the more specialized, or "marked", the terms become. In some cases, there may not be a clear superordinate term.

A number of problems may arise in the identification of superordinate terms and hyponyms. The hyponyms *brother* and *sister* have only the technical superordinate *sibling,* while the hyponyms *uncle* and *aunt* have none. The only possible superordinate term for the

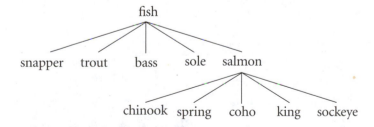

Figure 6.1. A Hierarchy of Fish Hyponyms

hyponyms *cow* and *bull* is *cow*, which is, of course, identical with one of the hyponyms; the term *cattle* is a collective term, while *bovine* is only technical. For the cohyponyms *chair*, *table*, *desk*, there likewise exists no simple superordinate term, but merely the phrase *a piece of furniture*. Color terms, such as *red, green*, and *pink*, also have no obvious superordinate since the term *colored* sometimes means 'not white' and sometimes 'not transparent'. The superdinate term *animal* (which contrasts with *vegetable* and *mineral*) is a hyponym of itself, where it contrasts with *human being*.

Lyons recognizes three different relationships of oppositeness. **Complementarity** (or "binary antonymy") is a relationship of contradiction, in which the denial of one term is the assertion of its complementary term. X is not Y and Y is not X (e.g., *right is not wrong* and *wrong is not right*). Other examples include the following:

single — married	male — female
dead — alive	pregnant — not pregnant
legal — illegal	on — off
asleep — awake	pass — fail
true — false	raw — cooked

Note that there are sometimes separate lexical items to express the complementary terms, while at other times negative prefixes such as *un-* or *in-* occur or the negative particle is used. In some cases, it may be possible to think of intermediate cases where the denial of one is not the assertion of the other, as in the case of *hermaphrodite* (which is not strictly either *female* nor *male*), *mermaid* or *satyr* (which is not strictly either *human* nor *nonhuman*), *retired* (which is not strictly either *unemployed* nor *employed*), *ambidextrous* (which is not strictly either *left-handed* or *right-handed*) and *divorced* (which is not strictly either *single* nor *married*), but these are not usual. Because complementary terms denote incompatible extremes, it is abnormal to compare or qualify them with *more* or *less*, though we may do so for humorous purposes when referring not to the quality itself, but to physical, emotional, or behavioral characteristics associated with a quality, as in *more (very) pregnant* or *more (very) married*.

A second relationship of oppositeness is **antonymy** (a term Lyons uses in a restricted sense), or "nonbinary antonymy". Antonymy refers to gradable concepts, which may be explicitly or implicitly compared, such as:

big — small/little	old — young/new
high — low	wide/broad — narrow
proper — improper	thick — thin/narrow
fat — thin	good — bad
small — large	many — few
hot — cold	rich — poor
warm — cool	sweet — sour/bitter
smart — dumb	noisy — quiet
wet — dry	intelligent — unintelligent

(Note that the prefixes *un-* and *in-* may denote antonymy as well as complementarity.) Such sets of adjectives are called **scalar adjectives.** In the use of these adjectives, there is always an implicit comparison to a norm. The norm varies from context to context, e.g., "A small elephant is a large animal" or "A large mouse is a small animal" or "Large for a child is small for an adult". A warm beer and a cold coffee may be the same temperature since the temperature norms for beer and coffee differ. Depending upon the context, the form that a scalar adjective is paired with may differ. For example, with animate beings, *young* is used, while for inanimate things, *new* is used, but *old* is used for both; beer is *bitter* or *sweet* whereas fruit is *sour* or *sweet*. In other instances, terms seem to be interchangeable; a river is *broad* or *wide*, or an animal may be *small* or *little*. Unlike complementary pairs, antonymous pairs, since they mark points on a scale, typically permit intermediate stages; thus, between *often* and *seldom*, we find *occasionally* and *sometimes*, between *love* and *hate*, we find *like* and *dislike*, and between *hot* and *cold*, we find *warm* and *cool*.

With scalar pairs, one is unmarked (positive, unbiased) and one is marked (negative, biased). The unmarked member will fit more naturally into the following slots than will the marked member:

> How _____ is it?
> Twice as _____
> Half as _____

Again, the markedness can be context-dependent; for example, in summer one might ask "how hot is it?", while in winter one might ask "how cold is it?". Some scalar adjectives are unidimensional, such as *hot — cold* or *tall — short*, while others are multidimensional, such as *attractive — unattractive* or *big — small*. We can also distinguish between the normal scalar adjective and the end-of-scale scalar adjective; the former fits the slot *very _____* (e.g., *big, tasty, interesting, beautiful, old, cold, hot*), while the latter fits the slot *absolutely _____* (e.g., *enormous/huge, delicious/scrumptious, fascinating, gorgeous/stunning, aged/ancient, freezing/ frigid, boiling/scorching/stifling*). Note that the end-of-scale adjective is much more varied and connotationally rich than the normal adjective.

The third relationship of oppositeness is **converseness**, which denotes a kind of reversal. Certain verb pairs, such as *buy/sell*, *rent/rent (lease)*, *lend/borrow*, and *give/receive*, are converse, as are kinship terms such as *husband/wife* and *brother/sister*. All converse terms permit reversal, for example, "Andy bought the car from Christy" entails and is entailed by "Christy sold the car to Andy" or "Bill is Trudy's son" entails and is entailed by "Trudy is Bill's mother". Other cases of converseness are terms expressing professional relationships such as *teacher/student*, *employer/employee*, *host/guest*, *master/servant*, and *lawyer/client* and terms expressing position in time and space, such as *in front of/behind*, *in back of*, *north of/ south of*, and *outside/inside*. Though logically "The bike is in front of the garage" entails "The garage is behind the bike", the second sentence is perspectively odd since we tend to place the figure in respect to the ground rather than the ground in respect to the figure. Syntactically, active sentences and their corresponding passives all denote converseness, though, again, the correspondences may sound odd because of the tendency for the topic of the discourse to be expressed in the subject position (e.g., "Sandy ate the strawberries" entails "The strawberries were eaten by Sandy"). Comparative expressions, though they usually contain scalar adjectives, are themselves converse (e.g., "The castle is larger than the fort" implies "The fort is smaller than the castle"). We must be careful to distinguish true cases of converseness from apparent ones, such as *ask/answer* (an answer is only expected, not necessary), *command/obey* (a command is not always obeyed), *seek/find*, *try/succeed* (seeking does not necessarily result in finding, nor trying with succeeding) and perhaps *teach/learn* (does teaching necessarily imply learning?).

A special kind of converseness is called **symmetry**. An example is *married*; while it is possible to say "Helen is married to David" and "David is married to Helen", it is also possible to say "Helen and David are married". Other examples of symmetry are *be {synonymous with, identical to, different from, adjacent to, related to, neighbors with, the same size as}*. The term *sister* can be symmetrical when the sex of both referents is female ("Dora is the sister of Sally", "Sally is the sister of Dora", and "Sally and Doris are sisters"), but when the sex differs, the symmetrical term *sibling* must be used (e.g., "Lois is the sibling of Don", "Don is the sibling of Lois", and "Don and Lois are siblings"). A verb such as *agree with* would appear to be symmetrical (e.g., "Tom agreed with Paul", "Paul agreed with Tom", and "Tom and Paul agreed"), but note that the relation may be unidirectional (when Tom and Paul agree, it may be that Tom agrees with Paul, but that Paul does not necessarily do anything). This type of unidirectional relationship is called **reciprocity**; other examples include *collide with, concur with, cooperate with, fight with*.

The set of privative verbs that we discussed in Chapter 4, such as *zip/unzip, tie/untie, wrap/unwrap*, and *connect/disconnect*, as well as a set of other verbs, including *appear/disappear, exhale/inhale, progress/regress*, and *inflate/deflate*, present an interesting case of oppositeness. These also seem to be a special case of converseness; they have been called **reversives** (Cruse 1986).

■ *Self-Testing Exercise*: Do Exercise 6.3. A concept related to that of hyponymy is that of the semantic field. Read about this in Exercise 6.4.

Semantic Features

Componential analysis is an attempt to give a semantic analysis of words in terms of **semantic features** or **components** (Katz and Fodor 1963). It consists in determining the basic components constituting the semantic content, or sense, of a word. These components, sometimes called *semantic primitives*, are assumed to be the most basic notions expressed by linguistic meaning, the "givens" of the semantic system which cannot be broken down further by semantic analysis. Furthermore, they are thought to be universal, not language specific, part of the cognitive and perceptual system of the human mind. According to the linguist Manfred Bierwisch, "all semantic structure might finally be reduced to components representing the basic dispositions of the cognitive and perceptual structure of the human organism". These components combine in different ways to form the meaning of individual words; thus, features are the shared semantic characteristics of words. Every word in the language consists of a unique bundle of semantic features. Semantic features combine in different ways in different languages; that is, they are lexicalized differently, resulting in the varied vocabularies of different languages.

Semantic features are usually presented as a matter of opposition, paired positive and negative features, denoting the presence or absence of the particular feature in the meaning of the word. Since semantic features are theoretical elements, not part of the vocabulary of the language, they are represented abstractly by capitalizing them and placing them in square brackets.

The determination of semantic features is a kind of "factoring out" of semantic components. This process can be seen most clearly in a semantic feature analysis of a livestock paradigm (see Table 6.1). The table is read as follows: all of the words in the second row, for example, share the features [−MALE] and [+ADULT], while all of the words in the third column share the feature [+BOVINE], and so on. While the words in the first column share the feature [+HUMAN], those in the other columns share the feature [−HUMAN]. However, for each word to be distinguished from every other word by at least one feature, [−HUMAN] is much too broad a category, suggesting that we need the further distinctions [+SWINE], [+BOVINE], and so on. But if we add one of these positive features to a column, we must, for completeness, also add all the others as negative features to that column, leading to a very cumbersome feature analysis. A second difficulty is deciding which is the positive and which is the negative member. Sometimes the choice is arbitrary, but often the positive term is more inclusive or more generalized than the negative term. For example, *dog*, which we analyze as [+ADULT], [+MALE] is often used to refer to both male and female canines (thus [±MALE]) and young and old canines (thus [±ADULT]). Likewise, the term *man* may be [±MALE] in the sense of "mankind" and [±ADULT] in its use, for example, on the door of a washroom. The positive feature often has more extended and metaphorical meanings than the negative feature, as can be seen with *stallion, cock,* or *bull* (*bitch* and *cow* are perhaps exceptions to this generalization).

Other sets of words can likewise be differentiated by the use of semantic features. For example, we could distinguish types of clothing as in Table 6.2a or bodies of water (6.2b). Departing from the livestock paradigm, it becomes clear how arbitrary the choice of supposedly universal features becomes, since the clothing terms given in (6.2a) could certainly be analyzed with quite a different set of features, for example, with a feature such as [±SLEEVE] rather than one such as [±UPPER BODY]. Once more specialized garments such as *vest, nightgown,* or *turtleneck* are included, it would become necessary to add many more specific semantic features. Another weakness evident in the examples in (6.2b) is that, although the eight terms are all distinguished by at least one feature, there is not a sense that the features used satisfactorily capture the meaning of the terms since, for example, *bay* and *inlet* contain some feature of [+INDENTATION].

Feature Analysis of Nouns

Despite the problems of feature analysis just mentioned, it is possible, at the minimum, to analyze nouns into their major syntactic subclasses (introduced in Chapter 4) by using the following set of **semantic features for nouns**:

[±COMMON]
[±COUNT]
[±CONCRETE]

Table 6.1. Componential Analysis of a Livestock Paradigm

man	boar	bull	cock	dog	stallion	ram	[+MALE] [+ADULT]
woman	sow	cow	hen	bitch	mare	ewe	[−MALE] [+ADULT]
child	piglet	calf	chick	puppy	foal	lamb	[±MALE] [−ADULT]
boy	shoat	bullock	chick	dog puppy	colt	ram lamb	[+MALE] [−ADULT]
girl	gilt	heifer	chick	bitch puppy	filly	ewe lamb	[−MALE] [−ADULT]
crowd	drove	herd	flock	pack	herd	flock	[+COLLECTIVE]
[+HUMAN]	[+SWINE]	[+BOVINE]	[+CHICKEN]	[+CANINE]	[+EQUINE]	[+SHEEP]	
			[−HUMAN]				

[±ANIMATE]
[±HUMAN]
[±MALE]
[±COLLECTIVE]

The definition of [±ANIMATE] is somewhat problematical; it usually refers to animal rather than vegetable life, with a secondary meaning of 'living'. Thus, *tree* and *beef* should be analyzed as [−ANIMATE], the first not being animal life and the second not being living. In Table 6.3 are some examples of the componential analysis of different types nouns. Note that there is a hierarchy of features: if something is [−ANIMATE], then [HUMAN] and [MALE] are irrelevant; if [−CONCRETE], then [ANIMATE] is irrelevant. For some terms, the semantic analysis depends on our conception of the object: a university, for example, may be thought of in terms of the concept, the physical structure, or the collective body of people constituting it.

Using these semantic features, however, we could not distinguish between the terms *father* and *man*. Certain classes of nouns, such as kinship terms, require a different kind of feature, namely **relational** or **contextual features**. The term *father* could be analyzed in the following way:

X [+PARENT OF] Y
  X [+ANIMATE], [+MALE], [+ADULT], [±HUMAN]
  Y [+ANIMATE], [±HUMAN], [±ADULT], [±MALE]

The term *daughter* would be analyzed as follows:

X [+OFFSPRING OF] Y
  X [+ANIMATE], [±HUMAN], [±ADULT], [−MALE]
  Y [+ANIMATE], [±HUMAN], [+ADULT], [±MALE]

Scalar adjectives and verbs also lend themselves to an analysis using relational features:

high: Y [+GREATER THAN] Norm
    Y [+DIMENSION OF] X
    Y [+VERTICAL]

Table 6.2. Componential Analysis of (a) Types of Garments and (b) Bodies of Water

(a) garments

coat	*jacket*	*shirt*	*blouse*	*skirt*	*pants*	*shorts*
[+UPPER BODY]	[+UPPER BODY]	[+UPPER BODY]	[+UPPER BODY]	[–UPPER BODY]	[–UPPER BODY]	[–UPPER BODY]
[±FULL LENGTH]	[–FULL LENGTH]	[–FULL LENGTH]	[–FULL LENGTH]	[±FULL LENGTH]	[+FULL LENGTH]	[–FULL LENGTH]
[±MALE]	[±MALE]	[±MALE]	[–MALE]	[–MALE]	[±MALE]	[±MALE]
[+OVER GARM.]	[+OVER GARM.]	[–OVER GARM.]	[–OVER GARM.]	[–OVER GARM.]	[–OVER GARM.]	[–OVER GARM.]

(b) bodies of water

lake	*sea*	*ocean*	*river*	*brook*	*pond*	*bay*	*cove*
[–FLOWING]	[–FLOWING]	[–FLOWING]	[+FLOWING]	[+FLOWING]	[–FLOWING]	[–FLOWING]	[–FLOWING]
[–SALINE]	[+SALINE]	[+SALINE]	[–SALINE]	[–SALINE]	[–SALINE]	[±SALINE]	[±SALINE]
[±LARGE]	[±LARGE]	[+LARGE]	[±LARGE]	[–LARGE]	[–LARGE]	[±LARGE]	[–LARGE]

Table 6.3. Feature Analyses of Sample Nouns

butter	cabbage	commitment
[+COMMON]	[+COMMON]	[+COMMON]
[−COUNT]	[+COUNT]	[−COUNT]
[+CONCRETE]	[+CONCRETE]	[−CONCRETE]
[−ANIMATE]	[−ANIMATE]	[−ANIMATE]

weather	sunrise	experience
[+COMMON]	+COMMON]	[+COMMON]
[−COUNT]	[+COUNT]	[+COUNT]
[+CONCRETE]	[+CONCRETE]	[−CONCRETE]
[−ANIMATE]	[−ANIMATE]	[−ANIMATE]

attack	aid	leftovers
[+COMMON]	[+COMMON]	[+COMMON]
[+COUNT]	[+COUNT]	[+COMMON] [− COUNT]
[±CONCRETE]	[±CONCRETE]	[−CONCRETE]
[−ANIMATE]	[−ANIMATE]	[−ANIMATE]
		[+COLLECTIVE]

cook	aide	measles
[+COMMON]	[+COMMON]	[+COMMON]
[+COUNT]	[+COUNT]	[+COMMON] [− COUNT]
[+CONCRETE]	[+CONCRETE]	[−CONCRETE]
[+ANIMATE]	[+ANIMATE]	[−ANIMATE]
[+HUMAN]	[±HUMAN]	
[±MALE]	[±MALE]	

whale	lioness	clergy
[+COMMON]	[+COMMON]	[+COMMON]
[+COUNT]	[+COUNT]	[−COUNT]
[+CONCRETE]	[+CONCRETE]	[+CONCRETE]
[+ANIMATE]	[+ANIMATE]	[+ANIMATE]
[−HUMAN]	[−HUMAN]	[+HUMAN]
[±MALE]	[−MALE]	[±MALE]
		[+COLLECTIVE]

university		
[+COMMON] or	[+COMMON] or	[+COMMON]
[+COUNT]	[+COUNT]	[+COUNT]
[−CONCRETE]	[+CONCRETE]	[+CONCRETE]
	[−ANIMATE]	[+ANIMATE]
	[+HUMAN]	
	[±MALE]	
	[+COLLECTIVE]	

take:	X take Y from Z	give:	X give Y to Z
	Z [HAVE] Y		X [HAVE] Y
	X [CAUSE] (X [HAVE] Y)		X [CAUSE] (Z [HAVE] Y)

We will return to this type of analysis of verbs in Chapter 10; it is termed "predication analysis".

■ *Self-Testing Exercise: Do Exercise 6.5.*

Feature Analysis of Verbal Predicates

While a complete analysis of verbs requires relational features, it is possible to characterize the inherent temporal nature of the situation[3] named by the verb by using a number of semantic features. The temporal nature is referred to by the name inherent aspect or by the German word *Aktionsart* 'type of action'. As the use of the term "aspect" suggests, inherent aspect is a concomitant of and interacts with verbal aspect (perfective/imperfective), as discussed in Chapter 5. There are a number of ways in which inherent aspect can be defined, but it is sufficient for our purposes to identify four **semantic features for verbal predicates**:

1. [**±STATIVE**]: this feature recognizes whether the situation denoted by the verb involves change [−STATIVE] or not [+STATIVE]; it is said that the [−STATIVE] (or dynamic) situation requires the input of energy, whereas a [+STATIVE] situation does not;
2. [**±DURATIVE**]: this feature recognizes whether the situation goes on in time [+DURATIVE] or occurs at a moment in time (punctual/instantaneous) [−DURATIVE];
3. [**±TELIC**]: this feature recognizes whether the situation has an endpoint or goal which is necessary for the situation to be what it is [+TELIC] or has no necessary conclusion [−TELIC]; and
4. [**±VOLUNTARY**]: this feature recognizes whether the situation is a matter of an agent's voluntary or willful action [+VOLUNTARY] (intentional) or not [−VOLUNTARY].

(The last feature is, strictly speaking, not a matter of the temporal qualities of a situation, but it has traditionally been treated with inherent aspect.)

On the basis of these features, different situation types are identifiable. The best-known typology is that of Zeno Vendler (1967), which distinguishes four situation types, as presented in Table 6.4.

States denote unchanging situations such as emotional, cognitive, and physical states, conditions, or qualities. States are continuous over the entire time period in which they exist. Examples of states are the predicates in *Philip {loves, suspects, resembles, expects, doubts} Brigit*. Stative expressions can be identified by a number of formal properties:

– states are generally expressed in the simple, not the progressive form (**Philip is loving Brigit*), because the progressive indicates a situation which is "ongoing" and changing.
– A state lasts in time indefinitely, for a given period of time, with no necessary end; it answers the question "for how long?".
– A person cannot be commanded, forced, or persuaded to be in a state (**Love Brigit! *His mother forced him to love Brigit*) because a state is not a matter of volition or will; it can only "be".

Table 6.4. Typology of Situation Types

state e.g., *love, resemble*	activity e.g., *push, run*
[+STATIVE]	[−STATIVE]
[+DURATIVE]	[+DURATIVE]
[−TELIC]	[−TELIC]
[−VOLUNTARY]	[±VOLUNTARY]
accomplishment e.g., *dress, use up*	achievement e.g., *kick, blink*
[−STATIVE]	[−STATIVE]
[+DURATIVE]	[−DURATIVE]
[+TELIC]	([+TELIC])
[±VOLUNTARY]	[±VOLUNTARY]

– For the same reason, no manner adverbs can accompany a stative expression: Philip cannot love Brigit *deliberately, studiously, attentively,* or *carefully*.
– A stative cannot occur in a pseudocleft sentence such as *What Philip did was love Brigit*, since states are not "done".
– States start and stop, but they cannot be finished: *Philip {started, stopped, *finished} loving Brigit*.

Other examples of states (taken from Vendler) are the following:

know	believe	be X
be married	dominate	think that
like/dislike	see	know that/how
have	possess	believe that/in
desire	want	understand
hate	rule	see

Activities are dynamic situations which go on in time (potentially indefinitely). Examples of activities are the predicates in *Jesse is {reading, pushing the cart, daydreaming, talking with Janice, staring at the picture, sitting on the bed}*. Activities last for a period of time and answer the question "for how long?"; they do not take any definite time nor have any definite end and hence cannot be "finished", though like states, they can begin and end. Activities go on in a homogeneous way; they are constant over the period of time in which they happen. With activities, one can "spend a certain amount of time V-*ing*". An activity may be either continuing (e.g., *argue, talk, walk*) or changing (e.g., *grow, improve, decline*). A test for activities is that if *one stops* V-*ing*, then *one has* V-*ed* (if *Jesse stops pushing the cart*, then *he has pushed the cart*). Other examples of activities from Vendler are the following:

run	swim	think about
walk	watch	housekeep
look	observe	keep in sight
pull	gaze upon	follow with one's eyes
pay attention to	scrutinize	focus one's eyes on

Although activities are frequently [+VOLUNTARY], they may also be [−VOLUNTARY], as is the case with, e.g., *The water is flowing, Her hair is turning gray, The child is growing*. Such activities cannot be commanded.

Accomplishments are dynamic situations with a terminal point or "climax" which is logically necessary for them to be what they are. Thus, in the examples *Sybil {wrote a letter, went to the store, cooked dinner}*, it is necessary for the endpoint to be reached (i.e., the letter to be produced, the store to be reached, and the dinner to be completed) for the accomplishment to occur. Therefore, a test for accomplishments is that if *one stops V-ing*, then *one has not V-ed* (if *Sybil stops writing the letter*, then *she has not written a letter*); she has simply worked on a letter, walked in the direction of the store, or prepared part of dinner. Accomplishments, unlike states and activities, can be "finished": if *Sybil finishes writing the letter*, then *she has written a letter*). Because of their necessary ends, accomplishments take a certain amount of time and answer the question "how long did it take?". With accomplishments, one V's "in a certain amount of time", not "for a certain amount of time". Accomplishments do not go on in a homogeneous way, but consist of an activity phase and a terminal point, which are different in nature. Finally, accomplishments are ambiguous with *almost*; if *Sybil almost wrote a letter*, then she may have written a partial letter or she may not have even begun the letter (just thought about it). Other examples of accomplishments drawn from Vendler are the following:

run a mile	draw a circle	recover from an illness
write a letter	get exhausted	get ready
paint a picture	make a chair	see *Carmen*
build a house	write/read a novel	play a game of chess
deliver a sermon	give/attend a class	grow up
watch (the passage of Venus across the sun)		

Note that accomplishments can be [+VOLUNTARY], e.g., *run a mile, get ready*, or [−VOLUNTARY], e.g., *get exhausted, grow up*.

Achievements are dynamic situations that are conceived of as occurring instantaneously, as in *Roger {reached the top of the mountain, flicked the switch on, solved the problem}*. They are punctual acts or changes of state. [TELIC] is not really a relevant category here because achievements, since they are punctual, end as soon as they begin (though they are often described as [+TELIC]). Achievements occur at a single moment in time and answer the question "at what time?". They can also answer the question "how long did it take?", but the meaning of achievements in this case is different from the meaning of accomplishments; "It took Sybil an hour to write a letter" implies that at any point during that hour she was working on the letter, but "it took Roger an hour to solve the problem" does not imply that at any point during that hour he was working on the problem: he may have been working on the problem during the time (an activity) or not. In fact, achievements seem to fall into two subclasses: those that are truly instantaneous (such as *kick, flick, tap*) and those that, though they name a culminating point, usually involve a preliminary process (such as *find*, generally preceded by looking for, *reach the top*, generally preceded by working one's way towards the top). When the process leading up to the endpoint and the endpoint are named by the same verb, the progressive is possible: *He died at 5:00/He is dying, The plane arrived at 5:00/The plane is arriving.* Otherwise, the progressive is either incompatible with achievements (*She is recognizing a friend*) or denotes the repetition of the achievement either by a singular subject (*He is kicking the ball*) or multiple subjects (*The guests were arriving gradually*). Other examples of achievements from Vendler are the following:

die	topple the tree	understand
win the race	spot (something)	get married
recognize	find	know
start V-ing	stop V-ing	notice
realize	lose	see
cross the border	resume V-ing	catch a dog
be born	?think of	

Note that achievements are incompatible with *start* and *stop*, which themselves are achievements (e.g., *She stopped recognizing a friend*). Achievements are often [−VOLUNTARY] (e.g., *find, spot, catch a dog*), though they can be [+VOLUNTARY] as well (e.g., *cross the border, kick the ball, tap the window*).

In Vendler's lists given above, the verbs *understand, see,* and *know* occur in both the categories of states and of achievements. As states, these verbs denote an unchanging condition (e.g., *I understand German, I see poorly, I know how to tune a car*), while as achievements, they denote the dynamic event of coming into a state (e.g., *Now I understand what you mean, I see a parking spot over there, Now I know what to do*). This exemplifies the multivalency of verbs, that they are often able to name more than one situation type.

You may have noticed that it is often not just the verb alone, but also other parts of the predicate that figure in the determination of situation type. First, the addition of a nominal object may contribute the notion of goal and thus change an activity into an accomplishment:

She sang. (activity) > She sang a song. (accomplishment)
I worked. (activity) > I worked the crossword puzzle. (accomplishment)

Moreover, the count qualities of the object are significant; with mass and indefinite plural objects, the activity status is unchanged, while with definite plural objects, the activity is converted into an accomplishment:

She sang {folk music, songs}. (activity)
She sang two songs. (accomplishment)

Prepositional phrases which denote either a spatial goal or temporal limit may also convert an activity into an accomplishment:

He walked. (activity) > He walked {to the store, from dawn to dusk}. (accomplishment)

Particles such as *up, down, out, off,* and *through* may have the same effect:

She used the paper. (activity) > She used up the paper. (accomplishment)

However, not all prepositional phrases and particles change an activity into an accomplishment:

> He walked in the woods. I worked at/on the crossword puzzle.
> He walked along/on.
> I worked on the machine.

The count qualities of the subject may affect the situation type as well:

> The runner crossed the line. (achievement)
> Two runners crossed the line. (accomplishment)
> Runners crossed the line. (activity)

For these reasons, we speak of *situation type* rather than *verb type*.

The situation type interacts in complex ways with verb aspect, as suggested in the previous chapter. Here it is sufficient to emphasize that changing the aspect of an expression does not alter its situation type. Thus, *she was singing* and *she sang* are both activities, although the first is viewed imperfectively (as ongoing) while the second is viewed perfectively (as a whole or "bounded"). In contrast, *she sings* is an activity which is viewed habitually, that is, is seen as happening in bound segments on different occasions; this constitutes the situation type of **habit**.[4] Any situation type can be seen as occuring on different occasions over time, e.g., *He writes poems* (accomplishment), *He crosses the border everyday* (achievement), *She runs* (activity), *He enjoys every movie he sees* (state).

■ Self-Testing Exercise: Do Exercise 6.6.

Feature Analysis of Modals

Another application of semantic features is in the analysis of the meaning of the modal auxiliaries: *will* (*would*), *can* (*could*), *shall* (*should*), *may* (*might*), and *must*. We can apply the same analysis to the phrasal equivalents of the modal auxiliaries: *have to* [hæftə], *have got to*, [hævgatə], *ought to* [atə], *need to*, *be supposed to* [spoustə], and *be able to*.

The modals can be analyzed using two features of meaning:

1. **epistemic meaning**: meaning which is a matter of belief (inference, deduction), such as potentiality, possibility, probability, prediction, or certainty; or
2. **deontic (root) meaning**: meaning which is a matter of action, such as permission, duty, responsibility, obligation (weak or strong), ability, or command.

Epistemic meanings answer the question "How do you know?", while deontic meanings answer the question "What should I do?". Epistemic modality relates to the entire proposition: *It may rain* = 'it is possible that it will rain'. Deontic modality is subject-oriented: *You may leave the table* = 'you are permitted to leave the table'. Sentences with modal auxiliaries or their phrasal equivalents are either epistemic or deontic in meaning, or ambiguous between the two readings. Each of the modals may denote both types of meaning, but the different modals are distinguished by the intensity or strength of epistemic or deontic meaning they express. Note that the past-tense forms *would*, *could*, *should*, and *might* do not express past-time meaning (except in indirect speech), but rather different degrees of epistemic or deontic meaning.

Table 6.5 contains examples of the different modals in their epistemic and deontic meanings.

While the distinction between epistemic and deontic is often quite obvious (e.g., *I must be dreaming* = 'it is possible that I am dreaming' or *I must leave now* = 'I am obliged to leave now'), it may also be rather subtle (e.g., *This car is able to go very fast* = 'it is possible that this car will go very fast' vs. *He is able to run very fast* = 'he has the ability to run very fast'). Note that permissive *may* is often replaced by *can* for many speakers and that *had to* is the only way to express obligation in the past (because *must* is unpaired). For most North American speakers, the modal auxiliary *shall* is now quite rare, having been replaced by *will*, so the examples given above may not be very meaningful;[5] however, we can still see the contrast between *will* and *shall* in the questions *Will we eat before we leave?*, which asks for a prediction, and *Shall we eat before we leave?*, which asks for a recommendation.

The negation of modality may work in two ways. There may be negation of the main verb (modality + neg + main verb), as in:

> *You mustn't pay the fine* 'it is obligatory that you not pay the fine'
> *She may not be in her office* 'it is possible that she is not in her office'.

Or there may be negation of the modal (neg + modality + main verb), as in:

> *She can't be in her office* 'it is not possible that she is in her office'
> *You don't have to pay the fine* = 'it is not necessary for you to pay the fine'.

Sentences may also be ambiguous between epistemic and deontic readings. For example, *They must (have to) be married* may mean either that the speaker surmises, perhaps from appearances, that the couple is married (the epistemic reading) or that the couple is obliged to be married, perhaps in order to do something (the deontic reading). In contrast, *They have to get married* can be only deontic in meaning. The sentence *You might have said something* can mean that the speaker believes either that the hearer did probably say something (epistemic) or that the hearer should have said something (deontic). A sentence appearing in a departmental memorandum read *A student whose file of essays is incomplete may not be considered for appeal*; this can interpreted epistemically as a statement of a possible outcome or deontically as a statement of an impermissible course of action. *Bill won't go* is either the speaker's prediction about Bill's not going (the epistemic reading), 'I don't believe he will go', or the speaker's report of Bill's statement about his volition (the deontic reading), 'Bill says that he is unwilling to go'. Below are some further examples of ambiguous modals. Try to paraphrase the two readings in each case:

> You must help your mother.
> Frank may go out to buy a newspaper.
> He should have gone {by now, by then}.
> She must not care.
> You may see him.

Table 6.5. Epistemic and Deontic Meanings of the Modal Auxiliaries

Epistemic	Deontic
may	
He may commit suicide.	You may go to the movies.
April may have left.	May I be excused from the table?
must	
I must be dreaming.	I must convince him to reform.
The author must be a young man.	You must not do that.
will	
John will know the answer.	I will certainly be there.
She will be home soon.	I will marry you.
shall	
I shall be in my office today.	Lesley shall see to it.
We shall finish it by tomorrow.	He shall be there.
can	
Oil can float on water.	She can sing beautifully.
Winters can be very cold.	He can write well
It can't be five o'clock already.	Can I be excused from the table?
should	
We should be home soon, children.	You should see that movie.
You should know our decision soon.	I should go.
would	
He would know, if anyone does.	Would you please be more attentive.
Would it be safe to travel there?	Would you open the door for me?
could	
She could have known.	She could help you more often.
She could die.	As a child I could climb trees.
might	
That might be the correct answer.	You might check into it.
You might have killed yourself.	You might have been more helpful.
ought to	
The book ought to appear soon.	The children ought to go to bed now.
have to	
This has to be the right house.	I have to finish my paper today.
	I had to return the library book.
have got to	
This has got to be the one he was referring to.	I have got to be going now.
be supposed to	
It is supposed to rain today.	I am supposed to be there now.
be able to	
This car is able to go very fast.	He is able to wiggle his ears.

Epistemic and deontic meaning can be expressed by parts of speech other than the modal auxiliaries, as exemplified below:

1. modal verbs:
    I assume that he's left. (epistemic)
    I suggest that he learn the answer. (deontic)
    I suggest that he knows the answer. (epistemic)
    I insist that he do it. (deontic)
    I insist that he did it. (epistemic)
    I {guess, think} that you're right. (epistemic)
    We recommend that he step down. (deontic)

I expect him to go is ambiguous: either 'it is possible that he will go' (epistemic) or 'I place him under some obligation to go' (deontic).

2. modal adjectives:
    It is obligatory to understand modals. (deontic)
    It isn't necessary to read that chapter. (deontic)
    It is possible to understand modals. (epistemic)
    It is probable that the results are known. (epistemic)

3. modal adverbs: *probably, possibly, certainly*

4. modal nouns:
    It is your {duty, obligation} to look after your parents. (deontic)
    There is a {likelihood, probability, possibility} of rain today. (epistemic)

5. epistemic parentheticals:
    You are right, I {guess, think, suspect, believe, reckon, feel, assume}.
    Your cat will come back, I'm {certain, sure, confident}.

■ *Self-Testing Exercise: Do Exercise 6.7.*

Strengths and Weaknesses of Semantic Features

With the concept of semantic features, we can define more precisely certain relationships that we have already discussed. Synonymous words W_1 (W = word) and W_2 are analyzable in terms of the same components. Polysemy and ambiguity both involve a word's having more than one complex of components assigned to it, either out of or in context. Antonymy (in the broad sense, not Lyons' restricted sense) is a case where W_1 and W_2 share the same features except for one feature of W_1 being [+] and the same feature of W_2 being [−]. Hyponymy may be defined as follows: W_1 is a hyponym of W_2 if the meaning of W_1 contains all the features of W_2 but not vice versa. For example, *woman* is a hyponym of *adult*:

Adult W_2	Woman W_1
[+HUMAN]	[+HUMAN]
[+GROWN]	[+GROWN]
[±MALE]	[−MALE]

That is, all features of W_1 are features of W_2 but not vice versa.

However, the goal of feature analysis — the analysis of all words of a language in terms of combinations of semantic features — has never been met because of innumerable difficulties once one departs from the clear-cut cases of livestock terms or even concrete nouns. The concept of semantic features involves a fundamental circularity. We argue that components are abstractions, not the words of the language, but we have no metalanguage to refer to them. We must use the words of the language, and in so doing, must choose which words are the most "basic". We must somehow decide what the primitive components of meaning are, which concepts cannot be further analyzed. But when does one stop making distinctions? No one has yet determined all the possible semantic components of a one language (let alone a universal list). To do so, it would probably be necessary to postulate many semantic components that occur in only one word. But components are supposed to be recurrent, so such unique features undercut the entire purpose of semantic feature analysis. Moreover, many aspects of meaning are not binary and are not susceptible to analysis into binary features. We also saw that for different parts of speech, we had to postulate very different kinds of semantic features. Furthermore, in any particular use of a word, only some or perhaps none of the postulated semantic features may be relevant. As we will see below, in cases of metaphorical language, it appears that only certain features of a word may be important: in a sentence such as *He's a pig* (meaning 'he has terrible table manners'), the intrinsic feature of [+ANIMATE], [−HUMAN], [+SWINE] are not relevant to the intended meaning; rather, the emphasis is on certain behavioral characteristics. We can remove features and still identify the thing. We seem to use different features for different purposes, such as to identify something, to give synonyms or definitions, or to make inferences. It is uncertain how clearly features are marked, especially in our passive vocabulary. In fact, there is no real evidence that semantic features have any psychological reality, that when we use words, we "think" of any of the constituent components, or even that the features are relevant in our understanding of the meaning of the word.

Prototypes

An alternative to feature analysis, which is intended to have psychological validity is called **prototype** theory (proposed by psychologist Eleanor Rosch 1973). It argues that we understand the meaning of a word because we have a prototypical concept of the category to which the thing belongs; all members of the category are judged in relation to this prototype. This is a case of graded membership in a category: things are more or less good exemplars of a category. When members can be ranked in this way, the set is said to be "fuzzy". Thus, for example, we have a prototypical concept of a dog, or canine (perhaps a beagle), and we understand all other dogs in relation to this prototype. **Core members** would be those dogs most closely resembling the prototypes, such as shepherds, terriers, collies, poodles, and huskies, whereas more **peripheral members** would include those which are not as easily, or quickly, identified as a dog, including coyotes, jackals, wolves, and foxes. The defining characteristic of a dog would seem to have something to do with its being a domesticated animal, not, as the dictionary suggests, with the type and number of teeth it has. Or if we consider the concept of jewelry, we would certainly judge necklaces, pins, and rings to be core members; there might be some disagreement about items such as wristwatches, tie-clasps, and cufflinks, while many would probably reject altogether items such as eyeglasses, medic-alert bracelets, and belt buckles. Thus, our prototype of jewelry seems to have the notion of 'purely ornamental, nonfunctional' as central. In an experiment, psycholinguist Lila Gleitman (1983) asked subjects to rank things as good or bad members of a particular category (e.g., fruit, sport, vegetable, vehicle, even numbers, odd numbers, female, plane geometry) and timed their responses: they were faster with familiar, typical things, thus suggesting the validity of prototypes.[6]

Let's look at one extended example of prototypes. If we consider the concept of "vehicles", we might first divide the concept into three divisions — land, air, and water vehicles — and then list the core and peripheral members as a means of arriving at the defining characteristics of the category (see Table 6.6). It is obvious that there would be a fair amount of disagreement among speakers concerning both the members of this category and the division into core and peripheral. The general definition of 'a conveyance for the transport of people or cargo' would undoubtedly be unproblematical. However, for some speakers, the prototype of a vehicle includes the concept of movement over land, so neither air nor water conveyances are considered "vehicles". Many speakers might include in their prototype a notion of running on wheels or tires and thus exclude water conveyances and perhaps trains as well. Most speakers view a vehicle as motorized or capable of moving independently, thus excluding conveyances propelled through human or animal power, such as wagons or rickshaws; conveyances such as wheelchairs or go-carts, which may or may not be motorized, also create a problem. Students asked to perform this exercise with the concept

Table 6.6. Core and Peripheral Members of the Category "Vehicle"

Type	Core Members		Peripheral Members	
Land	car	truck	bicycle	tricycle
	motorcycle	scooter	skateboard	wagon
	limousine	van	baby carriage	shopping cart
	bus	ambulance	wheel barrow	sled
	hearse	taxi	toboggan	rickshaw
	tractor	go-cart	wheelchair	cart
	combine	train	buggy	carriage
Air	airplane	helicopter	hot air balloon	glider
	spaceship	satellite	zeppelin	gondola
	jet		chair-lift	parachute
Water	ferry	yacht	canoe	kayak
	tanker	motorboat	sailboat	(life)raft
	ship	tugboat	rowboat	punt
	hovercraft	steamboat	dinghy	catamaran
	hydrofoil	tugboat	barge	

of vehicle have actually come up with a wide variety of defining characteristics for vehicles — such as that a vehicle must be enclosed or that it must be something one sits in — suggesting that individual speakers may have quite divergent prototypes of categories.

■ *Self-Testing Exercise: Do Exercise 6.8.*

Semantic Anomaly

One of the basic semantic concepts mentioned at the beginning of the chapter was **semantic anomaly**. How is it that speakers of the language are all able to recognize that certain expressions — say *the birth of a peanut* or *the birth of a lamp* — are meaningless? How is it also possible that we can provide an interpretation, a figurative interpretation, for other expressions — say *the birth of the morning, the birth of the/a nation,* or *the birth of linguistics* — which on the surface are equally anomalous, since only animate beings are born?

Selectional Restrictions

It would appear that there are restrictions on the compatibility or combinability of words. Not only does a word contain certain semantic features, but it may also require that words with which it cooccurs contain certain features. These are called its **selectional restrictions**. Frequently a verb selects features in its noun arguments (subject or object). In Table 6.7, we see examples of selectional restrictions for certain words. Keep in mind that we are considering only absolutely literal uses of language.

When selectional restrictions are violated, when there is an incompatibility in the selectional restrictions of a word and the inherent features of a word in combination with it, we have semantic anomaly. There is generally an implied rather than an explicit contradiction, as in **The rooster laid an egg: lay an egg* requires a [−MALE] subject, while *rooster* is [+MALE]. (Compare the explicit contradiction of **The rooster is a hen,* where *rooster* is [+MALE] and *hen* is [−MALE].)

Figurative Language

To this point, we have been concerned with literal or "normal" uses of language, because figurative uses of language (personification, metaphor, etc.) routinely violate or break selectional restrictions. With figurative uses of language, as opposed to true anomaly, however, we can supply some interpretation. We do this, it seems, by allowing certain semantic features to override others in context. Compare the following three sentences:

> An intruder attacked me. (literal)
> Envy attacked me. (metaphorical)
> The rock attacked me. (anomalous)

Both the second and third sentences violate the selectional restriction that *attack* requires a [+ANIMATE] subject, but the second one permits interpretation, while the third one does not.

Table 6.7. Examples of Selectional Restrictions

trot — requires [+QUADRUPED] subject
  *{The horse, *the money, *the spider} trotted home.*
fly — requires [+WINGED] subject
  *{The airplane, the bird, *the goat} flew north.*
sing — requires [+HUMAN] or [+AVIAN] subject
  *{The woman, the bird, *the motor} sang sweetly.*
  cf. *The motor hummed softly.*
talk, think, dream — require [+HUMAN] subject (or possibly [+ANIMATE])
  *{The man, *the rock} is talking/thinking/dreaming.*
  ?*My dog is talking to me/thinking about his dinner/dreaming about cats.*
admire — requires [+HUMAN] subject
  *{Judy, *the goldfish} admires Mozart.*
pray — requires [+HUMAN] [±COLLECTIVE] subject
  *{The man, the nation, *the treaty} is praying for peace.*
pregnant — requires [+ANIMATE] and [−MALE] subject
  *{Mary, the mare, *the bull} is pregnant.*
marry — requires [+HUMAN] subject and object
  *Carl married Susan. *The goose married the gander.*
terrify — requires [+ANIMATE] object
  *The thunder terrified {the dog, the child, *the house}.*
anger — requires [+ANIMATE] object
  *Intruders anger {dogs, homeowners, *houses}.*
drink — requires [+ANIMATE] subject and [+LIQUID] object
  *{The child, *the glass} drank {the milk, *the candy}.*
melt — requires [+SOLID] object or subject
  *The sun melted {the candy, *the smoke, *the water}. The candy melted.*
fall — requires [+CONCRETE] subject
  *{The book, *the water} fell to the floor.*
shatter — requires [+SOLID] subject or object
  *The hammer shattered {the rock, *the pudding}. The rock shattered.*
tall — requires [+VERTICAL] object
  *{The building, the person, *the road} is tall.*
long — requires [+HORIZONTAL] object
  *{The ribbon, *the tree} is long.*

Types of figurative language. Let's first consider some of the different ways in which selectional restrictions may be violated. When these violations are interpretable, we are dealing with types of figurative language:

1. **Oxymoron (paradox)** refers to expressions which contain an explicit contradiction, such as *delicious torment, living death, sweet sorrow, silent scream, cold comfort, good grief, pleasing pain,* or the Shakespearean "I must be cruel only to be kind".

2. **Tautology** refers to expressions which are "true by definition", offering no new information, such as *A gander is a male goose* or *Word endings come at the end of words.* Most dictionary definitions are tautologies of sorts. Other examples of tautologies include the following:

free gift	Boys will be boys.
new innovation	War is war. Business is business.
past history	He is his father's son.
end result	What will be will be.
main protagonist	It ain't over till it's over.
scrutinize carefully	His moustache is on his upper lip.

The purpose of a tautology such as *free gift* seems to be to emphasize or highlight the feature [+FREE] inherent in the word *gift* by expressing it in a separate word. However, in the case of an expression such as *boys will be boys* we appear not to have a true tautology, but an **apparent tautology**, since the second instance of *boy* is not understood in respect to its core inherent features [+HUMAN], [+MALE], [−ADULT], as is the first instance of *boy*, but in respect to certain behavioral characteristics of boys, for example, loudness, rowdiness, carelessness, and so on. (Which of the above are true tautology and which apparent tautology?)

3.   **Synesthesia** refers to expressions which combine a word from one sensory domain with a word from another sensory domain, such as *cold response, sweet sound, cool reception, sharp rebuke, flat note, quiet color,* or *soothing color.* A common type of synesthesia is the use of a color terms (from the visual domain) in conjunction with an emotional states (*blue/black mood, green with envy, yellow with cowardice, red with anger*). Again, it appears that secondary features of a word are brought to the forefront so that, for example, the soothing or calming features of *quiet,* not its feature of low audition, are emphasized in *quiet color.*

4.   **Synecdoche** refers to expressions which refer to a thing by naming part of it, such as *a new face* or *new blood* (=a new person). A typical kind of synecdoche is the naming of something by naming the material of which it is composed, such as *a cork, an iron,* or *a glass.*

5.   **Metonymy** refers to expressions which denote a thing by naming something associated with it, *the bar* (=the legal profession), *the church* (=religion), *(man of) the cloth* (=clergyman, priest), *the crown* (=the king), *the block* (=one's neighbors), and more recent examples such as *the law* (=the police), *a suit* (=a businessman, and perhaps businesswoman).

6.   **Personification** refers to expressions which attribute human qualities to nonhuman or inanimate objects, such as *The idea grabbed me, The vending machine ate my money.*

7.   **Metaphor** refers to expressions which transfer a word from one conceptual domain to another, such as the following, which all violate the selectional restrictions given in Table 6.7 for the relevant words:

Stock prices are falling.	The bell sang out when struck.
There was a pregnant pause.	He flew into a rage.
The bad news shattered her.	She was away a long time.
That is certainly a tall order.	He eagerly drank up the new ideas.

A typical type of metaphor is the use of body parts to name the parts of other entities:

lip of a glass	mouth of a river
eye of a storm	shoulder of a road

heart of a problem	ribs of a ship
legs of a table	head of a committee
neck of a bottle	guts of a machine

The transference of terms from the physical domain to the mental domain, as in *grasp the point*, *get a joke*, or *wrestle with an idea*, is also very common; in fact, much of our Latinate vocabulary denoting cognitive processes, such as *translate, deduce, abstract, explain, compose, conceive,* and *affirm,* originally denotes physical processes. The use of animal terms to denote human beings held in low esteem is also typical: *a rat, wolf, snake (in the grass), pussycat, tiger,* and so on.

The interpretation of metaphors. In metaphor, selectional restrictions may be violated in one of two ways, depending on whether the noun or the verb must be interpreted metaphorically:

a.   The noun is not selected by the verb:

Ralph is married to a gem.
Juliet is the sun.
Billboards are warts on the landscape.

The verb "to be" selects subjects and objects with the same semantic features; thus, *gem, sun,* and *warts* are incompatible with the verb and are read figuratively.

b.   The verb is not selected by the noun:

My car drinks gasoline.
Craig ate up the compliments.
Kevin is married to his work.
The moonlight sleeps upon the bank.

The selectional restrictions of the subjects of these sentences are incompatible with the features of *drink, eat, be married,* and *sleep,* and thus the verbs are read figuratively. Sometimes, however, there is no apparent violation of selectional restrictions in the immediate context, as in *They have swerved from the path* or *He bit off a larger bite than he could chew.* The larger context will undoubtedly reveal a violation of selectional restrictions.

While the interpretation of metaphors is a difficult matter, it seems that in general we interpret them by selecting only some, but not all of the features of a word, and often not the core but rather the peripheral features. Thus, for *the vending machine ate my money*, it is not the feature of putting food into the mouth for *eat* which is evoked, but the features of devouring, using up, and consuming (without giving anything obvious in return). By substituting these secondary features, we arrive at the literal meaning: *the vending machine used up my money.* However, such a reading overlooks the specifically figurative meaning — that of attributing human qualities to a machine — which motivates the use of the figurative expression. We also seem to transfer the features of eating (of intentional action) onto the inanimate subject to arrive at the metaphorical meaning, thus animating or personifying an inanimate object.

Looking specifically at the novel metaphors of literary works, linguist Tanya Reinhart (1976) has proposed a system for analyzing metaphors which takes into account this two-part process of literary and metaphorical reading. She uses as an example the following metaphor from T. S. Eliot's "The Love Song of J. Alfred Prufrock":

The yellow fog that rubs its back upon the window-panes …

We first assign this metaphor a **focus interpretation**, which yields its "literal" meaning, what the metaphor is about. In this reading, the features of rubbing one's back which are relevant in context are transferred to the movement of fog. Thus, the fog is seen to be moving and touching up against the window panes. Literally, the fog is swirling up against the window panes. But there is also a **vehicle interpretation**, in which the features of cats relevant in context — such as their fuzziness, yellowness, sensuousness, even stealth — are transferred to the fog. This evokes the intended image of the fog as a cat. Notice that the vehicle interpretation is much more open-ended than the focus interpretation.

Reinhart discusses a second metaphor from the same poem:

I have seen the mermaids riding seawards on the waves …

In the focus interpretation, the relevant features of riding — the rising and falling motion — are transferred to the mermaids' movement. Literally, the mermaids are advancing by sitting on the waves. In the vehicle interpretation, the relevant features of horses — their force, their nobility, their need to be tamed, and so on — are transferred to waves. This evokes the image of the waves as horses.

Another approach to the interpretation of metaphors, especially the more conventionalized metaphors of everyday speech, is provided by George Lakoff and Mark Johnson in their book *Metaphors We Live By* (1980). They argue that most language is metaphorical (often "dead metaphors"), and that cognitive processes themselves are metaphorical. Furthermore, they claim that the metaphors in language function quite systematically, forming coherent networks of metaphor. Recognizable principles underlie most common metaphors, e.g.:

ideas are objects (to be sensed)
    building: The argument is shaky.
    food: That notion is half-baked.
    people: He is the father of linguistics.
    plants: The seeds of the idea were planted.
time is money

I've invested a lot of time.	I haven't enough time.
You're running out of time.	You've wasted my time.
He's living on borrowed time.	Can you spare me a moment.
Put aside some time this evening.	That cost me a day's delay.

love is a physical force
    There isn't any electricity between us.
    They gravitated towards each other.

love is a patient
>   Their relationship is {sick, healthy}.

love is madness/illness
>   She drives me crazy.   He is mad about her.
>   Love is blind.

love is magic
>   She cast her spell.   She charmed him.

love is war
>   He made a conquest.   He made an advance.
>   She has to fend off suitors.

time is a line
>   the days ahead/behind   Don't look back/ahead.
>   the weeks to come   That is behind us.
>   We set the meeting back/forward.

We are able to interpret these metaphors, Lakoff and Johnson argue, because they are based on cognitive principles which we recognize.

■   *Self-Testing Exercise:* Do Exercise 6.9.

■ Chapter Summary

Now that you have completed this chapter, you should be able to:

1.   identify semantic relationships such as entailment, inclusion, contradiction, anomaly, ambiguity, connotation/denotation, hyponomy, polysemy, part-whole, and presupposition;
2.   recognize the structural relations of synonymy, hyponymy, antonymy, complementarity, and converseness between words;
3.   analyze nouns using seven inherent features and verbal predicates using four inherent features;
4.   determine whether modal forms are epistemic, deontic, or ambiguous, and give paraphrases of these readings;
5.   recognize and name different kinds of figurative language — oxymoron, paradox, tautology, apparent tautology, metonymy, synecdoche, personification, and synesthesia; and
6.   identify general principles underlying metaphors in the language and give a vehicle and focus interpretation of a novel metaphor.

■ Recommended Additional Reading

Elementary overviews of many of the topics discussed in this chapter may be found in Dillon (1977, Chapter 1) and Finegan (1999, Chapter 6, pp. 182–202). General discussions of lexical semantics include Leech (1974), Palmer (1981), Cruse (1986), and Lyons (1996). Hurford and Heasley (1983) contains a series of practice exercises and answers which cover most of the topics in this chapter. Comprehensive treatments of semantics are Lyons (1977) and Allan (1986). An excellent discussion of English semantics is Kreidler (1998).

More specialized treatments of the topics of this chapter include Kiparsky and Kiparsky (1971) on presupposition; Lyons (1977, Chapter 9) and Cruse (1986) on structural semantics; Katz and Fodor (1963) as well as Lehrer (1974) on componential analysis; Taylor (1995) on prototypes; Lakoff and Johnson (1980) and Reinhart (1976) on metaphor. The modal auxiliaries in English have been treated extensively; for good discussions, see Coates (1983), Perkins (1983), Leech (1987, Chapter 5), Palmer (1990), and Frawley (1992, Chapter 9). Discussions of inherent aspect, or situation types, may be found in Vendler (1967, "Verbs and Times"), Brinton (1988, Chapter 1), Smith (1991, Chapters 2–3), and Frawley (1992, Chapter 4).

■ Notes

1. Another example is the expression *hoi polloi*, from Greek meaning 'the (ordinary) people'. Again, current usage differs, with the directly opposite meaning of 'the upper classes' predominating. Dictionaries tend to list the etymological meaning, while perhaps noting that the expression is used "improperly" with the meaning 'people of distinction'. One dictionary simply lists both meanings without comment. Imagine the difficulties for a learner of the language when faced with such a contradictory definition! These examples were discussed by Justice (1987).

2. Lexical ambiguity differs from structural ambiguity, where no single word in a sentence is ambiguous, but the structure permits more than one interpretation, as in *He found her home* (which may mean either that he found her at home or that he found the home belonging to her).

3. Terminology in this area is quite confusing, so in recent years the term *situation* has come to be used as a neutral term to denote any state, event, process, act, or activity named by a verb.

4. Some scholars consider habits to be states, but because of their being volitional and consisting of multiple events, they are better understand as a separate situation type.

5. The use of *shall* and *will* in dialects which contain both modals is controlled by a complicated set of rules known as the "Wallis Rules" (originally formulated by John Wallis, who wrote a grammar of English — in Latin — in the seventeenth century). In declarative sentences, in the 1st person *shall* makes a prediction (e.g., *I shall be there in an hour*), while *will* expresses the speaker's intention (e.g., *I will marry you*). In the 2nd and 3rd persons, the situation is reversed so that *shall* expresses obligation, while *will* expresses a prediction (e.g., *you shall help your mother* vs. *he will be there in an hour*). In interrogative sentences, the modals operate differently: in the 1st and 3rd persons, *shall* is deontic and *will* is epistemic, while in the 2nd person *shall* is epistemic and *will* is deontic.

6. Oddly, while the range of acceptability for categories like fruit was quite large, Gleitman also found a range for even and odd numbers, which should not logically be rankable.

The Structure of English Sentences

CHAPTER 7

Phrasal Structure and Verb Complementation

■ Chapter Preview

This chapter treats the syntax of simple sentences in English. It begins with a brief description of constituent structure grammar, introducing the formalisms of phrase structure rules. It then defines the notion of a syntactic constituent and discusses the different relations of dependency holding between members of a constituent. The remainder of the chapter is concerned with constructing a phrase structure grammar for English, beginning with the distinction between subject and predicate. The internal structure of the noun phrase, the adjective phrase, the adverb phrase, and the prepositional phrase is then considered. Finally, the complement structures found in the verb phrase are treated, a number of grammatical functions are identified, and a categorization of verb types emerges.

■ Commentary

Introduction to Phrase Structure Grammar

We move now from the study of individual words to the study of the sequences of words which form the structure of sentences. This is the study of syntax. Although there are many ways to approach this study, we will take a primarily "generative" approach. Since it was developed in the early 1960s, the form of generative grammar has undergone many changes. The version of generative grammar presented here is not the most recent one, which has become highly theoretical and quite abstract, but takes those aspects of the various generative models which are most useful for empirical and pedagogical purposes.

We begin with a distinction upon which generative grammar was founded, between two types of rules, **phrase structure rules** and **transformations**. These rules are constitutive rules (determining grammatical structure) rather than regulatory rules (legislating the "good" forms to use, see Chapter 1). They are finite in number, yet they are intended to "generate" any possible sentence of English; this finite set of rules must account for the infinite number of sentences that can be produced and comprehended by speakers of a language. In the "classical" form of generative grammar, the phrase structure rules generate **deep** (or **underlying**) **structure** (**D-structure**) — the abstract level in which all meaning resides — determining the linear order of words in a simple, active, positive, and declarative sentence, the lexical and phrasal categories to which the words belong, and the hierarchical relationships in which the words enter. The transformational rules, which rearrange, add, and delete elements but which do not change meaning, generate the varied sentence types of **surface structure** (**S-structure**) — the concrete realization of D-structure. It is important to distinguish between the two levels for two reasons:

1. similar or identical sequences on the surface may have different meanings, as in a case of structural ambiguity such as *We bought the house on the hill*, where the D-structure will differentiate them; and
2. different sequences on the surface, as in an active sentence and its passive counterpart such as *The dog uncovered the bone* and *The bone was uncovered by the dog*, may have the same meaning, which can be seen in their identical D-structure.

Generative grammar is concerned exclusively with the form of sentences, distinguishing between "grammatical" (or "acceptable") and "meaningful". For example, the sentence (coined by Noam Chomsky) *Colorless green ideas sleep furiously* is grammatical, though not necessarily meaningful, while the sentence *Furiously sleep ideas green colorless* is ungrammatical (unacceptable) since it violates the rules of syntax. In other words, it is believed that syntax and meaning are completely separate: "grammar is autonomous and independent of meaning". (We will look at the semantics of sentences in Chapter 10.)

The predecessor to phrase structure rules was an approach to syntax used by structural linguists called "immediate constituent analysis", which accounted for the linear order of words on the surface and the hierarchical structure of the sentence; it was based on the principle that words enter into relationships with one another within coherent units known as "constituents", the proper subparts of sentences. (An even older form of phrase structure grammar is the sentence "diagramming" of traditional grammar; see the chapter on pedagogy on the CD-ROM.) In a book entitled *Syntactic Structures* published in 1957, however, Noam Chomsky argued that immediate constituent analysis, though not wrong, was insufficient since it dealt only with the surface order. It could not account for the relation between an active and corresponding passive sentence or a declarative and corresponding interrogative sentence, the difference between structurally similar sentences such as *Samantha is eager to please* and *Samantha is easy to please*, and the structural ambiguity of sentences such as the following:

> The missionary is ready to eat.
> Norah's writing occasioned him some surprise.
> Visiting relatives can be tiresome.
> Flying planes can be dangerous.
> The shooting of the hunters occurred at dawn.
> There's one of the Chinese lecturers.
> The tourists objected to the guide that they couldn't hear.
> They took the animal to the small animal hospital.

(Try to determine the ambiguity in each case.) Chomsky added the distinction between deep and surface structure and the concept of the transformation.

In this chapter and the next two chapters, we will study the phrase structure rules and transformational rules needed to account for the syntax of English.

The Form of Phrase Structure Rules

A phrase structure grammar consists of a set of ordered rules known as rewrite rules, which are applied stepwise. A rewrite rule has a single symbol on the left and one or more symbols on the right:

$$A \rightarrow B + C$$
$$C \rightarrow D$$

More than one symbol on the right constitutes a string. The arrow is read as 'is rewritten as', 'has as its constituents', 'consists of', or 'is expanded as'. The plus sign is read as 'followed by', but it is often omitted. The rule may also be depicted in the form of a **tree diagram**:

B and C are called labeled nodes; a node is a point on the tree diagram. Two metaphors are used here. In the family tree metaphor, B and C are daughters of A and they are sisters of each other; less often, A is referred to as the "mother" or "parent" of B and C. (The view taken here is entirely matriarchal!) Also, in the tree metaphor, A is seen as a branching node, as opposed to C, which is a nonbranching node. In the domination metaphor, a distinction is made between immediate domination and domination: a node dominates everything below it (hence, A dominates B, C, and D); a node immediately dominates those nodes for which there are no intervening nodes (hence, A immediately dominates B and C, but not D). Finally, B and C form a constituent: a **constituent** is all and only the nodes dominated by a single node, in this case, A (constituents are treated in the following section).

The phrase structure rules also allow for choices. The optional choices are indicated with parentheses:

$$A \rightarrow (B) \, C$$

This rule reads that A is expanded as optionally B and obligatorily C. In every rewrite rule, at least one element must be obligatory. There may also be mutually exclusive choices of elements in a string; these are indicated with curly braces:

$$A \rightarrow \{B, C\} \text{ or } A \rightarrow \begin{Bmatrix} B \\ C \end{Bmatrix}$$

This rule states that if you choose B, you can't choose C, but you must choose one — either B or C, but not both. Whether the mutually exclusive items are written on one line separated by commas or on separate lines does not matter, as long as they occur within braces.

These two types of choices can be combined:

$$A \rightarrow (\{B, C\})\,D$$

This rule leads to the following possibilities:

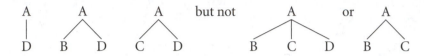

In every phrase structure rule, there must be an initial symbol, a first left-hand symbol, such as A above. Thereafter, every symbol appearing on the left has already been introduced on the right-hand side. The symbols that occur on the right, but never on the left are the terminal symbols; another way of defining them is that they occur at the bottom of a tree diagram. In our brief grammar above, B and D are terminal symbols. They immediately dominate lexical items, or words.

Phrase structure rules account for the linear order of elements in a sentence in deep structure, as well as for the hierarchical arrangement of sentence structure. They can also account for the infinite generating capacity of language. If a symbol introduces itself, it is known as a recursive symbol, as A in the following rule:

$$A \rightarrow B + C + (A)$$

Or if one of the symbols A introduces later introduces it, it is also recursive, as in the following:

$$A \rightarrow B + C$$
$$B \rightarrow (A) + D$$

(Note that if we don't make the second occurrence of A optional, there would be no end to our expansion.) Recursiveness leads to the "nesting" property of language, the embedding of elements within other elements. Thus, recursiveness, along with the options provided by the parentheses and curly braces formalism and with the choices to be made among a large number of lexical items, accounts for the infinite nature of language.

In addition to tree diagrams, there is the "notational variant" known as labeled bracketing. In this system, the terminal symbols are placed on the line and the nodes dominating them are subscripted. Square brackets indicate constituents. Our brief grammar immediately above would permit expansions such as the following with labeled bracketings:

$$_A[_B[D]C] \text{ or } _A[_B[_A[BC]D]C]$$

Note that there must be as many left-facing as right-facing brackets. While you are free to use this notation if you wish, most people find tree diagrams much clearer.

■ *Self-Testing Exercise:* If you are having trouble understanding this formalism, do Exercise 7.1.

Constituents

The study of syntax is the analysis of the constituent parts of a sentence: their form, positioning, and function. Constituents are the proper subparts of sentences. There are different types of constituents classified by the categories which constitute them; these have different functions and internal structures with elements arranged in a specific way. And they may themselves be complex, containing other constituents. The structure of a sentence is hence hierarchical.

In traditional grammar, sentences (or clauses) are composed of words and phrases, which are groups of words (without subject and predicate) forming a coherent group. In generative grammar, sentences are likewise composed of phrases, but **phrases** are defined as sequences of words — or a single word — having syntactic significance: that is, they form a constituent. Since tree diagrams indicate the phrases functioning as constituents, they are also called phrase markers.

Note that not all sequences of words function as constituents. It is the context which determines whether a particular sequence forms a constituent or not. The sequence of words *beautiful flowers* is a constituent in *I received beautiful flowers for my birthday* but not in *Though they are beautiful, flowers cause me to sneeze.* The sequence *the house on the hill* is a constituent in one reading of the ambiguous sentence *I bought the house on the hill,* but not in the other; it is a constituent in the sense 'I bought the house which is on the hill', but not in the sense 'I bought the house while standing on the hill'.

Syntactic constituents are identified by a number of different constituency tests, which are based on the principle that only entire constituents are moveable, replaceable, or deletable. For example, the constituent *beautiful flowers* in the first sentence above can be moved (*It was beautiful flowers that I received for my birthday*), replaced by pro-forms (*I received* <u>them</u> *for my birthday.* <u>What</u> *did you receive for your birthday? Beautiful flowers*), and conjoined (*I received beautiful flowers and chocolates for my birthday*).

■ *Self-Testing Exercise:* For more practice in applying constituency tests, do Exercise 7.2, question 1.

Before we look at the internal structure of specific constituents, we must consider the various relationships possible between the members of a constituent. These are the relations which hold between sisters. There are two possible relationships:

1. one-way dependency, or **modifier-head**: one of the sisters, the modifier (**Mod**), can be omitted, but the other, the head, cannot. The head is the essential center of the constituent and is obligatory; the modifier depends upon the head and cannot occur without it. The modifier expresses some quality or aspect of the head. The relation of adjective to noun is one example of modifier-head. In *blue eyes*, the modifier *blue* modifies the head *eyes*. In *deep blue eyes*, *deep* modifies *blue*, and *deep blue* modifies *eyes*. It is not the case that *blue* modifies *eyes* and *deep* modifies *blue eyes*, because this would suggest the incorrect reading "blue eyes which are deep" rather than the correct "eyes which are deep blue". In *the woman beside me, beside me* is the modifier of the head *woman*. The modifier also follows the head in *he swam quickly*, where *quickly* is the modifier of the head *swam*.

2. mutual dependency, or **governor-complement**: neither sister can be omitted and one sister cannot occur without the other; neither sister is more central. The first "governs" or controls the presence of the second, and the second "completes" the first. The relation between the subject and the predicate of sentence is a special case of mutual dependency (as in *The weather/is improving*). Other relations of governor to complement hold between a preposition and its complement (as in *on/the shore*), an adjective and its complement (as in *dear/to me*), a verb and its complement (as in *be/a fool*), and a verb and its object (as in *swim/a race*):

A Phrase Structure Grammar of English

We will now attempt to construct a phrase structure grammar of English, a set of rules of the form discussed above, that will "generate" any possible sentence of English. In reality, our grammar will be incomplete, partial, possibly wrong, but it will be illustrative. We will not be overly concerned with syntactic argumentation — with the niceties of arguments or the merits of alternative accounts — but you will learn to analyze most of the basic structures and types of English sentences. When trying to write rules to generate all possible but no impossible structures in English, it is reassuring to remember that no one has yet written a complete and flawless generative grammar of English. The grammar we write will always be subject to revision and testing: the phrase structure rules can be changed if they aren't formulated correctly, or a particular structure might be accounted for in a different component of the grammar (by transformations rather than phrase structure rules or the reverse).

Subject and Predicate

In constructing our phrase structure grammar of English, we begin with the initial symbol S = **sentence**. We all have an intuitive idea of what counts as a sentence. It is a tenet of both traditional and generative grammar that S consists of two constituents: the **subject** (**Su**) and the **predicate** (**pred**). The subject is variously defined as the topic, the actor, or that which is spoken about. The predicate is defined as the comment, the action, or that which is said about the subject; it says something true or false about the subject.

Note the different structures serving the function of subject in the following sentences:

The <u>man</u> could open the door.   <u>Truffles</u> are a kind of fungus.
The <u>house on the corner</u> is for sale.   <u>She</u> went to see who was at the door.
The <u>rain and fog</u> dissipated.   <u>There</u> are five cats in the hall.
The <u>film that I saw last night</u> was depressing. <u>It</u> is raining.
<u>It</u> is possible that Alfred will know the answer.

There are two tests for identifying subject:

– subject–auxiliary inversion, or the "question test", e.g., *Could [the man] open the door?*; and
– the "tag question" test, in which the pronoun in the tag agrees with the subject in gender, number, and person, e.g., *[The man] could open the door, couldn't [he]?*

The main element constituting the subject appears to be the noun with its accompanying modifiers; we will see below that this is the phrasal category of the noun phrase. Note that a noun may stand alone as subject (*truffles* above); a pronoun may also stand alone as subject since it replaces an entire noun phrase (*she* above). *It* and *there* are special kinds of "dummy" subjects called *expletives*; structurally they fill the position of subject but are lexically empty. There are two kinds of meaningless *it*, the impersonal *it* in *It is raining*, where there is no personal subject, and the anticipatory *it* in *It is possible ...*, where the real subject *that Alfred will know the answer* occurs at the end of the sentence and *it* fills the normal subject position.

The predicate is generally what remains of a simple sentence after the subject is removed. As you can see in the sentences above, a verb stands alone in the predicate (*dissipated*) in one example and is the main element constituting the predicate in the other examples. The category of the predicate is thus the verb phrase. A test for predicate is to see whether the sequence may be replaced by *do so/do too*:

Ronny <u>swam a race</u> and <u>so did</u> Matty/Matty <u>did too</u>.

We can formalize our recognition of the subject and predicate as key elements in the sentence in the following phrase structure rule:

$$S \rightarrow NP + VP$$

This gives us a formal definition of subject as the NP immediately dominated by S and of predicate as the VP immediately dominated by S. The rule will account for declarative sentences, but not for imperatives, which have no subject (e.g., *Remove the pan from the fire!*) or for interrogatives, which have a different word order (e.g., *Are you hungry?*). We treat these types of sentences later by a different mechanism (see Chapter 8). It is important to keep in mind that subject and predicate are **functions**, not categories; not all noun phrases serve the function of subject, nor do all verb phrases serve the function of predicate.

■ *Self-Testing Exercise:* Do Exercise 7.2, questions 2, 3, and 4.

Now that we have established that two phrasal categories, noun phrase and verb phrase, perform the major functions of the sentence, subject and predicate, we can look more closely at the internal structure of these categories. We will assume that there are **phrasal categories** corresponding to the major parts of speech, or **lexical categories**, namely noun, verb, adjective, adverb, as well as preposition (the parts of speech were treated in Chapter 5). The category of each phrasal category is determined by the lexical category of the head of a modifier-head construction or by the governor of a governor-complement construction; the head or governor is always obligatory. Phrases can be classified as belonging to the same phrasal category if they have the same internal structure and the same distribution in the sentence.

Noun Phrase

The **noun phrase** (**NP**) can be expanded in many different ways (see Table 7.1).[1]

The noun (N) is the only obligatory element in the first seven expansions of NP below and serves as head; the other elements are all optional. The adjective (A) or adjective phrase (AP) precedes the N and the prepositional phrase (PP) follows the N; both serve as modifiers of the noun, expressing a quality of the noun, answering the question "which dogs?".

"Det" here stands for determiners (introduced in Chapter 5), a set of grammatical words that are somewhat like modifiers, but actually serve the function of **specifier** (a one-way dependency), making more precise or definite the phrase that follows. Det includes quite a diverse set of grammatical words: demonstratives (Dem), consisting of *this, these, that,* and *those*; articles (Art), consisting of *a/an,* and *the*; *wh*-words (*Wh-*), consisting of *which, what,* and *whose*; possessives (Poss), consisting of possessive adjectives such as *my, your,* or *his* and possessive nouns such as *John's* or *Sally's*; and quantifiers (Q) such as *some, any, every, each, more,* or *neither*. We can write a rule for Det as follows:

Det → {Dem, Art, *Wh-*, Poss, Q}
Dem → {*this, that, these, those*}
Art → {*a, an, the*}
Wh- → {*which, what, whose*}
Poss → {*my, our, their, John's, the man's* … }
Q → {*some, any, every, each, neither, more* … }

The ellipses (…) indicate that these are not complete listings of the members of the sets Poss and Q. Poss may also include an entire noun phrase, as in *that angry man's (dog)*. Here the -*'s* inflection is being attached to an entire noun phrase *that angry man*. We can account for this phenomenon by the following rule:

$$\text{Poss} \rightarrow \left\{ \begin{array}{l} \text{NP -'s} \\ \textit{my, our, their} \ldots \end{array} \right\}$$

In the last two cases in Table 7.1, the pronoun (Pro)[2] and the proper noun (PN) stand alone and cannot cooccur with the AP, the Det, or the PP:

*The fierce he in the yard
*The fierce Goldy in the yard

Our rule for NP, therefore, must indicate the optionality of Det, AP, and PP and the mutual exclusiveness of Pro and PN with the other elements.

Table 7.1. Expansions of NP

NP →		
	N	*dogs*
	Det N	*the dogs*
	Det A N	*the large dogs*
	Det AP N	*the loudly barking dogs*
	Det N PP	*the dog in the yard*
	Det A N PP	*the ferocious dog behind the fence*
	Det AP N PP	*the wildly yapping dog on the sofa*
	Pro	*He*
	PN	*Goldy*

A preliminary structure for the NP *the large dogs* might be the following:

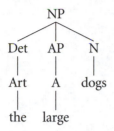

Here, Det is shown as sister of both AP and N. In fact, the determiner really relates to the rest of the noun phrase as a whole, not the AP and N separately. For this reason (and for reasons that will become clearer in Chapter 9), we will introduce the intermediate category of **N-bar** (N̄):

$$\bar{N} \rightarrow (AP)\ N\ (PP)$$

Our rule for NP is then the following:

$$NP \rightarrow \left\{ \begin{array}{l} (Det)\ \bar{N} \\ PN \\ Pro \end{array} \right\}$$

And our revised structure for *the large dogs* would be the following:

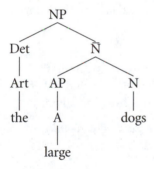

The validity of this "nested" structure is shown by the fact that the word *one*, which is a kind of substitute noun, can replace both *dogs* and *large dogs*:

> I like large dogs rather than small ones. (ones = dogs)
> The ones that I like best are rotweilers. (ones = large dogs)

By our rule for NP, a more complex phrase, *that angry man's fierce dog*, would have the following phrase marker:

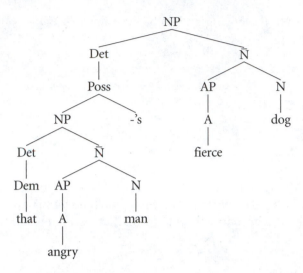

We are ignoring the presence in the NP of what are called predeterminers (*all, both, half*) and postdeterminers, such as some quantifiers (*many, few*) and the numerals, as in the following:

[all] the [many] very happy people

We are also not accounting for structures such as *all of (the dogs)* or *some of (the dogs)*.[3]

To this point in our grammar, the only function for NP that we have examined is that of subject (S→NP VP); numerous other functions will be recognized later in this chapter.

Adjective Phrase

The **adjective phrase** (**AP**) can be expanded in several different ways (see Table 7.2).

The category of degree adverbs (Deg) (introduced in Chapter 5) includes words which are traditionally defined as adverbs, since they modify both adjectives and adverbs:

Deg → {*more, most, less, least, very, quite, rather, least, exceedingly, awfully, absolutely, pretty* … }

However, they occupy a special syntactic position; unlike other adverbs — "general adverbs" — degree words cannot be modified by other adverbs. Degree words express a quality, intensity, or degree of the following adjective or adverb; in other words, they function, much like determiners, as specifiers of the head.

Table 7.2. Expansions of AP

AP →	A	*fierce*
	Deg A	*very fierce*
	Adv A	*fiercely barking*
	Deg Adv A	*very fiercely barking*
	A PP	*dear to me, tired of him, glad about that*

We can see that in all cases above, A is the obligatory element and head of the phrase; all of the other elements are optional. The elements preceding the A are modifiers or specifiers, but the PP following bears a different relationship to the A; it serves as complement. Although we will indicate it as optional in our rules, it is not optional if a complement-taking adverbial structure such as *aware of, afraid of, curious about, obvious to,* or *angry at* is selected. Note that the PP does <u>not</u> express a quality or degree of the A but rather "completes" it; the A serves as governor of the PP.

The initial tree structure for the NP *the very fiercely barking dog* might be the following:

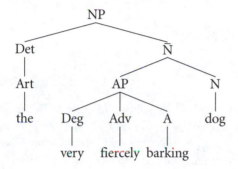

However, this structure incorrectly shows *very, fiercely,* and *barking* as sisters, all modifying *dog*, that is, a 'very dog', a 'fiercely dog', and a 'barking dog'. Obviously, this is not what is being said, but rather "very fiercely" is modifying "barking", and "very" is modifying "fiercely". As we will see in the next section, the sequence [Deg Adv] constitutes an adverb phrase, so the correct structure is the following:

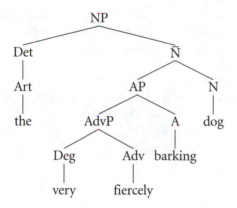

We must also recognize in our rule that Deg can modify A directly, as in *the very fierce dog*:

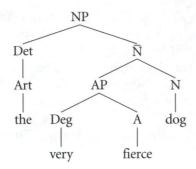

Thus, the following is our formulation of the rule for AP:[4]

$$AP \rightarrow \left(\left\{ \begin{matrix} Deg \\ AdvP \end{matrix} \right\} \right) A \ (PP)$$

Participles which occur before the noun can be treated as simple adjectives. Because of semantic restrictions on gradability, they often cannot be modified by Deg (*very smiling, *rather broken), though they can be modified by AdvP (*very sweetly smiling, rather badly broken*).[5] Participles which occur after the noun (e.g., *the girl smiling sweetly* …) will be treated differently in Chapter 9.

We are also ignoring adjectives that can follow the noun, as in *the people responsible for the budget* or *the members present*, or even the pronoun, as in *someone responsible*

We have seen above that the AP is introduced in our phrase structure rules under Ñ, functioning as modifier of the noun; we now have a structural definition for the "attributive" position of the adjective mentioned in Chapter 5: it is the adjective dominated by Ñ. Later in this chapter we will also introduce AP under the verb phrase, functioning as complement of the verb; this is the "predicative" position. Note that if an adjective has a complement, it can only occur in predicative position in English (*the lake is near to me* but not *a near to me lake*) unless it is compounded (*twenty-year-old house*).

It is quite common for more than one adjective to occur as modifier of the N, as in *the long, blue, silken scarf*. Moreover, each of the adjectives can be modified by Deg or AdvP, as in *the very long, quite pale blue, silken scarf*. To account for this possibility, we must introduce a modification to our rule for NP which permits more than one AP in a single NP. One way to do so would simply be to allow for multiple APs in a "flat" structure as follows:

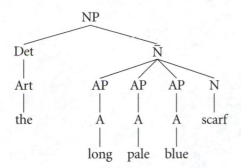

Apart from the fact that we don't actually have a mechanism in our rules for generating more than one AP, a hierarchical, or "nested", structure such as the following better captures the meaning of the phrase:

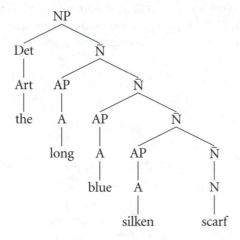

That is, rather than being a 'scarf which is silken and blue and long', it is a 'silken scarf which is blue' and a 'blue silken scarf which is long'. Note that changing the order of the adjectives produces unnatural phrases: ?*blue long silken scarf*, ?*silken blue long scarf*.

In order to account for this structure, our rule for Ñ must be rewritten as follows:

$$\bar{N} \rightarrow \begin{Bmatrix} (AP)\ \bar{N}\ (PP) \\ N \end{Bmatrix}$$

Adverb Phrase

The **adverb phrase** (**AdvP**) can be expanded as in Table 7.3a. We note that Deg is an optional modifier and that the Adv is head; our rule for AdvP is thus formulated as follows:

$$AdvP \rightarrow (Deg)\ Adv$$

So far we have looked at the AdvP only as modifier of the adjective, but we will look at its other functions in the next chapter.

Table 7.3. Expansions of (a) AdvP and (b) PP

(a)	AdvP →	Adv	*quickly*
		Deg Adv	*very quickly*
(b)	PP →	P NP	*on the beach*
		P P NP	*from behind the door*
		P P P NP	*out from under the table*

Prepositional Phrase

The **prepositional phrase** (**PP**) may be expanded as in Table 7.3b. Again, we observe that the P is the head of the PP, but unlike the other categories we have examined, the P cannot stand alone in the PP. It must be followed by an NP, what is traditionally known as an **object of the preposition** (**OP**).

It also appears that P's can have specifiers as well as objects. Like determiners or degree adverbs, these forms specify or limit the prepositional phrase. They include the words *right*, *straight*, and *slap* (in some dialects) and phrases measuring time and space, such as *three seconds* or *one mile*:

> right after lunch
> straight along this route
> two feet behind me
> two minutes before my arrival

For lack of a simpler name, we will term these **prepositional specifiers** (**PSpec**):

> PSpec → {*right, straight, slap, one mile, three seconds* ... }

Finally, we must also account for the sequences P P NP and P P P NP. Writing the rule as PP → P (P) (P) NP would incorrectly show the NP as object of all the P's, when it is actually complement of only the last P. Thus, we write our rule as follows:[6]

$$PP \rightarrow (PSpec)\ P \begin{Bmatrix} NP \\ PP \end{Bmatrix}$$

So far, we have seen PP's functioning as modifier of the N and complement of the A; further functions will be identified later in this chapter and in the next chapter.

The rule for PP is a recursive rule since PP (on the left) introduces a PP (on the right). And since NP introduces PP which introduces NP, NP is also a recursive symbol. The latter recursion leads to structures such as the following:

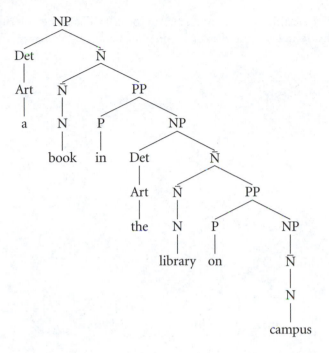

Here, "in the library" modifies "book" and "on campus" modifies "the library". Note that *a cat on the mat in the hallway* would have the structure given above, but the superficially similar *a cat on the mat with long whiskers* would not since "with long whiskers" modifes "the cat", not "the mat". A possible analysis of the phrase with a "flat" structure would give the following:

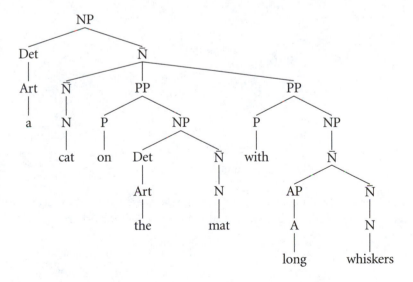

But the revision of our rule which permits more than one AP in the NP will also permit more that one PP, so the correct phrase marker for *the cat on the mat with long whiskers* is the following:

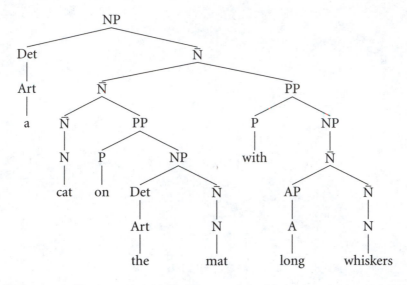

A further complication arises if there is a modifier both preceding and following the noun, as in *heavy rain in the night*. Should this be analyzed as a "flat" structure?

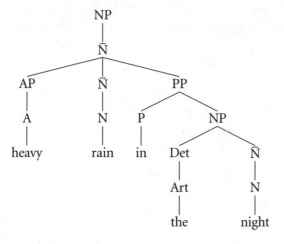

While this structure is probably not correct, it will suit our purposes, since there seems to be no reason to prefer one of the following hierarchical structures over the other:

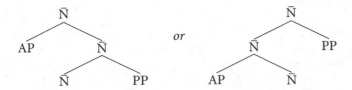

The phrase marker on the left would be 'night-rain which is heavy' and the phrase marker on the right would be 'heavy rain which is in the night'.

Conjunction

Our phrase structure rules do not yet account for the **conjunction** of elements (with *and, but, or*). It is possible to conjoin two or more <u>like</u> constituents, either phrasal or lexical categories (see Table 7.4).

The combined category will be the same as the individual categories conjoined. Thus, the supercategory of two conjoined Ps is P, while the supercategory of two conjoined APs is AP. The conjunction of lexical categories (Ps) *[in and out] the window*, is shown below:

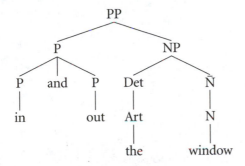

The conjunction of phrasal categories (APs) is found in *a [rather expensive and ugly] car*:

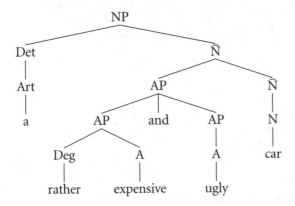

Note that we interpret *ugly* as AP rather that just A in order to have the conjunction of two like constituents. Generally, it is not possible to conjoin unlike categories, such as AP + NP,

Table 7.4. Conjunction

PP + PP	*on the table and under the chair*
P + P	*over or under the covers*
NP + NP	*the tortoise and the hare*
Ñ + Ñ	*cold coffee and warm beer*
N + N	*cats and dogs*
AP + AP	*very slow and quite tedious*
A + A	*long and boring*
AdvP + AdvP	*very cautiously but quite happily*
Adv + Adv	*quietly and smoothly*

very polite and the quick response, unless the unlike categories are functioning the same way; in *The instructor will be away [on Tuesday] and [next week],* for example, the PP *on Tuesday* and the NP *next week* are both functioning adverbially.

A phrase such as *a very rich and fattening dessert* is ambiguous; either *very* modifies *rich* only or it modifies both *rich* and *fattening*:

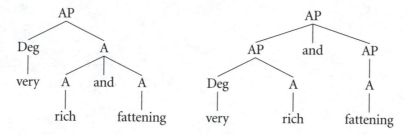

A phrase such as *soup or salad and french fries* is also ambiguous, as shown below:

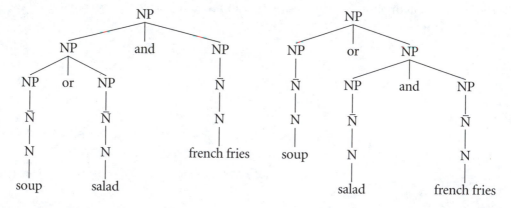

When AP's are conjoined, and the A's are of the same semantic type, it is common to omit the conjunction, as in *a happy and carefree child* > *a happy, carefree child* or *a delicious and bracing burgundy* > *a delicious, bracing burgundy.* Note that unlike the nested AP structures discussed above (i.e., *a long blue silken scarf*), it is entirely natural in these cases to change the order of above (i.e., *a long blue silken scarf*), it is entirely natural in these cases to change the order of the adjectives, i.e., *a carefree, happy child*, or *a bracing, delicious burgundy*.

Nominal compounding (which we treated in Chapter 4 as a matter of word formation), such as *french fries* and *ice cream* could also be represented in our syntactic trees as a kind of conjunction without an explicit conjunction, but we will not do so here:

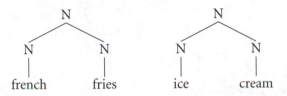

■ Self-Testing Exercise: Do Exercise 7.3.

Verb Phrase

In order to study the structure of the VP, we will introduce the intermediate category of V_{gp} = **verb group** consisting of the lexical verb with or without a particle. More importantly, we will for now ignore the specifiers of the verb, the auxiliaries, which we will deal with in Chapter 8. For our present purposes, then, the V_{gp} may be thought of as the verb in its base form.

Verb complementation. What we will consider now is the type(s) of complements that may follow a verb. They determine the (strict) **subcategorization** of the verb (as we noted briefly in Chapter 5). The particular structure or structures in which a verb can occur can be represented formally in a subcategorization frame:

    _____ NP   _____ AP   _____ PP

The verb occurs in the slot indicated by the line, with the possible complement(s) specified afterwards. Note that only <u>obligatory</u> complements (NPs, APs, and PPs) figure in the subcategorization of a verb, not the optional PP's which often follow a verb or verb phrase. Distinguishing obligatory from optional PP's can often be very difficult. Generally, it is the case that the obligatory complements cannot be omitted without affecting the grammaticality or meaning of the sentence, while the optional PP's, which are functioning as adverbials, can be omitted or can be moved to the beginning of the sentence. (This topic will be treated in detail in Chapter 8.)

Based on the type of complement a verb takes, a number of subcategories of verbs can be identified:

1. **Transitive** (or **monotransitive**), abbreviated [trans], e.g., *hit, eat, kill,* or *break*, with the following subcategorization frame:

    _____ NP   Reginald broke the vase.

The complement of the verb here is a noun phrase functioning as a **direct object (dO)**. While traditionally a direct object is defined as the person or thing affected by the action of the verb, we are now able to give it a formal definition: it is the NP immediately dominated by the VP, or it is the NP which is sister of the V_{gp}. A direct object can also be a subordinate clause:

     ____ S   Vivian wrote that she was unhappy.

However, since we will be considering subordinate clauses in Chapter 9, I will omit them from our current discussion.

2. **Intransitive**, e.g., *arrive, cry, laugh,* or *swim,* labeled with the feature [intrans] and with the following subcategorization frame:

     ____ #   The package has arrived.
                 After the argument, she cried.

With an intransitive verb, no complement is required or allowed. Note, however, that intransitive verbs are frequently followed by optional adverbs (e.g., *The package arrived a few minutes ago, The baby cried loudly for five minutes this morning*); these do not affect the verb's subcategorization.

3. **Ditransitive**, abbreviated [ditrans], e.g., *give, send, tell, lend, buy, offer,* or *show,* with the following subcategorization frames:

     ____ $NP_1\ NP_2$ Henk sent Olga roses.

or

     ____ $NP_2\ _{PP}[\textit{to/for}\ NP_1]$ Henk sent roses to Olga.

We can write this subcategorization frame more economically as follows:

     ____ NP {NP, $_{PP}[\textit{to/for}\ NP]$}

Note that the PP here is not an optional modifier, but an obligatory complement. NP_1 serves the function of **indirect object** (**iO**), while NP_2 serves the function of direct object. An indirect object is the goal or benefactive of the action; it always denotes something which is animate or is conceived of as animate. It is important to distinguish the indirect object *to* marker (a) from the one meaning 'place to which' (b), and the indirect object *for* marker (c) from the one meaning 'in the stead of', 'in the place of' (d):

a.   Jerry sent a letter to Elaine/the university.
b.   Jerry sent a letter to Toronto.
c.   Susan made a dress for her friend.
d.   Annabel answered the phone for Marianne.

The test to distinguish indirect objects from the other cases is known as the **indirect object movement** transformation: if the noun following *to* or *for* is an indirect object, it should be able to move to a position before the direct object (V NP_2 *to/for* NP_1 $\Rightarrow$ V $NP_1\ NP_2$):[7]

a. ⇒   *Jerry sent Elaine/the university a letter.*
b. ⇒   **Jerry sent Toronto a letter.*
c. ⇒   *Susan made her friend a dress.*
d. ⇒   **Annabel answered Marianne the phone.*

(⇒ means 'is transformed into'.) The test works no matter how lengthy either of the NP's is, that is, how many modifiers it has preceding or following it:

Calvin built a cabin in the woods for his six children. ⇒
Calvin built his six children a cabin in the woods.

Michael sent a paper he had written to his friend from school. ⇒
Michael sent his friend from school a paper he had written.

There are, however, certain restrictions with pronouns. If both the direct and indirect object are pronouns (a), or if the direct object alone is a pronoun (b), then indirect object movement cannot normally occur, but if the indirect object alone is a pronoun (c), then it can occur:

a.   I gave it to her.   ⇒   *I gave her it.[8]
b.   I gave it to Ingrid.   ⇒   *I gave Ingrid it.
c.   I gave the book to her.   ⇒   I gave her the book.

(This restriction results from the weakly stressed nature of pronouns.)

4. **Copulative** (or **copula**), abbreviated [cop], e.g., *become, seem, appear, feel, be, grow,* or *look,* and with the following subcategorization frame:

_____ NP   Priya is a chemist.
_____ AP   Priya seems tired.
_____ PP   Priya is in a good mood.

Or, more concisely:

_____ {NP, AP, PP}

The complement here serves the function of **subject complement** (**sC**). (You may know this function by one of its other names: *predicative nominative, subject(ive) predicative,* and so on.) It is important to distinguish an NP serving as direct object from an NP serving as subject complement. A subject complement characterizes the subject: it identifies, locates, or describes the subject, as in *Bill is the leader, Bill is in the living room,* and *Bill is irritable.* It expresses either a current state or a resulting state of the subject, as in *Bill is rich* and *Bill became rich.* A test distinguishing dO from sC is that the dO can become the subject of a passive sentence, while the sC cannot:

Martina became a lawyer. ⇒ *A lawyer was become by Martina.
Martina saw a lawyer.   ⇒ A lawyer was seen by Martina.

5. **Complex Transitive**, abbreviated [complex trans], with the following subcategorization frame:

____ NP NP	We consider him a fool.
____ NP AP	She made him unhappy.
____ NP PP	They regard that as the best design.

Or more concisely:

____ NP {NP, AP, PP}

There are two subclasses of verbs in this category:

a. nonlocative: *find, consider, make, think, elect, call, hold, regard (as), take (for), devote (to);* and
b. locative: *hang, put, place, lay, set, touch, shoot, pierce.*

The complex transitive verb combines the transitive and the copulative structures. The first NP is a direct object; the second element is an **object complement** (oC) (also known as an *object(ive) predicative*). The object complement characterizes the object in the same way as the subject complement characterizes the subject: it identifies, describes, or locates the object (as in *We chose Bill as group leader, We consider him a fool, She laid the baby in the crib*), expressing either its current state or resulting state (as in *They found him in the kitchen, She made him angry*). Note that "be" or some other copula verb can often be inserted between the direct object and the object complement (e.g., *I consider him to be a fool, We chose Bill to be group leader, They found him to be in the kitchen*). Like the subject complement, too, the object complement cannot usually become the subject of a passive sentence (though the direct object can):

We consider him a fool ⇒ *A fool is considered him (by us).
He is considered a fool (by us).

6. **Prepositional**, abbreviated [prep], with the following subcategorization frame:

____ PP	He agreed to the terms.
	She stood on the ladder.

There are two subclasses of verbs in this category:

a. locative: *stand, lie, lean, hang, sit, flow;* and
b. nonlocative: *agree (to), work (for), depend (on), look (into), refer (to), insist (on), respond (to).*

In the latter case, the verb and preposition seem to form a close syntactic and semantic unit; the particular preposition occurring with a verb is idiosyncratic and must be learned. The PP here serves as a complement (rather than as modifier, which is its function in the NP). To avoid confusion with the OP, we will call this a **prepositional complement** (pC).

7. **Diprepositional**, abbreviated [diprep], e.g., *confer, talk, consult,* with the following subcategorization frame:

_____ PP PP   She argued with him about money.

Thus, for the category VP, we have the possible expansions shown in Table 7.5.

We need to write a single rule for the verb phrase. There are a number of ways to do so; we will do it in the following way:

$$\text{VP} \rightarrow \text{V}_{\text{gp}} \left\{ \begin{array}{l} \left(\text{NP} \left(\left\{ \begin{array}{l} \text{NP} \\ \text{PP} \\ \text{AP} \end{array} \right\} \right) \right) \\ \text{AP} \\ \text{PP} \quad (\text{PP}) \end{array} \right\}$$

We must make sure that our rule generates all possible structures and does not generate any impossible structures. You should see if it might be possible to write the rule differently.

Latent objects. One of the difficulties for verb subcategorization in English is that it is sometimes possible to omit the direct object when it is understood from context, as in the case of *He ate* being understood as 'He ate dinner' in a certain context. In such cases, the object can be understood as being latent. How can you tell, then, when the verb is really transitive with a latent object, and when it is really intransitive? A few tests can be applied to the verbs in question. When the verb has a remarkably different meaning without an object than with an object, then we can assume that it is truly intransitive, not transitive with a latent object:

–   The workers struck last month. [intrans]
     The worker struck the match. [trans]
–   He played outside all afternoon. [intrans]
     He played the piano all afternoon. [trans]

If the object is irrelevant, then the verb is likewise intransitive since the object is not necessary at all:

Groucho smokes. [intrans]
I was reading all the time. [intrans]
Wyatt left yesterday. [intrans]

In the first sentence, it is not important what Groucho smokes; you are simply saying that 'Groucho is a smoker'. In the second sentence, what you are reading is immaterial, as is where Wyatt departed from (home, town, country) in the third sentence.

If the object is completely predictable, however, then the object is latent because in those cases the object is understood from context:

We held an election for president.		We elected Carolyn (president).
Machiko plays the violin.		She plays (the violin) very well.
Hannah bathed/woke up.	cf.	Hannah bathed/woke up herself.
		Hannah bathed/woke up the baby.

Table 7.5. Expansions of VP

VP →	V NP	*open a package*
	V NP NP	*write a friend a letter*
	V NP PP	*give an excuse to the teacher*
	V AP	*feel lonely*
	V NP AP	*make the dog angry*
	V PP	*jump into the pool*
	V PP PP	*talk about the problem with a friend*

President is a required element with the complex transitive verb *elected*, and *the violin* is a required element with the transitive verb *play*. The transitive verbs *bathe* and *wake up* must have an object, either the latent reflexive object (i.e., *herself*) or an explicit object (*the baby*).

Taking the verb *write* as an example, we might question whether it is intransitive, monotransitive, or ditransitive on the basis of the following sentences:

a. Margaret writes.
b. Margaret wrote yesterday.
c. Margaret wrote to George yesterday.
d. Margaret wrote a letter yesterday.
e. Margaret wrote a novel.

There is no missing object in (a) because an object is irrelevant; the sentence means 'Margaret is a writer'. The object in (b) and in (c) is latent because an object must be understood from context (e.g., *a poem, a letter, a memo*). In (d), the indirect object is latent because it must be understood from context (e.g., *to her mother, to Nadine*). Sentence (e), on the other hand, has no latent indirect object, because novels, unlike letters, are not written to anyone. Therefore, we need to assign *write* to all three verb subcategories, intransitive (a), transitive (b, e), and ditransitive (c, d).

In the following case, while *start* does not appear to have radically different meanings in the two uses, it is impossible to recover from the context who or what started the car in the second case:

Phyllis started the car.
The car started.

Thus, *start* is analyzed as both transitive and intransitive.

■ *Self-Testing Exercise: Do Exercise 7.4.*

Review of Phrase Structure Rules

The following are the phrase structure rules for English which we have established so far:

S → NP VP
NP → {(Det) N̄, PN, Pro}
N̄ → {(AP) N̄ (PP), N}
Det → {Art, Dem, Poss, Q, *Wh-*}
Dem → {*this, that, these, those*}
Art → {*a, an, the*}
Wh- → {*which, what, whose*}
Poss → {NP-'s, *my, our, their* ... }
Q → {*some, any, every, each, neither, more* ... }
AP → ({Deg, AdvP}) A (PP)
AdvP → (Deg) Adv
PP → (PSpec) P {NP, PP}
VP → V$_{gp}$ ({NP ({NP, PP, AP}), AP, PP (PP)})

We have identified the following grammatical functions:

Subject (Su)	Object of the Preposition (OP)
Direct Object (dO)	Prepositional Complement (pC)
Indirect Object (iO)	Modifier (Mod)
Subject Complement (sC)	Specifier (Spec)
Object Complement (oC)	Complement of Adjective (Comp of A)

The phrasal categories we have studied can serve the following functions:

- NP: Subject, Direct Object, Indirect Object, Subject Complement, Object Complement, Object of Preposition;
- AP: Modifier of Noun, Subject Complement, Object Complement;
- PP: Modifier of Noun, Subject Complement, Object Complement, Indirect Object, Prepositional Complement of Verb, of Preposition, or of Adjective; and
- AdvP: Modifier of Adjective.

■ *Self-Testing Exercises:* Do Exercise 7.5 as a review of the material covered in this chapter.

■ Chapter Summary

Now that you have completed this chapter, you should be able to:

1.   manipulate the formalisms of phrase structure rules;
2.   determine the type of dependency relation (subject–predicate, modifier-head, governor-complement) between elements within a constituent;
3.   analyze the structure of noun, adjective, adverb, and prepositional phrases in English using tree diagrams and identify their grammatical functions; and
4.   determine the subcategory of verbs in English on the basis of their complement structures.

■ Recommended Additional Reading

Treatments of English syntax which are similar in depth and level of formality to the treatment in this chapter include Wekker and Haegeman (1985, Chapters 2–3), Burton-Roberts (1997, Chapters 1–4, and 7), Thomas (1993, Chapters 1–3, and 5, pp. 80–95), Brown and Miller (1991, Chapters 1–6, 8), Kaplan (1995, Chapter 6, pp. 207–250, and Chapter 7) and Hopper (1999, Chapters 3–5 and 8–9). Less formal treatments include Huddleston (1984), Delahunty and Garvey (1994, Chapters 7–8), and Wardhaugh (1995, Chapters 2–4). You should be aware that the order in which the material is presented may differ quite markedly from the order followed here and that the formal system used may differ from the form of the grammatical rules introduced in this text.

More advanced textbook treatments of generative syntax (with a focus, but not an exclusive focus on English) include van Riemsdijk and Williams (1986), Radford (1988), Borsley (1995), Napoli (1993), Haegeman (1994), and Ouhalla (1999). Baker (1995) treats English syntax exclusively, as does Haegeman and Guéron (1999). References to the primary works in this field can be found in the texts cited. Sells (1985, Chapter 2) and Horrocks (1987, Chapter 2) present concise overviews of generative syntax in comparison to a number of competing approaches to syntax.

■ Notes

1. For the present, we are simplifying the structure of the NP by not considering the presence of subordinate clauses in the NP, that is:

    NP → Det N S   *the fact that I bought a dog*
                   the dog which I bought
          S   *that I own a dog*

    In this chapter, we will be simplifying the structure of the AP and the PP in a similar way by ignoring the possibility of subordinate clauses as complements to A and as objects of P:

    AP → A S   *worried that he might bite*
    PP → P S   *about what it takes*

    These phenomena will be treated in Chapter 9.

2. Certain pronouns are identical in form to determiners and take the place of the entire NP (e.g., *That is a fierce dog*); however, the determiner form sometimes differs slightly from the pronominal form, as in *My dog is gentle* vs. *Mine is a gentle dog*.

3. We are adopting here a formalism from a version of generative grammar called "X-bar theory". In this theory, all phrasal categories are seen as having the same structure, namely:

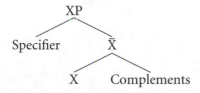

By a process of "adjunction", X̄'s can be stacked or nested, giving us the structure we see in the NP:

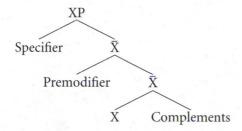

4. Although a nested structure with an intermediate category Ā — dominating A and PP — is warranted here, we will ignore it because it is not important for our purposes.

5. Just as one cannot say *very married* (except humorously), but one can say *very happily married*.

6. This rule is actually too powerful, since it would allow PSpecs to precede all P's, whereas they appear to be possible only before the first P: cf. *right out from under the table* but not **out right from under the table* or *?out from right under the table*. Again, a "nested" structure in which an intermediate category P̄ dominates P and its complements would solve this problem:

$$PP \rightarrow (PSpec) \ \bar{P}$$
$$\bar{P} \rightarrow P \ \begin{Bmatrix} NP \\ PP \end{Bmatrix}$$

However, since PSpecs are comparatively rare, we will not worry about this difficulty.

7. We are assuming that the order V NP$_2$ *to/for* NP$_1$ is the order in D-structure and that V NP$_1$ NP$_2$ is the derived order (as S-structure), though this assumption can be debated.

8. British English allows *I gave it her*, and colloquially one might find both of the asterisked sentences in North American English.

CHAPTER 8

Adverbials, Auxiliaries, and Sentence Types

■ Chapter Preview

This chapter continues discussion of the syntax of simple sentences in English. Three types of adverbial modification, which must be distinguished from verbal complements, are discussed first. The chapter then turns to the form of the verb specifiers — the auxiliary phrase — consisting of tense, mood, aspect, and voice. The structure of the passive sentence and the interaction of passive with verb subcategories are then treated. The chapter continues with a discussion of the structure of *yes/no* questions and negatives in English, followed by a consideration of tag questions and imperative sentences. A review of phrase structure rules, grammatical functions, and verb types ends the chapter.

■ Commentary

Adverbials

In the previous chapter, we discussed the obligatory complements within the verb phrase. We turn now to optional modifiers, both at the level of the verb phrase and at the level of the sentence. These are traditionally called *adverbs*. Three different types of adverbial functions may be distinguished:

1. adjunct adverbial,
2. disjunct adverbial, and
3. conjunct adverbial.

We will see that the adverbial function may be filled by a number of different categories: AdvP, PP, NP, and S (the last will be treated in Chapter 9).

Adjunct Adverbials

Adjunct adverbials (**aA**) generally answer one of the following questions:

–	How? (manner)	e.g., *enthusiastically, with enthusiasm*
–	When? (time)	e.g., *yesterday, on Tuesday, after I left*
–	Where? (place)	e.g., *there, in the kitchen, where I was*

- Why? (reason)   e.g., *for no reason, since I am poor*
- How many times?   e.g., *twice*
- How long?   e.g., *for two years*
- How often?   e.g., *monthly*

The four most common types of adjunct adverbials are manner, time, place, and reason. The examples given above show AdvPs, PPs, and Ss functioning as adverbials. NP's can also occasionally function as adverbials; these fall into a number of different types:

directional adverbs: *home, upstairs, outside*
measure phrases: *ten miles, two hours*
time expressions: *today, this morning, last year, Tuesday*

Adverbials are optional modifiers. Traditionally they are said to be modifying the verb, but they are better understood as modifying the verb together with its complements, which we can call **V-bar** ($\bar{V}$). Thus, we will introduce adverbials into our phrase structure grammar as optional sisters of the $\bar{V}$ in the following way (ignoring S for the present):

$$VP \rightarrow \bar{V} \left(\left\{ \begin{array}{l} PP \\ AdvP \\ NP \end{array} \right\} \right)$$

Our rule for $\bar{V}$ is then the following:

$$\bar{V} \rightarrow V_{gp} (\{NP (\{NP, AP, PP\}), AP, PP (PP)\})$$

It is common for more than one type of adverbial to appear in a sentence, as in *Jonathan ran a race for fun last weekend*, where there is an adverbial of reason and an adverbial of time. If there is more than one adverbial present, there will have to be more than one $\bar{V}$ node; thus we need to revise our rule for $\bar{V}$ as follows:

$$\bar{V} \rightarrow \left\{ \begin{array}{l} V_{gp} (\{NP (\{NP, AP, PP\}), AP, PP (PP)\}) \\ \bar{V} (\{PP, AdvP, NP\}) \end{array} \right\}$$

The sentence above would have the following tree diagram. (Note that in this tree we are using a shorthand "triangle notation" where we do not indicate the internal structure of minor phrasal categories or those that are irrelevant for our purposes. I will call these "generalized" trees.)

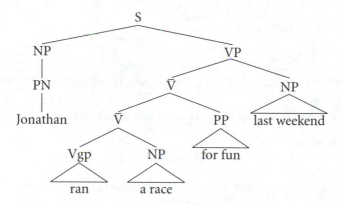

(In drawing your tree diagram, it is best in these cases to work backwards from the end of the sentence.) As many as four adverbials may occur, although the order does not seem to be entirely fixed, e.g., *He left [for town] [quickly] [a few minutes ago] [for help].*

In reality, adverbials are very free in their placement, appearing in different positions in the sentence, not just sentence final:

- sentence initial — *[Yesterday], I ran a marathon.*
- sentence final — *I ran a marathon [yesterday].*
- preverbal — *I [always] run well in the heat.*
- postverbal — *I handed the baton [quickly] to the next runner.*
- within the verb group — *I have [never] won a race.*

The various types of adverbials behave differently, however; while all can occur sentence finally, time adverbials are acceptable sentence initially and sometimes preverbally, place adverbials are clumsy sentence initially, and manner adverbials frequently occur preverbally but are less good sentence initially. One position which is impossible for adverbials is between the verb and the direct object. We will ignore the different positions of the adverbial, assuming them to be generated in D-structure sentence in sentence-final position and moved to their other positions later in derived structure.

Disjunct Adverbials

The second type of adverbial is the **disjunct adverbial** (dA). Traditionally, these are known as *sentence adverbs*. They denote the speaker's attitude toward or judgment of the proposition, expressing, for example, the speaker's degree of truthfulness or his manner of speaking. As in the case of adjunct adverbials, AdvPs or PPs (or Ss) may serve as disjunct adverbials:

- AdvP: *seriously, truthfully, frankly, certainly, hopefully, sadly, personally, confidentially, literally, foolishly, stupidly, oddly*
- PP: *in all frankness, to my surprise, in broad terms, to my regret*

Unlike adjunct adverbials, disjunct adverbials modify the entire S, not just the VP, so they are generated by the phrase structure rules as the optional sister of S, as follows:

$$S \to S \quad \left(\left\{ \begin{array}{l} AdvP \\ PP \\ NP \end{array} \right\} \right)$$

Note that disjunct adverbials appear most naturally at the beginning of the sentence, in which case our rule would be $S \to (\{AdvP, PP\})\, S$.

Sometimes, the same lexical item can be both an adjunct and a disjunct:

Bonnie spoke <u>seriously</u> about her problems. (aA)
<u>Seriously</u>, that's the most shocking news I've heard. (dA)

In the first sentence, *seriously* means 'in a serious manner', while in the second it means 'I am being serious when I say'.

Conjunct Adverbials

The third type of adverbial is the **conjunct adverbial** (**cA**). Traditionally, these are known as *conjunctive adverbs*. They express textual relations, serving to link clauses; they have no function in their own clause. They may be AdvP's or PP's:

– AdvP: *moreover, however, nonetheless, nevertheless, furthermore, next, finally, consequently, therefore, thus, instead, indeed, besides, hence*
– PP: *in addition, in conclusion, on the contrary, on one/the other hand, in other words, for example, as a result, in the second place*

Like disjunct adverbials, they are sisters of S; the rule given in the preceding section thus generates conjunct as well as disjunct adverbials.

■   Self-Testing Exercise: Do Exercise 8.1.

Functions of Postverbal Prepositional Phrases

PP's which follow the verb — postverbal PP's — can serve a number of different purposes. The **functions of postverbal PP's** include prepositional complement, adjunct adverbial, and postmodifier of the noun, but these can often be difficult to distinguish.

The first difficulty arises with the sequence V PP, which can represent the following structures:

$\bar{V}\ [V_{cop}\ PP]$	Farris is in the living room.	(sC)
$\bar{V}\ [V_{prep}\ PP]$	Wilma changed into work clothes.	(pC)
$_{VP}[\bar{V}\ [V_{intrans}]\ PP]$	Vancouver has changed in the last two years.	(aA)

That is, the PP can be either an obligatory complement of the verb (as in the first two cases) or an optional modifier of the $\bar{V}$, an adjunct adverbial (as in the third case).

If the PP has at least some of the following qualities, then it is likely to be an adjunct adverbial:

1. it is optional and hence can be omitted; the sentence is grammatical without it;
2. it can usually (but not always) be moved to the beginning of the sentence;
3. it expresses time, place, manner, or reason, answering the questions "when?", "where?", "how?", or "why?", not "what?" or "whom?" (but note that many prepositional complements answer these questions as well);
4. it can occur in a separate predication, as in *It happened on Tuesday, at school, for no good reason, quickly*;
5. it cannot occur with copulative verbs;
6. it can occur in a *do so/too* structure, as in *Phyllis reacted angrily and Isabel did so with resignation* (here, *do so* substitutes for the VP);
7. it may be replaced by a lexical adverb; and
8. it does not figure in the subcategorization of the verb.

No PP will meet all of the tests for adjunct adverbials, but it will meet at least some of them. Look at the following three sentences:

They agreed on the terms.
They agreed in an instant.
They agreed on the boat.

The PP in the first sentence is a complement of a prepositional verb, while the PP in the second sentence is an adjunct adverbial. The third sentence is structurally ambiguous since the PP can serve either of these functions. The two meanings are that 'They decided while they were on the boat' (the aA reading) or 'They decided (to buy) the boat' (the pC reading). The following (generalized) tree diagrams represent the two structures:

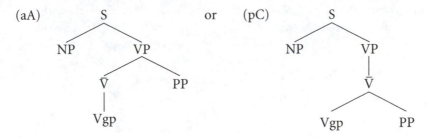

A second difficulty arises with the sequence V NP PP. This may represent a complex transitive verb structure, a transitive verb structure followed by an adjunct adverbial, or a transitive verb structure whose direct object is postmodified by a prepositional phrase, as in the following sentences:

$_{\bar{V}}[V_{gp}\ NP\ PP]$ Isaac played the violin with a new bow.   (pC)

$_{VP}[_{\bar{V}}[V_{gp}\ NP]\ PP]$ Isaac played the violin with great skill.   (aA)

$_{\bar{V}}[V_{gpNP}[\bar{N}\ PP]]$ Isaac played the violin with the loose bridge.   (Mod of N)

These different possibilities may yield ambiguous sentences such as *I beat the dog with the stick*, meaning either that 'I beat the dog using a stick' (the pC reading) or 'I beat the dog who had a stick' (the modifier reading), represented by the following generalized trees:

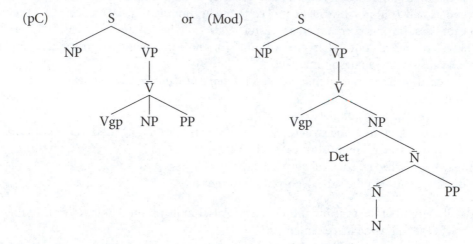

A third difficulty arises with the sequence V PP PP, where the second PP may be an adjunct adverbial, the modifier of the preceding noun, or the second prepositional complement in a diprepositional verb structure, as in the following sentences:

Monica stepped on a bee on Tuesday.	(aA)
Monica stepped on a bee with a large stinger.	(Mod of N)
Monica consulted with her doctor about the bee sting.	(pC)

Again, structural ambiguities arise, as in the case of the sentence *I ran into the girls with the flowers*. Here, "with the flowers" may be either an prepositional complement ('I ran into the girls with (using) the flowers') or a modifier of the noun "girls" ('I ran into the girls who had the flowers'), as shown below:

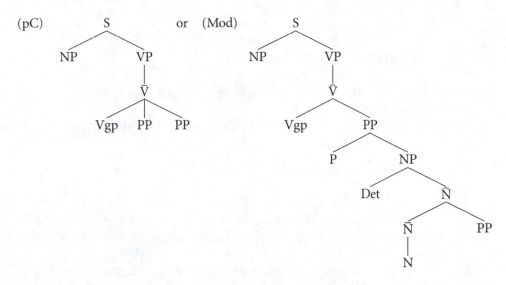

The last difficulty arises with **phrasal verbs** (introduced in Chapter 4), which must be distinguished from prepositional verbs. Transitive phrasal verbs consist of a verb, a direct object, and a particle, which is movable, occurring either before or after the object (unlike prepositions which can occur only before their objects). Compare the following phrasal verbs with the corresponding prepositional verbs:

- phrasal verb: *He slipped on the jacket/slipped the jacket on.*
  prepositional verb: *He slipped on a banana peel. *He slipped a banana peel on.*
- phrasal verb: *The terrorists blew up the power station/blew the power station up.*
  prepositional verb: *The ashes blew up the chimney/*blew the chimney up.*
- phrasal verb: *The children ate up the strawberries/ate the strawberries up.*
  prepositional verb: *The neighbors ate up the street/*ate the street up.*
- phrasal verb: *The official looked over the documents/looked the documents over.*
  prepositional verb: *The cat climbed over the fence/*climbed the fence over.*

The two types of verbs have the following underlying structures:

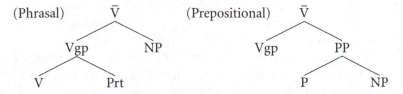

As you can see, the phrasal verb is really a monotransitive verb, with the particle associated with the verb. The particle is generated next to the verb. When it moves, it becomes the sister of the NP, as follows:

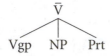

When the NP is a pronoun, this movement is obligatory. That is, one can say *He looked it up*, but not **He looked up it.*

There are a number of syntactic criteria you can use for distinguishing phrasal verbs from prepositional verbs:

1. in transitive phrasal verbs, the particle is movable, but the preposition in a prepositional verb is not;
2. the NP is the object of the verb in phrasal verbs rather than of the preposition;
3. in both transitive and intransitive phrasal verbs, the particle carries stress, as in *She took the cap óff* or *The plane took óff*, while prepositions are unstressed, as in *We knocked on the dóor.*
4. adverbials cannot intervene between the verb and the particle whereas they can between the verb and the preposition, **looked quickly up the information,* but *looked quickly into the oven.*

(Remember that phrasal verbs can also be intransitive, e.g., *catch on, get by, give in.*)

■ *Self-Testing Exercise:* Do Exercises 8.2.

Auxiliary

To this point, we have assumed that the verbal element in the V̄ consists of the lexical verb in its base form and nothing else. But just as there are specifiers of the noun, there appear to be specifiers of the verb. These are traditionally called "auxiliary verbs", which we saw in Chapter 5 include the primary auxiliaries (*have* and *be*), the dummy auxiliary *do*, and the modal auxiliaries (*will, can, shall, may,* and *must*) as well as a number of phrasal equivalents and borderline auxiliaries (e.g., *dare, need, let, ought to, have to*). When we considered auxiliaries as a word class, we looked at their special inflectional features (the "defective morphology" of modals in that they do not take -*s* in the 3rd p sg nor have nonfinite forms) and their special distribution, e.g., preceding *not* or -*n't,* the subject in a question, or emphatic markers *so, too.* They cannot stand alone in a sentence; instead, there must be a **lexical or main verb** present which functions as head of the verb group.

Table 8.1 presents the possible specifiers of the verb with the main verb *bite* (in the active voice only). We note that more than one auxiliary, in fact, up to three auxiliaries, can occur in a single sentence. But these must appear in a certain order and form; there is a complex internal structure to the verb group. And the main verb always comes last in the verb group; that is, unlike the noun, the verb allows no modifiers following it.

Let's look at the different elements in the verb group. We begin with **Tense (T).** Tense is expressed as a bound morph (an inflection) on the first element in the sequence, whether this is an auxiliary or the main verb. Tense is always present; it is an obligatory element. In English the only tense distinctions are past and present (or, more accurately, nonpast; see the discussion of tense in Chapter 5):

T → {past, pres}

Tense is later attached to the first element in the verb group. The verb or auxiliary carrying tense is called **finite**, all other forms (nontensed) are called nonfinite (not restricted in terms of tense, person, and number).

The second element in the verb group is **Modal** (**M**). The modal auxiliary is the first independent element in the verb group, but it needn't be present. M is optional. If a modal is present, it carries tense. (However, past tense forms of the modals do not usually express past time.) The form of the auxiliary (*have* or *be*) or main verb which follows the modal is the basic stem form, also called the "bare infinitive".

M → {*shall, can, will, may, must*}

The third element in the verb group is **Perfect** (**Perf**). Like M, Perf is optional. It contains the auxiliary *have*; the form following *have*, whether it is another auxiliary or the main verb, is in the form of a past (or perfect) participle. We account for this sequence with the following phrase structure rule:

Perf → (*have -en*)

Here, *-en* is an abstract marker for past participle (realized as *-en, -ed*, and so on), which will later be attached to the form following *have*. If the perfect occurs without a modal, then *have* carries tense; if a modal precedes the perfect, then *have* is in the basic stem form.

The fourth element in the verb group is **Progressive** (**Prog**). Prog is also optional. It contains the auxiliary *be*; the form following *be* is in the form of a present (or "progressive") participle. In the active voice, the form following *be* is always the main verb. We account for this sequence with the following phrase structure rule:

Prog → (*be -ing*)

-ing will later be attached to the form following *be*. If progressive is the first element in the

Table 8.1. Specifiers of the Verb (Active)

Those dogs				bite/bit	those cats
			are/were	biting	
		have/had		bitten	
		have/had	been	biting	
	can/could			bite	
	can/could		be	biting	
	can/could	have		bitten	
	can/could	have	been	biting	

verb group, then *be* carries tense, but if either the perfect or a modal (or both) precede, *be* will be nonfinite.

All of the specifiers of the verb are grouped together under the category of **Auxiliary** (**Aux**), which is expanded as follows:

Aux → T (M) (Perf) (Prog)
T → {past, pres}
M → {*shall, can, will, may, must*}
Perf → *have -en*
Prog → *be -ing*

Thus, the auxiliary in *could have been biting* would have the following tree representation:

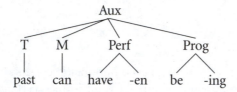

To finish accounting for the form of Aux, we need to attach the affixes (past, pres, -*en*, and -*ing*) to the following elements. We do this by means of a rule called **affix hopping**. This rule stipulates that each affix attaches to the <u>verbal</u> element immediately following it and forms the relevant word. In the example above, affix hopping attaches past to *can*, -*en* to *be*, and -*ing* to the main verb (*bite*). The attachment of affixes is written as follows, where # indicates word boundaries:

#can + past# have #be + -en# #bite -ing#

Rules of word formation give *could*, *been*, and *biting*, and thus the "past perfect progressive (active)" phrase *could have been biting*.[1]

It remains to determine where Aux is generated in the structure of the sentence. As specifiers, auxiliaries are often thought of as sisters of the V or the V_{gp}, as follows:

V_{gp} → Aux V ...   or   V̄ → Aux V_{gp}

However, Aux would differ from all other specifiers in being obligatory, not optional. An alternate view is to see Aux as sister of the VP and daughter of S, since, in fact, the Aux elements are relevant to the entire sentence.

```
        S
    ┌───┼───┐
   NP  Aux  VP
```

Our complete rule for S is then the following:[2]

S → { NP Aux VP
      S ({AdvP, PP, NP}) }

Above, we considered only active forms of Aux. There is a corresponding set of passive forms (see Table 8.2). (Although all of these forms are possible, some are quite rare.) These differ from the active forms in having a *be* auxiliary followed by an *-en* form. The *be* auxiliary is always the last auxiliary in the string, and hence the main verb is always in the past participle form. The phrase structure rule for **Passive** (**Pass**) and the revised rule for Aux would be as follows:

Aux → T (M) (Perf) (Prog) (Pass)
Pass → *be* - *en*

Note that passive too is optional.

■ *Self-Testing Exercises:* Do Exercises 8.3 and 8.4.

Passive Sentences

Although it is possible to generate a passive sentence directly in the D-structure by simply adding Pass to the phrase structure rule for Aux, as we just did, a passive sentence is typically seen as being directly related to its active counterpart — rather than as a completely different structure — since the choice of the passive, unlike the choice of any other auxiliary, affects the structure of the entire sentence.

Consider this active and passive pair:

The art expert could have detected the forgery. ⇒
The forgery could have been detected by the art expert.

The passive sentence compares with the active sentence in the following way:

1. the passive verb group contains the *be* - *en* sequence just before the main verb;
2. the subject of the active sentence (the agent) is the object of the preposition *by* at end of the passive sentence; and
3. the direct object of the active sentence is the subject of the passive sentence.

Passive sentences are thus best understood as deriving from their active counterpart by a

Table 8.2. Specifiers of the Verb (Passive)

Those cats					
				are/were	bitten by those dogs
			are/were	being	bitten
		have/had		been	bitten
		have/had	been	being	bitten
	could			be	bitten
	could		be	being	bitten
	could	have		been	bitten
	could	have	been	being	bitten

transformation involving the following sequence.[3] The passive auxiliary is inserted in the verb specifier position, which causes the agent NP (if there is an explicit one) to move to the *by* phrase. The subject position then becomes empty, and since it is not possible in English for the subject to be empty, the object NP moves to fill that position.[4] When it does so, it leaves behind a **trace** (*t*) in its former position. Traces, which encode the base position of a moved constituent, will become more important as we progress.

If NP_1 and NP_2 stand for the active subject (*the art expert*) and object (*the forgery*), respectively, then the two sentences above have the following tree representations on the surface level:

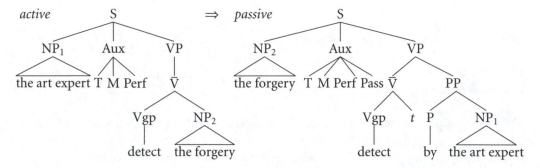

Note that the PP containing the agent phrase becomes the sister of the $\bar{V}$ and hence functions adverbially.

However, the most frequent kind of passive sentence in English is the **agentless passive** in which the *by* phrase is not present. Its omission is related to the rhetorical functions of the passive (see Chapter 11). However, we will analyze agentless passive sentences as containing an agent in D-structure, an agent which is not specified since it is recoverable from the context or is generally known This agent will be indicated by Ø in the tree in subject position of the D-structure active sentence. You can also think of this Ø as representing an indefinite pronoun such as "someone".

Verb Subcategorization and the Passive

Not all active sentences are susceptible to the passive. In order for a sentence to be passivized, the subject must be an agent (a doer or performer of an action) and the verb must have a direct or prepositional object which can move to the subject position. The subcategorization of the verb is therefore very important in the formation of the passive:

1. monotransitive verbs may be passivized: the dO of active becomes the Su of the passive sentence;
2. intransitive verbs cannot be passivized since they have no dO;
3. copulative verbs cannot be passivized since they have no dO (rather a sC) and the subject is not an agent;
4. ditransitive verbs may be passivized: either the dO or the iO of the active becomes the Su of the passive sentence (e.g., *The collector gave a forgery* (dO) *to the museum* ⇒ *A forgery*

was given to the museum by the collector or *The collector gave the museum* (iO) *a forgery* ⇒ *The museum was given a forgery by the collector*), but note that it must always be the NP immediately following the verb which becomes subject (e.g., *The collector gave the museum a forgery* ⇒ **The collector gave the museum a forgery* ⇒ ***A forgery was given the museum by the collector*);

5.   complex transitive verbs (both locative and nonlocative) may be passivized: the dO (but not usually the oC) of the active becomes the Su of the passive sentence (e.g., *They elected Felicity president* ⇒ *Felicity was elected president by them* but not **President was elected Felicity by them* or *Kyle hung the picture on the wall* ⇒ *The picture was hung on the wall by Kyle* but not **The wall was hung the picture on by Kyle*);

6.   prepositional verbs, when they are nonlocative, may usually be passivized: the OP of the active becomes the Su of the passive sentence (e.g., *The negotiating team agreed to the terms* ⇒ *The terms were agreed to by the negotiating team*; cf. *The picture hung on the wall* ⇒ **The wall was hung the on by the picture*);

7.   diprepositional verbs may sometimes be passivized: the OP of the first PP in the active becomes the Su of the passive sentence (e.g., *He conferred with the boss about the problem* ⇒ ?*The boss was conferred with about the problem*); and

8.   transitive phrasal verbs may usually be passivized (intransitive phrasal verbs cannot be): the dO of the active becomes the Su of the passive sentence (e.g., *The construction crew knocked down the fence* ⇒ *The fence was knocked down by the construction crew*).

Certain apparently transitive verbs cannot be passivized. These are ones in which the verb is stative in meaning (see Chapter 6), as in the following cases:

> Jake resembles his father.
> Maggie hates chocolates.
> Florence speaks French fluently.
> The color suits you.
> The dress fits me.

The subjects in these cases are not agents performing an action; the grammatical objects are also not affected by the action of the verb and are hence not direct objects.

■ Self-Testing Exercise: Do Exercise 8.5.

Yes/No Questions and Negative Sentences

To this point, we have considered only sentences which are declarative and positive. We turn now to negative and interrogative sentences; we will see that these can be treated together because they both make reference to the same sequence of elements in the auxiliary. As with passive sentences, we will consider both types of sentences to be derived via transformations from the corresponding positive and declarative sentences. That is, we are assuming that sentences in D-structure are positive, declarative, and active; we then convert them to negative, interrogative, and passive sentences on the surface by transformations (which permute, add, or delete elements, but do not fundamentally alter the meaning of the sentence). Generating the sentences in this way allows us to show the relationship, for example, between a declarative sentence and the corresponding interrogative — both have the same D-structure.

Yes/No Questions

The following examples show the formation of *yes/no* (or truth) questions from the corresponding declarative sentences:

Zelda is leaving for Paris tomorrow. ⇒ Is Zelda leaving for Paris tomorrow?
Zelda has been to Paris before. ⇒ Has Zelda been to Paris before?
Zelda has been planning this trip for a long time. ⇒ Has Zelda been planning this trip for a long time?
Zelda can afford this trip. ⇒ Can Zelda afford this trip?
This trip was arranged by Zelda ⇒ Was this trip arranged by Zelda?

(A second kind of question — the *wh*-question — will be treated in Chapter 9.)
    What happens in the formation of each of the questions above is a transformation called **subject–aux(iliary) inversion**, in which the order of the subject of the sentence and the <u>first</u> auxiliary element is reversed, or, more specifically, the first auxiliary moves to a position preceding the subject. The auxiliaries *is, has, can*, and *was* move in front of the subject *Zelda* in the examples above. Since the first auxiliary element carries tense, it is more correct to say that tense and the first auxiliary precedes the subject.
    The S-structure tree for the first question takes the following form:

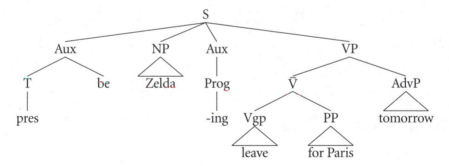

The part of the Aux node containing T and the first independent auxiliary attaches in front of the subject and becomes the daughter of S.[5]
    Subject–aux inversion also occurs in some noninterrogative sentences, namely, those beginning with a restricted set of negative adverbs:

{Never, seldom, rarely, scarcely} have I seen such sights as I saw in Europe.
No sooner had I arrived than I lost my passport.

Negative Statements and Questions

The following sentences show the formation of negative statements from the corresponding positive statements given above:

⇒ Zelda is not leaving for Paris tomorrow.
⇒ Zelda has not been to Paris before.
⇒ Zelda has not been planning this trip for a long time.
⇒ Zelda can not afford this trip.

In this case, the negative element (*not*) is placed after tense and the first auxiliary element. The contraction of *not* to -*n't* is optional and follows insertion of *not* into the string.

The following sentences show the formation of negative questions from the sentences given above:

⇒ Isn't Zelda leaving tomorrow?
⇒ Hasn't Zelda been to Paris before?
⇒ Hasn't Zelda been planning this trip for a long time?
⇒ Can't Zelda afford this trip?

In negative questions there is both subject–aux inversion and placement of the negative element after tense and the first auxiliary. Normally the negative element also inverts with the auxiliary; in this case, contraction is obligatory:

*Is not Zelda leaving tomorrow?
*Has not Zelda been to Paris before?

However, it is possible to leave the negative element behind. Such sentences involve word negation, rather than sentence negation, and the scope of negation is different in them:

Cf.   Is Zelda not leaving tomorrow?
        Has Zelda not been to Paris before?
        Can Zelda not afford this trip?

That is, these sentences involve the negation of an individual word, as in *happy/unhappy/not happy*. Both kinds of negation can occur in the same sentence:

Charley did<u>n't</u> deliberately <u>not</u> pay his taxes.
You simply ca<u>n't</u> <u>not</u> take advantage of this offer.
Joan is<u>n't</u> <u>un</u>happy about the news (nor is she happy).

Do-Support

What happens if you wish to form a negative or interrogative sentence from a sentence that has no auxiliary other than tense:

Zelda went to Paris last year.
⇒ Zelda didn't go to Paris last year.
⇒ Did Zelda go to Paris last year?

Placing tense before the subject or the negative after tense results in what is called "tense stranding" because by the rule of affix hopping there is nothing for tense to attach to: it must attach to the immediately following element and that element must be verbal, but in the interrogative the subject (NP) follows, and in the negative *not* follows. So a verbal element must be supplied by inserting the **dummy auxiliary *do***. This serves the function of an auxiliary when there is no other independent auxiliary present. This insertion transformation is called ***do*-support**.[6]

The surface tree produced by *do*-support is the following:

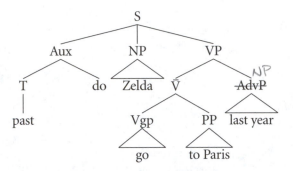

Do is initially inserted after T in Aux when it stands before V; then this portion of Aux is moved in front of the subject. This leaves a gap in the second portion of Aux. The verbal element following *do* occurs in its basic stem form.[7]

Note that there are several different *do*'s in English:

– main verb: *John always <u>does</u> the dishes. Let's <u>do</u> lunch.*
– pro-verb: *Katy writes poetry and so <u>does</u> Alfred.*
– auxiliary: *<u>Does</u> Susan work full-time?*

The pro-verb *do* is like a pronoun; just as a pronoun replaces the entire NP, the pro-verb replaces an entire VP. The dummy *do* behaves in all respects like an auxiliary; it is used when an auxiliary is necessary — in questions, tag questions, negatives, contrastive stress — and none is present in the corresponding noninterrogative, positive, nonemphatic sentence. However, dummy *do* is purely structural, a mere tense carrier; since it is empty of lexical meaning, its addition does not change the meaning of the sentence.

With main verb *be* and *have*, *do*-support works somewhat differently:

Zelda is in Paris. ⇒   Is Zelda in Paris?
                       Zelda is not in Paris.
Zelda has enough money for the trip. ⇒
                       Has Zelda enough money? or Does Zelda have enough money?
                       Zelda hasn't enough money. or Zelda doesn't have enough money.

When *be* is functioning as a main verb and it is the only verbal element present, it behaves as an auxiliary in respect to subject–aux inversion and negative placement; it is not necessary to insert *do*. When *have* is functioning as a main verb, it behaves either as an auxiliary or a main verb, depending on your dialect. Most of you probably treat it as a main verb and insert *do*, except perhaps in some fixed expressions. One way to account for the behavior of *be* and *have* would be to give them the feature [+Aux] in the lexicon.

Note that main verb *do* is consistently treated as a main verb, with dummy *do* inserted in questions and negatives (giving two *do*'s in a single sentence):

Candy does her own packing. ⇒ Does Candy do her own packing?
Candy does not do her own packing.

■ **Self-Testing Exercise:** Do Exercise 8.6; note that you must change questions into statements, passive into active sentences, and negative into positive sentences to arrive at the D-structure.

Tag Questions

In the sections above, we studied the structure of the *yes/no* question. An additional type of question is the tag question:

Andy is coming over, isn't he?
The stores haven't closed already, have they?
Farrah will be leaving soon, won't she?
You don't understand, do you?
It broke down, didn't it?

The "tag" follows the comma and consists of the following:

1.   tense and the first auxiliary of the main clause (or *do* if there isn't one);
2.   a pronoun identical in person, number, and gender with the subject of the main clause; and
3.   a marker of negative polarity; that is if the main clause is positive, *-n't* occurs (note that the negative element is obligatorily contracted), and if the main clause is negative, no negative element occurs.

Point (1) above should remind you of subject–aux inversion. However, in the formation of tag questions, tense plus the first auxiliary are copied rather than reordered. Also, rather than moving the subject, its features of person, number, and gender are duplicated in a pronoun. Note that tag questions are ill-formed if the pronoun does not have the same features as the subject or if a different auxiliary than that in the main clause is used:

Alison will be leaving soon, won't {she, *he, *they, *you}?
Alison will be leaving soon, {won't, *can't, *isn't, doesn't} she?

Certain modal auxiliaries do not work particularly well in tag questions, so some other auxiliary is sometimes substituted:

He may be at home, {*mayn't, won't} he?
He might not be at home, {ʔmight, ʔwill} he?

The phrasal equivalents of the modals and the borderline auxiliaries are particularly awkward in tags:

> I ought to be at home, {ᵗoughtn't, hadn't, shouldn't} I?
> He used to have long hair, {*usedn't, didn't} he?
> You needn't have come, {ᵗneed, ᵗdid} you?
> cf. He needs to leave, doesn't he?
> You daren't have answered, {*dare, had, ᵗshould} you?
> He has to resign, {hasn't, doesn't} he?

Note the behavior of main verb *have* and *be* in tag questions:

> She is happy, isn't she?
> He has the money, {hasn't, doesn't} he?
> cf. You had a good time, {didn't, *hadn't} you?
> Forrest had a long bath this evening, {didn't, *hadn't} he?

As in *yes/no* questions, *be* behaves universally as an auxiliary, and *have* (in the meaning of 'possess') behaves as either, depending on dialect. However, where *have* does not have the meaning of 'possess', *do* is required in tags:

> He has the money, {hasn't, doesn't} he?
> They had a party, {didn't, *hadn't} they?

Imperatives

We have so far accounted for the formation of declarative and interrogative sentences, but not for the formation of imperative sentences such as the following:

> Pass the salt!
> Take me to your leader!
> Don't smoke in the restaurant!

Our rule for S will not account for these because they have no subject. Traditionally, it is said that a *you* subject is "understood", or elliptical. Is there any validity to this? There are a number of tests for *you* in imperatives. First, consider reflexive pronouns. These are forms with -*self* or -*selves* attached to a personal pronoun which are co-indexed with (have the same referent as) the subject of the clause; that is, they agree in person, number, and gender with the subject:

> Jake shot {himself, *themselves, *myself}.
> Fiona talked about {herself, *themselves, *yourself} to Terry.
> I said that she should come to know {herself, *myself}.

(The last example shows that the reflexive must agree with the subject of the clause in which it occurs, not with the subject of some higher clause.) In imperatives, only *yourself*, not any other reflexive pronoun, can occur:

Shoot {yourself, *himself, *myself}!
Dress {yourself, *themselves, *itself}!

Furthermore, the 2nd person pronoun must be the reflexive, not the nonreflexive form:

*Shoot you!
*Dress you!

Second, consider the following sentence:

Andrew {lost/found} {his, *her, ?their} way.

In this idiom, only a possessive pronoun co-indexed with the subject can occur. When this idiom occurs in an imperative, only *your* can occur:

Don't lose {your, *my, *their} way home!

Third, consider the behavior of tag questions with imperatives:

Help me, won't {you, *she, *he, *they}?

As discussed in the previous section, the pronoun in a tag question is co-indexed with the subject of the main clause. With imperatives, only *you* can occur. These tests all suggest, therefore, that there is an understood, or underlying, *you* in the subject position of imperative sentences.

The last test also suggests that there is an underlying *will* in imperatives, because as you will recall from the previous section, the auxiliary of the main clause is copied in the auxiliary of the tag with reversed polariry:

Help me, {won't, *can't, *isn't} you?

The presence of an underlying *will* accounts for the occurrence of the basic stem form of the verb in imperatives as well. Since tense is copied from the main clause to the tag, the same test also argues for an underlying present tense in imperatives:

Help me, (won't, *wouldn't} you?

In D-structure, therefore, an imperative will have a subject *you*, present tense, and *will* plus the rest of imperative:

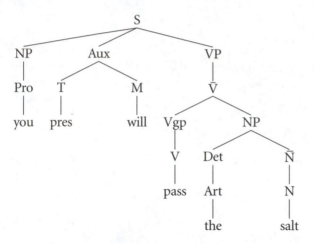

These are deleted in an imperative transformation to produce the appropriate S-structure. Imperatives cannot occur with a modal or auxiliary *have/be* in S-structure:

> *Have opened the door!
> *Be writing a letter![7]
> *Can pass the salt!

Modals are restricted because the modal position (in D-structure) is already occupied by *will* (there may be semantic reasons for the restriction as well); *have* and *be* are restricted because a command must relate to a future action, not to a past (completed) or present (ongoing) action.[8]

Generally, states cannot occur in the imperative because someone cannot be commanded to be in a state. A state is not a matter of will and hence cannot be brought about volitionally (see Chapter 6):

> *Resemble your father!
> *Be six feet tall!
> *Have brown eyes!

Only if the stative verb can be given an active reading can the verb appear in the imperative.

> Know the answer by tomorrow! = Learn the answer!
> Don't be a fool! = Don't act like a fool!

While *have* and *be* sentences are usually stative, note that the sentences below express actions ('do such things as be content/have a good time') rather than states:

> Have a good time!
> Be content with what you've got!

In the formation of negative imperatives, *do*-support is always required, even in the case of *be*

> Don't open the window!
> Don't forget the drinks!

Don't be so sad!
Don't have another drink!

■ *Self-Testing Exercise:* Do Exercise 8.7.

Review of Phrase Structure Rules

As we have now learned all the phrase structure rules (see Appendix II for a complete listing), except those accounting for complex sentences, it is perhaps useful to review what these rules do. They tell us the following:

– the lexical categories of words;
– the order of elements in D-structure; and
– the hierarchical relationships of the categories (what is a constituent of what, what dominates what, and what modifies or is a complement of what).

The terminal symbols of the phrase structure rules are abstract symbols that need to be filled by particular instances of the category, which we select from the lexicon, a kind of dictionary, which lists the morphemes of the language, along with phonological information, semantic information (selectional restrictions), inherent subcategorization (the lexical category), and strict subcategorization (the syntactic environments in which the word can occur). For example, the entry for the word *bite* might contain the following information (in addition to a feature analysis of the meaning of the word):

[baɪt] V; _____ NP (PP)
[baɪt] + {past} → /bɪt/
takes animate subject

The lexicon gives all irregular or idiosyncratic information. We also need a set of lexical insertion rules which tell us to insert the appropriate word under the relevant phrase marker, i.e., the word of the proper class with the subcategorization properties required by the phrase marker. Because of the recursive nature of the phrase structure rules as well as the choices allowed by both the phrase structure rules and the lexicon, different applications of the finite set of phrase structure rules can produce an infinite number of surface strings.

The phrase structure rules and the lexicon together form the **base**. The base derives deep or underlying structures, which are unambiguous and contain all meaning. Remember that the same D-structure may have different surface manifestations and the same S-structure (a structurally ambiguous string) will have more than one D-structure. These D-structure sentences are active as opposed to passive, declarative as opposed to interrogative or imperative, and positive as opposed to negative; so far in the course, they are also simple as opposed to complex. Such sentences are known as kernel sentences. Then to produce passive, interrogative or imperative, or negative sentences, what is needed is another kind of rule, a transformation, which converts a D-structure into a S-structure.

Phrase Structure Rules + Lexicon = Base
↓
D-Structure
↓
Movement Transformations
↓
S-Structure

Below is a listing of all of the grammatical functions, verb subcategories, and phrase structure rules that we have studied so far:

Functions	Verb Types
Subject (Su)	Intransitive
Direct Object (dO)	(Mono)transitive
Indirect Object (iO)	Ditransitive
Subject Complement (sC)	Complex Transitive
Object Complement (oC)	Phrasal
Adjunct Adverbial (aA)	Prepositional
Disjunct Adverbial (dA)	Copulative
Conjunct Adverbial (cA)	Diprepositional
Modifier (Mod)	
Specifier (Spec)	
Prepositional Complement (pC)	
Object of the Preposition (OP)	
Complement of Adjective (Comp of A)	

■ Chapter Summary

Now that you have completed this chapter, you should be able to:

1. identify adjunct, disjunct, and conjunct adverbials;
2. distinguish between prepositional phrases functioning as verbal complements, as adverbials, and as noun modifiers;
3. name and analyze the structure of the possible auxiliary phrases in English;
4. account for, by means of tree diagrams, the generation of passive sentences, *yes/no* questions, imperatives, and negative sentences from the corresponding active, declarative, and positive sentences;
5. explain the formation of tag questions by a rule of copying; and
6. disambiguate certain English sentences using D-structure tree diagrams.

■ Recommended Additional Reading

Treatments of English syntax which are similar in depth and level of formality to the treatment in this chapter include Wekker and Haegeman (1985, Chapters 3–4), Burton-Roberts (1997, Chapters 5–6), Thomas (1993, Chapters 4), Brown and Miller (1991, Chapters 7, and 10, pp. 125–32), Kaplan (1995, Chapter 8, pp. 306–26) and Hopper (1999, Chapters 6–7). Less formal treatments include Huddleston (1984), Delahunty and Garvey (1994, Chapter 11), and Wardhaugh (1995, Chapters 6–7).

For more advanced treatments, see the references in Chapter 7.

■ Notes

1. The finite verb is also marked in the present tense for person and number to agree with the subject, but this is very limited in English, only the 3rd p -*s* for most verbs. We will ignore subject–verb agreement.

2. In X-bar theory, Aux — known as I or INFL (for "inflection") — is seen as head, with the VP as complement, the subject NP as specifier, and S as IP:

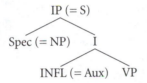

   This view has the advantage of representing S as having the same structure as all the other phrasal categories (namely XP → Spec X̄ and X̄ → X Complements). If a flat structure of this is given, it looks like our tree:

3. An alternative account of the passive as base-derived is discussed in Exercise 8.5, question 3.

4. The movement of the object to subject position is called "NP Movement".

5. It is thought that Aux moves to the complementizer position, as will be discussed in the following chapter. For the present, we will not worry about exactly where Aux attaches.

6. An alternative account, *do*-deletion, generates all sentences with *do* in D-structure and deletes it when it is not necessary, that is, when there is a verbal element adjoining to which tense can be affixed.

7. It is not possible to account for negatives and questions simply by rewriting the phrase structure rules to allow tense and the first auxiliary to be generated optionally before the subject and to allow for the optional placement of the negative element after tense and the first auxiliary element. If we attempted to do so, we would need a rule for the negative something like the following since *not* can follow any of the independent auxiliaries:

Aux → T (M) (*not*) (*have* (*not*) -*en*) (*be* (*not*) -*ing*) (*be* (*not*) -*en*)

The problem with this rule is that we cannot rule out multiple negation since the rule allows us to select all of the negative elements (and there is no mechanism for rewriting the rule to forbid this). It is similarly difficult to write such a phrase structure rule for the interrogative since we need to allow *have* and *be* to either precede or follow the subject:

S → (M) (have -*en*) (be -*ing*) NP (have -*en*) (be -*ing*) VP

With this rule, we would be able to select *have* and *be* more than once and to move more than one auxiliary before the subject, which are not permitted by the rules of English.

8. If a framing temporal clause is added, the progressive command sounds much better (*Be cleaning your room when I return*). *Have your room cleaned by the time I return* is not a true perfect, but rather a stative with a focus on the actions bringing about the state ('do such things as will bring your room into a cleaned state', see below).

CHAPTER 9

Finite and Nonfinite Clauses

■ Chapter Preview

This chapter treats the syntax of complex sentences in English. It begins by looking at the structure, function, and behavior of *that*-clauses. A similar treatment is accorded adverbial clauses. *Wh*-clauses are then discussed, including main clause *wh*-questions and embedded *wh*-clauses. The roles of the *wh*-words are examined, and the internal structure of the clauses is accounted for by a rule of *wh*-movement. An analysis is given of the functions and behavior of embedded *wh*-clauses, both relative clauses and indirect questions. Brief attention is paid to the distinction between restrictive and nonrestrictive relative clauses, to "headless", indefinite, and sentential relative clauses, and to cleft and pseudocleft sentences. The final section of the chapter deals with nonfinite clauses: with forms of the nonfinite verb, with omissions from the nonfinite clause, either controlled or indefinite, with complementizers in nonfinite clauses, and with the various functions of nonfinite clauses.

■ Commentary

We move now from the simple sentence to the complex sentence, that is, to a sentence that consists of more than one clause: a main clause (also called a higher S [referring to its position in the tree diagram], a matrix S, or a superordinate clause) and one or more dependent clauses (also called lower Ss, embedded Ss, or subordinate clauses). Dependent clauses are related to the main clause by a process of embedding. There are a number of different types of dependent clauses, each serving a variety of functions in respect to the main clause.

(On the teaching of complex sentences by a method called "sentence combining", see the chapter on pedagogy on the CD-ROM.)

Finite Clauses

Finite clauses are those clauses containing a subject and finite verb (marked for tense, person, and number). There are three main types of finite dependent clauses: *that*-clauses, adverbial clauses, and *wh*-clauses. *Wh*-clauses may also be independent.

That-Clauses

That-**clauses** are so named because they usually begin with the subordinating conjunction *that*, as in the examples in Table 9.1.

Form. We begin with the internal structure of the clause. The subordinating conjunction *that* which begins the clause has no function within the clause, but serves to connect the clauses. We say that it syntactically subordinates the second clause to, makes it dependent on, or embeds it in the first clause. *That* is thus a marker of subordination which we call a **complementizer** (**Comp**). The remainder of the clause after *that* is a fully formed S:

- it has a finite verb;
- it may have any number of auxiliaries: *that coffee might have been growing in Brazil*;
- it may be passive: *that coffee was grown in Brazil*;
- it may be negative: *that coffee doesn't grow in Brazil*; and
- it may itself be complex: *that though coffee tastes good, it is bad for your health.*

The two restrictions on the form of the *that*-clause are that it may not be a question (**that does coffee grow in Brazil*) and it may not be an imperative (**that buy some Brazilian coffee!*). In other words, there may be no disruption of the normal clausal order.

Function. In all cases, the *that*-clause has a nominal function; it is functioning as an NP would: it answers the question "what?". In fact, *that*-clauses may serve virtually all of the functions served by NP's. In the examples in Table 9.1, we see a *that*-clause serving as:

1. subject
2. direct object
3. direct object after indirect object
4. subject complement
5. complement of A
6. complement of N̄

(Example (7) will be discussed below.) A *that*-clause cannot serve the nominal function of indirect object because it does not denote an animate being, but rather an abstract proposition; it also cannot serve as an object complement.

The functions of Su, dO, and sC (sentences (1)–(4)) are nominal functions with which you are already familiar. Note that because all of these are obligatory positions, if the *that*-clause is removed, the main clause becomes grammatically incomplete. *That*-clauses frequently act as direct objects after a verb of communication:

Table 9.1. That-Clauses

(1)   That coffee grows in Brazil is well known to all.
(2)   I know that coffee grows in Brazil.
(3)   He told his mother that coffee grows in Brazil.
(4)   My understanding is that coffee grows in Brazil.
(5)   He is certain that coffee grows in Brazil.
(6)   His claim that coffee grows in Brazil is correct.
(7)   It is well known that coffee grows in Brazil.

I {said, stated, thought, believed} <u>that the world is flat</u>.

In these cases, they are reporting the speech or thought of others; these structures are called *indirect speech* (or "indirect discourse"). When a direct object is clausal, it must follow the indirect object, as in (3); it cannot precede, as in *He told that coffee grows in Brazil to his mother*. This restriction may be due to the tendency in English to put "heavy" elements (such as *that*-clauses) at the end of the sentence (see below).

You have not before encountered the functions exemplified in (5) and (6), complement of A and complement of N̄, as nominal functions. Until now you have seen only PPs functioning as complements of adjectives (e.g., *close to the door*); however, *that*-clauses may also serve this function, as in (6). The only postnominal function that you have seen so far is the PP as modifier (e.g., *the book on the shelf*); the postnominal *that*-clause in (6) has a different function, namely, as complement of the noun. Such *that*-clauses follow abstract nouns such as *claim, fact, idea, hope, notion, proposal,* and *lie* and express the content of the abstract noun. They bear a relation to the noun which is analogous to the relation a direct object bears to the related verb: *His claim that coffee grows in Brazil ... = He claimed that coffee grows in Brazil.* The clause complements the entire N̄, not just the N; e.g., in *his incorrect claim that coffee grows in Brazil*, the clause gives the content of his "incorrect claim", not just of his "claim".

In order to account for *that*-clauses in our phrase structure rules, we need to modify the rules in various ways. First, we need a rule for the form of embedded S's, which we will term **S-bar (S̄):**[1]

$$\bar{S} \rightarrow \text{Comp S}$$
$$\text{Comp} \rightarrow \textit{that}$$

Then we need to account for the different functions of the *that*-clause. To indicate its function as subject NP and as object of P, we add S̄ to the possible expansions of NP:

$$NP \rightarrow \{(\text{Det}) \ \bar{N}, \text{PN}, \text{Pro}, \bar{S}\}$$

We also have to allow S̄ to serve as complement of an adjective:

$$AP \rightarrow (\{\text{Deg, AdvP}\}) \ A \ (\{\text{PP}, \bar{S}\})$$

In order to account for S̄ as a complement of N̄, we have to create a new syntactic position following N̄:

$$NP \rightarrow (\text{Det}) \ \bar{N} \ (\bar{S})$$

What about S̄ as complement of the verb? These revised rules could be seen as accounting for S̄ as direct object and subject complement since they allow S̄ to be generated under NP, and NP is a position following the verb. However, there seems to be little justification for analyzing postverbal clauses as NPs since S̄ figures in verb subcategorization quite separately from NP. That is, certain verbs take both NP and S̄ complements, while others take only one or the other:

We expected bad news. We expected that the news would be bad.
Sally lifted my spirits. * Sally lifted that I feel happier.
*Tom hoped good results. Tom hoped that he had done well.

Thus, we rewrite our rule for V as follows

$$\bar{V} \rightarrow V_{gp} \left(\left\{ \begin{array}{l} NP(\{NP, PP, AP\}) \\ AP \\ PP \ (PP) \\ (NP) \ \bar{S} \end{array} \right\} \right)$$

The (generalized) tree diagrams for sentences (1) and (2) differ as follows:

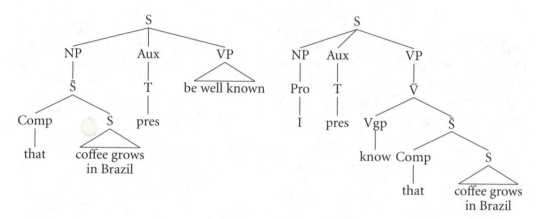

Extraposition. There is a tendency in English not to like heavy elements, such as clauses, at the beginning of a sentence, but to prefer them at the end. This preference is a result of the basic Su-V-O structure of English, where objects are typically longer than subjects (in older stages of the language, subjects were not even separately expressed but were indicated by the inflectional ending on the verb). Thus, while sentence (1) above is perfectly grammatical, it is much more natural to use the synonymous sentence (7) given in Table 9.1.

Because sentences (1) and (7) are synonymous and because the *that*-clause is logically functioning as subject in both sentences, we will derive sentence (7) from sentence (1) by a rightward movement transformation called **extraposition**. Such a transformation moves an element to an "extra" or added "position" at the end of the sentence. When the clause is extraposed, the original subject position, which is an obligatory position in the sentence that cannot be deleted, is filled by a "dummy" place-holder, anticipatory *it*; *it* has no lexical meaning here, but serves merely as a structural device. The moved clause — the extraposed subject (eS) — becomes a daughter of the main S and sister of the VP. We will assume that in D-structure, extraposition has not yet occurred. The sentence *It is false that the world is flat* has the following D-structure and S-structure:

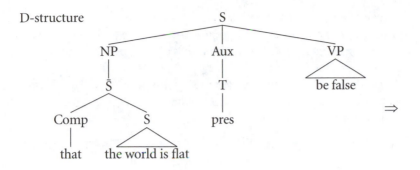

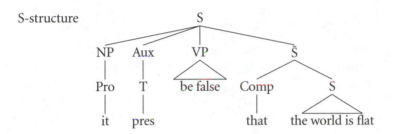

This is extraposition from subject position, which is almost always optional. However, there is a small set of verbs where extraposition is obligatory, including *seem, appear, transpire,* and *happen.* Thus, you cannot say ** That the world is flat seems,* but must say *It seems that the world is flat.* Nonetheless, we will generate such surface sentences from a D-structure in which the *that*-clause is in subject position; in other words, the verbs are treated as intransitive.

We also find, much less frequently, extraposition from object position, such as:

I hear <u>it</u> said <u>that the world is flat.</u>
He thinks <u>it</u> likely <u>that the world is flat.</u>

Normally, such extraposition is obligatory and occurs in a number of fixed expressions such as *{break, put} it to me that, bring it about that,* and *see to it that.*

You must be careful to distinguish extraposed structures such as (7) from structures with the *that*-clause as complement of the A such as (5) above. Consider the following two sentences:

a.   eSu: It is regrettable <u>that the picnic had to be canceled.</u>
b.   complement of A: Harry is regretful <u>that he forgot my birthday.</u>

Although both have the surface sequence V A S̄, in the first sentence, the S̄ can be moved back to subject position, replacing the *it* (*That the picnic had to be canceled is regrettable*). You must also be careful to distinguish extraposed structures from structures with the *that*-clause as complement of the Ñ such as (6) above. Consider the following two sentences:

a.   eSu: It is a proven fact <u>that the world is flat.</u>
b.   complement of Ñ: It contained a recommendation <u>that we cancel the program.</u>

While the first sentence is equivalent to *That the world is flat is a proven fact*, the second structure is <u>not</u> equivalent to ** That we cancel the program contained a recommendation*. In the first sentence, *it* is a dummy marker, while in the second *it* is a meaningful pronoun, referring to some previous noun phrase such as *the report*.

A phenomenon similar to extraposition is right movement, where the *that*-clause moves to an extraposition at the end of the sentence, but it is not necessary to insert *it* in the position vacated since it is not an obligatory position:

a.   complement of A: He was certain <u>that the world was flat</u> when I saw him yesterday. ⇒ He was certain when I saw him yesterday <u>that the world was flat</u>.
b.   complement of N̄: His belief <u>that coffee grows in Brazil</u> is correct. ⇒ His belief is correct <u>that coffee grows in Brazil</u>.

Speaker judgments may vary concerning the grammaticality of sentences with right movement.

Deletion of the complementizer. Sometimes *that* does not appear, as in *He thinks the world is flat*. In these cases, we assume that the Comp position was originally filled and that there was then deletion of the complementizer.[2]

We find that *that* can always be deleted when the clause has the following functions; the numbers here refer to the sentences in Table 9.1, with Ø denoting the deleted *that*:

2.   direct object: *I know Ø coffee grows in Brazil.*
3.   direct object after indirect object: *He told his mother Ø coffee grows in Brazil.*
6.   complement of A: *He is certain Ø coffee grows in Brazil.*

It is perhaps possible to delete *that* in the following cases, though speakers might disagree about the acceptability of these deletions:

4.   subject complement: *My understanding is Ø coffee grows in Brazil.*
6.   complement of N̄: *His claim Ø coffee grows in Brazil is correct.*
7.   extraposed subject: I*t is well known to all Ø coffee grows in Brazil.*

However, it is never possible to delete *that* when the clause serves as subject:

1.   **Coffee grows in Brazil is well known to all.*

The reason for this restriction relates to sentence processing. Since the first sequence "coffee grows in Brazil" forms a complete clause, when the sentence continues with "is well known to all", the speaker has to go back and adjust his or her reading of the structure, and interpretive difficulties may result.

Passive and interrogative. If one begins with the complex sentence *Everyone believes that the police falsely accused Ramona*, passive can work in the following ways:

–   the *that* clause is passive: *Everyone thinks that Ramona was falsely accused by the police;*
–   the main clause is passive: *That the police falsely accused Ramona is believed by everyone;* or
–   both clauses can be passive *That Ramona was falsely accused by the police is believed by everyone.*

Extraposition may also apply to the second two sentences, giving *It is believed by everyone that the police falsely accused Ramona* and *It is believed by everyone that Ramona was falsely accused by the police*, respectively.

Interrogative interacts in a more limited way because only the main clause, not the *that*-clause, may be a question. In (a) the *that*-clause functions as direct object; the corresponding question is (b). In (c) the *that*-clause functions as subject; one would expect to find the corresponding question (d), but this is ungrammatical; in these cases, extraposition is obligatory, as in (e):[3]

a. Jacob said that he had seen the movie already. ⇒
b. Did Jacob say that he had seen the movie already?
c. That Jacob has seen that movie already is possible. ⇒
d. *Is that Jacob has seen that movie already possible?
e. Is it possible that Jacob has seen that movie already?

You may also have multiple embedding, of course. Below is the D-structure tree for the sentence *It is possible that Ferdinand could have believed that the world is not flat*:

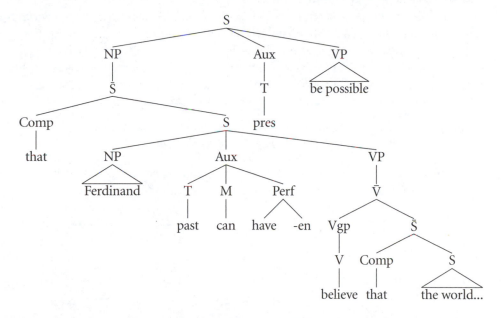

■ *Self-Testing Exercise: Do Exercise 9.1*

Adverbial Clauses

In the previous chapter, we saw PPs, AdvPs, and occasionally NPs functioning adverbially. In this section, we look at clauses which can have an adverbial function; these are called **adverbial clauses**. Table 9.2 provides examples of clauses functioning as adjunct adverbials. These clauses express the adverbial notions of time (1), manner (2), and reason (3) — that is,

Table 9.2. Adjunct Adverbial Clauses

(1) The student left the room <u>before I had finished the lecture</u>.
(2) She looked around the room <u>as if she knew people there</u>.
(3) He lied <u>because he was afraid</u>.
(4) We won't have our picnic <u>if it rains</u>.
(5) I tried to finish it <u>although I was very tired</u>.
(6) Joshua spends his spare time reading, <u>while Bill watches television</u>.
(7) It's <u>such</u> a hot day <u>that I'm going to the beach</u>.
(8) She works harder <u>than her sister works (does)</u>.
(9) We climbed higher <u>so that we could get a better view</u>.

they answer the questions when?, how?, and why? — and are comparable to PPs and AdvPs such as (1) {*at noon, yesterday*}, (2) {*curiously, with a happy expression*}, and (3) *out of fear.* However, adverbial clauses can express a wider range of adverbial notions, such as condition (4), concession (5), contrast (6), result (7), comparison (8), and purpose (9).

Adverbial clauses may also function as disjunct and conjunct adverbials: e.g., *if I may speak frankly* (dA), *if I judge accurately* (dA), *unless I am mistaken* (dA), *although these are important considerations* (cA). Conjunct adverbial clauses appear to be infrequent.

Like the *that*-clause, the adverbial clause includes a fully formed S, with the similar restriction that it cannot be interrogative or imperative. Also like the *that*-clause, it begins with a complementizer, but in adverbial clauses, a much greater variety of lexical items serve as complementizers. We will need to revise our rule for Comp as follows:

Comp → {*while, since, because, although, if, when, so that, as, such, before, after, until, as long as, as soon as, by the time that, now that, once, inasmuch as …* }[4]

Note that this is not an exhaustive listing of the complementizers. An adverbial clause is thus an S̄. We need to revise our phrase structure rules for both adjunct adverbials (in the VP) and conjunct/disjunct adverbials (in the S) in the following ways to account for adverbial clauses:

VP → V̄ ({AdvP, PP, NP, S̄})
S → S ({AdvP, PP, S̄})

We generate adverbial clauses at the end, but like other adverbials, they move fairly freely to the beginning of the sentence.

Abridgment of adverbial clauses. Consider the following sentences:

1. <u>When doing her school work</u>, she listens to music.
2. <u>Though new at the job</u>, she is very good.
3. <u>When apprehended by the police</u>, he had the stolen goods on him.
4. <u>If necessary</u>, you may have more time to finish the exam.

The underlined sequences express adverbial notions, but they do not seem to be complete clauses. Each sequence begins with a complementizer, but is missing a subject and some form of the verb *be* as well as tense: in (1) the progressive auxiliary, in (2) the main verb, in (3) the passive auxiliary, and in (4) the main verb are omitted. The tense omitted is the same as the tense in the main clause. In (1)–(3), the subject omitted is the same as the subject in main clause: "when <u>she</u> is doing her school work", "though <u>she</u> was new at the job", and "when <u>it</u> (=experience) is dearly bought". In (4), an impersonal "it" must be supplied: "whenever <u>it</u> is possible". We can therefore analyze these sequences as elliptical adverbial clauses because the subject, tense, and verbal can be supplied from the context (the main clause). We assume that in D-structure these are complete clauses.

Ambiguity of modification. Consider the following sentence:

He said when we met he would help me.

It is ambiguous, with two possible interpretations:

a. the helping and meeting coincide: He said <u>that</u> when we met he would help me. He said <u>that</u> he would help me when we met.
b. the saying and meeting coincide: He said when we met <u>that</u> he would help me. When we met, he said <u>that</u> he would help me.

"When we met" is a so-called *squinting modifier* since it can modify either the preceding clause ("he said") or the following clause ("he would help me"). In (a) the adverbial clause ("when we met") is an adjunct adverbial modifying the V̄ "would help me"; it is then moved to the beginning of the S which dominates it. In (b) the adverbial clause is an adjunct adverbial modifying the V̄ "said that he would help me"; the *that*-clause is then moved to the right following the adverbial clause. Study the following trees, which show the two D-structures and the movement of the adverbial clause (shown by arrows):

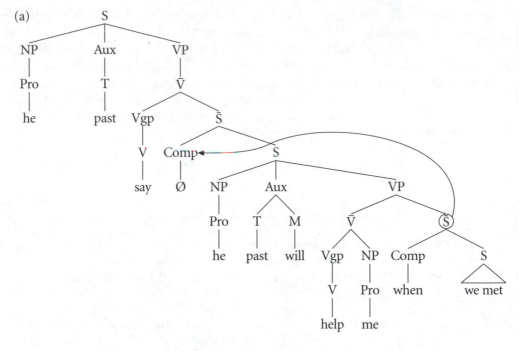

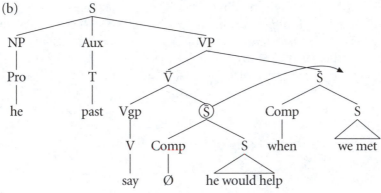

■ *Self-Testing Exercise:* Do Exercise 9.2 on nominal and adverbial clauses.

Wh-Clauses

In this section, we will study three types of *wh*-clauses:

1. *wh*-questions;
2. relative clauses; and
3. indirect questions.

The first is a type of main clause; the second two are types of subordinate clauses.

Wh-questions. In the previous chapter, we looked at two types of questions, *yes/no* (or truth) questions and tag questions. A third type of question is the *wh-* (**or content**) **question**.

Like an adverbial clause, the *wh*-question always begins with a complementizer, in this case, *who, whom, whose, what, which, why, when, where,* and *how.* Note that with the exception of *how,* all of the complementizers begin with *wh-,* hence the name **wh-words.** However, an important difference between adverbial clauses and *wh*-questions is that the complementizer in the *wh*-clause, the *wh*-word, always has <u>a function in its own clause</u>. If the *wh*-word is removed, the clause usually becomes incomplete. Furthermore, the form of the *wh*-complementizer depends upon its function (see Table 9.3). (You can perhaps more easily determine the function of the *wh*-word by putting the question in the form of a statement: e.g., You did see <u>whom</u> last night, You did leave early <u>why</u>.)

Who, whom, and *what* function as interrogative pronouns (Table 9.3a). They are standing for NP's (or clauses functioning nominally) which could serve as answers to the questions:

> Who called you last night? Felipe.
> What did you say? That I would be late.

The pronoun *who* is the subject form and *whom* is the object form, though it is common, especially in colloquial English, to use the *who* form for both. *Whose, which,* and *what* are interrogative determiners (Table 9.3b) since they precede nouns or adjectives, as in:

> Whose car did you take? Gunter's.
> Which car did you buy? The red one.
> What dessert do you want? Ice cream.

The answers provided to questions containing interrogative determiners are usually possessives or NP's, especially with the dummy noun *one. Why, when, where,* and *how* are called interrogative adverbs (Table 9.3c); the answers provided are generally adverbial phrases or clauses:

> Where did you eat dinner? At home/In a restaurant.
> Why did you do is? Because I felt like it.

However, interrogative adverbs may also stand for an obligatory element in the sentence, as in:

> <u>Where</u> did you put my glasses?
> <u>Where</u> are my glasses?

In the first case, *where* stands for the object complement of the complex transitive verb *put* (*You did put my glasses <u>where</u>*); in the second case, it stands for the subject complement of the copula verb *be* (*My glasses are <u>where</u>*). Finally, *how* is also an interrogative degree word (Table 9.3d); like all degree words, these may modify either adverbs or adjectives.

In the formation of questions, the *wh*-word is moved from its D-structure position in the sentence (the "extraction site"), which is determined by its function, to the beginning of the sentence. We will say that the *wh*-word moves into Comp position.[5] The difficulty of introducing the Comp position here is that *wh*-questions are main clauses, and S̄ is otherwise always subordinate. While there are good reasons for believing that all S's are, in fact, S̄'s (see

Table 9.3. Forms of the Interrogative Wh-Complementizer

(a) Pronoun
<u>What</u> happened to you last night? (subject)
<u>Who</u> called you last night? (subject)
<u>What</u> did you do last night? (direct object)
<u>Whom</u> did you see last night? (direct object)
<u>Whom</u> did you give the money to? (indirect object)
<u>Whom</u> did you go to the movie with last night? (object of preposition)
<u>What</u> did you call me? (object complement)

(b) Determiner
<u>Whose</u> car did you take?
<u>Which</u> movie did you see?
<u>What</u> movie did you see?

(c) Adverb
<u>Why</u> did you leave early?
<u>When</u> did the movie let out?
<u>Where</u> did you park?
<u>How</u> did you get to the theatre?

(d) Degree Word
<u>How</u> expensive was the show? (modifying A)
<u>How</u> quickly can you get here? (modifying Adv)

footnote 1), we will introduce $\bar{S}$ only when it is necessary to account for the presence of a complementizer. This transformation which moves the *wh*-word is called **wh-fronting** or **wh-movement**.[6] When the *wh*-word moves, there is a **trace**, an empty constituent (represented by *t*), left behind.

In *wh*-fronting, different constituents may move to the front, but they always contain the *wh*-word:

1. when the *wh*-word is a pronoun serving as a direct object, the NP moves:

    You did see $_{NP}$[whom] last night. ⇒ <u>Whom</u> did you see [*t*] last night?

2. when the *wh*-word is a pronoun serving as object of a preposition, either the NP or the PP moves:

    Alexandra went to the movie $_{PP}$[$_P$[with] $_{NP}$[whom]] last night. ⇒
    <u>Whom</u> did Alexandra go to the movie with [*t*] last night? or
    <u>With whom</u> did Alexandra go to the movie [*t*]?

You have a choice whether to move the NP or the entire PP. The former option results in preposition stranding, a preposition left in place (often at the end of the sentence) without its accompanying object. The latter option is called rather colorfully *pied piping*, but it is usually restricted to more formal style. Sometimes, however, pied piping appears to be obligatory:

*What classes should we meet between [*t*]?
Between what classes should we meet [*t*]?

(On the question of preposition stranding and the teaching of usage, see the chapter on pedagogy on the CD-ROM.)

3.   when the *wh*-word is an adverb or degree word, the entire AdvP or AP moves:

You left early $_{AdvP}$[$_{Adv}$[why]]. ⇒ Why did you leave early [*t*]?
You can get here $_{AdvP}$[$_{Deg}$[how]$_{Adv}$ [quickly]]. ⇒ How quickly can you get here [*t*]?
The show was $_{AP}$[$_{Deg}$[how] $_{A}$[expensive]]. ⇒ How expensive was the show [*t*]?

It is not possible to move Deg alone:

*How can you get here [*t*] quickly?
*How was the show [*t*] expensive? (However, this can sometimes be interpreted 'in what manner')

4.   when the *wh*-word is a determiner, the entire NP moves:

You like [$_{Det}$ [what] fruit]. ⇒ What fruit do you like [*t*]?

It is not possible to move Det alone:

*What do you like [*t*] fruit?

In addition to *wh*-fronting, there is subject–auxiliary inversion, as there is in *yes/no* questions. *Do*-support applies if necessary. In the following examples, [t_1] denotes the moved Aux and [t_2] denotes the moved *wh*-word:

Sean will buy a new computer when. When will Sean [t_1] buy a new computer [t_2]?
Joey bought a new computer when. When did Joey [t_1] buy a new computer [t_2]?

Note that the order of the fronted elements is *wh*-word and then Aux. This order can be accounted for if we assume that these elements move into different positions (see note 5), though, for our purposes, it suffices to say that they both move to Comp and to specify the order.

In *wh*-questions in which the *wh*-word is subject, as in *Who is going to the movie with me?*, the D-structure and the S-structure order appear to be the same. One might question, then, whether *wh*-movement and subject–aux inversion have taken place. There are three possible answers to this question:

1.   There is no *wh*-movement and no subject–aux inversion.
2.   *Wh*-fronting occurs but not inversion. There is vacuous movement of the *wh*-word to Comp ("vacuous" because it shows no effects on the surface):

$_{Comp}$[Who] $_{S}$[[*t*] is going to the movie with me]

Once the *wh*-word is fronted to Comp position, there is nothing in subject position and hence subject–aux inversion cannot occur.
3.   Both rules apply "vacuously" For this to be the case, subject–aux inversion occurs first and then *wh*-fronting, which thereby restores the original order:

_{Comp}[Who is] _S[[*t₁*] [*t₂*] going to the movie with me]

The third solution provides a consistent treatment of all *wh*-questions.

We find in *wh*-questions a phenomenon known as long *wh*-movement, in which a *wh*-word moves out of a dependent clause to the beginning of the main clause; movement in this case is said to be "unbounded" since it crosses clause boundaries. The movement occurs in successive cyclic steps, with the *wh*-word moving first to the Comp position of its own clause and then to the Comp position of the main clause. Below is the D-structure for *What did Fraser say that Elise was doing tonight?*, with the movement of *what* indicated.[7]

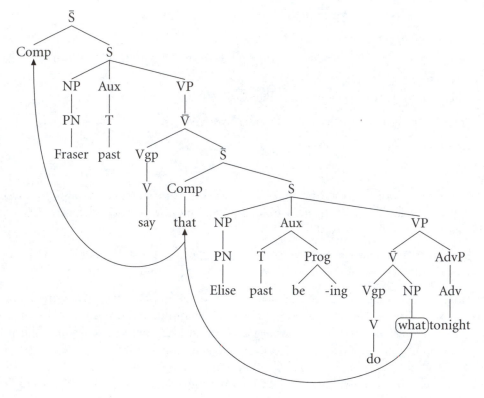

Another kind of question with a *wh*-word, the echo question,[8] has neither *wh*-fronting nor subject–aux inversion. The D-structure and the S-structure orders are the same:

Johnny did <u>what</u>?

The echo question involves rising intonation and stress on the *wh*-word. It serves to echo a statement by another speaker, questioning part of the statement.

Wh-fronting may also be involved in noninterrogative main clauses, namely in exclamations, which are formed with either *what a* or *how.*:

What a stupid remark he made!
How happy I am to see you!

Such clauses do not have subject–auxiliary inversion.

Relative clauses. The second kind of *wh*-clause is the **relative clause** (see Table 9.4).

The internal structure of relative clauses is similar to that of *wh*-question: both begin with a *wh*-word which serves a function in its own clause and which has been fronted. Just as in *wh*-questions, the *wh*-words have different forms depending on the function they serve within their clause:

– relative pronouns: *who(m), which, that*[9]
– relative adverbs: *why, when, where*
– relative determiner: *whose*

Note that the inventory of *wh*-relatives differs somewhat from the inventory of *wh*-interrogatives. Relative pronouns may serve most of the nominal functions:

Su: <u>who</u> [*t*] had done the work
dO: <u>whom</u> he had hired [*t*] (< he had hired <u>whom</u>)
OP: <u>which</u> he stood on [*t*] (< he stood on <u>which</u>)
iO: <u>whom</u> he owed it to [*t*] (< he owed it to <u>whom</u>)

(As noted in the previous section, it is often best to put the *wh*-word back into its D-structure position — to "undo" *wh*-movement — in order to identify its function. Thus, *when the Olympics are held* becomes *the Olympics are held when.*) There are certain restrictions on the use of the pronoun forms: *which* is always used for inanimate referents, *who(m)* for animate referents, *whose* and *that* for either. (*Whose* may be used for inanimates and *that* for animates, contrary to what you may have been taught.)

Wh-movement operates in relative clauses just as it does in *wh*-questions. The *wh*-word moves to the Comp position. A complete NP, PP, or AdvP is fronted; a Det alone cannot be fronted (**I enjoy reading books whose I know author*). Pied piping may occur optionally: e.g., *which he stood on* or *on which he stood.* And *wh*-movement applies "vacuously" when the relative pronoun is subject of its clause, e.g., <u>which</u> [*t*] belongs to me.

Unlike *wh*-questions, however, there is no subject–auxiliary inversion in relative clauses since inversion can only occur in main clauses. Moreover, the *wh*-word in a relative clause has a dual function; in addition to its function within its own clause, it functions as a complementizer, subordinating the dependent clause in the main clause. This embedding function is analogous to the function of *that* in *that*-clauses.

The function of relative clauses is different from the functions of the other embedded clauses that we have studied. Relative clauses always serve an adjectival function; they are modifiers which follow the noun, analogous to PPs:

The girl <u>with red hair</u> = The girl <u>who has red hair</u>

Relative clauses express a quality or feature of the noun modified. They answer the question "which?". The noun that is modified is called the head noun or the **antecedent** ('that which

Table 9.4. Relative Clauses

He paid the money to the man	{who, that} had done the work
	{who(m), that} he had hired.
	to whom he owed it.
	who(m) (that) he owed it to.

The chair	{which, that} he broke	is being repaired.
	{which, that} belongs to me	
	on which he stood	
	which he stood on	

I gave the book to the woman whose sister is my friend.

I enjoy reading books { whose author I know. / the author of which I know. }

This is the year when the Olympic Games are held.

Give me one good reason why I should do it.

I told him the place where I had hidden the gift.

---

goes before'); in Table 9.4, you can see that the head noun can serve any function in the main clause. The relative pronoun, determiner, or adverb is co-indexed with the head noun; that is, it refers to the same person or thing — the same referent. Or it can be seen as referring back to the head noun. The head noun therefore "goes before" the relative. You can understand the relative clause as deriving from a full clause, as shown below; the relative pronoun then replaces the full NP:

The girl [the girl has red hair] > The girl [who has red hair]

We must modify our phrase structure rule for N̄ to account for relative clauses:

N̄ → (AP) N̄ (PP) (S̄)

We show in this revised rule that the relative clause, S̄, is the sister of the other modifiers of N̄, namely AP and PP. Furthermore, the rule shows that it is possible for both PP and S̄ to occur, as in *the girl in the front row who has red hair*. (In contrast, the S̄ serving as complement of N̄ is the sister of Det.)

Deletion of the relative pronoun or adverb is permitted in certain cases, similar to the deletion of *that*:

He paid the money to the man { Ø he had hired [*t*]. / Ø he owed it to [*t*]. }

The chair { Ø he broke [*t*] / Ø he stood on [*t*] } is being repaired.

?This is the year Ø the Olympic Games are held [*t*].

?Give me one good reason Ø I should do it [*t*].

?I told him the place Ø I had hidden the gift [*t*].

The relative pronoun can be deleted when it is serving as direct object, indirect object, or object of the preposition. It may also be possible to delete the relative adverb. But the relative can never be deleted if:

–   it is a subject pronoun[10]
      *He paid the money to the man Ø [t] had done the work.
      *The chair Ø [t] belongs to me is being repaired.
–   it is a determiner
      *I gave the book to the woman Ø sister is my friend.
      *I enjoy reading a book Ø author I know.
–   pied piping has occurred
      *He paid the money to the man to Ø he owed it [t].
      *The chair on Ø he stood [t] is being repaired.

(On the relation between the structure of relative clauses in English and other languages to the teaching of English, see the chapter on pedagogy on the CD-ROM.)

As with *wh*-questions, there can also be long *wh*-movement in the case of relative clauses:

The party which Julian said that Sarah was going to [t] this weekend is at Fred's
< The party Julian said that Sarah was going to which this weekend is at Fred's
< The party [Julian said Sarah was going to the party] is at Fred's

Similar to the extraposition of *that*-clauses, it possible to move relative clauses to an extra-position at the end of the sentence in certain cases. However, since the relative clause is an optional modifier, it is not necessary to fill its original position with a place-holder such as *it*

I heard a woman Ø talk yesterday whom I admire [t].
A woman Ø spoke at the meeting whom I admire [t].

This is called extraposition from NP. Speakers do not always agree on the acceptability of these structures.

There are, in fact, two types of relative clauses, traditionally called **restrictive** and **nonrestrictive** (or appositive). A restrictive relative clause is necessary to identify which person or thing (denoted by head noun) is being talked about; it "restricts", limits, or picks out the referent(s) from a larger set or referents. In a nonrestrictive relative clause, the head noun is sufficiently restricted or limited in order to be identified; the relative clause simply adds additional (or parenthetical) information. Consider the following examples:

1.   I just bought a new recording of Mozart's 35th Symphony, which I enjoy listening to.
2.   I just bought a new recording of a Mozart symphony which I enjoy listening to.
      I will listen to any Mozart symphony that you care to play.

The relative clause is (1) is nonrestrictive because the head noun has a unique referent and is hence identifiable; the relative clause adds only additional, nonnecessary information. The relative clauses in (2) are restrictive because the head noun is indefinite. The relative clause is needed to restrict the referent in each case (to only those Mozart symphonies I enjoy listening to or you care to play); without the relative clause, you would not know which Mozart symphonies were being discussed. Note that the relative clause following a proper noun is always nonrestrictive (as in 1), and the relative clause following an indefinite or generic NP (with *a, any,* as in 2) is always restrictive. Usually, however, it is the context which determines whether a noun phrase is sufficiently identified (without the relative clause) or not.[11]

There are formal differences between the two types of relative clauses as well:

– nonrestrictive clauses are set off by commas in writing, by comma intonation (pauses) in speech;
– *that* cannot be used in a nonrestrictive relative clause (e.g., **Janine, that I met years ago, is returning*); and
– nonrestrictive clauses do not allow deletion of the relative pronoun (e.g., **Janine, I met years ago, is visiting*).
– nonrestrictive clauses do not allow extraposition from NP (e.g., *?I ran into Erica on my way home from work, who is a friend from my childhood*).

We are going to analyze the two types of relative clauses differently:

restrictive: N̄ → (AP) N̄ (PP) (S̄)
nonrestrictive: NP → NP S̄

That is, for the nonrestrictive clause, the noun phrase is complete without the relative clause, which is outside of and independent of the head noun phrase; it is outside the scope of the determiner as well. In contrast, the restrictive clause is part of the noun phrase and is specified by the determiner.

Relative clauses may also be ambiguous between a restrictive reading and a nonrestrictive reading, as in *Children who have vivid imaginations should avoid this program*. Either (a) all children have vivid imaginations (the nonrestrictive reading) or (b) only some children — those who should avoid the program — have vivid imaginations. Below are D-structure trees for the two readings:

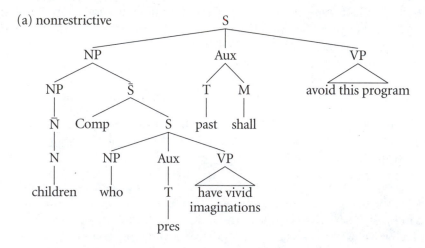

(a) nonrestrictive

(b) restrictive

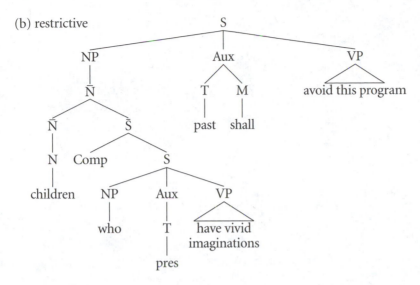

The use of *that* as both a relative pronoun and a pure complementizer can lead to confusion between appositive *that*-clauses and relative clauses:

a.   The suggestion that he might fail is disturbing.
b.   The suggestion that he made is disturbing.

In (a) is a clause functioning as a complement of N̄ (equivalent to a direct object of the verb *suggest*: Someone suggested that he might fail). The complementizer *that* has no function in its own clause, and the embedded clause is complete without *that* and can stand alone as a complete sentence *He might fail.* The *that*-clause can also function as an NP: *That he might fail is disturbing.* In (b) is a clause functioning as a modifier of N̄. The relative *that* has the function of direct object in its own clause, and hence the embedded clause is not complete without the relative: **He made.* The embedded clause cannot function as an NP: **That he made is disturbing.* Note that *which* can substitute for *that* in this case but not in the other: *The suggestion which he made is disturbing, *The suggestion which he might fail is disturbing.* Generalized D-structure trees for the sentences are given below:

(a)

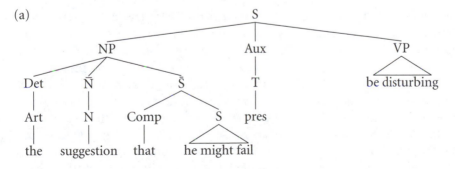

(b)

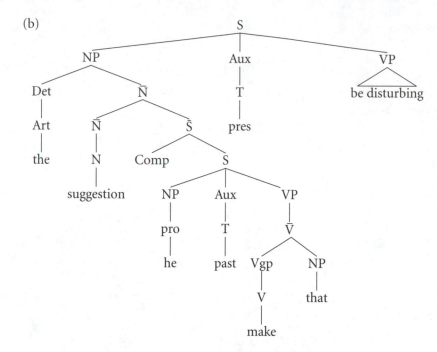

The surface similarity of these two types of clauses can lead to ambiguity:

– The idea that he proposed made her laugh.
that-clause: his proposing made her laugh (that he proposed made her laugh)
relative clause: his idea made her laugh (he proposed the idea)
– The fact that Bill forgot was verified.
that-clause: Bill's forgetting was verified (that Bill forgot was verified)
relative clause: the fact was verified (Bill forgot the fact)
The following embedded clauses resemble relative clauses:

> I sold <u>what you gave me</u>.
> I know {<u>where, why, when, how</u>} he went.
> He announced <u>what room it was in</u>.

Note that the *wh*-word begins the clause and serves a function in it (in this case, direct object, adjunct adverbial, and determiner, respectively). However, the problem is that there is no head noun in the main clause for the underlined clauses to modify; for this reason, such clauses have been called **free** or **headless relatives**. One way to analyze these clauses is to interpret *what* as *that which*; then, the clause can be understood as a relative clause modifying the head noun *that* (*I sold that which you gave me*). Note that such a paraphrase is more difficult with the other forms. A preferable analysis is to understand the free relative clause as filling the direct object position (as a *that*-clause fills the dO position in *I know <u>that he will attend</u>*), rather than a modifying position, and hence as functioning as a nominal clause (for this reason, free relatives are also called "nominal relative clauses"). While the free relatives shown above all occupy the dO position in the main clause, they may also be Su, sC, or OP:

<u>What he did</u> disturbed me.
The question is <u>what he should do</u>.
We argued about <u>what he should do</u>.

In a tree diagram, the free relative should be generated under NP, as is the *that*-clause, e.g.

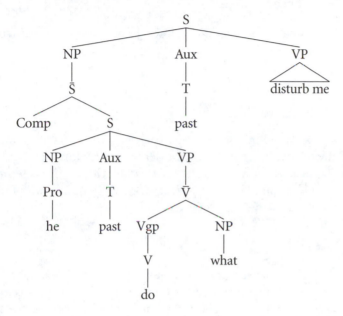

An embedded clause similar to the free relative is the **indefinite relative clause**, beginning with an indefinite pronoun ending with -*ever*:

He will agree to <u>whatever you say</u>.
Give the prize to <u>whoever enters first</u>.
He asked <u>whomever he saw</u>.
<u>Whatever he says</u> is correct.
You can call me <u>whatever you want</u>.

Again, the *wh*-word fills a function in its own clause (dO, Su, dO, dO, and dO above), and the entire clause fills a nominal function (OP, iO, dO, Su, and oC above). Indefinite relatives can also function like adverbial clauses:

<u>Whenever he is gone</u>, it is very quiet here.

Pseudocleft sentences (see Chapter 11) contain a headless relative clause, the verb *be*, and a NP or VP:

<u>What Sam got for his birthday</u> is a computer.
<u>What Judith did</u> was slam the door.
<u>What Judith slammed</u> was the door.
<u>What surprised Frances</u> was your answer.

Cleft sentences, (see Chapter 11), on the other hand, consist of *it*, the verb *be*, a NP or PP, and a true relative clause:

> It was a computer <u>that Sam got for his birthday</u>.
> It was the door <u>that Judith slammed</u>.
> It was after lunch <u>that they planned to meet</u>.

One last problem is posed by sentences such as the following containing nonrestrictive relative clauses:

> Jack helped me move, <u>which was very kind of him</u>.
> We rented a truck, <u>which made the move easier</u>.
> I'm very tired, <u>which is a result of gardening all day</u>.

The trouble here is that the relative pronoun does not refer back to any specific head noun, rather to the entire S. Strict prescriptive grammarians consider these structures wrong, but they are very common in colloquial and even more formal usage. These can be termed **sentential relative clauses**. We could account for these with some modification of our phrase structure rules, making the relative clause the sister of S.

■ Self-Testing Exercise: Do Exercise 9.4

Indirect questions. The third kind of *wh*-clause is **indirect questions** (see Table 9.5).
    The functions of the indirect question clause are the same as those of the *that*-clause. That is, they serve various nominal functions; in the sentences in Table 9.5, we see the following functions exemplified:

1. subject
2. direct object
3. direct object after indirect object
4. subject complement
5. object of preposition
6. complement of adjective
7. complement of $\bar{\text{N}}$
8. extraposed subject

Like the *that*-clause, the indirect question clause cannot function as indirect object nor as object complement and is normally extraposed when serving as subject of the main clause, as in (8).

Table 9.5. Indirect Questions

(1)	{<u>How he gets the money</u>, <u>Whether he gets the money</u>} is his own affair.
(2)	I asked {<u>when he was going to do it</u>, <u>whether she will get the fellowship</u>}.
(3)	He asked his friend {<u>when he was leaving on his holidays</u>, <u>whether he was taking holidays</u>}.
(4)	The question is {<u>how he will get the money</u>, <u>whether the work will get done</u>}.
(5)	We are concerned about {<u>how soon he can get here</u>, <u>whether he will lose his job</u>}.
(6)	She is uncertain {<u>which one that he should choose</u>, <u>whether she will be on time</u>}.
(7)	The question <u>whether he did it</u> is troubling.
(8)	It has often been asked <u>who did it</u>.

Indirect questions are a type of indirect speech; in our discussion above, we saw that indirect statements following verbs of communication were expressed by *that*-clauses. Both *yes/no* and *wh*-questions can be reported in a similar fashion:

–   direct *yes/no*: Rosie asked Paul, "Is your sister going to Toronto tomorrow?"
    indirect: Rosie asked Paul whether his sister was going to Toronto the next day.
–   direct *wh-*: Rosie asked Paul, "Why is your sister going to Toronto tomorrow?"
    indirect: Rosie asked Paul why his sister was going to Toronto the next day.

A number of changes occur when direct discourse is shifted to indirect discourse, including the shifting of verb tenses, pronouns, and certain adverbs (such as *here* and *now*). For our purposes, the important changes are the following:

–   subject–auxiliary inversion is "undone"; and
–   a complementizer — either *if* or *whether* — is supplied for *yes/no* questions.

For *wh*-questions, *wh*-movement is retained; the *wh*-word is base-generated in the position corresponding to its function and then moved to Comp position. The form of these *wh*-words is as discussed above for direct questions. In the sentences in Table 9.5, the *wh*-words (but not *whether*) have the following functions in their own clauses: (1)–(4) adverb, (5) degree word, (6) determiner, and (7)–(8) pronoun (subject). The *wh*-words thus have a dual role, as they do in relative clauses, as complementizers embedding the indirect question into the main clause and as pronouns, determiners, adverbs and degree words within their own clauses. However, *if* and *whether* have no function within their own clause but, like *that*, serve merely as complementizers; they are base-generated in Comp position. Note also that subject–aux inversion does not occur in either type of indirect question since this transformation is restricted to main clauses.

We have now studied a number of different subordinate clauses which have a surface similarity. Can you identify the type of subordinate clause in each of the following?

a.   I asked when the meeting would finish.
b.   I don't know the time when the meeting will finish.
c.   I will leave when the meeting is finished.

The first (a) is an indirect question, functioning as direct object of *asked*, with the interrogative adverb *when*. The second (b) is a relative clause, modifying *the time*, with the relative adverb *when*. The third (c) is an adverbial clause, with the complementizer *when*.

Indirect exclamatory sentences, like their direct counterparts, are formed with *what a* or *how*+A and *wh*-movement, but no inversion:

> It's strange <u>how old he looks</u>.
> I'm happy about <u>what a good time you had</u>.
> I've read of <u>what a fine reputation he has</u>.

■   *Self-Testing Exercise:* As a review of all *wh*-clauses, do Exercise 9.5.

Hint: When analyzing complex sentences with one or more dependent clauses, your first step should be to identify the main clause. Then bracket all of the dependent clauses and identify their function. Remember that to arrive at the D-structure all passive clauses must be returned to active, interrogative to declarative, and negative to positive; extraposition must be reversed. For example, below is the D-structure tree for *Did Matthew say whether the movie he saw yesterday was interesting?*. It consists of a main clause question containing an indirect question (functioning as direct object) which itself contains an embedded relative clause.

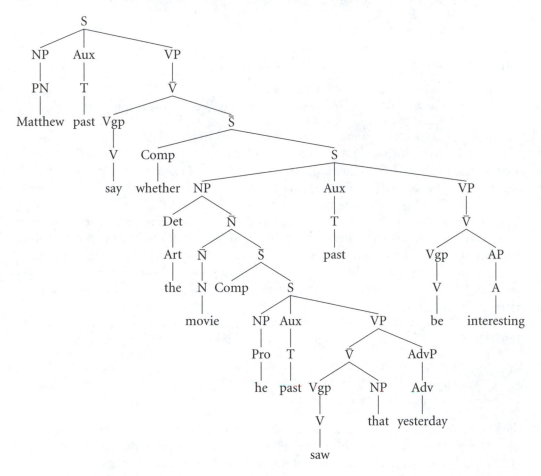

Nonfinite Clauses

In the first half of the chapter, we treated the various types of finite clauses; we turn now to **nonfinite clauses,** where the verbal element is not marked for person, number, or tense. By definition, nonfinite clauses are always dependent, or embedded, since a main clause must have a finite verb.

Forms of Nonfinite Clauses

The verbal element in nonfinite clauses may take one of four forms, usually determined by the verb in the main clause.

The first nonfinite form is the **bare infinitive** (what we have encountered before as the stem form of the verb), as in the following:

The teacher made me <u>do</u> it.
I saw Aaron <u>leave</u>.

We will denote all nonfinite forms with the feature [−tense] in Aux since the lack of tense is their most salient characteristic.[12] A tree diagram for Aux + V in the second sentence above would be as follows:

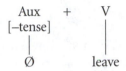

The bare infinitive is, in fact, quite limited, occurring after verbs of causation (e.g., *make*) and of perception (e.g., *see*), as well as modal auxiliaries.

The second nonfinite form is the *to*-**infinitive**. It consists of *to* followed by the stem form of the verb or auxiliary. It can also include the perfect, progressive, and passive in the order and with the endings that you will recognize from our analysis of the finite Aux:

simple active: I want <u>to give</u> you a present.
perfect active: He seems <u>to have left</u>.
progressive active: Sally appears <u>to be doing</u> well.
perfect progressive active: He seems <u>to have been doing</u> better recently.
simple passive: She wants <u>to be given</u> more responsibility.
perfect passive: He seems <u>to have been overlooked</u>.
progressive passive: [?]<u>To be being asked</u> stupid questions all the time bothers him.
perfect progressive passive: <u>To have been being asked</u> stupid questions all the time
                             bothered him.

The progressive passive and perfect progressive passive are awkward, perhaps because of the presence of two *be* auxiliaries. The Aux of the *to*-infinitive, which like all nonfinites has the feature [−tense], includes *to* and, as necessary, Perf, Prog, or Pass. Thus, *to have been being asked* (admittedly, a rare form) would be represented as follows:

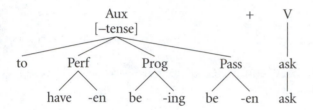

To arrive at the S-structure form, one has to perform affix hopping. Note that modals cannot occur here because they have no nonfinite forms.

The third nonfinite form is the *-ing* **participle**, or present participle. It too occurs in a number of different forms, always beginning with an *-ing* form:

> simple active: He stopped <u>working</u> there a year ago.
> perfect active: <u>Having arrived</u> late, she missed much of the concert.
> progressive active: *<u>being asking</u>[13]
> perfect progressive active: <u>Having been writing</u> for a long time, she took a break.
> perfect passive: He resents <u>having been asked</u> to help.
> progressive passive: She doesn't like <u>being left</u> out of the plan.
> perfect progressive passive: <u>Having been being given</u> so much attention pleases him.

When the *-ing* participle has a nominal function, it is known as a **gerund**. The sequence *having been writing* is represented as follows:

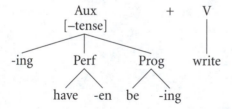

Affix hopping would attach the affixes appropriately here.

The fourth nonfinite form is the *-en* **participle**. It has only one form:[14]

> simple passive: The book <u>given</u> to him yesterday is very valuable.

```
Aux     +     V
[−tense]
  |           |
 -en         give
```

Note that modals cannot occur in either the *-ing* or *-en* form because they have no participial forms.

Omissions from Nonfinite Clauses

A characteristic of nonfinite clauses is that they are often incomplete, missing obligatory elements such as subject or direct object. For this reason, nonfinite clauses are called "phrases" in traditional grammar. But they are better understood as deriving from complete clauses by the omission of obligatory elements. These omissions are called **PRO**, or "big PRO" (PRO for "pronoun"); PRO refers to the phonetically null subject and object NPs of nonfinite clauses. PROs may be of two types: controlled or indefinite (arbitrary). A **controlled PRO** is one in which the missing element in the nonfinite embedded clause is identical to an element in the main clause, such as the subject, object, or indirect object. The omitted element can be supplied from the main clause to reconstitute a complete clause, as follows:

> I want [PRO to do well]. < I want [I do well]

In the sentence above, the PRO in the nonfinite clause is said to be "controlled" by the subject of the main clause, and since the PRO is the subject of the nonfinite clause, we call it a "subject PRO". Thus, it is a subject PRO controlled by the subject of the higher S (note that the controller NP needn't be in the main clause, but just in the next higher clause). We can represent this as follows:

> I want $_\bar{S}$[PRO to do well]. Leslie said that she wanted $_\bar{S}$[PRO to do well].

The various possibilities of controls and PROs are shown in Table 9.6a. You will note that there may be both subject and object PROs and that the two types of PRO can occur in the same clause.[15]

The second type of PRO is an **indefinite PRO**. This is one in which the missing element in the nonfinite clause can be filled with the general "you" or "one", not with any specific element from the higher clause (see Table 9.6b). The two types of PROs can occur in the same clause (see Table 9.6c).

Complementizers in Nonfinite Clauses

Unlike finite embedded clauses, nonfinite clauses are usually not preceded by a complementizer. However, complementizers are used in two situations.

The complementizer *for* occurs in the so-called *for*-**infinitive**. This is a *to*-infinitive with a nonnull subject. *For* is used when an infinitive with an explicit subject has one of the following functions (the functions are discussed below):

> subject: $_\bar{S}$[For Sue to see a doctor] is important.
> complement of A: We are anxious $_\bar{S}$[for John to do well].
> adverbial: $_\bar{S}$[For him to do well], he must try harder.
> postmodifier of N̄: Here is a letter $_\bar{S}$[for you to mail].
> complement of N̄: We issued a command $_\bar{S}$[for him to return].

Table 9.6. Controlled and Indefinite PRO in Nonfinite Clauses

(a)   Controlled PRO:

(1)   subject PRO controlled by subject of higher S:

The man ₛ[PRO sitting at the desk] is the clerk. < the man is sitting at the desk

I wondered when ₛ[PRO to call him]. < I call him

She demonstrated her determination ₛ[PRO to succeed]. < she succeed

ₛ[PRO Faced with an ultimatum], they gave in. < they are faced with an ultimatum

(2)   subject PRO controlled by object of higher S:

We persuaded him ₛ[PRO to try again]. < he try again

ₛ[PRO Running five miles] exhausted me. < I run five miles

I saw a picture ₛ[PRO painted by Renoir]. < a picture painted by Renoir

(3)   subject PRO controlled by indirect object of higher S:

I told Karen ₛ[when PRO to leave]. < Karen leave when

(4)   object PRO controlled by subject of higher S:

The question is too difficult ₛ[for Bill to answer PRO]. <Bill answer the question.

(5)   object PRO controlled by object of higher S:

We have a job ₛ[for Paul to do PRO]. < Paul do the job

(6)   more than one controlled PRO in the same clause:

She gave John the book ₛ[PRO to return PRO]. <John return the book

   subject PRO controlled by indirect object of higher S
   object PRO controlled by object of higher S

I need a knife ₛ[PRO to cut the bread with PRO]. <I cut the bread with a knife

   subject PRO controlled by subject of higher S
   object (of preposition) PRO controlled by object of higher S

(b)   Indefinite PRO:

ₛ[PRO Running five miles] is exhausting. < you run five miles

ₛ[PRO To leave now] would be wrong. < you leave now

It's time ₛ[PRO to start dinner]. < you start dinner

Table 9.6 (continued)

(c)   Controlled and Indefinite PRO in the same clause:

That question is too difficult ₛ̄[PRO to answer PRO]. < you answer that question

object PRO controlled by subject of higher S
indefinite subject PRO

The best answer ₛ̄[PRO to give PRO] is no answer. < you give the answer

object PRO controlled by subject of higher S
indefinite subject PRO

Explicit subjects are not permitted when the infinitive functions as object of P. The only situation in which *for* is almost never used is when the infinitive functions as direct object of the verb, whether it is a *to*-infinitive or a bare infinitive:

> We wanted (*for) him to return.
> We made (*for) him return.
> cf. We arranged for him to return.

For never precedes PRO. The subject of an *-en* or *-ing* participle never takes *for*.[16]

The second situation in which a complementizer is used is with **wh-infinitives**. Like all *wh*-clauses, *wh*-infinitives have *wh*-movement of a *wh*-word serving some function in the embedded clause. The fronted *wh*-word fills the complementizer position. Below are examples of nonfinite indirect questions (1) and free relatives (2):

(1)   I asked ₛ̄[where PRO to put it [*t*]].
We are concerned about ₛ̄[what PRO to do [*t*]].
We wondered ₛ̄[when PRO to leave [*t*]].
She is uncertain ₛ̄[whether PRO to apply for the job].
He agonized over the question ₛ̄[whether PRO to report the fraud].
ₛ̄[Which sofa PRO to buy [*t*]] is his current concern.

(2)   I know ₛ̄[{what PRO to do [*t*], where PRO to report it [*t*], when PRO to open it [*t*], whom PRO to speak to [*t*]}].

Both indirect *yes/no* and *wh*-questions may appear as nonfinite indirect questions; in *wh*-question there is a moved *wh*-constituent, whereas in *yes/no* questions there is not. Note that nonfinite indirect questions always contain a subject PRO controlled by the subject of the higher clause.

We will use S̄ in all cases of subordinate clauses, but see Comp as empty in cases where there is not an explicit complementizer.

■   *Self-Testing Exercise: Do Exercise 9.6.*

Functions of Nonfinite Clauses

The grammatical functions of nonfinite clauses are the same as those we identified for finite clauses (nominal, adjectival, and adverbial), but not all forms of clauses can serve all functions.

Subject and subject complement. Both *to*-infinitives (including *wh*-infinitives) and *-ing* participles (gerunds) can function as subject of the sentence. Like finite clauses, nonfinite subject clauses freely extrapose to the end of the sentence. Examples are as follows:

- Su $_\bar{s}$[PRO To run a small business] is difficult.
  eSu It is difficult $_\bar{s}$[PRO to run a small business].
- Su $_\bar{s}$[For him to be well prepared] is important.
  eSu It is important $_\bar{s}$[for him to be well prepared].
- Su $_\bar{s}$[PRO Running five miles] is exhausting.
  eSu It is exhausting $_\bar{s}$[PRO running five miles].
- Su $_\bar{s}$[Jane('s) running five miles] is impressive.
  eSu *It is impressive $_\bar{s}$[Jane's running five miles].
- Su $_\bar{s}$[What PRO to do [*t*] with her money] preoccupied her.
  eSu It preoccupied her $_\bar{s}$[what PRO to do [*t*] with her money].

Extraposition is not always possible when the gerund has an explicit subject (as in the fourth example above). The same forms may also function as subject complements:

Her first job was $_\bar{s}$[PRO selling computers].
What you must do is $_\bar{s}$[PRO rewrite the last paragraph].
Your first task is $_\bar{s}$[PRO to wash the windows].
The question is $_\bar{s}$[where PRO to eat in this town [*t*]].

-en participles may also function as subject complements:

The cat stayed $_\bar{s}$[PRO hidden under the bed].

Another type of sentence which should be analyzed as containing a subject nonfinite clause is the following:

That politician seems to be honest.

You will recall that sentences of the type *It seems that that politician is honest* were analyzed above as containing a *that*-clause subject which was obligatorily extraposed. Similarly, we analyze this sentences as having the following D-structure:

$_{NP}$[$_\bar{s}$[that politician to be honest]] [seems]

The S-structure results from extraposition of the $\bar{S}$ with "raising" of the subject NP *the politician* to subject of the matrix clause. (Raising is discussed in more detail below.)

Complement of A. Both *to*-infinitives and *-ing* participles can serve as the complement of an adjective:

> He is happy ₛ[PRO attending school].
> He is determined ₛ[PRO to do well].
> We are anxious ₛ[for the term to end].
> This dessert is easy ₛ[PRO to make PRO].
> This game is enjoyable ₛ[for children to play PRO].

There are two classes of adjectives which take such a complement. With the first class, the nonfinite clause has a subject PRO controlled by the subject of the upper clause; included in this class are adjectives like *determined, anxious, eager, hesitant, unwilling, furious, happy, liable, quick, reluctant, likely, bound, afraid, delighted,* and *able.* With the second class, the nonfinite clause has an object PRO controlled by the subject of the upper clause. Included in this class are adjectives like *difficult, impossible, easy, hard, tough, tiresome, boring, enjoyable,* and *delicious.*[17] Note that a *to*-infinitive clause or *-ing* participle may serve as subject of a sentence with one of these adjectives in the predicate; both may also be extraposed:

– Su ₛ[PRO {Answering, To answer} all these questions] is tiresome.
  eSu It is tiresome ₛ[PRO {answering, to answer} all these questions].

Object of P. Only *-ing* participles (gerunds) can serve as objects of prepositions. Nonfinites can occur as OPs no matter what the function of the PP as a whole:

– We talked [about ₛ[PRO going to a movie]].
    PP is complement of V
– You will find the answer [by ₛ[PRO turning the page]].
    PP is adjunct adverbial (expressing manner)
– The results [of ₛ[PRO investing in that stock]] were very good.
    PP is modifier of N̄
– He was close [to ₛ[PRO finding the answer]].
    PP is complement of A
– He was happy [about ₛ[Mary('s) being chosen]].
    PP is complement of A
– [With ₛ[his parents visiting]], he is too busy to attend class.
    PP is adjunct adverbial (expressing reason)

Adverbial. *To*-infinitives may function as adjunct adverbials (1)–(3), disjunct adverbials (4)–(5), and conjunct adverbials (6):

1. ₛ[PRO To get ahead], you need to work hard.
2. The lecturer used slides ₛ[PRO to make the talk more interesting].
3. ₛ[For him to win the election], his campaign workers will need to work very hard.
4. ₛ[PRO To judge by her reaction], she must be angry.
5. ₛ[PRO To tell you the truth], I haven't completed my assignment.
6. ₛ[PRO To change the subject], what are you doing tomorrow night?

Both -*ing* and -*en* participles may also serve an adverbial function as adjunct adverbials (7–12), disjunct adverbials (13), and conjunct adverbials (14):

7. ₛ[PRO Arriving late], we were not seated until the intermission.
8. ₛ[PRO Disappointed by the results], the scientist gave up the project.
9. ₛ[The plane arriving late], we missed our connection.
10. ₛ[Her fingers being numb], she couldn't button her coat.
11. ₛ[Their home ruined by fire], they had to seek shelter with relatives.
12. ₛ[The plot discovered], the conspirators fled.
13. ₛ[PRO Generally speaking], I don't watch television.
14. ₛ[PRO Putting it briefly], your computer cannot be repaired.

The nonfinite clauses in (9)–(12), as well as *With his parent visiting* in the previous section, have the special name of **absolute constructions**. They consist of a participle and an explicit subject (not PRO) and sometimes a preposition. Absolute constructions are thought to have no grammatical connection with the rest of the sentence (hence the term "absolute"). However, since they generally express the adverbial notion of "circumstance" (cause or time) or provide added detail to the sentence, we will analyze them as adverbial. In certain cases, a *being* participle has been deleted, leaving a predicate PP, AP, or NP: *Her head (being) to one side, she looked at him curiously*; *Her eyes (being) wide with astonishment, the child watched the clown*; *We pitied the victims, many of them (being) children*. These are called "small" (or verbless) clauses. It would seem that the causal meaning in not as strong when *being* is omitted (compare *His cap being in his hand, he couldn't hold the box* and *His cap in his hand, he left the room*), nor is it as strong when the absolute is in mid or final position rather than initial position (e.g., *The participants, some elderly, were very eager*; *The report is divided into sections, each devoted to a different aspect of the problem*). It might be possible to analyze absolute constructions with -*en* participles as having an elliptical *being*, as in *His house now (being) ruined, he reflected on his future.*[18]

Modifier of N̄ or of NP. Both -*ing* and -*en* participles and *to*-infinitives can function as modifiers of N̄; that is, they can have a restricted adjectival function. These nonfinite clauses have at least one element missing; in the case of the -*en* and -*ing* participles, the element missing is always the subject, which is controlled by the immediately preceding noun; for infinitives, there may be an object PRO:

The letters ₛ[for you to mail PRO] are on the counter.
There are lots of mouths ₛ[PRO to feed PRO] in that house.
The letters ₛ[PRO lying on the counter] are for you to mail.
The book ₛ[PRO written by Chomsky] is on the table.

The function of these nonfinite clauses is identical to that of adjectives (including participles) which precede the noun and of PPs or finite relative clauses which follow the noun. This equivalency can be seen in the following finite relative clause paraphrases of the above nonfinite clauses:

which {you should mail, are for you to mail}
which you have to feed
which are lying on the counter
which was written by Chomsky

The only difference between participial relative clauses and the finite relative clauses is the presence of the relative pronoun subject *which* and a form of *be*.[19] Note that the difference between participial clauses which follow the noun and participles functioning as adjectives which precede the noun (as discussed in Chapter 7) is the presence of a complement PP. A simple participle cannot follow the noun, as a complemented participle cannot precede the noun:

the ripped flag	*the flag ripped
the flag ripped by the wind	*the ripped by the wind flag

Nonfinite clauses may also serve as nonrestrictive adjectives, that is, as modifiers of the NP, as in the following examples:

Chomsky's book, ₛ[PRO lying on the table over there], is difficult to read.
Chomsky's book, ₛ[PRO written just last year], is difficult to read.
He described his one goal in life, ₛ[PRO to be a bus driver].

It is sometimes difficult to distinguish adverbial from nonrestrictive adjectival participial clauses since both can be moved to the beginning of the sentence:

– Adverbial: Disgusted by the movie, we left. < We left, disgusted by the movie.
– Adjectival: Discussed by everyone in the class, the movie seemed to generate lots of interest. < The movie, discussed by everyone in the class, seemed to generate lots of interest.

But note that the adverbial clause answers the question "why?" while the adjectival one does not; the adverbial clause can be replaced by a *because* clause ("because we were disgusted by the movie", but not "because the movie was discussed by everyone"). On the other hand, it is possible to replace the adjectival participial clause with a relative clause, but the adverbial clause lends itself less naturally to such a replacement ("the movie, which was discussed by everyone", but not "we, who were disgusted by the movie").

There appears to be a rule — in writing at least — that the PRO of the fronted participial clause must be controlled by the subject of the matrix clause. If this is not the case, then one has the error known as a *dangling participle*,[20] which may sometimes be (unintentionally) funny, as in:

Being completely untamed, George warned us that the animals were dangerous.
Having worked in the capital, the methods of lobbyists are very familiar to me.
From talking to others, the prevalent opinion favors our cause.

Complement of N̄. To-infinitives, like *that*-clauses, may function as complement of N̄ following an abstract noun:

- The suggestion [PRO to go home] wasn't well received.
  cf. The suggestion that he go home wasn't well received.
- We thought it was a good suggestion [for him to leave].

The relationship of the clause to the abstract noun is comparable to that of a direct object to a verb: *We suggested [that he go home]*. Just as it was important to distinguish *that*-clauses functioning as complement of Ñ from relative clauses (see above), it is important to make the same distinction here. If the nonfinite clause is functioning as complement of Ñ, it cannot be replaced by a relative clause: *the suggestion which he go home*. Furthermore, the PRO is not controlled by the head noun: *the suggestion [he (*the suggestion) go home]*.

Below are generalized trees exemplifying all of the functions discussed.

a. Subject: *Running a small business is difficult.*

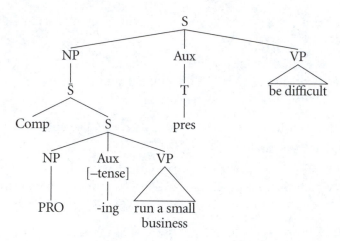

b. Subject Complement: *Her first job was selling computers.*

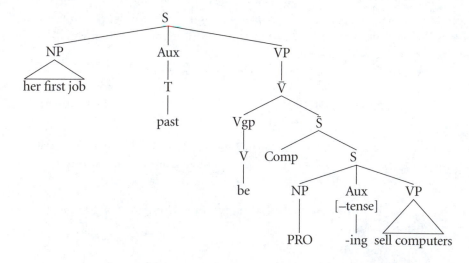

c. Complement of A: *The question is difficult to answer.*

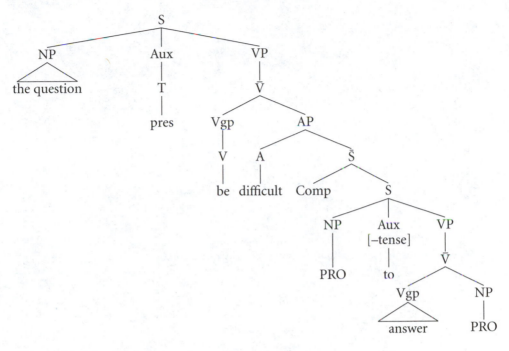

d. Object of P: *We talked about going to the movies.*

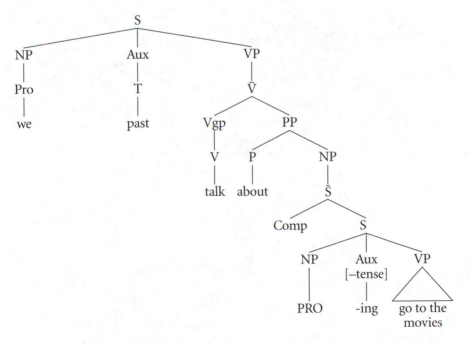

e.　Adjunct Adverbial: *You must work hard to get ahead.*

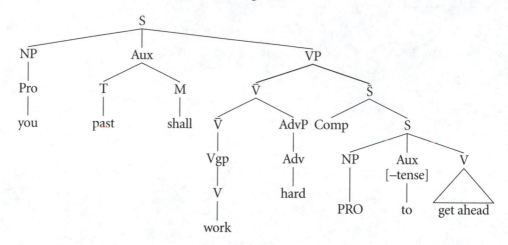

f.　Modifier of N̄: *The tree toppled by the wind was very old.*

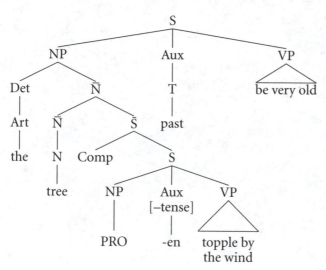

g.   Complement of N̄: *The proposal to erect a new building is absurd.*

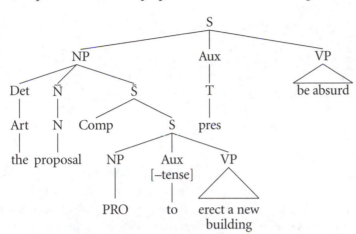

For (f) note that although the *-en* participle is logically passive, we are not changing it to active in D-structure.

Nonfinite Clauses as Complements of V

The most important function of nonfinite clauses is as complement of the verb, but this is also the most difficult function to analyze and discuss. A full treatment of it would require several chapters and is beyond the scope of this text. First, it is not clear that the verbal-complement functions of clauses are comparable to those of the noun phrases, and other phrasal categories, though it is traditional to see clauses as serving as direct objects and object complements. (Clauses cannot be indirect objects, since they do not have animate referents.) For this reason, clausal verb complements have been seen as directly dominated by V̄, not NP. Second, if clausal complements are included, an entirely new sub-categorization system of verbs is required. For example, a preliminary classification of verbs which considers only infinitive and *that*-clause complements yields at least ten different types:

expect {to V, NP to V, that S}	remind {NP to V, NP that S}
claim {to V, that S}	arrange {for NP to V, that S}
believe{NP to V, that S}	hear {NP V, that S}
force NP to V	make {NP V}
try to V	cause {NP to V}

With non-finite complements, the crucial factor seems to be whether there is an explicit NP between the matrix and embedded clause. Note that some verbs optionally allow such an NP, others obligatorily require one, while others do not permit one.

When the NP is absent, the structure can quite easily be analyzed as follows:

Sally forgot S̄[PRO to close the door].

Patricia expects S̄[PRO to get a good mark].

Mary practiced S̄[PRO reciting the poem].

He tried S̄[PRO {to cut, cutting} the rope].

She {hates, likes} S̄[PRO {to vacuum, vacuuming}].

That is, the nonfinite clause has a subject PRO controlled by the subject of the upper clause. This is semantically quite obvious: if Lucy expects to leave, then it is Lucy's leaving that is expected; another way to look at it is as two main clauses: Lucy expect [Lucy leave]. There is also a formal test using reflexives. We know (from the last chapter) that a reflexive must be co-indexed with the subject of its own clause. Therefore, in the following sentences there must be a deleted subject of the nonfinite clause, namely PRO, which is coindexed to the subject:

Lucy expects [PRO to improve {herself, *themselves, *yourself}].
Graham said that Mary wanted [PRO to protect {herself, *himself}].

Only *to*-infinitives and *-ing* participles may occur in the structure without an intervening NP. Note that some verbs take only *to*-infinitives (e.g., *expect, hope, wish, want*), some verbs take only *-ing* participles (e.g., *admit, keep on, finish, practice, enjoy, give up, avoid, deny, appreciate*), and some verbs may take either (e.g., *begin, start, stop, continue, go on, try, regret, prefer, dread*), though, sometimes, the different nonfinite forms convey different meanings, as in:

We stopped {to eat, eating}.
He remembered {to mail, mailing} the letter.

When the NP is present, all four types of nonfinites may occur:

a. bare infinitive:
    She heard the prowler open the door.
    They made the tenants clean the apartment.
b. *to*-infinitive
    She convinced him to change the wording.
    They expected Kylie to be on time.
c. *-ing* participle
    I resent the student('s) interrupting all the time.
    We saw two large bears crossing the road.
d. *-en* participle
    They discovered the car deserted in the woods.
    He kept a snake caged in his house.

The structure is not easily analyzed because the status of the NP is in question: Is it the subject of the embedded clause or the object of the main clause? That is, which of these two bracketings is correct?

> She heard ₛ[the prowler open the door] OR
> She heard the prowler ₛ[PRO open the door]?

A complementizer, which would clearly delineate the embedded from the main clause, occurs with only a few verbs in English, such as *prefer* and *wish*. Furthermore, when a pronoun substitutes for the NP, it occurs in the objective form. While this might suggest the second analysis, one can argue that subjects of nonfinites always occur in the objective case (e.g., *for him to leave*) or perhaps the genitive case (e.g., *John's drinking*), but not the nominative case.

To try to decide this issue, let's look at two example sentences:

a. John wants Mary to see a doctor.
b. John persuaded Mary to see a doctor.

Semantically, in (a) John wants an entire state of affairs, namely Mary's seeing a doctor; the entire proposition (Mary see a doctor) is the object of John's wanting. In (b) John persuades a person to do something (he persuades Mary, Mary see a doctor); he does not persuade an entire proposition (Mary see a doctor). If we question the nonfinite clauses, our questions and answers take different forms for the two sentences:

a. <u>What</u> did John want? <u>For Mary to see a doctor.</u>
   not *<u>Who</u> did John want? <u>Mary.</u>
b. <u>Who</u> did John persuade (to see a doctor)? <u>Mary.</u>
   not *<u>What</u> did John persuade? <u>For Mary to see a doctor.</u>

It is syntactically possible to delete the second NP in the first case (*John wants to see a doctor*) but not in the second case (**John persuaded to see a doctor*); rather, we must insert a reflexive pronoun (*John persuaded himself to see a doctor*). If we passivize the embedded clause in the cases of *want* and *persuade*, we see a difference:

a. Cian wants Sybil to write a best-selling novel.
   Cian wants a best-selling novel to be written by Sybil.
b. John persuaded Mary to see a doctor.
   John persuaded a doctor to be seen by Mary.

In the *want* case, there is synonymy between the active and passive versions. Cian wants the same state of affairs in both cases. In the *persuade* case, however, there isn't synonymy because in the active version John acts upon Mary, while in the passive version he acts upon the doctor. In pseudocleft sentences, the two verbs also behave differently:

a. What Arni wanted was for Karim to be quiet.
b. *What Arni persuaded was for Karim to be quiet.

Another difference is that the NP following *persuade* must be animate, because only an animate being can be made to do something:

a. Ann wanted a paper to be written on that topic.
b. *Ann persuaded a paper to be written on that topic.

A final difference is that the NP following *want* may be one which is restricted to subject position (namely existential *there* and the dummy *it* in weather expressions), but these forms cannot follow *persuade*:

a. Bronwyn wants {it to rain, there to be sun} tomorrow.
b. *Gwendolyn persuaded {it to rain, there to be sun} tomorrow.

Because of these semantic and formal differences, we set up two classes of verbs. In *want*-type verbs, the NP is subject of the nonfinite embedded clause: V_{gp} [NP VP]. In *persuade*-type verbs, the NP is object of the main clause verb, but controls the deleted subject of the nonfinite clause: V_{gp} NP [PRO VP]. In the *want* case, we analyze the nonfinite clause as the direct object, while in the *force* case, we analyze it as an object complement, completing the direct object. Note the similarity between nominal/adjectival and clausal object complements in the following:

a. Harris made Aster {chair, angry}.
b. Harris made Aster empty the garbage.

There is a problem for our classification, however. Consider the verb *expect*. In most respects, it seems to pattern like *want*:

a. Barbara expects Megan to feed the dog.
b. What does Barbara expect? For Megan to feed the dog.
c. Barbara expects the dog to be fed by Megan.
d. What Barbara expects is for Megan to feed the dog.
e. Barbara expects {it to rain, there to be sunshine} tomorrow.

However, in one important respect, the *expect* case is like the *persuade* case and unlike the *want* case. First, the second NP can be questioned: *Who does Barbara expect to feed the dog? Megan*. Second, note what happens when the matrix clause is passivized:

a. *Megan was wanted by Barbara to feed the dog.
b. Megan was persuaded by Barbara to feed the dog.
c. Megan was expected by Barbara to feed the dog.

This evidence suggests that with *expect*, the second NP is object of the matrix clause since it can become the subject of a corresponding passive. Remember that the rule for passive instructs us to move the direct object to subject position. A variant passive, however — *For Megan to feed the dog was expected by Barbara* — moves the entire clause to subject position, treating *Megan* as subject of the embedded clause. Thus, *Megan* seems to behave as both subject of the embedded clause and direct object of the matrix clause. How can this be? To account for this apparently contradictory behavior, we say that the NP is **raised** from the position of subject of the lower clause to the position of object of the upper clause ("subject-to-object raising").

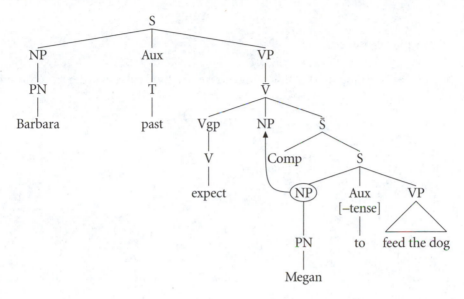

We will thus establish a third class of verbs that involve raising, the ***expect*-type verbs**. It is possible to classify verbs followed by infinitives, but also those followed by *-ing* or *-en* participles into these three categories. Table 9.7 contains a sample of verbs falling into these three classes.

Table 9.7. *Persuade-*, *expect-*, and *want*-type Verbs in English

persuade-type verbs

NP *to* V:	tell, order, ask, dare, forbid, beg, coax, advise, convince, encourage, permit, allow, oblige, force, cause
NP V:	make, have

expect-type verbs:

NP *to* V:	believe, assume, understand, consider, suppose, know, think, imagine, find, help
NP V-*ing* or NP V:	see, hear, witness, observe, notice, feel, taste
NP V-*ing*:	discover, catch, send, find, leave
NP V-*en*:	keep, make

want-type verbs:

NP *to* V:	wish, hope, prefer, like, desire, love, hate, dread
NP V-*ing*:	resent, regret
NP V-*en*:	have, want, see, get, need, see, hear

Review of Complex Sentences

In this chapter, we have modified the following phrase structure rules in order to account for embedded clauses:

$\bar{S} \rightarrow Comp\ S$

$$NP \rightarrow \begin{cases} (Det)\ \bar{N}\ (\bar{S}) \\ PN \\ Pro \\ \bar{S} \\ (NP)\ \bar{S} \end{cases}$$

$$\bar{N} \rightarrow \begin{cases} (AP)\ \bar{N}\ (PP)\ (\bar{S}) \\ N \end{cases}$$

$$AP \rightarrow \left(\begin{cases} Deg \\ AdvP \end{cases} \right)\ A\ \left(\begin{cases} PP \\ \bar{S} \end{cases} \right)$$

$Comp \rightarrow \{that,\ although,\ when,\ whether\ ...\}$

$$VP \rightarrow \bar{V}\ \left(\begin{cases} AdvP \\ PP \\ NP \\ \bar{S} \end{cases} \right)$$

$$\bar{V} \rightarrow \begin{cases} V_{gp}\ \left(\begin{cases} NP\ (\{NP, PP, AP\}) \\ AP \\ PP\ (PP) \\ (NP)\ \bar{S} \end{cases} \right) \\ \bar{V}\ (\{\ AdvP, PP, NP\ \}) \end{cases}$$

$$S \rightarrow S\ \left(\begin{cases} PP \\ AdvP \\ NP \\ \bar{S} \end{cases} \right)$$

We have examined the following types of finite main clause:

    wh-question

We have examined the following types of finite subordinate clauses:

that-clause	free or headless relative clause
adverbial clause	indefinite relative clause
relative clause (restrictive or nonrestrictive)	indirect question
sentential relative clause	

We have examined the following forms of nonfinite subordinate clauses:

bare infinitive	*wh*-infinitive (nonfinite indirect question)
to-infinitive	-*ing* participle or gerund
for-infinitive	-*en* participle

We have identified the following functions of subordinate clauses:

subject	extraposed object	complement of A
extraposed subject	object of P	modifier of Ñ
subject complement	disjunct adverbial	modifier of NP
direct object	adjunct adverbial	complement of Ñ
object complement	conjunct adverbial	absolute

Finally, we have encountered the following types of complementizers:

interrogative pronoun, determiner, adverb, degree adverb
relative pronoun, adverb, determiner
pure complementizer (base-generated under Comp) (*whether, that, since, because*, etc.)
for subject of infinitive

■ Chapter Summary

Now that you have completed this chapter, you should be able to:

1. identify the embedded finite and nonfinite clauses in a complex sentence;
2. determine the type and function of each embedded finite clause;
3. determine the form and function of each embedded nonfinite clause;
4. determine the type and function of each complementizer; and
5. give a tree diagram for any complex sentence, showing the hierarchical relation of each embedded clause, as well as its D-structure position and form.

■ Recommended Additional Reading

Treatments of English syntax which are similar in depth and level of formality to the treatment in this chapter include Wekker and Haegeman (1985, Chapters 1, 4–5), Burton-Roberts (1997, Chapters 8–10), Thomas (1993, Chapters 5, pp. 95–100, and Chapter 6),

Brown and Miller (1991, Chapters 9 and 10, pp. 132–40), Kaplan (1995, Chapter 6, pp. 251–67, Chapter 8, pp. 326–55, and Chapter 9) and Hopper (1999, Chapters 13–16). Less formal treatments include Huddleston (1984), Delahunty and Garvey (1994, Chapter 10), and Wardhaugh (1995, Chapters 5 and 8).

For more advanced treatments, see the references in Chapter 7.

■ Notes

1. In recent versions of generative grammar, there is assumed to be a phrasal category CP (= Complement Phrase), with Comp as its head and S as the complement; $\bar{S}$ is equivalent to $\bar{C}$, and there is also a Spec position:

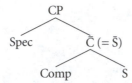

   It is further assumed that all S's, not just dependent clauses, have this structure.

2. An alternative account would be to make Comp optional. But since Comp serves to embed one clause in another — and embedding occurs whether or not there is a surface marker *that* — we reject this account.

3. The reason that subject–aux inversion is impossible in cases such as (d) has been explained recently by seeing the *that*-clause as filling the Comp position rather than the subject position. For the same reason, passive (which moves the subject) is impossible:

   > That Ali had read the book impressed me. ⇒
   > *I was impressed by that Ali had read the book.

   The same explanation may hold for subject clauses which are non-finite (see below).

4. As discussed in Chapter 5, there is an overlap between many of the forms which function as prepositions and those which function as conjunctions (e.g., *since, before, after, until*). It might be possible to analyze all of these forms as prepositions, which may take either NP or S complements. Note that some are complex forms incorporating *that*: *except that, given that, provided that, supposing that, assuming that, so that, such that*.

5. Current thinking is that the *wh*-word moves to the Spec position of CP (see footnote 1) and that Aux moves to Comp position. There are a number of reasons for believing this to be the case, not least of which is that it accounts for the order of the *wh*-word and the auxiliary.

6. *Wh*-movement, subject–auxiliary inversion, and passive (NP movement) are sometimes grouped together as "move α" since they all move an element (unspecified, hence α) to the left.

7. It used to be argued that the reason that the *wh*-word must move twice is that the Comp position of the dependent clause is already filled by *that* and two complementizers cannot fill a single Comp position (the so-called "Doubly-filled Comp Constraint"). In the current view, where the *wh*-word moves to Spec position (see footnote 5), this constraint no longer applies.

8. There are a number of constraints on *wh*-movement, where only echo questions can occur. *Wh*-movement cannot take place:

    a. from an indirect question:
    She wondered whether he said what ⇒ *What did she wonder whether he said [*t*]?

    b. from a complex NP, either one with a complement to N̄ or a relative clause:
    Tony spread the rumor that Jane said what ⇒ *What did Tony spread the rumor that Jane said [*t*]?
    Tony spread a rumor that who had already heard ⇒ *Who did Tony spread a rumor that [*t*] had already heard?

    c. from an adverbial clause
    We will leave when who arrives ⇒ *Who will we leave when [*t*] arrives?

    These constraints have to do with a bounding restriction called "subjacency". *Wh*-movement also cannot occur from coordinated structures:

    > We like ice cream and what ⇒ *What do we like ice cream and?

9. In current theory, the relative pronoun *that* is treated differently; it is base-generated directly in Comp position (like the *that* of *that*-clauses). Doing so accounts for certain restrictions on *that* (see below), for example, that it cannot follow a preposition nor occur in restrictive relative clauses. But it then becomes necessary to postulate a null *wh*-phrase (coindexed with the head noun) which moves to Comp. The same must be done for relatives with no overt complementizer.

10. Deletion of the subject relative pronoun may occur very colloquially, as in: *That's the guy Ø [t] gave me your name. I know someone Ø [t] can do it for you.* It was also possible in older English.

11. Prenominal modifiers (adjectives) are similarly restrictive and nonrestrictive. In the sentence *My rich sister just bought a new house*, if I have only one sister, *rich* must be nonrestrictive, but if I have more than one sister, *rich* is restrictive, for it identifies which of my sisters, namely the rich one, bought the house.

12. Nonfinite verbs also lack agreement features (hence are [−Agr]), but we are ignoring agreement.

13. The absence of this form, which was more common in earlier English and still appears colloquially today, has not been adequately explained (going under the name of the "double *-ing* constraint").

14. In traditional grammar, it is customary to categorize the passive forms of the *-ing* participle with the *-en* participle (as passive or past participles) because they are all passive in meaning.

15. In some versions of generative grammar, elliptical adverbial clause (see above) are treated as nonfinite clauses in which there is a subject PRO controlled by the subject of the main clause:

    > When PRO doing her homework, she listens to music
    > When PRO apprehended by the police, he had the stoled goods on him.

    Sentences such as *If necessary, you may have more time to finish he exam* present difficulties for this analysis.

16. The subject of the gerund usually appears in the possessive (either the inflected *-'s* form or the periphrastic *of* form):

    > The child's crying annoyed me.
    > The crying of the child annoyed me.

    When the gerund is formed from a transitive verb, a number of variations are possible with the subject:

possessive subject: <u>The Prince's</u> hunting foxes, the hunting <u>of the Prince</u> …
subject in *by* phrase: The hunting of foxes <u>by the Prince</u> …
subject gap: The hunting of foxes, Ø hunting foxes …

In current English, it is common to omit the possessive marker on the subject of the gerund, giving sentences such as *The Prince hunting foxes disturbs me*; this might sound more natural to you.

The object can also be expressed in different ways:

of preceding object: The Prince's hunting <u>of foxes</u> …
possessive object: the hunting <u>of foxes</u>, <u>foxes</u>' hunting …
object gap: The Prince's hunting Ø…

The possibility of both the subject and the object occurring in an *of*-phrase leads to ambiguity, as in the phrase *the shooting of the hunters*, where *hunters* can be either the subject or the object, namely 'the hunters shoot something' or 'someone shoots the hunters'.

Finally, both subject and object can be omitted: *Hunting* …

17. Sentences with these adjectives have also been analyzed by a type of raising called "*tough*-movement" (see Chapter 11). That is, the sentence *this dessert is easy to make* is seen as having the following D-structure:

$$_{NP}[_{\bar{S}}[\text{To make this dessert}] \text{ [is easy]}$$

The subject nonfinite clause is extraposed (*It is easy to make this dessert*) and the object NP (*this dessert*) is then "raised" to subject position in the matrix clause.

18. Object complement structures are sometimes also analyzed as "small clauses" with the infinitive of the verb "to be" understood: *They found the idea (to be) ridiculous.* However, in some object complements, the presence of "to be" is less natural, e.g., *We made him (?to be) captain.*

19. In earlier versions of generative grammar, it was the practice to derive adjectival participial clauses from relative clauses by a process of deletion: e.g., *the book awarded the prize < the book which was awarded the prize.* It is also possible to derive appositional phrases from reduced relative clauses: e.g., *my friend, the physicist < my friend, who is a physicist.*

Among other difficulties, there are certain participial clauses, such as those containing stative verbs, which cannot be so derived: *the student knowing the answer < *the student who is knowing the answer.*

20. In speech, "dangling participles" are quite common, as in:

Not knowing the facts, it's hard to make a judgment.
To work efficiently, frequent maintenance is necessary.
Having cleaned the house and prepared dinner, there was nothing more to do before the guests arrived.

The subject of the non-finite clause, in these cases, is available only from the larger discourse. For this reason, linguists have questioned whether PRO really occurs in adverbial non-finite clauses. We will, however, stick to the more traditional view.

The Meaning of English Sentences and their Communicative Functions

CHAPTER 10

Sentence Semantics

■ Chapter Preview

The chapter considers the semantic relationships holding between the verb and the nominal elements within a sentence. We begin by analyzing the core semantic content of sentences as propositions, consisting of nominal arguments and a predicate. We then consider the semantic functions that arguments can serve, using the notion of thematic roles — roles such as Agent, Force, Source, Goal, and so on. The roles are defined, their surface manifestations in English are exemplified, and dual roles are examined. We explore how predicates uniquely select arguments serving particular thematic roles. The chapter next explores the ways in which predicates relate nominal arguments to one another. Using various relational semantic features, different aspectual types — stative, inchoative, continuative, egressive, causative, and agentive — and different semantic classes of predicates — descriptive, cognitive, locative, and possessive — are analyzed.

■ Commentary

In Chapter 6, we considered the semantics of individual lexical items. We will now consider the semantic relationships holding between nouns and verbs in a sentence. In the preceding chapters on syntax, we followed the approach of many linguists, who believe that it is possible to treat syntax as autonomous, or syntax and semantics as essentially separate, with semantics purely interpretative. In this chapter, we will follow the approach of other linguists who believe that syntax and semantics are intrinsically linked; in their view, semantics is, in fact, fundamental, and D-structure is a *semantic* representation using semantic features. It is a much more abstract logical representation than we considered in the previous chapters.

Note that just as there are many different ways to approach word meaning, there are alternative approaches to sentence meaning, only a couple of which will be examined in this chapter. Moreover, for many linguists, sentence meaning incorporates many of the concepts that will be treated in Chapter 11.

Propositions

Our analysis of sentence semantics begins with the concept of the proposition (prop), the semantic content of a clause minus any particular syntactic structure as well as its intended communicative force (communicative force will be treated in Chapter 11). For example, the proposition [Harriet call the doctor] may be expressed in the following forms, among others:

Did Harriet call the doctor?	Will Harriet call the doctor?
Harriet called the doctor.	for Harriet to call the doctor
Harriet's calling the doctor	It was Harriet who called the doctor.
It was the doctor whom Harriet called.	The one who called the doctor was Harriet.

Thus, the proposition may occur in different sentence types, in nonfinite as well as finite form, and in utterances with different focuses. Note that the proposition itself crucially lacks tense, aspect, modality and agreement marking.

A proposition is divided into a predicate (pred) and its arguments (arg). An argument is any of the various elements of the sentence that are set in relation to one another by the predicate, typically noun phrases. The predicate is the operation carried out on an argument or arguments; it places the arguments in relation to one another. Predicates are typically verbs (including accompanying prepositions and particles), prepositions, and (predicate) adjectives. Predicates differ in respect to valency, the number of arguments that cooccur with a predicate. There are different types of valencies, Ø-, 1-, 2-, and **3-place predicates**; these, along with the less common 4-place predicate, are exemplified in Table 10.1. Note the different verb types occurring in each structure. Zero-place predicates consist of a class of impersonal constructions called weather expressions in which the subject is a dummy *it* which does not refer. One-place predicates consist of what are traditionally known as intransitive verbs (*burn, choke*), intransitive phrasal verbs (*fly away, run out*), and some copula + subject complements (*be Irish, be depressed, be a dancer, become a lawyer*). Two-place predicates consist of transitive verbs (*break, sand, surprise, write, left*), transitive phrasal verbs (*write down, press flat*), prepositional verbs (*belong to, look into, start at*), as well as adjectival structures with *be* (*be similar to, be behind, be upset with*). Note the contrast between the identifying statement *Violet is the lead ballerina*, which is a 2-place predicate, and the descriptive statement *Violet is a dancer*, which is 1-place. Elliptical structures such as the following would also be considered 2-place structures because of the presence of a latent object:

Jack is eating (something).
Fiona is jealous (of someone).

Three-place predicates include ditransitive, complex transitive, and diprepositonal verbs.

The predicate and argument(s) of a proposition may be represented in tree diagrams, as follows:

Table 10.1. Ø-, 1-, 2-, 3, and 4-Place Predicates

Ø-place:

It is sunny.	It is snowing.
It is hot.	It felt chilly.

1-place:

The house is burning.	The bird flew away.
Frank is Irish.	The child choked.
His time ran out.	Sam is depressed.
There are two answers.	Violet is a dancer.
Janet became a lawyer.	

2-place:

Mary broke the glasses.	The carpenter sanded the desk.
The book belongs to Peter.	The news surprised us.
Diana left the gym.	The teacher is upset with him.
Gary wrote a paper.	Violet is the lead ballerina.
Frank is similar to John.	The coat is behind the door.
The contest starts at noon.	He pressed the papers flat.
He wrote the address down.	The witch looked into the cauldron.
Alice is my aunt (=is an aunt to me).	

3-place:

The police officer gave a ticket to the speeder.
Mary put the keys on the table.
We donated the clothes to charity.
The baby crawled from the chair to the sofa.
Santa Cruz is between Los Angeles and San Francisco.
The road extends from coast to coast.

4-place:

He flew from New York to Havana via Miami.

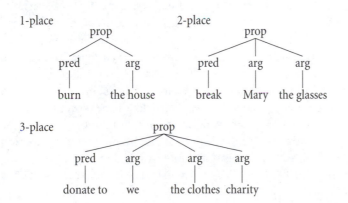

Note that arguments include only the nuclear elements of sentences, not adverbial elements.

Thus, in the sentence *Patsy is knitting a sweater in the living room*, "in the living room" is not an argument (because *knit* is a transitive verb), while in the sentence *Patsy put the sweater in the living room*, "in the living room" is an argument (because *put* is a complex transitive verb). The second sentence is a single 3-place predicate:

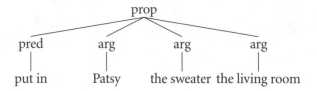

(An analysis of the first sentence is given in the Self-Testing Exercise.)

Now that propositions have been analyzed into the predicate and argument(s), we can examine how these parts are related semantically.

■ Self-Testing Exercise: Do Exercise 10.1.

Thematic Roles

The concept of **thematic roles** (or **θ-roles**) is a means of accounting for the functions of arguments in respect to the predicate; thematic roles are the "grammatically relevant semantic relations between predicates and arguments" (Frawley 1992:201). This approach was first proposed by Charles Fillmore (1968, 1977) and was originally known as case grammar. To define the roles of arguments, Fillmore borrows the notion of case from traditional grammar, but uses the term in a slightly different way. Traditionally, nouns may be inflected for case, for nominative, genitive, dative, accusative, and so on (as we saw in Chapter 5). But the meaning of a case ending is difficult to determine, as is perhaps most obvious with the genitive, which can express possessive, subjective, objective, descriptive, partitive, or adverbial meaning. The nominative case, which denotes the grammatical function of subject of the sentence, would seem to be fairly unified in meaning, but even it expresses a variety of concepts, including agent, cause, recipient, object, or instrument of an action. Traditionally, it is also unclear whether the notion of case should be restricted to case inflections — what is known as *morphological case* — which are used almost exclusively in a synthetic language such as Finnish, or should embrace other formal means to express the same grammatical functions, namely periphrases (using prepositions) and word order, which are the primary means for the expression of case in an analytic language such as English. Since languages seem to make use of various surface representations for the same grammatical function, Fillmore decides to use *case* in a new way: to indicate "semantic case" or the underlying semantic-syntactic functional relationships. He conceives of these semantic cases as finite in number and universal, not language specific, much like semantic features. They are a matter of D-structure, while their formal marking is a matter of S-structure.

This approach to the function of noun phrases offers certain advantages over the purely structural approach of syntactic analysis, where case refers to the position of a noun phrase in D-structure; for example, the "subject" is the NP to the left of the verb or directly dominated by S, while the "direct object" is the NP to the right of V or directly dominated by VP. As is obvious from the terms "right" and "left", these relations are considered for SuVO word order only. While the structural approach could be modified to account for other word orders, such as SuOV, VOSu, and OVSu, where O is adjacent to V, it would be more difficult to account for VSuO or OSuV. Case grammar abandons the idea that noun phrases are ordered in the base; rather, it sees them as assigned a particular surface position according to their thematic role. D-structure orders become universal since the structural notions of subject, object, and so on are eliminated.

Another advantage of case grammar is that it is able to recognize a relationship among sentences such as the following:

> The chef roasted the meat (over the fire).
> The fire roasted the meat.
> The meat roasted (over the fire).

In a purely structural approach, it would need to postulate three separate verbs *roast* with similar semantic features but different subcategorization rules:

> roast _____ NP (PP)
> _____ NP
> _____ (PP)

In case grammar, it is possible to see the three cases as a single verb selecting certain thematic roles, which then appear in different surface syntactic positions.

While Fillmore envisages a finite number of universal thematic roles, there is not yet general agreement on the inventory of these roles, on their designations, or on their definitions. Despite the fact that determination of thematic roles is described by one scholar as "intuitionism run wild" (Dillon 1977:73), we may consider the following as a list of some of the possible thematic roles served by arguments in a sentence:

1. **Agent** (also called "actor"): the animate initiator, causer, doer, or instigator of an action who acts by will or volition, takes responsibility for the action, and is its direct cause;
2. **Force** (also "author"): the inanimate cause of an action, which does not act by will or volition;
3. **Instrument** (also "means"): the means by which an event is caused, or the tool, generally inanimate, used to carry out an action; an instrument does not act but is acted upon; (Agent, Force, and Instrument together could be considered "Cause".)
4. **Experiencer** (also "dative" or "affected"): the animate being affected inwardly by a state or action;
5. **Source**: the place-from-which or person-from-whom an action emanates;
6. **Goal** (also "recipient"): the place-to-which or person-to-whom an action is directed, including indirect objects and directional adverbs;
7. **Path**: the path taken in moving from one place to another in the course of an action;

8. **Location** (also "place"): the place-at/in-which or the time-at-which an action occurs (also "temporal");
9. **Possessor**: the possessor of a thing, really a special kind of locative, since the thing and the possessor must coincide; there are two kinds of possession, depending on whether the possessor and the thing possessed are inherently connected, such as *Judy's head* (inalienable possession) or not, such as *Judy's car* (alienable possession);
10. **Benefactive**: the person or thing for which an action is performed or the person who derives something from the actions of another;
11. **Factitive** (also "result" or "effected"): the object resulting from an action or state, having no prior existence but coming about by virtue of the action or state;
12. **Patient** (also "affected", "object(ive)", or "theme"): the person or thing affected by an action, or the entity undergoing a change;
13. **Theme**: the person or thing which undergoes an action, or that which is transferred or moved by an event but otherwise unchanged;
14. **Neutral** (also "theme"): the person or thing which is not changed or even acted upon, but simply present at an action:
15. **Range** (also "extent"): the specification or limitation of an action; and
16. **Role**: a person playing a role or part in an action or state.

Note the differences between Patient, Theme, Neutral, and Factitive:

> Jane broke <u>the vase</u>. (Patient)
> Jane moved <u>the vase</u>. (Theme)
> Jane saw <u>the vase</u>. (Neutral)
> Jane made <u>a vase</u>. (Factitive)

A Patient is changed in some way by the action, while a Theme is affected by the action, often by changing location, but is itself unchanged. A Neutral is present at the event but does not undergo an action. A Factitive comes about by virtue of the action itself.

The Expression of Thematic Roles in English

Each underlying thematic role is expressed in a variety of ways on the surface in English, including case inflection, function word and word order. In Table 10.2 are examples of the most common ways in which the different cases are expressed syntactically.

Both Agent and Force are generally expressed as the subject of an active sentence or in the *by*-phrase of a passive sentence and only rarely as object. Instrument is most often expressed in a *with* or *by* phrase. Experiencer is normally the subject of a state verb. The roles of Source, Goal, Path, and Location are normally expressed prepositionally: Source typically with *from*, *out of*, or *off*, Goal with *to*, Path with *via*, *along*, or *over*, and Location with *on*, *in*, *over*, *behind*, or *under*. However, Goal is a complex role including indirect objects (occurring in three different positions in the sentence) as well as locative goals and directional adverbs. Note that the expression of inalienable possession is more varied than the expression of alienable possession. In fact, the only meaning attributable to *The brown hair belongs to her* or

Table 10.2. The Syntactic Expression of Thematic Roles in English

AGENT	The logger felled the tree.
	The tree was felled by the logger.
FORCE	The wind felled the tree.
	The tree was felled by the wind.
	The logger felled the tree with a single blow.
INSTRUMENT	The tree was felled with an axe.
	The sweater was knitted by hand.
	He used an axe to fell the tree.
	Liquor killed him.
	His insights impressed us.
	He impressed us with his insights.
EXPERIENCER	Marianne is lonely/feels lonely/is suffering.
	I like the book.
	The news pleases me. The news enraged me.
	The news is pleasing to me.
SOURCE	I got the book from the library.
	I got some money out of the bank.
	The child took the book off the shelf.
	I borrowed the book from my teacher.
	His leaving pleases me
	('is a source of pleasure to').
	The sun gives off heat.
	A caterpillar turns into a butterfly.
	The plane left (from) Boston.
GOAL	I sent a card to my grandmother.
	I sent my grandmother a card.
	My grandmother was sent a card.
	My grandmother got a card from me.
	She reached the coast.
	I sent the package to Europe.
	A new idea came to me.
	We hung the picture on the wall.
	Susy jumped onto the step.
	I sent the child home.
	I walked upstairs.
	She did it {for love, to gain attention}.
PATH	Hannibal traveled over the mountains.
	We walked along the railroad tracks.
	The package came via London.
LOCATION	The dog is in the house/on the chair/under the table/behind the couch.
	I will return on Tuesday/at noon.
	There are many people in the room.
	The room has many people in it.
	That bottle contains alcohol.
	People filled the room.
	Vancouver is a rainy city.

Table 10.2. (continued)

POSSESSOR *alienable*:	<u>He</u> has/owns/possesses a dog. The dog belongs <u>to him</u>. The dog is <u>his</u>. The jewels are <u>in his possession</u>. That dog <u>of his</u> is a nuisance. <u>His</u> dog is a nuisance. <u>The man</u> with the dog/<u>who</u> has the dog …
inalienable:	<u>She</u> has/?owns/?possesses brown hair. ?The brown hair belongs to <u>her</u>. ?The brown hair is <u>hers</u>. ?The brown hair is <u>in her possession</u>. That brown hair <u>of hers</u> is beautiful. <u>Her</u> brown hair is beautiful. <u>The man</u> with brown hair. <u>The man who</u> has brown hair
BENEFACTIVE	Jack answered the phone <u>for José</u>. The store special-ordered the book <u>for me</u>. The maitre d' reserved a place <u>for our party</u>.
FACTITIVE	They formed <u>a circle</u>. Wren designed <u>St. Paul's</u>. The coach turned into <u>a pumpkin</u>. He baked <u>a cake</u>.
PATIENT	I baked <u>the chicken</u>. <u>The chicken</u> was baked by me. <u>The chicken</u> baked in the oven.
THEME	I put <u>the letter</u> on the table. <u>The letter</u> flew out of the window We read <u>the letter</u>.
NEUTRAL	<u>The house</u> costs a lot. <u>The table</u> measures three feet by three feet. Richard saw <u>a tree</u> on the horizon.
RANGE	The dress costs <u>a hundred dollars</u>. The man weighs <u>80 kilograms</u>. We drove <u>ten miles</u>. He hummed <u>a silly tune</u>. He lived out <u>his life</u> happily.
ROLE	We made Lise <u>treasurer</u> of the club. Hilda is <u>the principal</u> of the school.

The brown hair is hers is one of alienable possession — perhaps one of her hairs has fallen into the soup! Benefactive should not be confused with Goal, though they are both expressed in a *for* phrase: Benefactive is paraphrasable with 'in the place of' or 'in the stead of', and only animate Goal may undergo indirect object movement (note the ungrammaticality of **Jack answered José the phone*). While Factitive, Theme, Patient, and Range are all expressed by the noun phrase immediately following the verb in an active sentence, only Factitive, Patient, and Theme, but not Range, are what are traditionally known as direct objects since they can become the subject in a passive sentence (note the ungrammaticality of **A hundred dollars is cost by the dress*). Neutral is expressed by both subjects and direct objects. Role is denoted by subject and object complements.

Dual Thematic Roles

Often an argument may have more than one thematic role. Dual roles occur with arguments of certain classes of verbs. First, the animate subject of many verbs of motion, such as *run*, *walk*, *swim*, *wade*, *climb*, *stand up*, *roll over*, or *travel*, is both Agent and Theme:

Lucille sat down.   Lucille = Agent and Theme

The subject both performs an intentional action (sitting) and is acted upon, that is, changes location (from standing to sitting). However, some verbs of motion, such as *fall*, *slip*, *slide*, or *sink*, may be ambiguous in respect to thematic role:

Jack {fell down, slipped over the edge, slid down the slope}.

Here Jack may have intentionally performed these actions (in which case *Jack* is both Agent and Theme), but another interpretation of the sentences is that these are events that simply befell Jack, without his being responsible (in which case *Jack* is Theme but not Agent). The second reading is obvious if one inserts "accidentally" in the sentences above. Second, ditransitive verbs and related verbs such as *give*, *sell*, *lend*, *hire*, *rent*, *supply*, *furnish*, *award*, *issue*, *show*, or *tell* show the following thematic structures:

They presented an award to Sam.   They = Agent and Source
                                       Sam = Goal
                                       award = Theme
They presented Sam with an award.   They = Agent and Source
                                       Sam = Theme and Goal
                                       award = Neutral

In each case, the subject is both an Agent performing the action of presenting and the Source of the award, while the indirect object, Sam, is the Goal of the award. However, since the position immediately following the verb seems to be closely associated with the Theme (or Patient) role, the movement of the indirect object to this position makes it Theme as well, or part of what the sentence is "about", as we will see in the next chapter. Third, verbs such as *spray*, *cram*, *pile*, *stack*, *smear*, *mark*, *engrave*, *plant*, *beat*, or *hit* show the following thematic structures:

She sprayed paint on the wall.	She = Agent paint = Patient wall = Location
She sprayed the wall with paint.	She = Agent the wall = Patient and Location paint = Theme

Again, the position directly following the verb seems to correlate with the Patient role. The assignment of a secondary role to the Location role seems to affect the view taken of the situation. The second sentence has a strong implication of 'completeness' or 'total affectedness', that is, that the wall is completely covered, since the wall is not only Location but also Patient in this case — that is, the thing affected by the action — whereas in the other case the wall is merely Location. This sense of completeness seems to hold up even when the sentences are passivized (suggesting that thematic roles are assigned at D-structure, before arguments are moved):

> Paint was sprayed on the wall.
> The wall was sprayed with paint.

Further evidence that the sense of 'total affectedness' is associated with the role of Patient or Theme, rather than merely with the position immediately following the verb, is provided by sentences such as the following, in which the relevant argument is in subject position:

Bees swarmed in the garden.	the garden = Location
The garden swarmed with bees.	The garden = Location and Patient

Again, the second sentence has the implication of completeness. Note that not all verbs (with similar meanings) permit both variants. For example *cover* or *fill* allow only the first, while *put* allows only the second:

> She {covered the wall with a quilt, filled the glass with water}.
> *She {covered a quilt on the wall, filled water into the glass}.
> *She put the wall with a quilt.
> She put a quilt on the wall.

Fourth, verbs like *steal, take, borrow, rent, hire, snatch, grab, get, rob, strip,* and *empty* allow the following thematic structures:

The thief stole her jewels.	The thief = Agent and Goal her = Possessor jewels = Theme
The thief stole the jewels from her.	The thief = Agent and Goal her = Source jewels = Theme
cf. The thief robbed her of the jewels.	The thief = Agent and Goal her = Theme and Source jewels = Neutral

While the thief is Agent and Goal in all of these sentences, note that the three structures lead to different focuses, depending on the thematic roles of the other arguments. With all these verbs, then, the effect of moving a word to the position immediately following the verb is to give the noun the role of Patient or Theme, in addition to any other role it may have (though Patient supersedes Neutral). A final example of dual roles in simple sentences is the following:

<u>Howard</u> jumped <u>the horse</u> over <u>the fence</u>.   Howard = Agent
the horse = Theme and Agent
the fence = Location

Here, the horse is acted upon by Howard (hence Theme), but itself acts by jumping (hence Agent); this interpretation depends upon a view of horses as beings capable of intentional action. Note that in *Howard drove the car out of the driveway*, "the car" is only Theme, not Agent.

Dual roles also come about in embedded structures, where a noun phrase has one thematic role by virtue of being the direct object of the higher verb, and another role by virtue of being the subject of the lower verb:

<u>Susan</u> forced <u>Katy</u> to write <u>the letter</u>.   Susan = Agent *Theme*
Katy = ~~Patient~~ and Agent
the letter = Factitive

(Actually, it is PRO in the embedded clause that has the role of Agent, but we ignore this fine point here.) In contrast, the same argument, when it follows an *expect*-type verb, as in *Susan expects Katy to write the letter* has the sole role of Agent since it is the subject of *write*, but not the object of *expect*. If object complement structures are considered embedded structures[1], then the dual roles of the direct object becomes clearer, since it is also subject of the embedded clause:

<u>We</u> made <u>Rachel</u> (to be) <u>captain</u>.   We = Agent
Rachel = Theme and Experiencer
captain = Role

Here, Rachel is the entity acted upon by us (hence Theme) but is also the being affected inwardly by the role of captain (hence Experiencer). In the following sentences, Stu is the Goal of her teaching, but in the first sentence he also has — by virtue of his position as direct object of the upper clause — the role of Theme:

She taught <u>Stu</u> to cook.   Stu = Theme and Goal
She taught <u>cooking</u> to <u>Stu</u>.   Stu = Goal, cooking = Theme

Again, the Theme role carries the implication of completeness, so that to say *She taught Stu to cook, but he can't cook a thing* is illogical, while to say *She taught cooking to Stu, but he can't cook a thing* seems acceptable.

It is important to distinguish dual thematic roles from **ambiguous roles**, as in the following:

Crane made a speech for <u>Crawford</u>.
<u>Vanessa</u> drowned in the river.

Bill floated in the lake.
Alex tasted the wine.

In the first sentence, Crawford is ambiguous between Goal and Benefactive, depending on whether Crane made a speech in support of Crawford or whether he made a speech in his stead. In the second sentence, Vanessa is Agent (and Patient) if she intentionally drowned herself, but only Patient if she accidentally drowned; likewise, Bill is Agent (and Theme) if he made himself float in the lake, but only Theme if through no actions of himself he floated (if it were, for example, his dead body that was being talked about). Finally, Alex may be Agent (and Experiencer) if he deliberately sampled the wine, but Experiencer only if he just happened to detect wine in a dish he was eating.

Thematic Grids

The thematic roles of the arguments occurring with any particular predicate are specified uniquely by that predicate. It is said that the predicate "assigns" thematic roles to its arguments. Information concerning the thematic role assignment of a predicate is given in the lexicon. It is specified in a thematic grid, which is "the abstract specification of the thematic role possibilities for each predicate" (Frawley 1992: 241). A thematic grid — what used to be called a case frame — is much like the syntactic subcategorization frame of a verb. It indicates optional case roles by the use of parentheses and mutually exclusive choices by *or*. The verb *open*, for example, assigns only one obligatory role, Theme, and optionally either Agent or Force and optionally Instrument. Note that Agent or Force or Instrument cannot appear alone.

open   Theme + (Agent or Force) + (Instrument)
       The key (In) opened the door (Th).
       The intruder (Ag) opened the door (Th) with the key (In).
       The wind (Fo) opened the door (Th).
       The door (Th) opened.
     *The intruder (Ag) opened. *The wind (Fo) opened. *The key (In) opened.

Sample thematic grids are given in Table 10.3.

The verbs *melt* and *cook* are similar in both assigning the obligatory role of Patient and an optional Agent, Force, or Instrument. The verb *cook* differs in permitting Patient to be elliptical and also in allowing Factitive to replace Patient. Instrument can in fact occur with Agent, though not with Force, as in *Harry melted the butter with a Bunsen burner* or *Lily cooked the rice on a camp stove*, so instead of (Agent or Force or Instrument), our rule should probably read (Agent (Instrument) or Force). The semantically-related verbs *kill*, *die*, and *murder* differ in their thematic role assignments. While both *kill* and *murder* assign Agent and Patient roles, *kill* allows a nonintentional Force role to replace the Agent; *die* assigns only the Patient role. We are ignoring various circumstantial roles such as Location, which could optionally accompany these predicates, as in *Smithers died in the train station* (Location) or *The gangster murdered Smithers last night* (Location).

Perception verbs fall into sets, depending on whether the subject is Experiencer or Agent,

Table 10.3. Thematic Grids for English Verbs

melt	Patient + (Agent or Force or Instrument)
	Harry (Ag) melted the butter (Pa).
	The flame (Fo) melted the butter (Pa).
	The microwave (In) melted the butter (Pa).
	The butter (Pa) melted.
	*Harry (Ag) melted. *The heat (Fo) melted.
	*The microwave (In) melted.
cook	Patient or Factitive + (Agent or Force or Instrument)
	Lily (Ag) is cooking rice (Pa) / dinner (Fa).
	Lily (Ag) is cooking. (Patient is elliptical)
	The rice (Pa) is cooking.
	The rice-cooker (In) cooked the rice (Pa).
	The heat (Fo) cooked the rice.
	Dinner (Fa) is cooking.
kill	Agent (Instrument) or Force + Patient
	The {blow, gunshot, accident} (Fo) killed Smithers (Pa).
	The man (Ag) killed Smithers (Pa) with a knife (I).
	*The knife (In) killed Smithers (Pa).
	*Smithers (Pa) killed. *The {man, blow} (Ag, Fo) killed.
murder	Agent + Patient + (Instrument)
	The gangster (Ag) murdered Smithers (Pa) with a knife (In).
	The gangster (Ag) murdered Smithers (Pa).
	*The gangster (Ag) murdered.
	*Smithers (Pa) murdered.
die	Patient
	Smithers (Pa) died.
	*The man (Ag) died Smithers.
	*The accident (Fo) died Smithers.

as in:

	hear	Experience + Neutral	I (Ex) heard the noise (Neu).
vs.	listen (to)	Agent + Goal	I (Ag) listened intently to the lecture (Go).
	see	Experiencer + Neutral	I (Ex) saw a sudden light (Neu).
vs.	look (at)	Agent + Goal	I (Ag) looked at the old book (Go).

Another use of the verb *look* occurs in *The dog looked happy (to me)*, or *The room looked clean (to me)*, where Neutral or Location is an obligatory role and Experiencer is optional. In the case of visual and auditory perception, there are separate lexical verbs, but in the case of tactile perception (as well as olfactory and gustatory perception), there is only one verb:

feel$_1$	Experiencer + Neutral	He (Ex) felt the presence (Neu) of an intruder in the house.

feel₂	Agent + Theme or Location	He (Ag) felt the clothes (Th) to see if they were dry.
		He (Ag) felt under the blanket (Lo) to see what was there.

For *feel*, one would also need to account for *His hands (Th) felt moist (to me)* and *The room (Lo) felt damp (to me)*; in this case, Theme or Location is obligatory and Experiencer is optional. Thematic grids can also distinguish between other stative and active verbs in the same way:

	know	Experiencer + Neutral	I (Ex) know the answer (Neu).
vs.	learn	Agent + Neutral	I (Ag) learned the French vocabulary (Neu).

Learn can also have an Experiencer subject, as in *I learned a lesson from that experience*.

Finally, there appears to be a hierarchy among thematic roles in their filling of subject position. The subject hierarchy (Fillmore 1968) is roughly Agent > Instrument > Patient, which says that if Agent is present, it will be subject, then Instrumental will be subject, then Patient will be subject. Choices of subject which violate this hierarchy, such as a Patient in subject position when an Agent is expressed in the same sentence, always represent a marked option, as in the case described, the passive.

■ Self-Testing Exercise: Do Exercise 10.2.

Predications

Now that we have examined the roles that noun phrases serve in a sentence, we can look at the way that the verbal predicates set the noun phrases in relation to one another; this may be called predication analysis. It is a way of analyzing the relational features of verbs, a method mentioned briefly in Chapter 6. It is useful in analyzing predicates expressing different views of a situation (different aspects) as well as those belonging to a number of different semantic classes.

Descriptive Predicates

The first type of predicate that we will look at are **descriptive predicates**, which serve to qualify or identify the subject.

Stative and inchoative. Consider the following sets of sentences:

1.   The pages are yellow.
     The clothes are dry.
     The water is cool.
2.   The pages yellowed.
     The clothes dried.
     The water cooled.

3. The pages {got, <u>turned, became</u>} <u>yellow</u>.   The pages <u>came to be yellow</u>.
    The clothes {<u>got</u>, [?]<u>turned, became</u>} <u>dry</u>.   The clothes <u>came to be yellow</u>.
    The water {<u>got, turned, became</u>} <u>cool</u>.   The water <u>came to be cool</u>.

The sentences in (1) are **stative**, denoting an unchanging condition (of yellowness, dryness, coolness). The predicate is 1-place, and the subject is a Neutral (or in the case of animates, an Experiencer) role. States are assumed to be basic, not further analyzable. Thus, the predicates in the sentences in (1) are analyzed with the stative feature BE yellow, BE dry, or BE cool.

In contrast, the sentences in (2) and (3) are **inchoative**, denoting a change in state (from not yellow to yellow, wet to dry, or not cool to cool), or more precisely, the beginning of a new state. Again, this is a 1-place predicate, with a Patient (or, sometimes, Theme) role. Each set of sentences in (2) and (3) consists of structurally different but semantically synonymous sentences; they would have the same propositional analysis, with only the surface lexical items differing. The predicates in the sentences in (2) and (3) are analyzed with the appropriate stative feature plus an additional inchoative feature, which can be represented as CHANGE, BECOME, or simply COME; remember that semantic features are capitalized to distinguish them from actual words of the language (see Chapter 6). The feature analyses of the sentences is (2) are the following:

the pages (Pa) COME BE yellow
the clothes (Pa) COME BE dry
the water (Pa) COME be cool

Since we are analyzing the predicate, our feature analysis must include the arguments which are set in relation by the predicate. A kind of primitive paraphrase of our analysis of the first set of sentences is 'it come about that the pages be yellow' or 'the pages come to be yellow'. Another way of understanding relational features is as abstract predicates, each heading a separate proposition, as in the following tree for the first set of sentences in (2) and (3):

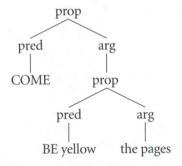

(Note that each proposition is an argument of the proposition above it.)

In (2), *The pages yellowed*, *The clothes dried*, and *The water cooled*, the inchoative feature and the stative feature are amalgamated, or lexicalized, as a single surface verb *yellow*, *dry*, or *cool* (by a process known as "predicate raising"). In (3), each feature is lexicalized separately, the inchoative element as *turn*, *get*, *become*, or *come* and the stative element as *yellow*, *dry*, or *cool*. We can consider the first option as synthetic and the second option as analytic, as in the following sentences:

Synthetic	Analytic
The sky {cleared, blackened}.	The sky became {black, clear}.
	The sky turned {black, clear}.
	The sky came to be {clear, black}.

One reason for the existence of synthetic as well as analytic forms is that the latter avoid bald Su-V sequences and easily allow modification, since adjectival modification, for example, *The pages became {slightly, very, more} yellow*, is considered to be easier than adverbial modification, for example, *The pages yellowed {slightly, ?very much, ?more}*.

Causative and agentive. Now consider the following sets of sentences:

4. The sunlight <u>yellowed</u> the pages.
    The heat <u>dried</u> the clothes.
    The breeze <u>cooled</u> the water.
5. The sunlight {<u>made</u>, <u>turned</u>} the pages <u>yellow</u>.
    The heat {<u>made</u>, ?<u>turned</u>} the clothes <u>dry</u>.
    The breeze {<u>made</u>, <u>turned</u>} the water <u>cool</u>.
6. The sunlight <u>caused</u> the pages <u>to become yellow</u>.
    The heat <u>caused</u> the clothes <u>to become dry</u>.
    The breeze <u>caused</u> the water <u>to become cool</u>.

These sentences are all **causative**, denoting something effecting a change of state in an entity. They involve a 2-place predicate, with a Force role and a Patient role. We will propose a causative feature CAUSE. Again, the sets of sentences in (4), (5), and (6) are structurally different yet semantically synonymous, and thus the predicates in each set are analyzable as follows:

The sunlight (Fo) CAUSE the pages (Pa) COME BE yellow
The heat (Fo) CAUSE the clothes (Pa) COME BE dry
The breeze (Fo) CAUSE the water (Pa) COME BE cool

A rough paraphrase of the first yields 'the sunlight cause the pages to come to be yellow'. As you can see, these sentences are both causative (the feature CAUSE) and inchoative (the feature COME) — hence inchoative-causative — as well as stative. The three features may find expression as a single lexical item, *yellow*, *dry*, or *cool* (as in 4), or the causative and inchoative feature may be lexicalized together as *make* or *turn* separate from the stative feature (as in 5), or each feature may be lexicalized separately (as in 6), where CAUSE surfaces as *cause*, COME as *become*, and the statives as *yellow*, *dry*, and *cool*. An analysis of the three features as separate predicates produces the following tree:

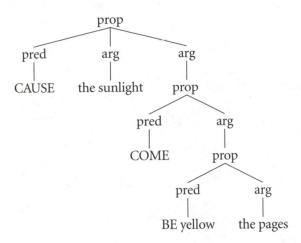

Finally, consider the following sentence:

7. ⁷Orlando <u>yellowed</u> the pages.
    Orlando <u>dried</u> the clothes.
    Orlando <u>cooled</u> the water.
8. Orlando {<u>made</u>, <u>turned</u>} the pages <u>yellow</u>. (cf. Orlando <u>painted</u> the pages <u>yellow</u>.)
    Orlando {ˀ<u>made</u>, *<u>turned</u>} the clothes <u>dry</u>.
    Orlando {<u>made</u>, ˀ<u>turned</u>} the water <u>cool</u>.
9. Orlando <u>caused</u> the pages <u>to become yellow</u>.
    Orlando <u>caused</u> the clothes <u>to become dry</u>.
    Orlando <u>caused</u> the water <u>to become cool</u>.

These sentences are **agentive**, involving a human agent who intentionally brings about a change in state in an entity. They consist of a 2-place predicate with an Agent and a Patient role. We analyze these sentences with the additional agentive feature **DO**, as follows:

Orlando (Ag) DO CAUSE the pages (Pa) COME BE yellow
Orlando (Ag) DO CAUSE the clothes (Pa) COME BE dry
Orlando (Ag) DO CAUSE the water (Pa) COME BE cool

(While CAUSE always cooccurs with DO and could probably be omitted, we retain it here, since DO does not always cooccur with CAUSE.) These sentences can be termed **inchoative-agentive**. Notice that the sentences in (7) lexicalize all of the features in one verb, those in (8) lexicalize the agentive, causative, and inchoative features as a verb and the stative feature separately as an adjective, and those in (9) lexicalize the agentive plus causative features as a verb, the inchoative feature as a second verb, and the stative feature as an adjective. While the agentive forms are almost identical to the causative forms, they are rather more restricted.

The propositional tree for the first set of agentive sentences would be the following:

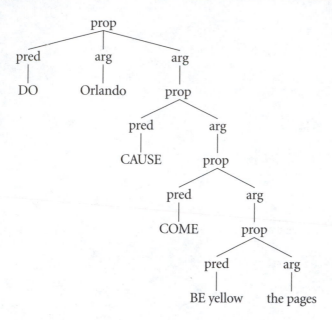

Note that the same surface form, *yellow* or *dry* or *cool* can be stative, inchoative, or inchoative-causative/agentive. Other examples in which the three forms are the same, with the possible addition of a particle are given in Table 10.4a. But the surface forms are not always the same. The stative (or adjectival) form may differ from the other two (10.4b). Or the past participle may serve as the stative form (10.4c); the past participle may be a "regular" form such as *closed* or a relic form such as *rotten* which is no longer used as a true past participle: *The food has rotted* not **The food has rotten*. *Melt* is an interesting case since the relic form seems to be restricted to describing only certain substances: *The lava is molten* but not **The cheese is molten*. Derivation may also be involved. The suffix *-en* can form the inchoative and causative/agentive forms (10.4d). (The form *strengthen* exhibits a minor phonological change which fronts the "o" vowel. Can you think of another example of this sort?) It is frequently the case that the inchoative form is missing and must be supplied by an analytic form; the causative/agentive may be formed in a variety of ways (10.4e). In other cases, the past participle serves as the stative form and analytical inchoative form, and a zero-derived "denominal" verb (one derived from the noun) serves as the causative/agentive form (10.4f). Finally, all three forms may be different, as with *dead — die — kill*, or one may be analytical and the others different, as with *cold — turn cold — cold — chill* or *clean — become clean — cleanse*.

While the sentences that we have examined all involve predicate adjectives, the same analysis also applies to sentences with predicate nominals:

stative: Rachel is president of the student body.
inchoative: Rachel became president of the student body.
inchoative-causative: The election made Rachel president of the student body.
inchoative-agentive: A majority elected Rachel president of the student body.

Table 10.4. Stative, Inchoative, and Causative/Agentive Forms

(a)	warm — warm — warm empty — empty — empty (out) slow — slow — slow (down) quiet — quiet — quiet (down)	open — open — open clear — clear — clear (away) thin — thin — thin (out) narrow — narrow — narrow
(b)	full — fill — fill	hot — heat — heat (up)
(c)	torn — tear — tear closed — close — close drained — drain — drain	rotten — rot — rot melted/molten — melt — melt locked — lock — lock
(d)	ripe — ripen — ripen wide — widen — widen black — blacken — blacken stiff — stiffen — stiffen	broad — broaden — broaden red — redden — redden deep — deepen -deepen strong — strengthen -strengthen
(e)	*-en* moist — become moist — moisten sharp — become sharp — sharpen	cheap — become cheap — cheapen
	-ify beautiful — become beautiful — beautify	
	-ize sterile — become sterile — sterilize modern — become modern — modernize	fertile — become fertile — fertilize passive — become passive — passivize
	en- large — become large — enlarge	rich — become rich — enrich
	Ø dirty — become dirty — dirty hollow — become hollow — hollow	free — become free — free ready — become ready — ready
(f)	brushed — become brushed — brush cashed — become cashed — cash hammered — become hammered — hammer	halved — become halved — halve sliced — become sliced — slice plowed — become plowed — plow

Continuative and egressive. Up to this point, we have been considering only the existence of states and the beginning of states, but it is also the case that states may come to an end and that states may continue. In order to provide an analysis of such situations, we need to introduce the feature negative, or **NEG**. The end or cessation of a state is termed **egressive** ('going out', in contrast to *ingressive* 'going in') and can be analyzed COME NEG, that is, 'to come to not be in a state'. To express the egressive, English does not have simple lexical verbs, as is the case with the inchoative, but must make use of auxiliary-like verbs called aspectualizers, including *cease*, *stop*, and *quit*. The end of a situation may simply come about, or it may be caused by a force or agent:

-   egressive: The pages ceased to be yellow. The clothes stopped drying. The water ceased to be cool. Rachel ceased to be president of the student body.

- egressive-causative: The sunlight stopped yellowing the pages. The heat stopped drying the clothes. The breeze quit cooling the water.
- egressive-agentive: Orlando stopped making the pages yellow. Orlando stopped drying the clothes. Orlando quit cooling the water.

To express the continuation of a state, the **continuative**, English makes use of the aspectualizers *continue*, *stay* and *remain* and causative-agentive *keep* or *retain*:

- continuative: The pages continued to be yellow. The clothes stayed dry. The water remained cool. Rachel continued to be president of the student body.
- continuative-causative: The heat kept the clothes dry. The breeze caused the water to remain cool.
- continuative-agentive: Orlando caused the pages to remain yellow. Orlando kept the clothes dry. Orlando caused the water to stay cool. The students {kept, retained} Rachel as president of the student body.

Note that the expression of continuation differs from the expression of the simple stative, since when we use a form such as *stay*, there is an implication that the situation might have stopped but did not; the stative has no such implication. For example, in the case of *The clothes stayed wet* as opposed to *The clothes are dry*, the expectation is that the clothes might have become dry, but didn't. Thus, we analyze continuative forms as containing the features NEG COME NEG 'to not come to not be in a state' (which is, of course, logically the same as COME, with the two negative "canceling" one another).[2]

Negative. Inchoative, continuative, and egressive may also be negated:

- negative-inchoative: The pages didn't become yellow. The clothes didn't dry. The water didn't cool. The sunlight didn't yellow the pages. Orlando didn't dry the clothes.
- negative-continuative: The clothes didn't stay dry. The water didn't remain cool. The breeze didn't keep the water cool. Orlando didn't keep the clothes dry.
- negative-egressive: The clothes didn't stop drying. The sunlight didn't stop yellowing the pages. Orlando didn't stop cooling the water.

Negative-inchoative is analyzed as NEG COME, negative-continuative as NEG NEG COME NEG, or COME NEG, and negative egressive as NEG COME NEG, with necessary causative and agentive features. Note that negative-egressive is equivalent to the continuative ('it didn't stop' = 'it continued') and negative-continuative is equivalent to egressive ('it didn't continue' = 'it stopped').

Cognitive Predicates

With the features, COME, CAUSE, and DO, and stative predicates, we can analyze a number of different types of predicates. The first that we will consider are cognitive predicates, which denote cognitive states and events within the mind. (In what follows, we will use BE to designate any kind of state; thematic roles will also be shown.)

1. stative: BE Ex + Neu

> Ryan knows Chinese.
> Kristin was aware of the facts of the case.
> Carol knows Alison.

2. inchoative: COME BE Ex + Neu

> Ryan learned Chinese as his mother tongue.
> Kristin became aware of the facts of the case.
> Carol {got, came} to know Alison. Carol met Alison.

3. inchoative-causative/agentive: DO CAUSE COME BE Ag + Ex + Neu

> Ryan learned Chinese as an adult. Shihong taught Ryan Chinese.
> Pete {told, informed} Kristin of the facts of the case.
> Beverly introduced Carol to Alison.

Since one learns one's first language apparently effortlessly, it might be possible to view the predicate *learn* as purely inchoative, as in (2). Generally, however, learning a language requires conscious effort by the learner, so in (3), *learn* is seen as agentive. Here, Ryan acts upon himself in order to learn Chinese: Ryan DO CAUSE Ryan COME KNOW Chinese.

4. continuative: NEG COME NEG BE Ex + Neu

> Ryan remembers Chinese.
> Kristin continues to be aware of the facts of the case.
> Carols continues to be acquainted with Alison. Carol remembers Alison.

5. continuative-causative/agentive: DO CAUSE NEG COME NEG BE Ag or Fo + Ex + Neu

> A short stay in China made Ryan remember Chinese.
> Pete kept Kristin aware of the facts of the case.
> Carol kept in touch with Alison.

6. egressive: COME NEG BE Ex + Neu

> Ryan forgot Chinese.
> Kristin ceased to be aware of the facts of the case.
> Carol ceased to know Alison. Carol forgot Alison.

7. egressive-causative/agentive: CAUSE COME NEG BE Fo + Ex + Neu

> Time away from China made Ryan forget his Chinese.

Locative and Possessive Predicates

If we introduce the stative feature COINCIDE, we are able to analyze a large number of locative and possessive predicates. Remember that possession can be treated as a special kind of location.

1. stative: COINCIDE Neu + Lo or Po
   locative:

   > Gabriel is {at school, in the house, behind the garage, under his bed}.
   > The vase sits on the mantle. The mantle has a vase on it.
   > The umbrella is standing in the corner.
   > The book is lying on the table.

   possessive:

   > Sam {has, owns, possesses} a book.
   > The book is Sam's.
   > Sam has brown hair.

The correct analysis of sentences with predicates such as *lie*, *sit*, or *stand* depends on the animacy of the subject. An inanimate subject is clearly static and does not "do" anything to remain in a position; thus, the sentence *The umbrella is standing in the corner* would be unambiguously analyzed as umbrella COINCIDE corner. But an animate subject must supply energy, that is, do something, to remain in a position; thus, it seems, *Kate is standing in the corner* is better analyzed as Kate DO CAUSE COINCIDE Kate corner, not as Kate COINCIDE corner.

2. inchoative: COME COINCIDE BE Th + Go
   locative:

   > Brigitte {got to, reached, arrived at} the top of the mountain.
   > The bus ran into the house.
   > The ball rolled into the street.
   > A fly fell into his drink.

   possessive:

   > Joe {got, acquired, obtained, received} a book.

Note that the place role is understood as Locative in the case of the stative expressions and Goal in the case of the inchoative expressions.

3. inchoative-causative: CAUSE COME COINCIDE BE Fo + Th + Go or Po
   locative:

   > The wind blew the dust into the house.
   > The waves carried the raft out to sea.
   > The hurricane flattened his house.
   > Lightening felled the tree.

   possessive:

   > ?His will donated his fortune to the university.

It is difficult to think of a force causing someone to come into possession of something (as distinct from the force causing something to be located with someone). In the case of sentences such as *The hurricane flattened his house* and *Lightening felled the tree*, the goal (the ground) is implicit.

4. inchoative-agentive: DO CAUSE COME COINCIDE Ag + Th + Go or Po
    locative:

> Carol {put, placed, stood, laid, piled} a book on the desk.
> Frederike {sat down, stood up, lay down, rolled over}.
> The mover {pushed, dragged} the box down the ramp.
> The child rolled the ball to his friend.
> The mad driver drove the car into the building.
> She {ran, skated, skipped} to the end of the block.
> The company {mailed, shipped, couriered} the package to the customer.
> He planted {ideas in her head, roses in the garden}.
> She {painted the wall, water the plants, saddled the horse, wrapped the package, loaded the car}.
> He {bottled the wine, landed the fish, seated the guests}.

    possessive:

> The teacher {gave, presented, rented, lent, took, sold, awarded, donated} the book to Maya.

Note that in a sentence such as *Kate sat down*, Kate acts upon herself to cause a change in her position (to an understood goal) — Kate DO CAUSE Kate COME COINCIDE (chair) — in contrast to a sentence such as *Kate is sitting down* (like *Kate is standing in the corner*, discussed above), where Kate acts upon herself to maintain a position.

The predicate often contains the means by which the change in location is effected, e.g.:

> She skipped to the end of the block. = She DO CAUSE herself COME COINCIDE the end of the block (by skipping)
> The company couriered the package to the customer. = The company DO CAUSE the package COME COINCIDE the customer (by couriering)

The verb may also lexicalize the Theme role, e.g., *water*, or the Goal role, e.g., *land*:

> She watered the plants. = She DO CAUSE water COME COINCIDE the plants
> He landed the fish. = He DO CAUSE the fish COME COINCIDE land

With the continuative, the place role is locative, as with the stative.

5. continuative: NEG COME NEG COINCIDE Neu + Lo
    locative:

> The papers {remained, stayed} on the table.

    possessive:

> The jewels continued in her possession.

6. continuative-causative: CAUSE NEG COME NEG COINCIDE Fo + Neu + Lo
    locative:

> The water kept him afloat.
> The tornado left his house standing.

Again, possessive meanings are difficult to imagine.

7.   continuative-agentive: DO CAUSE NEG COME NEG COINCIDE Ag + Neu + Lo
     locative:
>   She {stayed, remained} on the bucking horse.
>   She (intentionally) left her purse at home.
>   We keep our motor-home in the back yard.

 possessive:
>   She held on to her jewels.
>   He didn't sell his stocks.
>   They didn't give up the family home.

With the egressive, the place role is Source, in contrast to the inchoative, where it is Goal.

8.   egressive: COME NEG COINCIDE Th + So
     locative:
>   The leaves fell from the trees.
>   The ghost vanished from the room.
>   The train departed from the station.
>   The child disappeared.
>   The fog cleared.
>   The bird molted.

 possessive:
>   She lost her keys.
>   He dropped a few pounds.

The Source may be implicit, as in *The fog cleared (from the sky)*. A sentence such as *The bird molted* could be understood as Feathers COME NEG COINCIDE the bird.

9.   egressive-causative: CAUSE COME NEG COINCIDE Fo + Th + So
     locative:
>   The wind blew the leaves from the trees.

 possessive:
>   ?The cave gave up its secrets.

10. egressive-agentive: DO CAUSE COME NEG COINCIDE Ag + Th + So
     locative:
>   The sheriff {left, departed from} town.
>   Joanne stripped the wallpaper from the wall.
>   Amanda {took, removed, pulled, dragged} the box from the cupboard.
>   He dropped the ball from the roof.
>   Felicity drove the car out of the garage.
>   She {peeled the apple, dusted the furniture}.
>   She removed the spot from the shirt.
>   They {unearthed the treasure, mined the diamonds}.

possessive:
> Sam {rented, took, bought, borrowed} the book from Maya.
> Janice gave up her apartment.

For a number of verbs, whether the predicate is inchoative or egressive depends on whether a Goal or a Source role cooccurs, e.g., *He dropped the ball {into the pool, from the roof}*. The verb may lexicalize the Theme role, as in the case of *dust*, or the Source role, as in *unearth*:

> She dusted the furniture. = She DO CAUSE dust COME NEG COINCIDE the furniture
> He unearthed the treasure. = He DO CAUSE the treasure COME NEG COINCIDE the earth

The oppositeness of inchoative and egressive can be seen clearly in the morphology of English, as the privative marker *un-* attaches to many inchoative forms to create egressive forms, e.g., *wrap – unwrap, saddle – unsaddle, cork – uncork, cover – uncover, load – unload*. The verb lexicalizes the Theme role in both cases.

■ *Self-Testing Exercise:* **Do Exercise 10.3.**

One of the things that this approach to predicates and arguments does is to cast doubt on the traditional categories, N, A, V, etc., because in D-structure, there are no lexical categories, only thematic roles and relational features. Lexical categories seem to be just a surface structure phenomenon, added after transformations. They are an idiosyncratic aspect of language, unpredictable and accidental. D-structures may then be universal, while lexical categories and lexicalization are language specific.

■ Chapter Summary

Now that you have completed this chapter, you should be able to:

1. determine the propositional structure of utterances;
2. identify the thematic roles of the noun phrases in a proposition; and
3. analyze different types of predicates using a set of semantic features, or abstract predicates.

■ Recommended Additional Reading

The primary source on case grammar is Fillmore (1968, 1977). Good secondary discussions can be found in Dillon (1977, Chapter 5) and Frawley (1992, Chapter 5). Kreidler (1998) and Brown and Miller (1991, Chapter 18) are good textbook discussions of both thematic roles and predication analysis; Hurford and Heasley (1983, Chapter 19–20) contains exercises treating both topics. A rather old, but very clear discussion of predication analysis is Parisi and Antinucci (1976, Chapter 4). Also see Leech (1974, Chapter 7) and Lyons (1977, Chapter 12), which treat the issues from a somewhat different perspective.

■ Notes

1. On so-called "small clauses", see Chapter 9, note 18.

2. Another set of aspectualizers, *begin*, *commence*, and *start*, focus on the initial stages of a state and may be combined with causative and agentive:

   a.   The pages began to yellow. The clothes began to dry. The water began to cool.
   b.   The heat began to dry the clothes. The breeze started to cool the water.
   c.   Orlando began to dry the clothes. Orlando started cooling the water.

   These might be analyzed with the additional feature BEGIN. This view of an action is often called *ingressive* (or *inceptive* or *inchoative*), while what we are here calling *inchoative* might be better understood by the traditional aspectual term *perfective*.

CHAPTER 11

Information Structuring and Speech Acts

■ Chapter Preview

The first half of the chapter introduces certain functional concepts such as topic/comment and given/new and then explores how the options provided by the syntax of English have pragmatic consequences in how information is organized and presented in a text — what is known as "information structuring". The second half of the chapter then accounts for the functions of language in context using the framework of speech act theory. Direct speech acts and indirect speech acts are examined in detail, considering both their communicative force and the conditions on their appropriate use. The chapter ends with a brief discussion of the cooperative principle and the pragmatic maxims that control conversation.

■ Commentary

To this point in the text, we have been treating traditional concerns of phonology, morphology, syntax, and semantics, but have not considered language above the level of the sentence. Pragmatics is the study of how language is used, how the forms of language are matched with or adapted to the functions that it is serving in context, and how language is used to create discourse (**discourse** can be defined as a sequence of two or more sentences, either written or spoken, that cohere in some way). Another important part of pragmatics is the study of how contextual conditions influence the form of language used; contextual factors include such things as the social positions or roles of the participants in discourse and their interpersonal relations of intimacy and power, the psychological states of the speaker (Sp) and hearer (H), the intentions, beliefs, attitudes of Sp and H, and even the circumstances (physical and social) of speech. As competent communicators, we almost instinctively know how to adapt our speech to all of these many diverse conditions. This knowledge is known as **communicative competence**, the knowledge which enables Sp and H to understand and produce utterances in relation to communicative purposes and the speech context. Our study of pragmatics, then, will have two parts: the study of how language is used to create cohesive texts and the study of how language use is determined by social interactions between individuals. We will attempt to determine to what extent these aspects of language use follow identifiable principles.

Pragmatics and Syntax

In everyday language use, we are always making choices about how to express ourselves. The conscious choice of one formulation over another is not restricted to literary language. The syntax of the language provides alternate ways of saying the same thing. We have already seen, for example, how syntax may change thematic roles, and how such roles may be determined (in part) by syntax. Why do we choose one way of saying something over another? The choice often depends on contextual factors, especially the context of the immediate discourse. We organize our discourse in a particular way in order to create cohesive and coherent texts, for example, to emphasize (foreground) or deemphasize (background) aspects of our discourse or to fit our contribution into an ongoing discourse. This is called **information structuring**; the language provides a variety of means for achieving our ends of arranging material for specific effects in discourse.

Basic Distinctions

Before we look at the various options provided by English syntax for structuring information, we must define a number of distinctions. These are underlying semantic distinctions which are universal, not language-specific.

Given and new information. **Given** (or **old**) **information** is already known to the participants, having been "given" in the preceding discourse, while **new information** is not known to the hearer, being introduced into the discourse for first time. Given information may be evoked either textually or situationally or it may be inferrable (Prince 1981). That is, it may be mentioned explicitly in the previous discourse; it may be part of the communicative context (e.g., the 1st and 2nd persons are always given); or it may be information shared privately by the participants in the discourse, information assumed to be culturally known, or information implied by something already introduced into the discourse, for example by being part of the thing or in close association with it. Given information may be introduced by the same or another speaker. If assumed, it need not be overtly referred to at all. The subject of the sentence is typically given information. Given information is expressed in abbreviated ways, by, for example, pronouns or unstressed nouns. In contrast, new information is either brand new or unused for some period (Prince 1981). It must be expressed fully and explicitly, in full noun phrases, with more stress, and with modifiers spelled out in full. The predicate of the sentence is typically new information. Consider the following short discourse:

> I must tell you about my move. First, the movers arrived two hours late. Then, they damaged my new couch. The upholstery on the back is badly ripped. And they dropped two boxes of dishes. What a nightmare!

In the first sentence, the first person *I* (the speaker) and the telling are old information, being given in the communicative context and the move is new information. In the second sentence, though they are appearing for the first time, the movers are given information, since they can be assumed from the context of the move. The movers continue to be given information in the third sentence (and the fifth sentence) and are referred to pronominally;

the new couch is new information and set out in a full NP. In the fourth sentence, the upholstery is given information because it can be assumed from the context of the couch (almost all couches are upholstered); furthermore, the back is a subpart of the couch itself, so it too is given information and it is not necessary to specify "the back (of the couch)". The fifth sentence shows the usual pattern of given information ("they") and then new information ("dropped two boxes of dishes"). Finally, the subject (the move) can be omitted altogether in the last exclamatory sentence, since it is given information.

Topic and comment. The **topic** is what an utterance is about, its starting point, its center of attention, or the perspective from which it is viewed. It is usually the subject of the sentence. The **comment** is what is said about the topic; it is usually the predicate of a sentence.[1] The usual situation is for the topic to be given and the comment to be new information, as in *They damaged my new couch.* This is a sentence about the movers (the topic); it says of the movers that they damaged the new couch (the comment). A less typical, but possible, situation is for the topic to be new and the comment to be old information, as in the following: *As for my chair, it got ripped too.* Here, the chair is new information, introduced for the first time; it is the topic of the sentence. "getting ripped too" is in the context of the discourse old information, but it functions as a comment about the couch. *As for* and *speaking of* are special linguistic means for marking topic. A test for topic is that it answers the question "Tell me something about X [i.e. the topic]"; in this case, "Tell me something about your move" or, less likely, "Tell me what happened yesterday". Although the examples given have all equated the topic with the subject of the sentence, which is a simple NP, we will see below that there are many structures in which the topic is not the grammatical subject; furthermore, the topic may be an entire clause (e.g., *That my furniture was damaged was upsetting*) or another type of element moved to the front of the sentence.

Contrast. Information is in **contrast** if it is in opposition to another entity or is selected from a larger set of entities. Noun phrases in contrast may be linguistically marked by *only* and are typically expressed with stress. In the following "Phyllis" contrasts with "most of my high school friends":

Most of my high school friends have moved away; only <u>Phyllis</u> still lives in town.

Note that "Phyllis" would not be in contrast if the discourse were *(even) Phyllis has now left town.* The noun phrase to which a noun phrase stands in contrast may follow *rather than* (e.g., *Phyllis rather than Amanda still lives in town*), or it may not be expressed, but just implied or part of context. Furthermore, both the subject and the predicate may be contrastive, as would be the case if the above discourse continued *and Phyllis has died.*

Contrastive information bears some resemblance to new information; however, new information picks out one entity from an unlimited set of possibilities, whereas contrastive information picks out one entity as opposed to another entity or a limited set of other entities.

Definite and indefinite. Information is **definite** if the referent of the noun phrase is familiar to the hearer, while it is **indefinite** if the referent is novel, or unfamiliar to the hearer. Proper nouns, pronouns, and nouns preceded by the definite article or demonstratives are usually definite; the speaker assumes that the hearer will be able to identify the referent. Nouns preceded by the indefinite article or *any* are usually indefinite; the speaker assumes that the hearer cannot identify the referent. The combination of the notion of definiteness with the notion of givenness provides four possibilities:

1.   indefinite + new: <u>A couple</u> I know just returned from a vacation in Africa.
2.   indefinite + given: They visited four countries — <u>a vacation</u> they'll never forget.
3.   definite + given: <u>They</u> went on a photographic safari in Tanzania.
4.   definite + new: <u>The guide</u> on their trip was excellent.

While it is usual for new information to be indefinite and given information to be definite (as in cases 1 and 3), given information may be indefinite if it is not necessary for the hearer to identify the referent (case 2) or new information may be definite if it can have only one possible referent (case 4).

Specific, nonspecific, and generic. Information is **specific** if it denotes a particular entity in the real world, while it is **nonspecific** if it denotes no particular entity in the real world. Pronouns and proper nouns are usually specific, though some pronouns, such as general *you*, *one*, or *they*, are nonspecific, as in *You never can tell, One must consider all options, They never tell you anything*, where no person is being referred to. A test for specific is whether the noun can fit in the slot: *There is a certain _____.* Combining specificity with definiteness yields the following possibilities:

1.   specific + definite: Tomorrow I'm going to polish <u>the car</u>.
2.   nonspecific + indefinite: I dream of buying <u>an expensive car</u>.
3.   specific + indefinite: I saw <u>a car</u> I liked yesterday.
4.   nonspecific + definite: I'm going to buy <u>the first car</u> off the production line.

The underlined expression in (1) refers to a particular car in the real world which the hearer can identify; in (2) it refers to no particular car, and thus the hearer cannot identify it; and in (3) it refers to a particular car but the hearer cannot identify it. Note that it is rather odd to refer to no particular entity which the hearer can identify, though it can occur, as shown in (4).

    Generic refers to a set, whereas specific refers to particular members of the set. Generic nouns refer to the class or category ("genus") of an entity. They can be either definite or indefinite:

    generic + indefinite: <u>Houses</u> are expensive. <u>A house</u> is expensive.
    generic + definite: <u>The house</u> is the largest purchase you will make in your lifetime.

Contrast a specific reference such as *The house is beautiful* (the particular house that I am looking at). Note the use of the so-called "bare plural" *houses* with generic reference.

■ *Self-Testing Exercise: Do Exercise 11.1*

Syntactic Options and Pragmatic Considerations

We will now analyze different syntactic possibilities provided by English grammar that can be exploited in order to manipulate the semantic distinctions we have been considering. These syntactic structures provide means to structure information in different ways, and we will find that discourse functions are to some extent matched with syntactic form.

Fronting. **Fronting** consists in the movement of a word, phrase, or clause to the beginning of the sentence, as in the underlined NPs in each set below:

> Which holiday do you like best?
> <u>Christmas</u> I like best; <u>Thanksgiving</u> I like least.
> Do you swim or run for exercise?
> <u>Swimming</u> I do everyday, but <u>running</u> very seldom.

The fronted element must be given information in the context, and fronting results in its becoming the topic of the utterance. Fronting is thus a means of echoing topically what has been contextually given. Note that the fronted element may also be contrastive. The fronted element must be definite:

> *<u>A movie</u> I want to see.
> <u>That movie</u> I want to see.

The fronted element must also be the most salient or prominent element in the sentence:

> *<u>A run</u> I take every morning around the seawall.
> <u>A run around the seawall</u> I take every morning.

The fronted element is contextually most demanded: *Wilson his name is.* Fronting may serve to put in end focus the most important part of the sentence: *A very short run I can <u>handle</u>.* Note that fronting does not change the grammatical subject of the sentence, nor does it alter any of the functional relations within the sentence, but the fronted element necessarily becomes the new topic of the utterance.

In addition to the fronting of obligatory NPs, it is also common to front optional adverbial elements. **Adverb fronting** may move adverbial words, phrases, or clauses to the front of the sentence and topicalize them:

> <u>Suddenly</u> the car careered across the road.
> <u>The day after tomorrow/on Tuesday</u> I hope to return home.
> <u>Working late</u>, I missed my train.
> <u>If you don't stop playing that loud music</u>, I'll go crazy.
> <u>Because Rosa's leaving next week</u>, we're planning a party.
> <u>When we get home</u>, let's watch a video.

The fronting of adverbial subordinate clauses, especially conditional and causal clauses, is particularly common. Another phenomenon is adverb fronting + inversion (of subject and verb/auxiliary), which can occur with some locative and negative adverbs:

Out popped a clown.
On the porch sat a fierce dog.
Never have I seen such a sight.
Here comes my brother.
There is the book I was looking for.

Inversion has the effect of end-focusing the subject (see below).

Left-dislocation. Like fronting, **left-dislocation** moves a word, phrase, or clause to the beginning of the sentence, but it has the additional feature that it leaves a pronominal copy of the fronted element in its original place:

Annette, she'll be home late tonight.

Left-dislocation serves to re-introduce given information that has not been talked about for a while; this information becomes topic. It is frequently contrastive and usually definite. Left-dislocation is typically used when going through a list:

There are several interesting people we have met here, Mary, Sue, or Sarah. Sarah, we met her the first day we arrived.

Note that a NP can be left-dislocated from any position in the sentence; it may even be dislocated from an embedded sentence: *That party, Alison said that Susie had organized it for Dean.*

Cleft sentence. Clefting involves the following transformation of a standard declarative sentence. Beginning with *Jane gave this book to Bill on Saturday because it was his birthday*, clefting gives the following possibilities:

It was this book that Jane gave to Bill.
It was Bill who Jane gave this book to.
It was Jane who gave this book to Bill.
It was on Saturday that Jane gave this book to Bill.
It was because it was his birthday that Jane gave this book to Bill.

A **cleft sentence** consists of a dummy *it* subject, a form of *be*, an item in "cleft" position (underlined above), and a relative clause. Note that a NP, a PP, or an S̄ (aA) may be clefted. The clefted element is new information and comment, while the relative clause is given information and topic. The clefted element is frequently contrastive: e.g., *It was Jane (not Sally) who gave this book to Bill.* Cleft sentences have the effect not only of isolating the new information but also of putting the main focus towards the end of the sentence.

Though the information in the relative clause of a cleft is given information, the speaker does not assume that the hearer is thinking about it at the moment, merely that the hearer can readily deduce or recall it. For this reason, cleft sentences may begin a narrative.

It was in 1954 that I first visited London …

Occasionally, the information in cleft position is not new, as in the following short discourse:

His ego knew no bounds. It was his egoism (given) that I despised, but it was his brilliance (new) that I admired.

Finally, note that although the cleft sentence alters the syntactic form of the sentence, it does not alter the functional relations within the sentence (apart from moving an element into cleft position).

Pseudocleft sentence. Pseudoclefting involves the following transformation of the standard declarative sentence *Henry studied linguistics at university*:

What Henry studied at university was linguistics.
What Henry did was study linguistics at university.

A **pseudo-cleft sentence** consists of a headless relative clause, a form of *be*, and either a NP or a VP. New information follows *be*; it may be contrastive, as in *What Henry studied at university was linguistics (not mathematics)*. The pseudocleft structure thus postpones the sentence focus (the new information) to the end. The headless relative is given information, which the reader or hearer must be thinking about; hence, pseudocleft sentences cannot begin narratives. It is also the topic of the sentence. Note that reversing the order changes the topic: <u>*Linguistics*</u> (topic and given) *was what Henry studied at university*. A structure similar to the pseudocleft is what can be called a *one*-cleft sentence, which permits the same reversal of order:

The one who studied linguistics at university was <u>Henry</u> (comment and new).
<u>Henry</u> (topic and given) was the one who studied linguistics at university.

Stress. Both new information and contrastive information receive phonological **stress** (as well as higher pitch):

Sálly (not Júne) did that.
I did thát.

In neutral cases, the last major element (noun, verb, or adjective) in a sentence is stressed:

He stood on the dóck.
He stóod there.
He sáw them.

In these cases, either the stressed element is new or the entire sentence is:

Fido got bitten by a snáke.

But stress can move elsewhere in a sentence to mark information that is new or contrastive:

The ców jumped over the moon. (as opposed to the horse)
cf.   It was the ców that jumped over the moon.
The cow júmped over the moon. (as opposed to stepped)
The cow jumped óver the moon. (as opposed to around)
The cow jumped over the móon. (as opposed to the sun; or this is the neutral/unmarked case)

Note that the topic would also differ in these cases. (Stress is discussed in further detail in Chapter 3.)

Passive. Unlike the constructions discussed so far, an **agented passive** alters the functional relations within the sentence: the agent of the active sentence is expressed in a *by*-phrase and the direct or indirect object of the active sentence becomes the subject of the passive. This has the effect of making the passive subject given information and the topic of the sentence:

> Did you hear the news about Adele?
> She was given a commendation by the council.

Note that it would be odd to respond to the above question, which introduces "Adele" and makes her topic of the discourse, with a sentence such as *The council gave her a commendation*, since this suggests that the council is the topic and given information. Subjects of agented passives tend to be definite: ?*A cake was baked by Adelaide* (cf. *The cake was baked by Adelaide*). While **agentless passives** also make the passive subject topic, they are used in additional contexts:[2]

- when the agent is unknown: *A bomb was thrown*; *The school was vandalized*.
- when the speaker does not wish to specify the agent: *The expensive vase got/was broken*;
- when the agent is general, nonspecific, or obvious from context: *The tape should be rewound. All the employees were given lay-off notices. Tuition fees have been raised*; and
- when an NP other than the agent is topic: *The wording of the contract was changed. The house was knocked down. She was given a standing ovation. The terms were agreed to.*

The passive is also used to create cohesion in a text by beginning a sentence with the NP which ended the previous sentence (e.g., *Tanya walked up behind Harry. He was startled* vs. ?*She startled him*). (On the teaching of the passive to second-language learners, see the chapter on pedagogy on the CD-ROM.)

Note the alteration of topic in the following, as well as the effect of deleting the agent:

> You can buy a good computer for $2000.
> $2000 can get you a good computer.
> A good computer can be bought for $2000.

Another passive form is the so-called passive of experience, which uses *have*:

> She had her hopes dashed by the news. (< The news dashed her hopes.)
> He had his reputation tarnished by the rumors. (< The rumors tarnished his reputation.)

Rather than making the active object the topic (as in *Her hopes were dashed by the news*), the passive of experience makes the experiencer "she" the topic.[3] The construction of BE plus past participle has the same effect of making the experiencer the topic:

> We were amused by the movie. (< The movie amused us.)
> I am frightened by the prospect of tackling that job. (< The prospect of tackling that job frightens me.)

The past participles of *confuse, bore, disgust, amaze, puzzle,* and *worry* behave in the same way.

Other topicalizing transformations. English does not have as many options here as other languages, but it still provides a number of permutations of word order which move elements into topic position or make them part of the topic. This process is called **topicalization**. In the following cases, the underlined segment is part of the topic:

1.   *tough*-movement: So called because it may occur with the adjective *tough* (as well as *hard, easy,* and *impossible*), *tough*-movement moves the object of an infinitive to the subject (and hence topic) position of the matrix clause:

> The right answer is difficult to find. (< To find the right answer is difficult. It's difficult to find the right answer.)

2.   subject-to-subject raising: This transformation moves, or "promotes", the subject of the *that*-clause occurring with *likely, certain, happen,* and *seem* to the subject position in the matrix clause:

> Sam is certain to foot the bill. (< That Sam will foot the bill is certain, It is certain that Sam will foot the bill.)

3.   subject selection: Certain verbs in English permit "lexical packaging variants" (Foley and Van Valin 1985) in which a different NP is placed in subject, or topic, position. These may exist as matched pairs of verb:

> John bought a computer from Bill. Bill sold a computer to John.
> The news {pleased, amused} me. I liked the news.
> The volcano emitted poisonous fumes. Poisonous fumes emanated from the volcano.
> The newspaper account implied that the drive was drunk. I inferred from the newspaper account that the driver was drunk.

(Also *give/take, teach/learn, borrow/lend, rob/steal, regard/strike.*) Sometimes the same verb may permit the selection of different subjects, perhaps with a change in accompanying preposition or in the voice of the following infinitive:

> Canada grows a lot of wheat. A lot of wheat grows in Canada.
> The Smiths rented the cabin from Henry. Henry rented the cabin to the Smiths.
> I need to tune my bike. My bike needs to be tuned.

The construction with *take/have/get* and a deverbal noun may also permit a switch in subjects in certain instances:

> The waves battered the ship.
> The ship took a battering from the waves.

Finally, *there*-insertion (see below) also leads to a change in subject:

> The tent has a hole in it. There's a hole in the tent.

A variety of other transformations, although they do not move elements to subject position, allow some degree of leftward movement, altering the topical structure of the sentence:

1.   dative (or indirect object) movement:
As discussed in Chapter 7, ditransitive verbs allow variant orders, V dO *to/for* iO or V iO dO:

> I gave the report to George.
> I gave George the report.

Assuming unmarked sentence stress, the topic in the first instance might be considered "my giving the report to someone", with "George" being the comment, whereas the topic in the second instance might be considered "my giving George something", with "the report" being the topic. Contrastive stress could alter this topic/comment structure. Similar to dative movement are the types of sentences discussed in Chapter 10, where again the leftward movement of an NP alters the topic:

> They loaded the cart with hay. (topic = "their loading the cart"; comment = "with hay")
> They loaded the hay onto the cart. (topic = "their loading the hay"; comment = "onto the cart")
> We sprayed the wall with paint. (topic = "our spraying the wall"; comment = "with paint")
> We sprayed paint on the wall. (topic = "our spraying paint"; comment = "on the wall")

2.   particle movement:
As discussed in Chapter 8, phrasal verbs allow placement of the particle before or after the direct object:

> He wore out the brakes. (topic = "his wearing out (something)"; comment = "the brakes")
> He wore the brakes out. (topic = "his wearing the brakes"; comment "out")

The second sentence also conveys a completive sense resulting from the final placement of the particle *out*, which carries heavy stress. Note the completive sense — captured by the verbs *out* and *down* — in the second sentence in each set below:

> He cut down the tree. He cut the tree down. = He downed the tree by cutting.
> She rubbed out the error. She rubbed the error out. = She "outed" the error by rubbing.

Focusing transformations. There are two important positions in the sentence, the beginning and the end. We have just seen that by moving an element to the beginning, we can make it topic. We can also choose to move an element to the end of the sentence, the second prominent position. This has the effect of **focusing**, thus emphasizing, that element. Operations which focus include those exemplified in Table 11.1. Both *it*-extraposition, the movement of a *that*-clause to the end of the sentence, and extraposition from NP, the movement of a relative clause or other modifying element out of the NP to the end of the sentence, are discussed in Chapter 9. In the second example of *it*-extraposition given, extraposition is obligatory. Subject–verb inversion is similar to subject–auxiliary discussed in

Table 11.1. Focusing Operations in English

(1) *it*-extraposition:
It has been confirmed <u>that Boris won the election</u>.
< <u>That Boris won the election</u> has been confirmed.
It happens <u>that I'm related to the Russian royal family</u>.
< *<u>That I'm related to the Russian royal family</u> happens.

(2) extraposition from NP:
A new course will be offered <u>which explores the influence of global warming</u>.
< A new course <u>which explores the influence of global warming</u> will be offered.

(3) subject–verb inversion:
In the room were several people I knew.
< Several people I knew were in the room.
Down the hill careened an out-of-control car.
< An out-of-control car careened down the hill.

(4) *there*-insertion:
There were two children killed in the fire.
< Two children were killed in the fire. The fire killed two children.
There was a (*the) beautiful Ming vase on the mantelpiece.
< ?A beautiful Ming vase was on the mantelpiece.
There seems to be no solution.
< *No solution seems to be.

(5) heavy NP shift:
You should see before it leaves <u>the show at the art gallery</u>.
< You should see <u>the show at the art gallery</u> before it leaves.

(6) quantifier postposing:
The ships in the harbor <u>all</u> suffered damage in the storm.
< <u>All</u> the ships in the harbor suffered damage in the storm.

(7) right-dislocation:
<u>She's</u> gone out shopping, <u>your mother</u>.
We want <u>him</u> caught, <u>that criminal</u>.
<u>He's</u> amazing, <u>that man is</u>.
<u>He's</u> jilted her, <u>Jack has</u>.

Chapter 8, but involves a main verb; it occurs in cases where there is a sentence-initial locative or directional adverbial, or, less commonly, where there is an adjectival phrase (e.g., *Near the entrance stood a solemn-looking man*) or a participial phrase (e.g., *Destroyed in the fire were two large warehouses, Lying by the fire was a large dog*). *There*-insertion occurs with copula verbs and definite noun phrases; note that in cases of heavy subjects, *there*-insertion is the preferred structure while in other cases, it may be obligatory. Heavy NP shift is the shifting of a heavily modified NP to the end (see Chapter 9). Quantifier postposing is the movement of a quantifier such as *each* or *all* from its position before the NP to after the NP. Right-dislocation is the reverse of left dislocation (see above); however, right-dislocation differs from left-dislocation in that both a noun phrase and an auxiliary can right dislocate, as in the second example given in Table 11.1.

Relative clauses. Finally, we consider the differences between restrictive and nonrestrictive relative clauses in terms of information structuring. Nonrestrictive relative clauses modify only specific nouns, which may be either definite or indefinite:

> specific, definite: I am going to remodel <u>the kitchen</u>, which is fifty years old.
> specific, indefinite: Yesterday I saw <u>a beautiful kitchen</u>, which had granite counters.
> nonspecific, indefinite: *I dream of having <u>a new kitchen</u>, which has a gas stove.
> nonspecific, definite: *<u>The biggest kitchen</u>, which I can afford, costs $10,000.

Restrictive relative clauses modify either specific or nonspecific nouns, both definite or indefinite

> specific, definite: I'm going to buy <u>the cabinets</u> that I looked at yesterday.
> specific, indefinite: Yesterday I saw <u>a model kitchen</u> that I can afford.
> nonspecific, definite: I'm going to build <u>the biggest kitchen</u> that I can afford.
> nonspecific, indefinite: I dream of having <u>a kitchen</u> that has sufficient storage space.

Another way to view this restriction is to see the function of a restrictive relative clause as that of turning a nonspecific noun into a specific one.

Information Structuring in a Passage

One way of seeing the effects of syntactic differences on information structuring is to compare a "normal" passage (Text A) with an "odd" passage (Text B) (taken from Brown and Yule 1983: 128):

Text A: (1) The sun's shining, it's a perfect day. (2) Here come the astronauts. (3) They're just passing the Great Hall; (4) perhaps the President will come out to greet them. (5) No, its the admiral who's taking the ceremony.

Text B: (1) It's the sun that's shining, the day that's perfect. (2) The astronauts come here. (3) The Great Hall they're just passing; (4) he'll perhaps come out to greet them, the President. (5) No, its the ceremony that the admiral's taking.

The cleft sentence in sentence (1) in Text B treats the facts that something is shining and that something is perfect as given and topic, as well as in the forefront of the hearer's consciousness; furthermore, the sun and the day are possibly contrastive. In contrast, the corresponding sentence in Text A treats only the sun as given (in the sociophysical context). Sentence (2) of Text B treats the astronauts as given and topic, though they are obviously new information; the inverted sentence (2) of Text A has the advantage of end-focusing this new information. The fronting in sentence (3) of Text B topicalizes the Great Hall, which is treated as old information, whereas the unmarked structure in Text A rightly presents the astronauts as old information (expressed pronominally)/topic and the Great Hall as new information/comment. In the right-dislocated structure in sentence (4) in Text B, the President is end-focused; he is initially presented as given information (expressed pronominally), though he is in fact new information. The effect of adverb fronting in sentence (4) in Text A is to topicalize the notion of doubt and to make the rest of the sentence new information. Sentence (5) in both texts is a cleft sentence, but in Text B the cleft position is occupied by the wrong word; the new (and contrastive) information here is not the ceremony (ceremony can be inferred from the context), but the admiral, as in the version in Text A.

While this is an obviously concocted example, you should be able to see the importance of effective information structuring in the construction of cohesive and coherent texts.

■ *Self-Testing Exercises: Do Exercises 11.2 and 11.3.*

Speech Act Theory

An important means of accounting for the function of language in context, developed within the philosophy of language, is speech act theory. The first writer on this topic was the British philosopher J. L. Austin, whose Harvard lectures were published in a book entitled *How to Do Things with Words* (1962). Austin's student, the American philosopher John Searle, has carried on his work, first in a book entitled *Speech Acts* (1969) and in subsequent work. Linguists have utilized speech act theory in the area of pragmatic analysis; but it has also been applied to literary texts (see, e.g., Pratt 1977).

Austin observes that — contrary to the position of logicians — not all utterances have "truth value". He thus makes a fundamental distinction between constatives, which are assertions which are either true or false, and performatives, which cannot be characterized as either true or false, but are, in Austin's terms, "felicitous" (happy) or "infelicitous" (unhappy). These are utterances by which the speaker carries out an action, hence the term *speech act*. Examples of performatives are utterances such as the following:

I name this ship the "Queen Elizabeth".	I promise.
I refuse to answer that question.	I congratulate you.
I will pay you tomorrow.	I bet you a quarter.
We authorize the payment.	I swear it's true.

Simply by uttering each of these statements, the speaker performs an action, such as naming, congratulating, promising, and betting, These actions require no further action other than the linguistic action in order to be what they are. As in the examples given, speech acts may contain an explicit **performative verb**, which is normally first person and simple present tense (i.e., *I name, I congratulate, I promise, I bet,* and so on). Performatives can occur with "hereby". Austin says that there are 1,000 such verbs in English. Searle rejects Austin's distinction between constative and performative, interpreting all utterances as performatives, even those which we might understand as representing a state of affairs and hence true or false, for example, *It is raining*. He categorizes such a speech act as a Representative. Before looking at his categorization, however, we will consider how he analyzes speech acts and the bases he uses for his taxonomy.

Components of Speech Acts

Austin argues that every utterance can be understood as consisting of three parts:

1. a locutionary act, including both an utterance act and a propositional act; a locutionary act is the recognizable grammatical utterance (its form and meaning);
2. an illocutionary act, such as stating, promising, or commanding; an illocutionary act is the communicative purpose of an utterance, the use to which language is being put, or what the speaker is trying to do with his locutionary act, and
3. a perlocutionary act, such as persuading, annoying, consoling, or alarming; the perlocutionary act is the intended or actual effects of a locutionary act, the consequences these acts have on hearers' attitudes, beliefs, or behavior. The effects of a speech act are not conventional but depend upon the context.

The same locutionary act, such as *It's raining*, may be a statement of fact about the weather, advice to carry an umbrella, or a warning that one shouldn't go outside.

The semantic structure of a speech act consists of its **illocutionary force** (abbreviated **IF**), and its **propositional content** (abbreviated **prop**). Illocutionary force is the way in which the proposition is to be taken. Illocutionary force is expressed by performative verbs, but also by a variety of other means, including sentence type, word order, stress, intonation, punctuation, or mood or modal auxiliaries. The same proposition [He not smoke] may have different illocutionary forces:

He doesn't smoke.   Doesn't he smoke?   Would that he didn't smoke.

An utterance is thus analyzable as IF(prop). Either the illocutionary force or the proposition can be negated, represented ~IF(prop) and IF(~prop) (using the logical symbol for negation ~), for example *I do not promise to be there on time* and *I promise not to hurt you*.

Every illocutionary act, Searle postulates, can be understood in respect to three features:

1. its illocutionary point or force;
2. its direction of fit; and
3. its expressed psychological state.

Direction of fit refers to the way in which language relates to the external world: it may be word-to-world, where the speaker intends what he says to match things in the world, to be true or false statements about the world, or it may be world-to-word, where the speaker intends the world to come to match what he says, to bring about or effect a change by saying something. The British philosopher G. E. M. Anscombe (1957: 56) exemplifies these directions of fit with a story of a detective following a shopper in the food market. The shopper's list of things to buy has a world-to-word fit, but the detective's list of what the shopper has selected has a word-to-world fit. (The shopper may not get everything on his or her list, but note that we could not say that his or her list is "false" in this case. If the detective misses out an item, however, we could say that his or her list is wrong.) In the nonlinguistic domain, the word-to-world fit would be analogous to a drawing of a house, which is meant to be a true representation of an existing structure, whereas the world-to-word fit would be analogous to an architect's blueprint of a house, which is meant to lead to the construction of such a structure. If the house departs from the plans as construction proceeds, we would not say that the original blueprints were "false".

The **expressed psychological state** of a speaker of a speech act, also known as the **sincerity condition** of a speech act, consists of the beliefs and attitudes of the speaker, the psychological state of the speaker towards the propositional content of the speech act. If you say something and do not have the corresponding state of mind, then your speech act is insincere (what Austin called "infelicitous"), for example, promising to do something without intending to do so. If you say something and deny the corresponding psychological state, then your utterance is absurd, for example, promising to do something and then denying that you intend to do it.

Taxonomy of Speech Acts

In an article entitled "A Classification of Illocutionary Acts" (1976), Searle uses the three factors — illocutionary force, direction of fit, and expressed psychological state — as the basis for classifying all speech acts. He identifies six classes:[4]

1.   **Directives**: A directive speech act is an attempt by Sp to get H to do something. Examples of directives are ordering, commanding, requesting, pleading, begging, entreating, daring, inviting, questioning (an attempt to get H to perform the speech act of answering), insisting, suggesting, permitting, and challenging. Note that the action must be future and voluntary, because it is impossible to ask someone to perform an action in the past or to do something which is not a matter of human will. For example, *I command you to leave yesterday* or *I order you to grow taller* are "infelicitous" commands. (Volition here does not refer to one's liking to do what is commanded, but merely to its being humanly possible.) The expressed psychological state is that Sp must want or wish for H to do something; to say *Turn on the t.v., but I don't want you to* is contradictory. The direction of fit is world-to-word, for S is attempting to get the world to resemble his or her words.

With directives, as all speech acts, either the proposition or the illocutionary force can be negated. And we have names for these different negated forms:

Command	IF(prop) I command you to close the door.
Forbid, Prohibit	IF(~prop) I command you not to close the door. I forbid you to close the door.
Permit	~IF(prop) I don't command you to close the door.
	~IF(~prop) I don't command you not to close the door = you may close the door.

2.   **Commissives**: With a commissive speech act, Sp commits himself or herself to the performance of an action. Examples of commissives are promising, vowing, pledging, threatening, guaranteeing, pledging, agreeing, consenting, and refusing. Again, the promised action must be future and voluntary; note the infelicitousness of *I promise to leave yesterday* or *I promise to grow taller*. The expressed psychological state is that Sp intends to do something. The direction of fit is world-to-word.

3.   **Representatives** (also known as "Assertives"): Here Sp represents a state of affairs. Examples of representatives are affirming, declaring, describing, claiming, stating, explaining, classifying, insisting, telling, hypothesizing, claiming, recalling, mentioning, attesting, confiding, emphasizing, and predicting. A representative commits Sp to the truth of the proposition. The expressed psychological state is one of belief, though Sp's state of belief can be more or less strong, ranging from conviction (as in affirming) to tentativeness (as in predicting). The direction of fit of a representative is word-to-world in that the description is meant to match the situation in the world.

4.   **Expressives**: In an expressive speech act, Sp expresses a psychological state about the situation or state of affairs denoted by the proposition. Examples of expressives are thanking, apologizing, consoling, congratulating, greeting, welcoming, and deploring. The propositional content is something which affects Sp or H; note that it would be odd to say *I console you on the war in Bosnia* or *I congratulate you on the Queen's sixtieth birthday* unless these events somehow affected H. As you are aware, however, many, if not most, expressives are highly conventionalized; Sp may say *Congratulations on your promotion* even when he or she is intensely envious or *Thank you for the beautiful gift* even when he or she thinks the gift tasteless or useless. What is most important in these cases is that the utterance counts as an expressive, not that the psychological state is deeply felt. Expressives have no direction of fit, since the proposition is presupposed rather than asserted. For example, if Sp says *I am sorry about your car accident*, the occurrence of the car accident is being assumed, or presupposed, and this utterance would be infelicitous if a car accident had not occurred. The only exception is the optative mood (expressing a wish), which has a world-to-word direction-of-fit, for example *Would that it would rain*, *If only Noel would come*.

5.   **Verdictives**: Sp expresses a value judgment or rates something. Examples of verdictives are assessing, ranking, rating, estimating, grading, diagnosing, calculating, and measuring. Verdictives may be a subcategory of representatives since the expressed psychological state of the speaker is belief in the value judgment, and the direction of fit is word-to-world.

6.   **Declaratives**: Declaratives are the prototypical speech act. Here the Sp brings about a change in the world by uttering an locutionary act. Examples of declaratives are declaring war, seconding a motion, adjourning a meeting, firing, nominating, christening, finding guilty/innocent, betting, passing (in a game), divorcing, baptizing, arresting, and resigning. Generally Sp must hold some position in an **extralinguistic institution** in order for the speech act to be effective. However, there are two exceptions:

a.   in supernatural cases, as when God says "Let there be light", or
b.   for ordinary speakers, when making statements about language, for example, defining, abbreviating, naming, calling, and dubbing.

The direction of fit of a declarative is in both directions since the speaker is both representing a state of affairs and bringing it about at the same time. There is no psychological state expressed; the president can declare war or the prime minister can disband parliament no matter what his or her feelings about the action.

There may be hybrid speech acts which combine two different types of speech acts. For example, inviting is both a directive (Sp tries to get H to do something) and a commissive (Sp is committed to accepting H's actions) or a referee's declaring a foul is both a representative (Sp believes that a fouling action has occurred) and a declarative (by virtue of Sp saying that a foul has occurred, it is a foul, with the consequences that entail).

Appropriateness Conditions on Speech Acts

The conditions under which a speech act can successfully be performed are called its **appropriateness conditions**. Austin termed them "felicity conditions"; they are the "unspoken rules" by which a speech act is governed, or its pragmatic presuppositions. They dictate how, when, where, and by whom a speech act can be performed felicitously, such as the circumstances of speech, the relationship of Sp and H, the beliefs and attitudes of the participants, and even the form of the speech act itself. Generally, the speaker believes that all the appropriateness conditions are met and presupposes that the hearer takes this for granted.

General appropriateness conditions on speech acts. While each kind of speech act is subject to its own set of conditions, a number of general appropriateness conditions apply to all speech acts:

– **propositional content condition**: the content of the proposition of the speech act must be appropriate to its illocutionary force; for example, a prediction must concern a future event, and a report a present or past event.
– **preparatory conditions**: Sp and/or H must hold certain beliefs before a particular speech act can appropriately be performed, and the speech act must occur in a conventionally recognized context or the appropriate circumstances. Also, Sp must be in an appropriate position to perform the speech act.
– **nonobvious condition**: it must not be obvious that in the normal course of events the proposition of the speech act is or will be.
– **essential condition**: the utterace counts as, or must be recognized by H as counting as, the performance of a particular type of speech act.
– sincerity condition: Sp is responsible for what he or she is saying and is sincere. H will assume Sp is being sincere.
– the relation of Sp to H must be correct; the speaker must have the right to speak as he or she does. For example, a different relation of the speaker in respect to the hearer is necessary to perform the speech acts of commanding (Sp superior to H), pleading (Sp inferior to H), or urging (Sp and H equals).
– the interests of Sp and/or H in respect to the propositional content must be appropriate. Note the very different interests of Sp in boasting or complaining, and the very different interests of H who receives a warning or advice, or congratulations or condolences:

> Let me {boast/complain} for a moment about what just happened to me.
> I {congratulate/console} you on your marriage.
> I {warn, advise} you not to speak to him. I {advise, *warn} you to speak to him.

– the strength or commitment of Sp to the speech act must be appropriate. For example, Sp has different degrees of commitment to the proposition when suggesting and insisting:

> I suggest that we go to a movie tonight. Why don't we go to a movie tonight?
> I insist that we go to a movie tonight.

- the speech act must relate to the previous discourse in an appropriate way. For example, answers and replies cannot begin a segment of discourse, though they may end it; conclusions must necessarily end a segment of discourse; and interjections or interruptions cannot either begin or end a segment of discourse:

> I {begin, end, interrupt} by pointing out …

- the style or formality of the performance must be appropriate to the speech act. For example, one can announce on television, but generally not confide (daytime talk shows may be an exception!); one can assert, report, or inform explicitly, but one can hint, insinuate, or intimate only indirectly.
- an extralinguistic institution may be required for some speech acts, with Sp and/or H occupying certain positions within that institution, as is the case in excommunicating, arresting, convicting, or declaring man and wife.

It is important to distinguish rules of conversational politeness, or social decorum from the general appropriateness conditions on speech acts since violations of either set of rules have quite different results. If appropriateness conditions are violated, the speech act is not or cannot be performed; if rules of conversational politeness are violated, the speech act is performed — it would count as the speech act — but it would be judged as rude. In other words, appropriateness conditions are constitutive rules, while rules of conversational politeness are regulatory rules. Remember that regulatory rules control already existing behavior (e.g., *When cutting food, hold the knife in the right hand*), while constitutive rules create or define new forms of behavior (e.g., *Checkmate is made when the king is attacked in such a way that no move will leave it unattacked*).

Appropriateness conditions on promising. The appropriateness conditions on promising will serve as an example of the specific conditions relevant to one kind of speech act. The performer of the speech act of promising says the essential condition, expresses the sincerity condition, and presupposes the other appropriateness conditions:

- propositional content condition: the proposition denotes a future act committed or performed by Sp.
- preparatory conditions: Sp is able to do what he or she promises; H would prefer Sp's doing what is promised; and Sp believes H would prefer his doing it. Note the oddness of *I promise to kill you* as a promise, though it would work as a threat or warning.
- nonobvious condition: it is not obvious to both Sp and H that Sp will perform the action in the normal course of events.
- sincerity condition (expressed psychological state): Sp intends to do what he or she promises (and thinks it is possible to do it). If Sp meets the sincerity condition, the promise is sincere; if Sp does not have the proper intention, but purports to, the promise is insincere.

– essential condition: Sp intends that the utterance will place him or her under an obligation to do what is promised; and Sp intends H to recognize that his utterance counts as a promise.

Note that since "I promise" is one of strongest devices for indicating commitment, so it is often used not only when promising but also when uttering a forceful representative, as in:

> I didn't do it, I promise.
> I promise you'll go to jail for 10 years.

Now consider Table 11.2. It gives a list of the appropriateness conditions on two directives (*request, question*), three representatives (*assert, advise, warn*), and three expressives (*thank, greet, congratulate*). The following abbreviations are used: Ac = action and E = event.

> ■ Self-Testing Exercise: Do Exercise 11.4.

Indirect Speech Acts

We often perform speech acts indirectly rather than directly, especially in spoken discourse. That is, by means of one explicit speech act, we actually perform another implicit one. But for such **indirect speech acts** to be successful, there must be some principle underlying them. How they work is that we give expression to one of the appropriateness conditions of the speech act we want to perform. This expression itself is a the explicit speech act, a type of speech act such as a statement (representative), expressive, or question (directive), but it has the illocutionary force of the intended speech act. It "functions as" the implicit speech act. The clearest example of indirect speech acts is directives, because in polite social behavior, there is a tendency to avoid the direct imperative. In fact, in spoken discourse, there is a tendency to use no performatives at all, except as emphasis, often as parentheticals, "I tell you", "I promise", or "I declare".

Consider the directive *(I command you to) pass the salt*, expressed explicitly with a performative verb or imperative sentence. Appropriateness conditions on this directive are the sincerity condition (1) and the preparatory conditions (2). A speaker may perform this directive indirectly, then, by giving expression to either of these appropriateness conditions in the following ways:

1. Sp has a wish or desire for salt/for H to pass the salt:
   > I {would like, want} the salt.
   > I {would like, want} you to pass the salt.
   > It would be nice if you passed the salt.

2. the action to be performed is a future, voluntary (able and willing) action of H:
   > {Can, could, would} you pass the salt?
   > Can you reach the salt?
   > Would you mind passing the salt?
   > Is it possible for you to pass the salt?

Table 11.2. Types of Speech Acts and their Appropriateness Conditons

Type of condition

Request
Propositional Content: Future act Ac of H.
Preparatory: 1. H is able to do Ac. Sp believes H is able to do Ac.
2. It is not obvious to both Sp and H that H will do Ac in the normal course of events of his or her own accord.
Sincerity: Sp wants H to do Ac.
Essential: Counts as an attempt to get H to do Ac.
Comment: Order and command have the additional preparatory rule that Sp must be in a position of authority over H. Command probably does not have the pragmatic condition requiring nonobviousness. Furthermore, in both the authority relationship infects the essential condition because the utterance counts as an attempt to get H to do Ac in virtue of the authority of Sp over H.

Assert, state (that), affirm
Propositional Content: Any proposition prop.
Preparatory: 1. Sp has evidence (reasons, etc.) for the truth of prop.
2. It is not obvious to both Sp and H that H knows (does not need to be reminded of, etc.) prop.
Sincerity: Sp believes prop.
Essential: Counts as an undertaking to the effect that prop represents an actual state of affairs.
Comment: Unlike argue these do not seem to be essentially tied to attempting to convince. Thus "I am simply stating that prop and not attempting to convince you" is acceptable, but "I am arguing that prop and not attempting to convince you" sounds inconsistent.

Question*
Propositional Content: Any proposition or propositional function.
Preparatory: 1. Sp does not know 'the answer', i.e., does not know if the proposition is true, or, in the case of the propositional function, does not know the information needed to complete the proposition truly (but see comment below).
2. It is not obvious to both Sp and H that H will provide the information at the time without being asked.
Sincerity: Sp wants this information.
Essential: Counts as an attempt to elicit this information from H.
Comment: There are two kinds of questions, (a) real questions, (b) exam questions. In real questions Sp wants to know (find out) the answer; in exam questions, Sp wants to know if H knows.

Thank (for)
Propositional Content: Past act Ac done by H.
Preparatory: Ac benefits Sp and Sp believes Ac benefits Sp.
Sincerity: Sp feels grateful or appreciative for Ac.
Essential: Counts as an expression of gratitude or appreciation.
Comment: Sincerity and essential rules overlap. Thanking is just expressing gratitude in a way that, e.g., promising is not just expressing an intention.

* In the sense of "ask a question" not in the sense of "doubt".

Table 11.2. (continued)

Advise
Propositional Content: Future act Ac of H.
Preparatory: 1. Sp has some reason to believe Ac will benefit H.
              2. It is not obvious to both Sp and H that H will do Ac in the normal course of events.
Sincerity: Sp believes Ac will benefit H.
Essential: Counts as an undertaking to the effect that Ac is in H's best interest.
Comment: Contrary to what one might suppose advice is not a species of requesting. It is interest-
              ing to compare "advise" with "urge", "advocate" and "recommend". Advising you is
              not trying to get you to do something in the sense that requesting is. Advising is more
              like telling you what is best for you.

Warn
Propositional Content: Future event or state, etc., E.
Preparatory: 1. H has reason to believe E will occur and is not in H's interest.
              2. It is not obvious to both Sp and H that E will occur.
Sincerity: Sp believes E is not in H's best interest.
Essential: Counts as an undertaking to the effect that E is not in H's best interest.
Comment: Warning is like advising, rather than requesting. It is not, I think necessarily an at-
              tempt to get you to take evasive action, Notice that the above account is of categorical
              not hypothetical warnings. Most warnings are probably hypothetical: "If you do not
              do X then Y will occur".

Greet
Propositional Content: None.
Preparatory: Sp has just encountered (or been introduced to, etc.) H.
Sincerity: None.
Essential: Counts as courteous recognition of H by Sp.

Congratulate
Propositional Content: Some event, act, etc., E related to H.
Preparatory: E is in H's interest and Sp believes E is in H's interest.
Sincerity: Sp is pleased at E.
Essential: Counts as an expression of pleasure at E.
Comment: "Congratulate" is similar to "thank" in that it is an expression of its sincerity condi-
              tion.

(From John Searle, *Speech Acts: an Essay in the Philosophy of Language*, 66–67. © Cambridge University Press, 1969. Reprinted with the permission of Cambridge University Press.)

> Would it be possible for you to pass the salt?
> Would it be too much trouble for you to pass the salt?
> Do you think you can manage to pass the salt? (sarcasm)
> Why don't you pass the salt?
> Why not pass the salt? (there is nothing stopping you)

A test that these are all used as directives is the fact that they all take *please*, and negative responses to them could all include a phrase such as *I'm sorry*. Note the asymmetry here: it is usual to state Sp's desire and to question H's ability or willingness; the sincerity condition is related to the speaker, while the preparatory condition is related to the hearer:

> ?Do I want the salt?
> The salt is in front of you, Bill (so it is possible for you to pass it)
> You can pass the salt now.

It would also be possible to perform the directive indirectly by expressing the fact that Sp doesn't have what he wants, as in:

> The cook forgot the salt in this dish.
> This dish {needs, could use} salt.
> A little salt would help this dish.

(Note that these do not take final *please*, though they do take initial *please*).

Indirect speech acts are idiomatic English, so they are not always translatable into other languages. However, indirect speech acts are not idioms. That is, it is not the case that there is one speech act with idiomatic meaning, that "Can you pass the salt" has the idiomatic meaning "Pass the salt!", just as "kick the bucket" has the idiomatic meaning "die". The words in indirect speech acts have their literal meaning; they are not a case of "noncompositionality" (see Chapter 5 on idioms). It is also not the case that the explicit speech act is somehow "defective". The question "Can you pass the salt?" is not defective in the way that "Can you eat Mt. Everest?" is. The former functions as a request and the latter does not. Finally, we should not understand the indirect speech as ambiguous; rather, the explicit speech act is being used in two ways.

When performing a speech act indirectly, we are actually performing two speech acts at the same time:

1. the literal, or explicit speech act, which is secondary, and
2. the nonliteral, or implicit speech act, which is primary.

In some contexts, both speech acts are functional. A person could acknowledge the literal speech act by responding, for example:

> Can you reach the salt? No, it's too far away.
> Do you have the time? No, I don't wear a watch
> Do you have a match? No, I don't smoke.

In fact, all of the indirect forms of *Pass the salt* given above have uses where they are not directives, except those with *Why not, Why don't you,* and *How about.* Note also that in some contexts a speaker may want to deny the indirect speech act: *I'd like some salt, but I'm not asking you to pass it.* So the explicit speech act still has literal meaning and is used with literal meaning.

Look now at Table 11.3. It gives numerous examples of indirect directives, which are based on the appropriateness conditions of that type of speech act: Group 1 concerns the preparatory conditions on directives, Group 2 the sincerity conditions, Group 3 the propositional content, Group 4 the preparatory conditions, and Group 5 the reasonableness conditions.

Table 11.3. Sentences Conventionally Used in the Performance of Indirect Directives

GROUP 1:	Sentences concerning H's ability to perform Ac: Can/Could you be a little more quiet? You could be a little more quiet. You can go now (this may also be a permission = you may go now). Are you able to reach the book on the top shelf? Have you got change for a dollar?
GROUP 2:	Sentences concerning Sp's wish or want that H will do Ac: I would like you to go now. I want you to do this for me, Henry. I would/should be most grateful if you would/could do it for me. I would/should be most grateful if you would/could help us out. I'd rather you didn't do that any more. I'd be very much obliged if you would pay me the money back soon. I hope you'll do it. I wish you wouldn't do that.
GROUP 3:	Sentences concerning H's doing Ac: Officers will henceforth wear ties at dinner. Will you quit making that awful racket? Would you kindly get off my foot? Won't you stop making that noise soon? Aren't you going to eat your cereal?
GROUP 4:	Sentences concerning H's desire or willingness to do Ac: Would you be willing to write a letter of recommendation for me? Do you want to hand me that hammer over there on the table? Would you mind not making so much noise? Would it be convenient for you to come on Wednesday? Would it be too much (trouble) for you to pay me the money next Wednesday?
GROUP 5:	Sentences concerning reasons for doing Ac: You ought to be more polite to your mother. You should leave immediately. Must you continue hammering that way? Ought you to eat quite so much spaghetti? Should you be wearing John's tie? You had better go now. Hadn't you better go now? Why not stop here? Why don't you try it just once? Why don't you be quiet? It would be better for you (for us all) if you would leave the room. It wouldn't hurt if you left now. It might help if you shut up. It would be better if you gave me the money now. It would be a good idea if you left town. We'd all be better off if you'd just pipe down a bit.

Table 11.3. (continued)

This class also contains many examples that have no generality of form but obviously, in an appropriate context, would be uttered as indirect requests, e.g.:

You're standing on my foot.
I can't see the movie screen while you have that hat on.

Also in this class belong, possibly:

How many times have I told you (must I tell you) not to eat with your fingers?
I must have told you a dozen times not to eat with your mouth open.
If I have told you once I have told you a thousand times not to wear your hat in the house.

GROUP 6:   Sentences embedding one of these elements inside another; also, sentences embedding an explicit directive illocutionary verb inside one of these contexts.
Would you mind awfully if I asked you if you could write me a letter of recommendation?
Would it be too much if I suggested that you could possibly make a little less noise?
Might I ask you to take off your hat?
I hope you won't mind if I ask you if you could leave us alone.

■   *Self-Testing Exercise:* Do Exercise 11.5.

The Cooperative Principle and Conversational Implicature

How does the hearer recognize the presence of an implicit speech act? First, there are some conventional forms for performing various indirect speech acts. Second, the propositional content may make a difference, as in:

Can you reach the salt? versus Can you reach the ceiling?

Most importantly, there is an appropriateness condition on language use in general which is in force. This condition was identified by the philosopher Paul Grice (1975, 1981) and termed the **cooperative principle:** "Make your conversational contribution such as is required, at the stage at which it occurs, by the accepted purpose or direction of the talk exchange in which you are engaged" (1975:46). It is the principle that Sp has a communicative (or other) purpose in speaking and makes this purpose clear to H; likewise, H trusts that Sp has a purpose and will do his or her best to discern it. In order to ensure that hearers recognize their intent, speakers should make their conversational contribution such as is required at the stage at which it occurs in the discourse; it should adhere to the the accepted purpose or direction of the talk exchange in which the participants are engaged. According to Grice (1975:45–46), certain maxims should be followed by the speaker:

1.   the maxim of quantity: be as informative as necessary but not more informative than necessary;
2.   the maxim of quality: do not say what you believe is false, do not say what you don't have evidence for;
3.   the maxim of manner: avoid obscurity and ambiguity, be brief, be orderly;
4.   the maxim of relation: be relevant.

When the maxim seems to be intentionally "flouted" or violated, H will attempt to understand the utterance by taking contextual information into account and making certain inferences — called **conversational implicatures** — which conform to the cooperative principle (that Sp is trying to make his or her communicative purpose clear to H) and the maxims of conversation. For example, consider the following short conversations:

1.   Speaker A: Do you have any money?
      Speaker B: I have a ten-dollar bill.
2.   Speaker A: What color is her jacket?
      Speaker B: It's white.
3.   Speaker A: Is Jim coming to the party tonight?
      Speaker B: His parents are visiting for the weekend.
4.   Speaker A: Is Ellen at home?
      Speaker B: Her light is on.
5.   Speaker A: What on earth has happened to the roast beef?
      Speaker B: The dog is looking very happy (Levinson 1983: 126).

In (1) Speaker A would make the implicature that Speaker B has only ten dollars. However, if B has more than ten dollars, he or she is not uttering a false statement, but one that flouts the maxim of quantity. Likewise in (2) Speaker A would make the implicature that the jacket is entirely white. However, if it is white and black, then B has again flouted the maxim of quantity, without uttering a false statement. In (3), (4), and (5), Speaker B's response does not on the surface address Speaker A's question. But A will assume that it follows the maxim of relevance and attempt to interpret it, in (3) making the implicature that because Jim's parents are in town he will not be coming to the party and in (4) making the implicature that Ellen's light being on is an indication that she is at home. In (5), the maxim of relevance would lead A to the implicature that the dog has eaten the roast beef. Conversational implicatures have the feature that they are "defeasible" or cancelable; for example, in (1) above, Speaker B could continue by saying *I have a ten-dollar bill, in fact three ten-dollar bills*, thus canceling the implicature that he or she has only ten dollars, or in (3) above, Speaker B could continue by saying *His parents are visiting for the weekend, but he will be able to come to the party*.[5]

Indirect speech acts function much like examples (3) and (4), where the maxim of relevance is apparently flouted. The hearer must make certain implicatures, determining that some implicit speech act, rather than the explicit speech act, is relevant in context. This is known as the **principle of conversational relevance**. Of course, there are still cases where both direct and indirect speech acts are not recognized, and not communicated, where there are breakdowns in the communicative process. These may be either intentional (when Sp is lying, obscuring, purposely confusing, or disguising his or her illocutionary intent) and unintentional (when Sp's illocutionary intent is misunderstood or H fails to understand).

One way in which the relevance of one utterance to another is indicated is by means of forms called **discourse markers**. These are short words or phrases, such as *well, so, y'know, actually, anyway, then,* and *I mean,* which are hard to classify in terms of part of speech. They are seemingly devoid of meaning, but are of high frequency in speech, usually occurring at the beginning of utterances. Discourse markers were traditionally seen as empty fillers, but they are now understood as signaling the relevance of the utterance they introduce to the ongoing discourse (among other functions). Look again at example (3) above with the discourse marker *well* added:

3′.   Speaker A: Is Jim coming to the party tonight?
       Speaker B: <u>Well</u>, his parents are visiting for the weekend.

Well here indicates that the most immediately accessible context may not be the most relevant one for interpretation of the following utterance. Or consider a version of example (4) above with *so* or *then* added:

4′.   Speaker A: Ellen's lights are on.
       Speaker B: {<u>So, Then</u>} she must be at home.

The discourse marker here indicates that the following statement is a conversational implicature of the preceding statement. Note that the discourse marker *so* differs from the *so* expressing causal or result (e.g., *Ellen was hungry so she ate some potato chips*), just as the discourse marker *then* differs from the temporal *then* (e.g., *Ellen went home, then went to bed*).

■ Chapter Summary

Now that you have completed this chapter, you should be able to:

1. define concepts of information structuring;
2. analyze the effects of a variety of syntactic possibilities in English upon information structuring;
3. determine the illocutionary force, expressed psychological state, direction of fit, and speech act type of an utterance;
4. discuss the appropriateness conditions of different speech act types;
5. explain the operation of an indirect speech act in relation to the corresponding direct speech act; and
6. identify conversational implicatures in respect to Gricean maxims and the principle of conversational relevance.

■ Recommended Additional Reading

The classic treatment of the concepts of information structuring is Chafe (1976); a general exploration of the topic is Brown and Yule (1983, Chapters 3, 4, and 5) and a cross-linguistic approach is Foley and Van Valin (1985). A thorough discussion of the given-new contrast can be found in Prince (1981). Good textbook treatments of information structuring are Brown and Miller (1991, Chapter 20) and Finegan (1999, Chapter 8).

The primary discussions of speech act theory are Austin (1963) and Searle (1969, 1975, 1979) and of conversational maxims are Grice (1975, 1981). Secondary treatments of speech act theory are Lyons (1977, Section 16.1), Levinson (1983, Chapter 5), and Allan (1986, Vol. 2, Chapter 8). Finegan (1999, Chapter 9, pp. 295–307) is a textbook coverage of speech acts, and Hurford and Heasley (1983, Chapters 21–26) contains practice exercises on speech acts. Interesting articles on indirect speech acts are included in Cole and Morgan (1975). Conversational implicature is well treated in Levinson (1983, Chapter 3). The concept of conversational relevance is the subject of Sperber and Wilson (1995) and is well summarized in Blakemore (1988), who also discusses discourse markers.

■ Notes

1. Other terms used for topic and comment are *theme* and *rheme*, although sometimes these designate structural positions in the sentence, as opposed to conceptual notions.

2. Moreover, the passive is characteristic of certain styles of writing, such as instructions or technical/ scientific writing where the intended agent is general or understood. In scientific writing the use of the passive is connected with the replicability of results. Despite prescriptive prohibitions against the passive, it has legitimate uses in all types of discourse.

3. The passive of experience should not be confused with causative *have* + past participle, e.g., *She had her suit dry-cleaned* (= caused her suit to be dry-cleaned).

4. A number of different taxonomies have been proposed (see Hancher 1979).

5. It is common to distinguish between "conventional implicatures" and "conversational implicatures". Conversational implicatures are "nondetachable" (not attached to any one word in a sentence, paraphrases carrying the same implicatures) and nonconventional (not part of the conventional meaning of words), whereas conventional implicatures may be part of the conventional meaning of individual words. This distinction is being ignored here.

References

Adams, Valerie. 1973. *An Introduction to Modern English Word-Formation* [English Language Series, 7]. London: Longman.

Akmajian, Adrian, Richard A. Demers, Ann K. Farmer, and Robert M. Harnish. 1995. *Linguistics: An Introduction to Language and Communication.* 4th ed. Cambridge, MA and London: The MIT Press.

Allan, Keith. 1986. *Linguistic Meaning.* 2 vols. London and New York: Routledge and Kegan Paul.

Anscombe, G.E.M. 1957. *Intention.* Oxford: Clarendon Press.

Austin, J.L. 1962. *How to Do Things with Words,* edited by J.O. Urmson. Cambridge, MA: Harvard University Press.

Baker, C.L. 1995. *English Syntax.* 2nd ed. Cambridge, MA and London: MIT Press.

Bauer, Laurie. 1983. *English Word Formation* [Cambridge Textbooks in Linguistics]. Cambridge: Cambridge University Press

————. 1988. *Introducing Linguistic Morphology.* Edinburgh: Edinburgh University Press.

Biber, Douglas. 1988. *Variation across Speech and Writing.* Cambridge: Cambridge University Press.

Blakemore, Diane. 1988. "The Organization of Discourse". In *Linguistics: The Cambridge Survey.* Vol. 4: *Language: The Socio-cultural Context,* edited by Frederick J. Newmeyer, 229–50. Cambridge: Cambridge University Press.

Bloomfield, Leonard. 1933. *Language.* New York: Holt, Rinehart and Winston.

Bolinger, Dwight. 1986. *Intonation and its Parts: Melody in Spoken English.* Stanford: Stanford University Press.

Borsley, Robert D. 1995. *Syntactic Theory: A Unified Approach.* 2nd ed. London: Edward Arnold.

Brinton, Laurel J. 1988. *The Development of Aspectual English Systems: Aspectualizers and Post-Verbal Particles* [Cambridge Studies in Linguistics, 49]. Cambridge: Cambridge University Press.

Brown, Gillian and George Yule. 1983. *Discourse Analysis* [Cambridge Textbooks in Linguistics]. Cambridge: Cambridge University Press.

Brown, Keith and Jim Miller. 1991. *Syntax: A Linguistic Introduction to Sentence Structure.* 2nd ed. London: Harper Collins Academic.

Burton-Roberts, Noel. 1997. *Analysing Sentences: An Introduction to English Syntax.* 2nd ed. London and New York: Longman.

Carr, Philip. 1999. *English Phonetics and Phonology: an Introduction.* Oxford and Cambridge, MA: Blackwell.

Celce-Murcia, Marianne and Diane Larsen-Freeman. 1999. *The Grammar Book: An ESL/EFL Teacher's Course.* 2nd ed. Boston: Heinle and Heinle.

Chafe, Wallace L. 1976. "Givenness, Contrastiveness, Definiteness, Subjects, Topics, and Point of View". In *Subject and Topic,* edited by Charles Li, 25–55. New York: Academic Press.

Cheshire, Jenny. 1991. *English around the World: Sociolinguistic Perspectives.* Cambridge: Cambridge University Press.

Chomsky, Noam. 1957. *Syntactic Structures* [Janua Linguarum, Studia Memoriae Nicolai van Wijk Dedicata, Series Minor 4]. The Hague and Paris: Mouton.

Chomsky, Noam and Morris Halle. 1968. *The Sound Pattern of English.* New York: Harper and Row.

Coates, Jennifer. 1983. *The Semantics of the Modal Auxiliaries.* London: Croom Helm.

Cole, Peter (ed.). 1981. *Radical Pragmatics.* New York: Academic Press.

Cole, Peter and Jerry L. Morgan (eds). 1975. *Syntax and Semantics.* Vol. 3: *Speech Acts.* New York: Academic Press.

Couper-Kuhlen, Elizabeth. 1986. *An Introduction to English Prosody.* London: Edward Arnold.

Cruse, D. A. 1986. *Lexical Semantics* [Cambridge Textbooks in Linguistics]. Cambridge: Cambridge University Press.

Crystal, David. 1969. *Prosodic Systems and Intonation in English.* Cambridge: Cambridge University Press.

———. 1996. *A Dictionary of Linguistics and Phonetics.* 4th ed. Oxford and Cambridge, MA: Basil Blackwell.

———. 1997. *The Cambridge Encyclopedia of Language.* 2nd ed. Cambridge: Cambridge University Press.

Curme, George O. 1931, 1935. *A Grammar of the English Language.* 2 vols. Boston: Heath.

———. 1947. *English Grammar.* New York: Barnes and Noble.

Delahunty, Gerald P. and James J. Garvey. 1994. *Language, Grammar and Communication: A Course for Teachers of English.* New York: McGraw Hill.

Dillon, George L. 1977. *Introduction to Contemporary Linguistic Semantics.* Englewood Cliffs, N.J.: Prentice Hall.

Fillmore, Charles J. 1968. "The Case for Case". In *Universals in Linguistic Theory*, edited by Emmon Bach and Robert T. Harms, 1–88. New York: Rinehart and Winston.

———. 1977. "The Case for Case Reopened". In *Syntax and Semantics.* Vol. 8: *Grammatical Relations*, edited by Peter Cole and Jerrold M. Sadock, 59–81. New York: Academic Press.

Finegan, Edward. 1999. *Language: Its Structure and Use.* 3rd ed. San Diego: Harcourt Brace Jovanovich.

Foley, William A. and Robert D. Van Valin, Jr. 1985. "Information Packaging in the Clause". In *Language Typology and Syntactic Description.* Vol. 1: *Clause Structure*, edited by Timothy Shopen, 282–364. Cambridge: Cambridge University Press.

Fowler, H. W. 1983. *Modern English Usage.* 2nd ed., revised by Sir Ernest Gower. Oxford and New York: Oxford University Press.

Francis, W. Nelson. 1958. *The Structure of American English.* New York: Ronald.

Fraser, Bruce. 1975. "Hedged Performatives". In Cole and Morgan (eds.), 187–210.

Frawley, William. 1992. *Linguistic Semantics.* Hillsdale, NJ: Lawrence Erlbaum.

Fries, Charles Carpenter. 1952. *The Structure of English: An Introduction to the Construction of English Sentences.* New York: Harcourt, Brace.

Fromkin, Victoria and Robert Rodman. 1993. *An Introduction to Language.* 5th ed. Forth Worth: Harcourt Brace Jovanovich.

Giegerich, Heinz J. 1992. *English Phonology: An Introduction.* [Cambridge Textbooks in Linguistics]. Cambridge: Cambridge University Press.

Gleitman, Lila R. 1983. "Lexical Categories and Concepts". Talk presented at the University of British Columbia, Vancouver, B.C.

Greenbaum, Sidney and Randolph Quirk. 1990. *A Student's Grammar of the English Language.* London: Longman.

Grice, H. Paul. 1975. "Logic and Conversation". In Cole and Morgan (eds.), 41–58. [Reprinted in Grice 1989.]

———. 1981. Presupposition and Conversational Implicature. In Cole (ed.), 183–98. [Reprinted in Grice 1989.]

———. 1989. *Studies in the Way of Words.* Cambridge, MA: Harvard University Press.

Haegeman, Liliane. 1994. *Introduction to Government and Binding Theory.* 2nd ed. Oxford and Cambridge, MA: Blackwell.

——— and Jacqueline Guéron. 1999. *English Grammar: A Generative Perspective* (Blackwell Textbooks in Linguistics, 14). Oxford: Blackwell.

Hancher, Michael. 1979. "The Classification of Cooperative Illocutionary Acts". *Language in Society* 8: 1–14.

Hawkins, Peter. 1984. *Introducing Phonology.* London: Hutchison.

Hirtle, Walter H. 1982. *Number and Inner Space: A Study of Grammatical Number in English.* Laval, Québec: Les Presses de l'Université Laval.

Hopper, Paul J. 1999. *A Short Course in Grammar: A Course in the Grammar of Standard Written English.* New York and London: W. W. Norton.

Horrocks, Geoffrey. 1987. *Generative Grammar* [Longman Linguistics Library]. London and New York: Longman.

Huddleston, Rodney. 1984. *Introduction to the Grammar of English* [Cambridge Textbooks in English]. Cambridge: Cambridge University Press.

———. 1988. *English Grammar: An Outline.* Cambridge: Cambridge University Press.

Hurford, James R. 1994. *Grammar: A Student's Guide.* Cambridge: Cambridge University Press.

——— and Brendan Heasley. 1983. *Semantics: A Coursebook.* Cambridge: Cambridge University Press.

Jensen, John T. 1990. *Morphology: Word Structure in Generative Grammar* [Current Issues in Linguistic Theory 70]. Amsterdam and Philadelphia: John Benjamins.

Jespersen, Otto. 1909–49. *A Modern English Grammar on Historical Principles.* 7 vols. London: Allen and Unwin.

———. 1933. *Essentials of English Grammar.* London: George Allen and Unwin.

Justice, David. 1987. "The Lexicography of Recent Semantic Change". Paper presented at the annual meeting of the Modern Language Association, San Francisco, CA.

Kaplan, Jeffrey P. 1995. *English Grammar: Principles and Facts.* 2nd ed. Englewood Cliffs, NJ: Prentice Hall.

Katamba, Francis. 1989. *An Introduction to Phonology.* London and New York: Longman.

Katz, Jerrold J. and Jerry Fodor. 1963. "The Structure of a Semantic Theory". *Language* 39: 170–210.

Kiparsky, Paul and Carol Kiparsky. 1971. "Fact". In *Semantics: An Interdisciplinary Reader in Philosophy, Linguistics and Psychology*, edited by Danny D. Steinberg and Leon A. Jakobvits, 345–69. Cambridge: Cambridge University Press.

Klammer, Thomas P. and Muriel R. Schulz. 1995. *Analyzing English Grammar.* Boston: Allyn and Bacon.

Kriedler, Charles W. 1989. *The Pronunciation of English: A Course Book.* Oxford and New York: Basil Blackwell.

———. 1998. *Introducing English Semantics.* New York: Routledge.

Ladefoged, Peter. 1993. *A Course in Phonetics.* 3rd ed. New York: Harcourt Brace Jovanovich.

Lakoff, George and Mark Johnson. 1980. *Metaphors We Live By.* Chicago and London: University of Chicago Press.

Larsen-Freeman, Diane (ed.). 1997. *Grammar Dimensions: Form, Meaning, and Use.* 2nd ed. 4 vols. Boston: Heinle and Heinle.

Lass, Roger. 1984. *Phonology: An Introduction to Basic Concepts.* [Cambridge Textbooks in Linguistics]. Cambridge: Cambridge University Press.

Leech, Geoffrey N. 1974. *Semantics.* Harmondsworth: Penguin.

———. 1987. *Meaning and the English Verb.* 2nd ed. London and New York: Longman.

Lehrer, Adrienne. 1974. *Semantic Fields and Lexical Structure* (North-Holland Linguistic Series, 11). Amsterdam: North-Holland.

Levinson, Stephen C. 1983. *Pragmatics* [Cambridge Textbooks in Linguistics]. Cambridge: Cambridge University Press.

Lyons, John. 1968. *Introduction to Theoretical Linguistics.* Cambridge: Cambridge University Press.

———. 1977. *Semantics.* 2 vols. Cambridge: Cambridge University Press.

———. 1996. *Linguistic Semantics: An Introduction.* Cambridge: Cambridge University Press.

Marchand, Hans. 1969. *The Categories and Types of Present-Day English Word-Formation: A Synchronic-Diachronic Approach.* 2nd ed. München: C. H. Beck.

MacKay, Ian. 1991. *Phonetics: The Science of Speech Production.* 2nd ed. Boston: Allyn and Bacon.

Matthews, Peter H. 1991. *Morphology: An Introduction to the Theory of Word Structure* [Cambridge Textbooks in Linguistics]. 2nd ed. Cambridge: Cambridge University Press.

Murray, Thomas E. 1995. *The Structure of English: Phonetics, Phonology, Morphology.* Boston: Allyn and Bacon.

Napoli, Donna Jo. 1993. *Syntax: Theory and Problems.* New York and Oxford: Oxford University Press.

———. 1996. *Linguistics: An Introduction.* New York and Oxford: Oxford University Press.

O'Grady, William and Michael Dobrovolsky (eds). 1996. *Contemporary Linguistic Analysis.* 3rd ed. Toronto: Copp Clark.

Orwell, George. 1946. *A Collection of Essays.* New York: Harcourt Brace Jovanovich.

Ouhalla, Jamal. 1999. *Introducing Transformational Grammar: From Principles and Parameters to Minimalism.* New York: Oxford University Press.

Palmer, Frank R. 1981. *Semantics: A New Outline.* 2nd ed. Cambridge: Cambridge University Press.

———. 1990. *Modality and the English Modals.* 2nd ed. London and New York: Longman.

Parisi, Domenico and Francesco Antinucci. 1976. *Essentials of Grammar,* translated by Elizabeth Bates [Language, Thought, and Culture: Advances in the Study of Cognition]. New York: Academic Press.

Perkins, M. R. 1983. *Modal Expressions in English.* London: Frances Pinter.

Pinker, Steven. 1994. *The Language Instinct: How the Mind Creates Language.* New York: William Morrow.

Poutsma, H. 1904–26. *A Grammar of Late Modern English.* 4 vols. Groningen: Noordhoff.

Pratt, Mary Louise. 1977. *Toward a Speech Act Theory of Literary Discourse.* Bloomington: Indiana University Press.

Prince, Ellen F. 1981. "Toward a Taxonomy of Given-New Information". In Cole (ed.), 223–55.

Pullum, Geoffrey K. and William A. Ladusaw. 1996. *Phonetic Symbol Guide.* 2nd ed. Chicago and London: University of Chicago Press.

Quirk, Randolph, Sidney Greenbaum, Geoffrey Leech, and Jan Svartvik. 1985. *A Comprehensive Grammar of the English Language.* London and New York: Longman.

Radford, Andrew. 1988. *Transformational Grammar: A First Course* [Cambridge Textbooks in Linguistics]. Cambridge: Cambridge University Press.

Reinhart, Tanya. 1976. "On Understanding Poetic Metaphor". *Poetics* 5: 383–402. [Reprinted in *Linguistic Perspectives on Literature,* edited by Marvin K. L. Ching, Michael C. Haley, and Ronald F. Lunsford, 91–114. London, Boston, and Henley: Routledge and Kegan Paul.]

Rosch, Eleanor H. 1973. "Natural Categories". *Cognitive Psychology* 4: 328–50.

Sapir, Edward. 1921. *Language: An Introduction to the Study of Speech*. New York: Harcourt, Brace and World.

Saussure, Ferdinand de. 1986. *Course in General Linguistics*, edited by Charles Bally and Albert Sechehaye in collaboration with Albert Riedlinger, translated by Roy Harris. La Salle, IL: Open Court.

Searle, John R. 1969. *Speech Acts: An Essay in the Philosophy of Language*. Cambridge: Cambridge University Press.

———. 1975. "Indirect Speech Acts". In Cole and Morgan (eds.), 59–82. [Reprinted in Searle 1979, 30–57.]

———. 1976. "A Classification of Illocutionary Acts". *Language in Society* 5: 1–23 [Reprinted in Searle 1979, 1–29.]

———. 1979. *Expression and Meaning: Studies in the Theory of Speech Acts*. Cambridge: Cambridge University Press.

Sells, Peter. 1985. *Lectures on Contemporary Syntactic Theories: An Introduction to Government-Binding Theory, Generalized Phrase Structure Grammar, and Lexical-Functional Grammar*. Stanford: Center for the Study of Language and Information.

Smith, Carlota S. 1991. *The Parameter of Aspect* [Studies in Linguistics and Philosophy, 43]. Dordrecht, Boston, and London: Kluwer.

Spencer, Andrew. 1991. *Morphological Theory: An Introduction to Word Structure in Generative Grammar*. Oxford: Basil Blackwell.

Sperber, Dan and Deidre Wilson. 1995. *Relevance: Communication and Cognition*. 2nd ed. Cambridge, MA: Blackwell.

Stegner, Wallace. 1955. *Wolf Willow: A History, a Story, and a Memory of the Last Plains Frontier*. Lincoln and London: University of Nebraska Press.

Strang, Barbara M.H. 1968. *Modern English Structure*. 2nd ed. London: Arnold.

Taylor, John R. 1995. *Linguistic Categorization: Prototypes in Linguistic Theory*. New York: Oxford University Press.

Thomas, Linda. 1993. *Beginning Syntax*. Oxford and Cambridge, MA: Blackwell.

Thurber, James. 1931. "Ladies' and Gentlemen's Guide to Modern English Usage". In *The Owl in the Attic and other Perplexities*, by James Thurber, 73–113. New York: Harper and Row.

Trask, R.L. 1996. *Dictionary of Phonetics and Phonology*. London: Routledge.

van Riemsdijk, Henk and Edwin Williams. 1986. *Introduction to the Theory of Grammar* [Current Studies in Linguistics, 12]. Cambridge, MA and London: MIT Press.

Vendler, Zeno. 1967. *Linguistics in Philosophy*. New York: Cornell University Press.

Wardhaugh, Ronald. 1995. *Understanding English Grammar: A Linguistic Approach*. Oxford and Cambridge, MA: Blackwell.

Wekker, Herman and Liliane Haegeman. 1985. *A Modern Course in English Syntax*. London: Croom Helm.

Wells, J.C. 1982. *Accents of English*. 3 vols. Cambridge: Cambridge University Press.

White, E.B. 1934. *Essays of E.B. White*. New York: Harper and Row.

Appendices

■ Appendix I: Abbreviations

The following abbreviations are used in this textbook and accompanying CD-ROM:

A	adjective	IF	illocutionary force
aA	adjunct adverbial	intrans	intransitive verb
Ac	action	iO	indirect object
Adv	adverb	IPA	International Phonetic
AdvP	adverb phrase		Alphabet
Ag	Agent (thematic role)	Lo	Location (thematic role)
AP	adjective phrase	m	masculine gender
arg	argument	M	modal auxiliary
Art	article	Mod	modifier
Aux	auxiliary	n	neuter gender
C	consonant	N	noun
cA	conjunct adverbial	N̄	N-bar
Co	coda	Neu	Neutral (thematic role)
Comp	complementizer	Nom	nominal
complex trans	complex transitive verb	nomn	nominative case
compr	comparative degree	Nu	nucleus
cop	copula(tive) verb	obj	objective case
dA	disjunct adverbial	oC	object complement
Deg	degree word	On	onset
Dem	demonstrative	OP	object of the preposition
Det	determiner	p	person
ditrans	ditransitive verb	P	preposition
dO	direct object	Pa	patient (thematic role)
D-structure	deep structure	Pass	passive
eSu	extraposed subject	pC	prepositional complement
Ex	Experiencer (thematic role)	Perf	perfect aspect
f	feminine gender	pl	plural number
Fa	Factitive (thematic role)	PN	proper noun
Fo	Force (thematic role)	pos	positive degree
Go	Goal (thematic role)	poss	possessive
H	hearer	Po	Possessor (thematic role)
I	Instrument (thematic role)	PP	prepositional phrase

pred	predicate	V	verb
prep	prepositional verb	V̄	V-bar
pres	present tense	vd	voiced
Pro	pronoun	V$_{gp}$	verb group
PRO	gap in nonfinite clause	vl	voiceless
Prog	progressive aspect	Vo	vowel
prop	proposition(al context)	VP	verb phrase
prsprt	present participle	W	word
Prt	particle	*wh-*	*wh*-word
PSpec	prepositional specifier	*	ungrammatical
pstprt	past participle	?	questionable grammaticality
Q	quantifier	{ }	mutually exclusive choice
Rh	rhyme	( )	optional
Ro	Role (thematic role)	1st	first person
S	sentence	2nd	second person
S̄	S-bar	3rd	third person
sC	subject complement	#	word or syllable boundary
sg	singular number	→	is realized as, has as its allo-phones/allomorphs OR is rewritten/expanded as
So	Source (thematic role)		
Sp	speaker		
S-structure	surface structure	⇒	is transformed into
Su	subject	>	becomes
Sy	syllable	<	comes from
supl	superlative degree	Ø	zero-realized
T	tense	[ ]	narrow transcription
Th	Theme (thematic role)	/ /	broad transcription
trans	transitive (monotransitive) verb	~	(logical) negation

■ Appendix II: Phrase structure rules (simple sentences)

$$S \rightarrow \left\{ \begin{array}{l} S \left(\left\{ \begin{array}{l} PP \\ AdvP \\ NP \end{array} \right\} \right) \\ NP\ Aux\ VP \end{array} \right\}$$

$$NP \rightarrow \left\{ \begin{array}{l} (Det)\ \bar{N} \\ PN \\ Pro \end{array} \right\}$$

$$\bar{N} \rightarrow \left\{ \begin{array}{l} (AP)\ \bar{N}\ (PP) \\ N \end{array} \right\}$$

$$AP \rightarrow \left(\left\{ \begin{array}{l} Deg \\ AdvP \end{array} \right\} \right) A\ (PP)$$

$$AdvP \rightarrow (Deg)\ Adv$$

$$PP \rightarrow (PSpec)\ P \left\{ \begin{array}{l} NP \\ PP \end{array} \right\}$$

$$Det \rightarrow \left\{ \begin{array}{l} Art \\ Dem \\ Poss \\ Q \\ \textit{Wh-} \end{array} \right\}$$

$$Poss \rightarrow \left\{ \begin{array}{l} NP\ \text{-'s} \\ my,\ your,\ his \ldots \end{array} \right\}$$

$$VP \rightarrow \bar{V} \left(\left[\begin{array}{l} AdvP \\ PP \\ NP \end{array} \right] \right)$$

$$\bar{V} \rightarrow \left\{ \begin{array}{l} V_{gp} \left(\left\{ \begin{array}{l} NP\ (\{NP,\ PP,\ AP\}) \\ AP \\ PP\ (PP) \end{array} \right\} \right) \\ \bar{V} \left(\left\{ \begin{array}{l} AdvP \\ PP \\ NP \end{array} \right\} \right) \end{array} \right\}$$

$$V_{gp} \rightarrow V\ (Prt)$$

$$Aux \rightarrow T\ (M)\ (Perf)\ (Prog)$$

$$T \rightarrow \left\{ \begin{array}{l} past \\ pres \end{array} \right\}$$

$$Perf \rightarrow have\ \textit{-en}$$

$$Prog \rightarrow be\ \textit{-ing}$$

Subject Index

Numbers in **bold** indicate the page on which the term is defined.

A

absolute construction 246
accomplishment **145**, 146, 147
achievement **145**–146, 147
acronym **99**
activity 114, **144**–145, 146, 147
adjectivalizer **88**
adjective 81, 109–110, 117, **121**–**122**, 123, 124, 172–175
    attributive 62, **121**, 174
    incomparable 110
    predicative 62, **121**, 174, 280
    scalar **136**–137
adverb 109, 111, 112, 117, 122, **123**, 172, 175–176, 225, 226, 227, 229, 230, 237
    degree adverb **122**, 172
    interrogative **225**–226, 227, 237
    relative **229**, 230
adverbial 191–194, 195, 221–222, 245–246, 293
    adjunct **191**–**193**, 195, 221–222, 245–246
    conjunct **194**, 222, 245–246
    disjunct **193**–**194**, 222, 245–246
adverbializer **88**
affix 59, **77**–79, 86–91, 93, 97–98, 99, 103, 106, 120, 122, 280
    class changing **78**, 86, 87–88
    class maintaining **78**, 86–87
    derivational **78**
    infix **77**–78
    inflectional **78**, 103
    prefix **77**, 86–87
    suffix **77**, 87–89, 91, 93, 97–98, 106, 280; agentive **88**, 97, 120, 122; diminutive **87**, 99; feminine **87**

affix hopping **200**, 241
affricate **24**, 31–32, 45 n.
agent/agentive **279**–281, 282, 283, 285, 286, 288 n., 296; *see also* affix, suffix, agentive
allomorph **82**–85, 86
    root **85**, 86
allophone **48**, 49, 54
alveolar **24**, 25, 26, 29, 30–32, 33, 52, 53
alveolopalatal **24**, 25, 30–31, 53
ambiguity 108, 132, 150, 159 n., 164, 180, 195, 196, 211, 223–224, 260 n., 271, 273–274
    lexical **132**, 150
    structural 164, 180, 195, 196, 211, 223–224
ambisyllabic **66**–68
American English 28, 29, 33, 36, 38, 39, 45 n., 61, 62, 135, 189 n.
analytic 103, 278, 280
anaphoric **110**
animacy **105**
animal communication 7
anomaly **132**, 153–158
antecedent **229**–230
antonymy **136**–137, 150
appropriateness condition 303, 304, **305**–307, 308–309, 310
    essential **304**, 307, 308, 309
    nonobvious **305**, 306
    preparatory **305**, 306, 307, 308, 309
    propositional content **305**, 306, 308, 309
    sincerity **303**, 304, 305, 306, 307, 310
approximant **24**, 32–33, 52, 55
approximation **23**, 32, 35, 43

open 23, 32, 35, 43
close 23, 43
argument 264–266
article 120, 121; *see also* definiteness
articulation **23–25**, 34–35, 54
    manner of 24–25, 34, 54
    place of 23–24, 35, 54
articulator 21, 35
aspect **113**–115, 143, 147, 281–282, 288 n.; *see also* perfect *and* progressive
    imperfective **114**, 147
    inherent **143**
    perfective **114**, 147, 288 n.
aspectualizer 281–282, 288 n.
aspiration **28**, 34, 45 n., 48–49, 50, 53, 54, 68
assimilation **51**, 52, 54, 60
auxiliary (Aux) 80, **198–201**, 202, 207, 209, 213 n., 239–240, 258 n.

B

back formation **97**–98
base (morphology) **78**–79
base (syntax) **211**
be 105, 198, 206, 208, 210
bilabial **23**, 25, 26, 29, 31
blend **97**
British English 33, 39, 61, 62, 135, 189 n.

C

Canadian English 28, 39, 60, 62, 135
"Canadian" raising **39**–40
case 81–82, **107**–109, 253, 266–267
    common **107**
    dative **108**
    genitive **107**, 108–109, 266; *see also* possessive
    nominative 81–82, **107**, 266
    objective 81–82, **107**, 253
case grammar *see* thematic roles
category, lexical/phrasal **169**
causative 92, **278**, 280, 281, 282, 283, 284, 285, 286, 288 n.
cavity, oral/nasal **20**–22
clause 116, 188 n., 215, 256, 258 n., 259 n., 260 n., 260 n., 288 n.; *see also* question, indirect *and* relative clause
    adverbial **221–222**, 235, 237, 247, 250, 259 n., 260 n.; elliptical 222–223, 259 n.

dependent (subordinate) 116, 188 n., 215–256
finite **214**–238
main **214**
nonfinite **238**–256
small 260 n., 288 n.
that- 116, **216**–221, 233–234, 236, 244, 247, 258 n., 297, 298
wh- **224**–238
cleft sentence 236, 294
click 45 n.
clipping 97, **98**–99
co-index **208**, 230
cooperative principle 312
comma intonation **232**
comment **291**, 294, 298
comment clause 116
commonization **93**
communicative competence **289**
competence 6, 9, 10, 13 n.
complement **168**, 181, 183, 184, 216, 217, 219, 244, 245, 248, 249, 251–255
    subject **183**, 184, 216, 244, 248
    object **184**, 254, 260 n.
    of adjective 216, 217, 219, 245, 249
    of N̄ 216, 217, 219
    of verb **217–218**, 251–255
    prepositional **184**
complementarity **136**
complementizer **216**, 220, 222, 225, 230–231, 232, 233–234, 237, 241, 243, 253, 258 n., 259 n.
    deletion of **220**, 230–231, 232, 233–234
componential analysis **138**
compound 60, **93**–97, 106, 181
    vs. phrase 93–94
    amalgamated **96**–97
    head of **94**
    phrase **96**
    syntax of 94–95
conjunction 123, 179–181, 258 n.
connotation **132**, 135, 137
consonant **23**–34, 43–44
consonant cluster **55**–57
    final 56
    initial 55–56, 57
constative **301**
constituency test 167

constituent **165**, 167, 211
contextual conditions **289**
continuative 115, **282**, 283, 285, 286
contraction 78, 80
contradiction **132**, 136
contrast *see* stress, contrastive
conversational 312–314
   implicature **313**, 314
   maxims 312–**313**
   relevance, principle of **313**
converseness 137–138
conversion *see* functional shift
cooperative principle 312, 313

D

D-structure (deep structure) **163**, 203–204,
   211–212, 266–267
dative movement 182–183, 298
declustering 83
definiteness 105, **110**–111, 146, 291–292, 300
degree, 81, **109**–110
deixis **111**, 112
demonstrative 104, 111, 120
denotation **132**, 135
dental **23**, 25
dentalization **28**–29, 30, 31, 34, 51, 52, 54
deontic (root) 147–150
derivation 59, **86**–91, 97, 120, 280
determiner 106, 107, **120**, 121, 170, 188 n.,
   225, 226, 227, 229, 231, 237
   interrogative **225**, 226, 227, 237
   relative **229**, 231
devoicing **28**, 34, 52, 54, 83, 84
diacritic **28**, 29, 30, 31, 32, 33, 34, 50, 51, 52,
   53, 54
dialect 19, 20, 28, 33, 34, 45 n., 55, 56, 61,
   110, 206
dictionary 130, 159 n.
diphthong **35**–36, 38, 39–41, 45 n.
   falling **35**, 39–40
   rising **36**, 40
direction of fit 302–303
   word-to-world **302**, 304
   world-to-word **302**, 303, 304
discourse **289**
discourse marker **314**
dislocation 294, 299–300
   right- **299**–300

   left- **294**
distribution 48–49, 119–123
   complementary **48**–49
   parallel **48**
do 198, 206, 207
do-support **205**–207, 210–211, 227
domination **165**
durative 114, **143**–145

E

egressive 115, 281–282, 283, 286, 287
egressive pulmonic system **20**
"elsewhere" (phoneme/morpheme) **50**, 83
embedding **215**, 221, 229, 273
   multiple 221
-en participle *see* participle, past
enclitic **78**–79, 80
entailment **131**, 134, 135, 137
environment, phonetic 47, 48, 49
epistemic **147**–150
etymeme 77
exclamation **228**
   indirect **237**
expletive **169**
expressed psychological state *see* appropriateness condition, sincerity
extension **130**
extralinguistic institution **304**, 306
extraction site **225**
extraposition 218–220, 231, 232, 236, 244,
   245, 260 n.
   from subject **218**–220, 236, 244, 245,
   260 n., 298, 299
   from object **219**
   from NP **231**, 232, 298, 299
eye dialect **19**

F

factivity **134**
false morphological division 89
features, distinctive 45 n., 52, 138–151,
   277–287
   phonological 45 n., 52
   relational **140**, 143
   semantic **138**–151, 277–287
figurative language 153–158
flap **24**
flapping **28**, 51

focusing 293, 295, **295**–300
free variation 49, 82
fricative **24**, 30–31, 55, 56
fronting 52, 54, **293**–294
    of adverb 293
    of adverb, with inversion 293–294
functional shift **91**–93

G

gender 81, **105**–106, 126–127 n.
    common 105, 106, 126–127 n.
    feminine 105, 106
    grammatical **105**
    natural **105**
    neuter 81, 105
    masculine 81, 105
generic 105, 107, 110, 111, 112, **292**
gerund **240**, 244, 245, 259–260 n.
    subject of 259–260 n.
glide **25**, 32–33, 35, 36, 38, 39–41
glottal 22, 29, 33
glottalic system 45 n.
glottis **20**, 23
governor **168**, 169
grammar 7–10, 12, 13, 163–164, 259 n., 260 n.
    descriptive 7, 10
    generative 12, 163–**164**, 259 n., 260 n.
    prescriptive 8, 10
    traditional 12, 13, 259 n.
grammatical **164**
grammatical category **103**–104, 105, 107, 118
    covert 104, 105, 107
    overt 104

H

h 33, 50
habit 112, 113, 115, **147**, 159 n.
have 198, 206, 208, 210
head **167**, 169
heavy NP shift **299**
homograph 19, **75**
homonym **75**
homonymy **133**
homophone 19, 39, 41, **75**, 124
homorganic **24**, 33
hyponymy **135**–136, 150
    (co)hyponym **135**–136

I

idiom 59, **100**–101, 310
illocutionary force **302**, 303, 305, 307
imperative **116**, 208–209, 307
    formation of 208–209
implication *see* entailment
inchoative 92, **277**–278, 280, 281, 282, 283,
        284, 285, 287
inclusion **131**, 135
indirect object movement *see* dative move-
        ment
infinitive 122–123, 199, 239, 241, 243, 244,
        245, 246, 247, 252, 297
    bare 199, **239**, 252
    for- **241**, 243
    to- 122–123, **239**, 244, 245, 246, 247, 252
    wh- 243
inflection **78**–79, 104, 105, 106, 107, 108, 109,
        112, 115–116, 119–123
information 61, 290–291, 292, 293, 294, 295,
        296
    given (old) 61, **290**
    new 61, **290**
information structuring 290–301
-ing participle *see* participle, present
ingressive 115, 288 n.
initialism **99**
innateness **6**–7, 9
intension **130**
interdental **23**, 25, 30–31, 51, 52
International Phonetic Alphabet 10, 18, 26
interrogative *see* question
intonation 19, 22, **62**–65
inversion 168, 204, 207, 227, 229, 237, 258 n.,
        293, 298–299
    subject-aux(iliary) 168, **204**, 207, 227, 229,
        237, 258 n.
    subject-verb 293, **298**–299
-ist 88–89
it 169, 218, 254, 264, 294
    anticipatory 169, 218
    impersonal 169, 254, 264

J

juncture 69 n.

L

labeled
   node **165**
   bracketing 166
labialization **31**, 32, 52, 54, 55
labiodental **23**, 25, 30, 51
labiovelar **24**, 32–33
language **3–7**
   arbitrary nature of 5
   creative (infinite) nature of 7
   functions of 4, 11
   rule-governed nature of 6
larynx **20**–22, 35
lateral **25**, 32
lateral release **32**, 51, 69 n.
lexeme **75**, 124
lexicalization 277, 287
lexicon **211**
liquid **25**, 52, 54, 56
literary coinage 100
locative 283–286, 293; *see also* thematic role,
   Locative
logic 9
loudness 22

M

meaningful 164
metaphor **155**–158
   focus interpretation of 157
   principles underlying 157–158
   vehicle interpretation of 157
metonymy **155**
minimal pair **47**
modal 113, 116, 147–150, 159 n., 198, 199,
   207, 210, 239
   adjective 116, 150
   adverb 116, 150
   auxiliary 116, **147**–149, 198, 199, 207, 239
   verb 150
modifier **167**
monophthong **35**, 36, 39
monophthongization **41**, 45 n., 53
mood **115**–116, 304; *see also* imperative
   indicative 115
   subjunctive 115
morph **76**–77, 79–81
   bound **76**
   free **76**

   zero 76
morpheme **75**–76, 79–85, 103
   lexical 76
   grammatical 76, 103
morphemic analysis **79**–82
morphological analysis **79**–82
morphological realization rule **82**, 102 n.
   agglutinative 82, 102 n.
   fusional 82, 102 n.
   null realization 82
   zero 82, 102 n.
morphology **10**–11, 12
movement 197–198, 220, 298
   left 298
   particle 197–198, 298
   right 220

N

Ñ **171**
nasal **24**, 29–30, 52, 54, 55, 56
nasal release **30**, 51, 69 n.
negative 80, 86–87, 136, 148, 204, 205,
   213–214 n., 281, 282, 293, 302, 303
   modal 148
   negative sentence 205, 210–211
   sentence negation **205**
   word negation **205**
negative polarity 207
nominalizer **88**–89
noncompositionality 100
nonsyllabic 35–36, **42**–44
noun 80, 104, 105–106, 107–108, 110, 117,
   118, **120**–**121**, 124, 125, 127 n., 139–142,
   146, 147, 169–172 , 217
   abstract 120, 124, 217
   collective 120–121, 127 n., 140–141
   common 120, 124, 139–141
   concrete 120–121, 124, 139–141
   count 104, 120–121, 124, 127 n., 139–141,
   146, 147
   mass (noncount) 120–121, 124, 127 n., 146
   proper 120–121, 124
number 80, 81, 82–83, 84, **104**–105
   generic 105
   plural 80, 82–83, 84, 104
   singular 80, 81, 104

O

object   176, 181–182, 185–186, 201, 202, 216,
        217, 236, 245, 249, 254, 264, 267, 268,
        271
    direct   **181**–182, 201, 202, 216, 217, 254,
        267, 271
    indirect   **182**, 216, 236, 268
    latent   185–186, 264
    of preposition   **176**, 245, 249
obstruent   **32**, 53, 56
orthography   **18**, 73
oxymoron (paradox)   **154**

P

palatal   **24**, 25, 32, 52
palatalization   **53**
paraphrase   **131**
parenthetical   65, 116, 150
part of speech *see* word class
part-whole   **133**; *see also* synecdoche
participle   81, 122, 174, 199, 240, 244, 245,
        246, 247, 252, 255, 259 n., 260 n., 280,
        299, 296–297
    "dangling"   247, 260 n.
    past   81, 122, 199, **240**, 244, 246, 252, 255,
        259 n., 280, 296–297
    present   81, 122, 199, **240**, 244, 245, 246,
        252, 255, 259 n.
particle   92, 95, **123**, 146, 147
passive   117, 164, 183, 184, 200–203, 213 n.,
        220–221, 239, 240, 253, 254, 258 n.,
        296–297
    agented   296
    agentless   202, 296
    formation of   201–202
    functions of   296
    notional   117
    of experience   296
perfect   **114**–115, 199, 239
    continuative   114
    resultative   114
performance   **6**, 10, 13n, 19, 20
performative   **301**
performative verb   **301**, 307
periphrasis, periphrastic form   **103**, 108, 109,
        112, 114, 115, 122
person   81, **106**–107
    generic   107

personification   **155**
pharyngeal   **24**, 25
phoneme   **47**–49
    marginal   **49**
phonetics, articulatory   10, **18**, 20–23
phonology   10, 12, **18**, 47
phonotactics   **54**–57
phrase   59, 93–96, 100, 121, 122, 146, 147,
        169–179, 181–186, 217, 226–227, 299
    adjective   122, **172**–**175**, 299
    adverb   **175**–176
    noun   121, **169**–172
    prepositional   146, 147, **177**–179, 217,
        226–227; postverbal   194–197
    verb   169, **181**–**186**
phrase marker   **167**
pitch *see* intonation
pied piping   **226**–227, 229, 231
plosive   **26**
polysemy   **132**, 133, 150
possessive   80–81, 96, 108, 120, 170,
        259–260 n., **283**–287; *see also* thematic
        role, Possessor
potential pause   **74**
pragmatics   11, 12, **289**
predicate   169, **264**–266, 276–287, 290, 291
    cognitive   282–283
    descriptive   276–282
    locative/possessive   283–287
preposition   **123**, 176–179, 258 n.
preposition stranding   **226**
presupposition   **133**–134
privative   **86**–87, 138, 287
PRO   **241**–243, 245, 247, 252, 259 n., 260 n.,
        273
    controlled   **241**, 245
    indefinite   **241**
productivity   **78**–79, 84, 86, 87
progressive   **114**, 115, 127 n., 143, 146, 199,
        214 n., 239, 240
pronoun   81, 104, 105, 106, 107, 111, 117,
        188, 208–209, 225, 226, 229, 230, 231,
        233–234, 237, 252, 259 n.
    interrogative   **225**, 226, 237
    reflexive   **208**–209, 252
    relative   **229**, 230, 231, 233–234, 259 n.
proposition   **264**
propositional content   **302**

prospective 115
prototype **151**–153
proverbial (gnomic) 112
pseudocleft sentence 235, 253, 295
punctual 114, 145

Q
quantifier 120, 121, 299
   postposing **299**
question 64, 65, 134, 168, 204–205, 207–208,
      209, 213–214 n., 221, 225–228, 236–238,
      243, 253, 259 n.
   echo 64, 228
   indirect 134, **236–238**, 243
   tag 64, 168, **207–208**, 209
   wh- (content) 64, 134, **225–228**, 237, 243
   yes/no (truth) 64, **204–205**, 237, 243

R
r 33, 39
   intrusive *r* **33**
   linking *r* **33**
   nonrhotic dialect **33**
   rhotic dialect **33**
raising **254–255**, 260 n.
recategorization **124–125**
reciprocity **138**
recursive 166, 176
reduplication **91**
relative clause **229–236**, 237, 243, 246–247,
      259 n., 260 n., 298, 300
   free (headless) **234–235**, 243
   indefinite **235**
   restrictive **231–233**, 300
   nonrestrictive **231–233**, 236, 300
   sentential **236**
remnant (frozen) form **84**
retroflex **25**, 33
reversive **138**
root **76–77**, 100
   bound **77**
   creation **100**
rule 8, 49–54, 83–85, 89, 163, 165–166, 168,
      211–212, 213 n., 306
   constitutive **8**, 163, 306
   lexical **89**
   morphemic **83–85**
   phonemic **49–51**

phonological 6, **51–54**
phrase structure 163, 165–166, 168,
      211–212, 213 n.
regulatory **8**, 163, 306

S
S̄ 217, 225–226
S-structure (surface structure) **164**, 211–212,
      266–267
selectional restriction **153**, 154, 211
semantics 11, 12, **129**–131, 134–138, 263
   lexical 11, 129
   sentence 11, 129, 263
   structural **134–138**
   text (discourse) 11, 129
   traditional **129–131**
semivowel *see* glide
sense **131**, 134, 138
sibilant **31**
sign **4–5**
   iconic **4**, 5
   indexical **4**, 5
   symbolic **5**
simplicity **9**
situation **147**, 159 n.
sonorant **52**, 53
sound **20–23**, 35
   nasal **22**, 23
   nasalized **22**, 35
   oral **21**, 23, 35
   voiced **22**, 23, 35
   voiceless **22**, 23
specificity 110, **292**, 300
specifier **170**, 176, 189 n., 198, 200, 258 n.
   prepositional **176**, 189 n.
speech **18–19**
speech, indirect **217**, 237
speech act 4, **301–312**
   Commissive **303**, 306–307
   Declarative **304**
   Directive **303**, 307, 309
   Expressive **304**
   illocutionary **302**
   indirect **307**, 309–312, 313
   locutionary **302**, 304
   perlocutionary **302**
   Representative **304**
   Verdictive **304**

state/stative 112, 114, 127 n., **143**–144, 147,
    159 n., 203, 210, 260 n., 276–277, 280,
    281, 282, 283, 284, 285
stem **78**–79
stop **24**, 26, 28–29, 50, 52, 53, 54, 55
stress 19, 50, 51, **57**–62, 68, 74, 92–93
    contrastive 19, 61, 291, 293, 294, 295
    functions of 58–61
    primary **58**
    secondary **58**
strong form **60**
subcategorization (subclassification) 120,
    181, 211, 252, 267
subcategorization frame **181**
subject **168**–169, 201, 201, 216, 244, 248, 267,
    290, 291
subject hierarchy **276**
subject selection 297
subject-to-subject raising **297**
superordinate term **135**–136
suppletion **109**
suprasegmental features **57**–65
syllabic 35, **42**–44, 50, 51, 54
syllable 23, 34, 41, 42, **65**–68
    closed **41**
    coda of **65**–68
    nucleus of **23**, 34, 42, 65–68
    onset of **65**–68
    open **41**
    rhyme of **65**–66
symbol **165**–166, 168
    initial 168
    recursive **166**
    terminal **166**
symmetry **138**
synecdoche **155**
synesthesia **155**
synonymy **134**–135, 150
syntax **11**, 12, 163
synthetic 103, 278

T

tautology **154**–155
    apparent 155
telic **143**, 145
tense 81, 104, **111**–113, 115, 198–199
    nonpast (present) 81, 112
    past 81, 113

future 113
tense stranding 206
that 216, 217, 220, 229, 232, 233–234, 237,
    259 n.
thematic grid **274**–276
thematic role (θ-role) **266**–276
    Agent **267**, 268, 269, 276
    ambiguous 273–274
    Benefactive **268**, 270, 271
    dual roles 271–274
    Experiencer **267**, 268, 269
    Factitive **268**, 270, 271
    Force **267**, 268, 269
    Goal **267**, 268, 269, 271
    Instrument **267**, 268, 269, 276
    Location **268**, 269
    Neutral **268**, 270, 271
    Path **267**, 268, 269
    Patient **268**, 270, 271, 276
    Possessor **268**, 270
    Range **268**, 270, 271
    Role **268**, 270
    Source **267**, 268, 269
    Theme **268**, 270, 271
there-insertion **297**–298
tone group **63**
tonic syllable **63**
topic 61, 137, **291**, 293, 295, 296, 297, 298
topicalization 293–298, **297**
tough-movement 260 n., **297**
trace 202, **226**
transcription **26**
transformation 163, **164**, 212
tree diagram 89–91, **165**, 265
triangle notation **192**
trill **24**, 45 n.

U

universal 6, 9–10, 138
unreleased **28**, 34, 50, 51, 54
uvular **24**, 25

V

velar **24**, 25, 26, 29, 32, 37, 38, 52
velaric system 45 n.
velarization 32, 34, 53, 54, 69 n.
    dark (velarized) *l* **32**, 53
velum **21**–22, 23, 24, 35

verb   74, 81, 94–96, 111–117, 122, 123,
      143–147, 181–186, 197–198, 199,
      202–203, 213 n., 239, 254–255, 264, 273,
      274–276, 297, 298, 299
   complex transitive   184, 203
   copulative   122, **183**, 202, 264, 299
   diprepositional   **185**–186, 203
   ditransitive   **182**–183, 202–203, 299
   expect-type   254–255, 273
   finite   199, 213 n., **215**
   intransitive   122, **182**, 202, 264
   lexical (main)   **198**
   perception   239, 274–276
   persuade-type   254–255
   phrasal   74, 94–96, 123, 197–198, 203, 264,
      298
   prepositional   **184**, 203, 264
   transitive (monotransitive)   122, **181**–182,
      202, 264
   want-type   254–255
verbalizer   **88**
vocal cords   **20**, 22
vocal tract   20–22
vocative   **65**
voice   117; *see also* passive
voiceless vowel   33, 35, 50
voluntary   **143**
vowel   23, **34**–44, 51, 52, 53, 54, 59, 68, 69 n.
   acoustic properties of   23, 34
   articulation of   34–35
   back   **35**, 38–39
   central   **35**, 37–38
   front   **35**, 36–37
   function of   23, 34

   lax   **41**, 42, 53
   length   41–42, 51, 54, 68
   nasalized   35, 52, 54, 68, 69 n.
   reduced   **37**–38, 53, 59
   retracted   **53**, 54
   rounded (pursed)   **35**, 38–39
   tense   **41**, 42
   unrounded (spread)   **35**, 36, 37, 39

W
weak form   **60**
wh-movement (fronting)   225–**226**, 227, 228,
      229, 231, 237, 243, 258 n., 259 n.
   long   228, 231
wh-word   225, 226–227, 243, 258 n.
word   19, 59, **73**–75, 79, 103, 118
   criteria for   73–75
   function (grammatical)   76, 103, **118**
   lexical (content)   **118**
   morphosyntactic   75
   orthographic(al)   74
   phonological   74
   types of   79
word class   58–59, 76, **118**–126
   major (open)   76, 118
   minor (closed)   76, 118
   test for, distributional   119
   test for, inflectional   119–120
word order   103, 108
writing   19–20

Y
yod-dropping   **41**, 53